MACINTOSH METHODOLOGIES IN THEORY AND PRACTICE

A technical guide for experienced users

formerly *Macs For Dummies*

BY D. WELCH POGUE

Includes advanced treatment of these topics:

◆ Invoking the commencement of A/C 120V electric power to the CPU unit

◆ Propelling the cursor-control module on a horizontal plane

◆ Insertion and removal of magnetic-oxide data storage media

Look, we use the word *Dummies* on the cover with affection and a twinkle in the eye. Still, we understand if you're not thrilled about leaving a book on your desk called *Macs For Dummies*.

We hear you. And we've got the perfect solution: just rip off the real cover of the book! This phony cover will be all that's left. Leave it on your desk in plain sight, so everybody will know what a computer whiz you are.

TM

References for the Rest of Us! ®

BESTSELLING BOOK SERIES

Are you intimidated and confused by computers? Do you find that traditional manuals are overloaded with technical details you'll never use? Do your friends and family always call you to fix simple problems on their PCs? Then the *...For Dummies*® computer book series from IDG Books Worldwide is for you.

...For Dummies books are written for those frustrated computer users who know they aren't really dumb but find that PC hardware, software, and indeed the unique vocabulary of computing make them feel helpless. *...For Dummies* books use a lighthearted approach, a down-to-earth style, and even cartoons and humorous icons to dispel computer novices' fears and build their confidence. Lighthearted but not lightweight, these books are a perfect survival guide for anyone forced to use a computer.

> *"I like my copy so much I told friends; now they bought copies."*
>
> — *Irene C., Orwell, Ohio*

> *"Quick, concise, nontechnical, and humorous."*
>
> — *Jay A., Elburn, Illinois*

> *"Thanks, I needed this book. Now I can sleep at night."*
>
> — *Robin F., British Columbia, Canada*

Already, millions of satisfied readers agree. They have made *...For Dummies* books the #1 introductory level computer book series and have written asking for more. So, if you're looking for the most fun and easy way to learn about computers, look to *...For Dummies* books to give you a helping hand.

IDG
BOOKS
WORLDWIDE

MACS® FOR DUMMIES®
6TH EDITION

by David Pogue

IDG Books Worldwide, Inc.
An International Data Group Company

Foster City, CA ♦ Chicago, IL ♦ Indianapolis, IN ♦ New York, NY

Macs® For Dummies,® 6th Edition

Published by
IDG Books Worldwide, Inc.
An International Data Group Company
919 E. Hillsdale Blvd.
Suite 400
Foster City, CA 94404
www.idgbooks.com (IDG Books Worldwide Web site)
www.dummies.com (Dummies Press Web site)

Library of Congress Catalog Card No.: 98-87907

ISBN: 0-7645-0398-7

Printed in the United States of America

10 9 8 7 6 5 4

6B/SS/QU/ZZ/IN

Distributed in the United States by IDG Books Worldwide, Inc.

Distributed by CDG Books Canada Inc. for Canada; by Transworld Publishers Limited in the United Kingdom; by IDG Norge Books for Norway; by IDG Sweden Books for Sweden; by Woodslane Pty. Ltd. for Australia; by Woodslane (NZ) Ltd. for New Zealand; by TransQuest Publishers Pte Ltd. for Singapore, Malaysia, Thailand, Indonesia, and Hong Kong; by ICG Muse, Inc. for Japan; by Norma Comunicaciones S.A. for Colombia; by Intersoft for South Africa; by Le Monde en Tique for France; by International Thomson Publishing for Germany, Austria and Switzerland; by Distribuidora Cuspide for Argentina; by Livraria Cultura for Brazil; by Ediciones ZETA S.C.R. Ltda. for Peru; by WS Computer Publishing Corporation, Inc., for the Philippines; by Contemporanea de Ediciones for Venezuela; by Express Computer Distributors for the Caribbean and West Indies; by Micronesia Media Distributor, Inc. for Micronesia; by Grupo Editorial Norma S.A. for Guatemala; by Chips Computadoras S.A. de C.V. for Mexico; by Editorial Norma de Panama S.A. for Panama; by American Bookshops for Finland. Authorized Sales Agent: Anthony Rudkin Associates for the Middle East and North Africa.

For general information on IDG Books Worldwide's books in the U.S., please call our Consumer Customer Service department at 800-762-2974. For reseller information, including discounts and premium sales, please call our Reseller Customer Service department at 800-434-3422.

For information on where to purchase IDG Books Worldwide's books outside the U.S., please contact our International Sales department at 317-596-5530 or fax 317-596-5692.

For consumer information on foreign language translations, please contact our Customer Service department at 1-800-434-3422, fax 317-596-5692, or e-mail rights@idgbooks.com.

For information on licensing foreign or domestic rights, please phone +1-650-655-3109.

For sales inquiries and special prices for bulk quantities, please contact our Sales department at 650-655-3200 or write to the address above.

For information on using IDG Books Worldwide's books in the classroom or for ordering examination copies, please contact our Educational Sales department at 800-434-2086 or fax 317-596-5499.

For press review copies, author interviews, or other publicity information, please contact our Public Relations department at 650-655-3000 or fax 650-655-3299.

For authorization to photocopy items for corporate, personal, or educational use, please contact Copyright Clearance Center, 222 Rosewood Drive, Danvers, MA 01923, or fax 978-750-4470.

About the Author

Ohio-bred **David Pogue** never touched a computer — nor wanted to — until Apple Computer suckered him into it by selling Macs half-price at Yale, from which he graduated *summa cum laude* in 1985. Since then, Pogue has merged his two loves — the musical theatre and Macs — in every way he could dream up: by writing manuals for music programs like Finale; by being the computer-consultant guy for Broadway musicals; by teaching Mac music seminars around the country; and by becoming the Mac guru to every Broadway and Hollywood creative-type he could get his hands on — Mia Farrow, Carly Simon, Mike Nichols, Stephen Sondheim, Gary Oldman, and others.

In his other life, Pogue is a straight-ahead theatre musician, having conducted $1\frac{1}{2}$ Broadway shows (the second one flopped out of town), played piano for off-Broadway productions, and composed a number of small-time musicals (such as his wedding). In his other life, he's a magician and novelist (having written *Hard Drive,* a techno-thriller named a "notable book of the year" by *The New York Times*).

And in his *other* other life, Pogue is a contributing editor for *Macworld* magazine. His column, *The Desktop Critic,* appears on the back page of the magazine each month (and was declared the best computer column in America by the Computer Press Association).

Pogue's résumé also boasts some *real* accomplishments, like winning the Ohio spelling bee in seventh grade, being the only nonlawyer in three generations, and getting a Viewer Mail letter read on David Letterman.

He lives in Connecticut with his wife Jennifer, son Kelly, and dog Bullwinkle. Their photos lurk on the World Wide Web at *http://www.davidpogue.com.*

Also by David Pogue:

MORE Macs For Dummies
The iMac For Dummies
Macworld Mac Secrets (with Joseph Schorr)
Magic For Dummies
PalmPilot: The Ultimate Guide
Hard Drive (a novel)
The Microsloth Joke Book
The Great Macintosh Easter Egg Hunt
Tales from the Tech Line
The Weird Wide Web (with Erfert Fenton)
Classical Music For Dummies (with Scott Speck)
Opera For Dummies (with Scott Speck)

ABOUT IDG BOOKS WORLDWIDE

Welcome to the world of IDG Books Worldwide.

IDG Books Worldwide, Inc., is a subsidiary of International Data Group, the world's largest publisher of computer-related information and the leading global provider of information services on information technology. IDG was founded more than 30 years ago by Patrick J. McGovern and now employs more than 9,000 people worldwide. IDG publishes more than 290 computer publications in over 75 countries. More than 90 million people read one or more IDG publications each month.

Launched in 1990, IDG Books Worldwide is today the #1 publisher of best-selling computer books in the United States. We are proud to have received eight awards from the Computer Press Association in recognition of editorial excellence and three from Computer Currents' First Annual Readers' Choice Awards. Our best-selling ...For Dummies® series has more than 50 million copies in print with translations in 31 languages. IDG Books Worldwide, through a joint venture with IDG's Hi-Tech Beijing, became the first U.S. publisher to publish a computer book in the People's Republic of China. In record time, IDG Books Worldwide has become the first choice for millions of readers around the world who want to learn how to better manage their businesses.

Our mission is simple: Every one of our books is designed to bring extra value and skill-building instructions to the reader. Our books are written by experts who understand and care about our readers. The knowledge base of our editorial staff comes from years of experience in publishing, education, and journalism — experience we use to produce books to carry us into the new millennium. In short, we care about books, so we attract the best people. We devote special attention to details such as audience, interior design, use of icons, and illustrations. And because we use an efficient process of authoring, editing, and desktop publishing our books electronically, we can spend more time ensuring superior content and less time on the technicalities of making books.

You can count on our commitment to deliver high-quality books at competitive prices on topics you want to read about. At IDG Books Worldwide, we continue in the IDG tradition of delivering quality for more than 30 years. You'll find no better book on a subject than one from IDG Books Worldwide.

John Kilcullen
Chairman and CEO
IDG Books Worldwide, Inc.

Steven Berkowitz
President and Publisher
IDG Books Worldwide, Inc.

Eighth Annual
Computer Press
Awards ≥1992

Ninth Annual
Computer Press
Awards ≥1993

Tenth Annual
Computer Press
Awards ≥1994

Eleventh Annual
Computer Press
Awards ≥1995

IDG is the world's leading IT media, research and exposition company. Founded in 1964, IDG had 1997 revenues of $2.05 billion and has more than 9,000 employees worldwide. IDG offers the widest range of media options that reach IT buyers in 75 countries representing 95% of worldwide IT spending. IDG's diverse product and services portfolio spans six key areas including print publishing, online publishing, expositions and conferences, market research, education and training, and global marketing services. More than 90 million people read one or more of IDG's 290 magazines and newspapers, including IDG's leading global brands — Computerworld, PC World, Network World, Macworld and the Channel World family of publications. IDG Books Worldwide is one of the fastest-growing computer book publishers in the world, with more than 700 titles in 36 languages. The "...For Dummies®" series alone has more than 50 million copies in print. IDG offers online users the largest network of technology-specific Web sites around the world through IDG.net (http://www.idg.net), which comprises more than 225 targeted Web sites in 55 countries worldwide. International Data Corporation (IDC) is the world's largest provider of information technology data, analysis and consulting, with research centers in over 41 countries and more than 400 research analysts worldwide. IDG World Expo is a leading producer of more than 168 globally branded conferences and expositions in 35 countries including E3 (Electronic Entertainment Expo), Macworld Expo, ComNet, Windows World Expo, ICE (Internet Commerce Expo), Agenda, DEMO, and Spotlight. IDG's training subsidiary, ExecuTrain, is the world's largest computer training company, with more than 230 locations worldwide and 785 training courses. IDG Marketing Services helps industry-leading IT companies build international brand recognition by developing global integrated marketing programs via IDG's print, online and exposition products worldwide. Further information about the company can be found at www.idg.com.

1/24/99

Author's Acknowledgments

I can't tell you how much I've appreciated the patience of everyone whose projects got back-burnered for the sake of this book: my editors at *Macworld;* Dr. Jennifer Pogue, the loveliest plastic surgeon in Connecticut; and Bullwinkle the Wonder Dog.

Thanks to the unbelievably supportive, enthusiastic people at IDG Books: publisher John Kilcullen; Senior Project Editor Mary Goodwin; and everyone in the sprawling universe of IDG Books voicemail.

Above all, thanks to my students: the ranks of born-again Mac nuts whose first steps, questions, and impressive strides constitute my research.

Publisher's Acknowledgments

We're proud of this book; please register your comments through our IDG Books Worldwide Online Registration Form located at http://my2cents.dummies.com.

Some of the people who helped bring this book to market include the following:

Acquisitions, Editorial, and Media Development

Senior Project Editor: Mary Goodwin

Acquisitions Manager: Michael Kelly

Copy Editor: Phil Worthington

Technical Editor: Tim Warner

Editorial Manager: Kelly Ewing

Editorial Assistant: Paul Kuzmic

Production

Project Coordinator: E. Shawn Aylsworth

Layout and Graphics: Lou Boudreau, Valery Bourke, Linda M. Boyer, Angela F. Hunckler, Jane E. Martin, Brent Savage, Janet Seib, Kate Snell

Proofreaders: Michelle Croninger, Henry Lazarek, Nancy Price, Rebecca Senninger, Janet M. Withers

Indexer: Sherry Massey

General and Administrative

IDG Books Worldwide, Inc.: John Kilcullen, CEO; Steven Berkowitz, President and Publisher

IDG Books Technology Publishing: Brenda McLaughlin, Senior Vice President and Group Publisher

Dummies Technology Press and Dummies Editorial: Diane Graves Steele, Vice President and Associate Publisher; Mary Bednarek, Director of Acquisitions and Product Development; Kristin A. Cocks, Editorial Director

Dummies Trade Press: Kathleen A. Welton, Vice President and Publisher; Kevin Thornton, Acquisitions Manager

IDG Books Production for Dummies Press: Michael R. Britton, Vice President of Production and Creative Services; Cindy L. Phipps, Manager of Project Coordination, Production Proofreading, and Indexing; Kathie S. Schutte, Supervisor of Page Layout; Shelley Lea, Supervisor of Graphics and Design; Debbie J. Gates, Production Systems Specialist; Robert Springer, Supervisor of Proofreading; Debbie Stailey, Special Projects Coordinator; Tony Augsburger, Supervisor of Reprints and Bluelines

Dummies Packaging and Book Design: Patty Page, Manager, Promotions Marketing

◆

The publisher would like to give special thanks to Patrick J. McGovern, without whom this book would not have been possible.

◆

Contents at a Glance

Cartoons at a Glance

By Rich Tennant

page 5

"Well, right off, the response time seems a bit slow."

page 111

"He must be a Macintosh user - there's a wristwatch icon etched on his retina."

page 285

"Well, the first day wasn't bad—I lost the Finder, copied a file into the 'Trash, and sat on my mouse."

page 203

page 237

page 365

page 337

Fax: 978-546-7747 • E-mail: the5wave@tiac.net

Table of Contents

· ·

Introduction

●●

A Formal Welcome to the 20th Century

Something has driven you to learning the computer — your friends, your job, or fate. In any case, you couldn't have chosen a better time; technology and price wars have made computers comprehensible, affordable, and almost fun. The Macintosh is the primary example.

In 1984, the ad people called the Macintosh "the computer for the rest of us." The Macintosh was as simple as a toaster — nothing to assemble, nothing to install, no manual to puzzle through.

But Apple Computer learned about a funny catch-22 in the computer business. The people who influenced computer sales (like computer magazines and consultants) *liked* the jargon, the keyboard codes, the messy circuit board stuff! These were people who prided themselves on having *mastered* the convoluted, dim-witted design of pre-Mac computers . . . people who not only didn't appreciate the simplicity of the Macintosh but actually *resented* it. In reviews, editorials, and interviews, the Powers That Were kept saying that the Macintosh would never survive unless Apple gave it all the jacks, slots, and specs of the "Dark Side" computers — IBM and Windows.

Alas, that movement pushed the Mac out of its "computer for the rest of us" mold. Suddenly, there were more models. The computer weenies who ruled the press started imposing all their terminology and tech-talk on this poor little machine. Macintosh user groups sprang up — they're everywhere now — where you'd hear talk like, "How can I accelerate my 350 MHz G3 to get a decent frame rate out of QuickTime three-point-oh?"

The Mac wasn't a toaster anymore.

Why a Book for Dummies?

Today, the Mac sometimes seems almost as intimidating as the computers it was supposed to replace. The way the magazines and techno-nerds throw jargon around, you'd think the Mac was the private property of the dweeby intelligentsia all over again.

It's not. You hold in your hands a primal scream: "It's *not* as complicated as they try to make it sound!" Really, *truly,* almost everything said by the computer whizzes of the world is more complicated than it has to be. (Ever study psychology? A person who uses jargon where simple English would do is trying to appear superior.)

This book is designed to help you

- ✔ Translate the tech-talk into useful information
- ✔ Weed out the stuff you'll never need to know
- ✔ Navigate the hype when it comes to buying things
- ✔ Learn the Macintosh and get useful things done

By the way, of *course* you're not a dummy. Two pieces of evidence tell me so: For one thing, you're learning the Mac, and for another, you're reading this book! But I've taught hundreds of people how to use their Macs, and an awful lot of them start out saying they *feel* like dummies when it comes to computers. Society surrounds us with fast-talking teenagers who grew up learning English from their Nintendo sets; no wonder the rest of us some-times feel left out.

But you're no more a dummy for not knowing the Mac than you were before you knew how to drive. Learning the Mac is like learning to drive: After a lesson or two, you can go anywhere your heart desires.

So when we say *Dummies,* we're saying it with an affectionate wink. Still, if the cover bothers you even a little — I'll admit it, you wouldn't be the first — please rip it right off. The inner cover, we hope, will make you proud to have the book lying out on your desk.

How to Use This Book (Other Than as a Mouse Pad)

If you're starting from the very, *very* beginning, read this book from the end — with **Appendix A**, where you can find out how to buy a Mac (and which one to get) without getting scammed. It also contains an idiot-proof guide to setting up your computer.

Otherwise, start with the very basics in **Chapter 1**; turn to **Chapter 15** in times of trouble; and consult the other chapters as the spirit moves you.

The book winds down with **Appendix B**, "The Resource Resource" (which has contact info for a number of important Mac companies and publications), and **Appendix C**, "The Techno-Babble Translation Guide." (You'd probably call it a glossary.)

Macintosh conventions

Macintosh conventions? Sure. They're called Macworld Expos, and there's one in Boston and one in San Francisco each year.

Conventions in this book

Oh, *that* kind of convention.

So that we'll be eligible for some of the more prestigious book-design awards, I've marked some topics with these icons:

Nerdy stuff that's okay to skip but will fascinate the kind of people who read Tom Clancy novels.

The Macintosh is the greatest computer on earth, but it's still a computer. Now and then it does unexplainable stuff, which I'll explain.

A shortcut so you can show off.

Denotes an actual You-Try-It Experience. Hold the book open with a nearby cinder block, put your hands on the computer, and do as I say.

Indicates a deep glimpse into the psychology of Mac users: why people who already *know* how to use the darn things, for example, love to intimidate people who *don't*.

A few new, cool things about Mac OS 8 and later versions. (I'll explain what "Mac OS" means in Chapter 1.)

A few new, cool things about Mac OS 8.5 and later versions.

Apple and obsolescence

One more thing before you delve in: Apple is the gigantic Silicon Valley computer company that started out as a couple of grungy teenagers in a garage. Each time Apple introduces a new Macintosh model, it's faster, more powerful, and less expensive than the model *you* already bought. People love Apple for coming up with such great products — but feel cheated at having paid so much for a suddenly outdated machine.

Feel whatever you want, of course. But if you're going to buy a computer, accept the fact that your investment is going to devalue faster than real estate in Chernobyl.

Here's a promise: No matter how carefully you shop or how good a deal you get on a computer today, your model will be *discontinued by the manufacturer within a year.* (It'll still *work* just fine, and be more or less up-to-date, for about five years.)

With that quick and inevitable computer death looming, how can people psych themselves into laying out $2,000 for a computer? Simple: They believe that in those few short years, the computer will speed them up enough, and enhance their productivity enough, to cover the costs easily.

That's the theory, anyway.

Part I
For the Absolute Mac Virgin

The 5th Wave   By Rich Tennant

"Fortunately, at this grade level the Mac is very intuitive for them to use. Unfortunately so is sailing mouse pads across the classroom."

In this part . . .

There are three general ways to learn how to work your Mac. You can prevail upon the good graces of your local computer dealer, who, having pocketed your money already, would just as soon have you blow away. You can read the manuals, which have about as much personality as a walnut. Or you can read a book like this one. (Then again, no book is quite like this one.)

Tough choice, huh?

In this part, you'll learn, as kindly and gently as possible, what you need to know to get up and running on your Mac system — and nothing else.

Chapter 1

How to Turn On Your Mac (And What to Do Next)

• •

In This Chapter

▶ How to turn your Mac on (and off)

▶ Confronting weird new words like *mouse* and *menu*

▶ Doing windows

▶ Mindlessly opening and closing folders

• •

*1*f you haven't bought a Mac yet, go immediately to Appendix A. Don't speak to any salesperson until you've read it.

If you already *have* a Mac, but it's sitting in cardboard boxes on your living-room floor, read the second half of Appendix A, where you'll be gently guided through the not-harrowing-at-all experience of plugging everything in.

Box Open. Now What?

At this moment, then, there should be a ready-to-roll Mac on your desk and a look of fevered anticipation on your face.

Switching the Mac on

In this very first lesson, you'll be asked to locate the On button. It's in the upper-right corner of your keyboard. I can't exactly tell you what it looks like, because Apple Computer tends to express its creativity by changing this button's shape on each different kind of Mac. For example:

✔ On most Macs, the On/Off switch is a big fat key marked by a left-pointing triangle, like this:

✔ On an iMac, the On/Off button is round, marked by a logo like this:

✔ And on any recent PowerBook laptop, the On/Off switch is capsule-shaped, about the size of a Good-N-Plenty. If you look closely, you'll see, etched into the dark gray plastic, the same logo that the iMac's power button has, pictured above.

Try pressing your power button or key now. If hitting that key produces some kind of response — a sound plays, the screen lights up, missiles are launched from the Arizona desert — then your machine is working. Memorize the position of the power key, and skip ahead to "The startup slide show."

If pressing that key didn't do anything, you're probably using an elderly Mac model, manufactured during what's now known as the Era When the Power Button Was in a Different Place on Each Mac Model. For example, some very old Macs have a plastic rocker switch on the back panel; a few models, such as those whose model numbers begin with a 6, have a round push button on the front panel; and extremely old laptops have a round, concave button on the back panel (hidden by the flap).

Fortunately, after you locate your model's power button, it'll pretty much stay in that spot for as long as you own your Mac.

The startup slide show

Was your hunt for the elusive On switch successful? Then turn the Mac on! You should hear a ding or a chord, and after a few seconds, an image appears on the screen.

If the computer does, in fact, have power, you're in for a treat: You get to witness the Macintosh Startup Slide Show, revered by millions. First, you see a quick glimpse of the smiling Macintosh. It looks like this:

(In the rare event that your smiling Macintosh looks like this —

— your monitor is upside-down.)

Next slide: You see the famous Mac OS logo, looking like Picasso's portrait of a schizophrenic:

During this time, the bottom of your screen fills with little inch-tall pictures. In Macintosh lingo, the term for "little inch-tall pictures" is *icons.* These particular icons represent the different features of your Mac, each turning itself on and preparing for action: One represents your CD-ROM drive, another's for dialing the Internet, and so on. Much, much, much more about these startup-item doodads in Chapter 8.

At last, the colored full-screen pattern, called the *desktop,* appears. Congratulations! You've arrived.

If you saw anything else during the startup process — such as a blinking question-mark icon, a strange error message, or thick black smoke — you've just met your first computer problem. Proceed directly to Chapter 15. This problem and many others are explained — and solved — for you there.

Techie terms to read if you're really bored

You may occasionally hear cocky teenagers tell you to "boot up." They have no intention of taking you fly-fishing. That's computerese for turning on the Mac. You also hear people say *power up, start up,* and just *boot.*

Furthermore, after the computer is on, you're sometimes asked to turn it off and on again. This is called *rebooting,* or *restarting,* or sometimes *turning it off and on again.*

Your First Moments Alone Together

As any gadget lover can tell you, the most exciting period of appliance ownership comes at the very beginning. You're gonna love this stuff.

The big turn-off

Before we get into 3-D color graphs, space-vehicle trajectories, and DNA analysis, I guess I should tell you how to turn the Mac *off.*

In a pinch, sure, you can just yank the power cord out of the wall. But regularly turning off the Mac by chopping off its power can eventually confuse the poor thing and lead to technical problems. Instead, you're supposed to turn off your Mac using the Shut Down command; we'll get to that in a moment.

Moving the mouse

The *mouse* is the rounded, three-inch plastic box on the desk beside your keyboard. Having trouble visualizing it as a rodent? Think of the cord as its tail, and (if it helps you) draw little eyeballs on the sloping side facing you.

Now then, roll the mouse across the desk (or mouse pad), keeping the cord pointed away from you. See how the arrow pointer moves across the screen? For the rest of your life, you'll hear that pointer called the *cursor.* And for the rest of your life, you'll hear moving the mouse called *moving the mouse.*

Try lifting the mouse off the desk and waving it around in midair like a remote control. Nothing happens, right? The mouse controls the cursor only when it's on a flat surface. (A ball on the bottom of the mouse detects movement when you roll it around.) That's a useful feature — you can pick up the mouse when you run out of desk space, but the cursor will stay in place on the screen. Only when you set the mouse down and begin to roll it again will the cursor continue moving.

If you have a PowerBook laptop, by the way, you don't *have* a mouse. Studies have shown that rolling an egg-sized plastic box across the thigh of the guy next to you on the airplane can have, ergonomically and socially speaking, unpleasant results. Therefore, you've been given, instead, either a *trackball* (essentially an upside-down mouse) or a *trackpad.* The principle is the same: Roll your fingers away from you, and the cursor moves up the screen. Instead of a square mouse button, you have a broad, clicky button nestled against the pad. (If your older PowerBook model has *two* broad, clicky buttons, they're identical in function.)

I won't mention this distinction again, because if you're smart enough to have bought a PowerBook, you're smart enough to translate future references to the mouse into trackpad terms.

What's on the menu?

Let's try some real computing here. Move the cursor up to the white strip at the top of the screen. It's called the *menu bar,* named after a delightful little pub in Silicon Valley. Touch the arrow on the word Special. (The *tip* of the Mac's arrow is the part you need to worry about. Same thing with real-life arrows, come to think of it.)

Pointing to something on the screen in this way has a technical term: *pointing.* (Think you're going to be able to handle this?)

Now put your index finger on the button on the mouse and press the button down. Hold the button down. Don't let go. If all goes well, you should see a list of commands drop down from the word Special, as shown here:

Congratulations — you've learned how to *click the mouse* (by pressing the button), and you've also learned to *pull down a menu* (the list of commands). Try letting go of the mouse button; the menu disappears.

Shutting down

Click the word Special (hereafter known as the *Special menu*) again; keep the mouse button down. When the list of commands appears, roll the mouse downward so that each successive command turns dark. In Mac jargon, you're *dragging the mouse* (moving with the button pressed). And when each menu command turns dark, it's said to be *highlighted*.

The only commands that don't get highlighted are the ones that are dimmed, or *grayed out*. They're dimmed because they don't make any sense at the moment. For example, if no disk is in the floppy-disk drive, choosing Eject Disk wouldn't make any sense (and it wouldn't work, either). So the Mac makes that command gray, which means it's unavailable to you.

Roll the mouse all the way down to the words Shut Down so that they're highlighted.

If you've had enough for one session, release the mouse button. The Mac turns itself off completely. (Some very old models shut *mostly* down — and then a message on the screen tells you to use the On/Off switch to finish the job.)

Hey, you've only read a few pages, and already you can turn your Mac on and off! Told you it was no harder than a toaster.

If your thirst for knowledge is unquenched, and you want to slog ahead with this lesson, then don't let go of the button yet. Instead, slide the cursor off the menu in any direction and then let go of the mouse button. The menu snaps back up like a window shade and nothing else happens. (A menu command only gets activated when you release the mouse while the cursor is on a command.)

When you're ready to forge forth, read on.

Moving things around on the desktop

Take a look around the Mac screen. You've already encountered *menus* (those words File, Edit, View, and so on at the top of the screen). Near the upper-right corner of the screen, you see an *icon* (remember? — a small symbolic picture). If your Mac is brand new, that icon is called Macintosh HD.

Shutting down just gets easier every year

Extensive user polling has revealed a common thread among computer users: They tend to turn these machines *off* a lot. It figures, then, that Apple would try to make doing so easier and easier.

For example, on all recent Mac models (including iMacs), you can turn off the machine by pressing the On/Off key on your keyboard — the same key you use to turn the thing *on.* (See the beginning of this chapter for a recap.)

To make sure you didn't hit that key *accidentally* while reaching for your Sprite, the Mac then offers you choices like these:

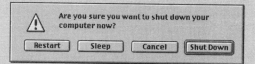

The Shut Down button will turn off your computer. The Cancel button will leave your Mac *on* — because you're *canceling* your decision to shut down, get it?

Restart turns the Mac off, then on again; and Sleep makes the screen go dark and the fan go quiet. Sleep is a lot like Off, except that (a) it uses a little bit more power than Off does, and (b) you don't have to wait 45 seconds for the computer to warm up when you want to use it again (you just press any key on the keyboard to revive the machine).

But if your Mac model is more than a couple of years old, pressing the triangle key on your keyboard doesn't do anything (once the computer is already on). You can't, in other words, shut down the Mac by pressing the same keyboard key.

If that's your situation, you probably have yet *another* Shut Down command. It's tucked away in a menu you may not even have recognized as a menu — the Apple logo at the upper-left corner of the screen.

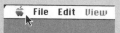

Click that logo (hereafter called the menu); hold the mouse button down; and check out the last command. See if the command is called •Shut Down.

My suggestion: Get into the habit of using *this* Shut Down command, the one in your menu, rather than the one in your Special menu.

Why? Because menus change, depending on what you're doing on your Mac; the Special menu I've just shown you may not always be there — but the menu's Shut Down command is *always* there.

If you have it at *all*, that is.

Icons represent everything in the Mac world. They all look different: One represents a letter you wrote, another represents the Trash can, another represents a floppy disk you've inserted. Here are some examples of icons you'll probably be seeing before long:

You can move an icon by dragging it. Try this:

1. **Point to the Trash icon and click.**
2. **Drag it to a new position (move the mouse while the button's down).**
3. **Let go of the mouse button.**

Hey, this thing isn't so technical after all, right?

Other than the fact that there's a Trash can, nobody's really sure why they call this "home-base" screen the desktop. It has another name, too: the *Finder.* It's where you file all your work into little electronic on-screen file folders so that you can *find* them again later. If you have a recent version of the Mac's built-in software, in fact, the *word* Finder even appears at the top of the screen, as shown in the following illustration.

Used in a sentence, you might hear it like this: "Well, no wonder you don't see the Trash can. You're not in the Finder!"

Icons, windows, and Macintosh syntax

Point to the hard-disk icon (a rectangular box, probably called Macintosh HD — for Hard Disk) in the upper-right corner of the screen.

This particular icon represents the giant disk inside your Mac, known as the *hard drive* or *hard disk,* that serves as your filing cabinet. It's where the computer stores all your work, all your files, and all your software.

So how do you see what's in your hard drive? Where do you get to see its table of contents?

It turns out that any icon can be *opened* into a window, where you'll see every item inside listed individually. The window has the same name as the icon you opened.

Before we proceed, though, it's time for a lesson in Macintosh syntax. Fear not; it's nothing like English syntax. In fact, everything you do on the Macintosh has this format: *noun-verb.* Shakespeare it ain't, but it's sure easy to remember.

Let's try a noun-verb command, shall we?

1. **Click the hard-disk icon in the upper-right corner of the screen.**

The icon turns black, indicating that it's *selected.* Good job — you've just identified the *noun.*

2. **Move to the File menu and choose Open.**

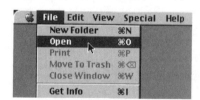

You guessed it — Open is the *verb.* And, sure enough, your hard disk opens into a window, where you can see its contents.

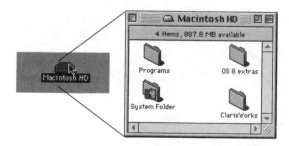

Did any of that make sense? In the world of Macintosh, you always specify *what* you want to change (using the mouse), and then you use a menu command to specify *how* you want it changed. You'll see this pattern over and over again: *Select* something on the screen and then *apply* a menu command to it.

The complete list of window doodads

Look over the contents of your hard-drive window, as shown in the following figure. (Everybody's got different stuff, so what you see on your screen won't exactly match these illustrations.)

Better yet, look over the various controls and gadgets around the *edges* of this window. Using these controls and buttons, you can do all kinds of neat things to a window: stretch it, move it, or make it go away. These various gadgets are worth learning about — you're going to run into windows *everywhere* after you start working.

CLOSE BOX — Click here to close the window, just as though you had chosen Close from the File menu.

TITLE BAR — Drag anywhere in this striped area to move the entire window.

TITLE BAR ICON — Drag this little icon to move the entire window to the Trash, to another disk, or to another window. (In Mac OS 8.5 and later.)

ZOOM BOX — Click here to make the window large enough to show all its contents.

COLLAPSE BOX — Click here to roll the window up like a windowshade, so that only the title bar is showing. Click here again to re-expand the window. (In Mac OS 8 and later.)

VERTICAL SCROLL BAR — It's white, indicating that you're seeing everything in the window (top to bottom).

SIZE BOX — Drag in any direction to make the window bigger or smaller.

WINDOW EDGES — You can move the entire window by dragging this narrow, puffy strip that runs all the way around. (In Mac OS 8 and later.)

HORIZONTAL SCROLL BAR — It's gray, indicating that you're not seeing everything in the window (there's something off to the side). You can drag the little square from side to side to adjust your view of the window.

Go ahead and try out some of the little boxes and scroll bars. Click them. Tug on them. Open the window and close it again. No matter what you do, *you can never hurt the machine by doing "the wrong thing."* That's the wonderful thing about the Macintosh: It's the Nerf appliance.

All systems are go

In that little window diagram, you may have noticed something peculiar about the item called the *collapse box* — as shown in the diagram, that little box is present only if your Mac has *Mac OS 8 or later.*

And what, you may understandably be shrieking, is *Mac OS 8 or later?*

Long story. Every year, Apple Computer piles neat new features onto the behind-the-scenes software that runs your computer. This backstage software was once called the *operating system.* But because everyone's in such a hurry these days, people now just call it the *OS.* (Say it "O.S.," not "oss.")

In August 1997, new Macs started coming equipped with *Mac OS 8,* or even 8-point-something — the newest, trendiest OS around. I bring up this point here because if you don't *have* OS 8 or later, your Mac will react differently to the lessons in this book. For example, if you click a menu (like the word Special at the top of your screen), you don't *have* to hold the mouse button down in Mac OS 8. If you *click-and-let-go* on the word Special, the menu stays down all by itself — until you click elsewhere (or wait for 15 seconds, glassy-eyed and motionless). What a huge savings of muscular effort!

Things *look* different in OS 8, too. Here's an example of the older look (left) side-by-side with the newer one (right):

See? The *things* on the screen are pretty much the same; they've just had a makeover on *Oprah.*

In this book, I'll mostly be showing the newer look — don't let it faze you. Even with an older Mac, you'll still find everything where it's supposed to be.

Tell you what: From now on, if something I'm teaching you seems odd, look for a Mac OS 8 icon or Mac OS 8.5 icon like the one beside this paragraph. Then you'll know you're not going crazy.

It would help, I guess, if you knew which OS version *your* Mac uses. Fortunately, finding out is easy.

Get a pencil.

See the logo in the upper-left corner of the screen? As you may recall, it's no ordinary logo. It's actually a menu, just like the ones you've already experienced. Point your arrow cursor tip on the apple, hold the button down, and watch what happens.

As with any menu, a list drops down. This one, however, has an extremely useful command. This command is so important that it's separated by a dotted line from the mere mortal list items after it. It's *About This Computer*.

Slide the pointer down until About This Computer turns black and then release the mouse button. A window appears:

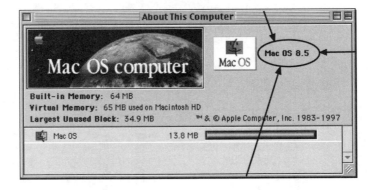

As my subtle drawn-in arrows indicate, this window reveals what version of the System software you have. The version is probably System Software 7-point-something or Mac OS 8-point-something. (It may even be 7- or 8-point-something-*point*-something, indicating that Apple uses a math even newer than New Math.)

In any case, the version is a number you'll need to know later in this book and later in your life. Therefore, take this opportunity to write it onto your Cheat Sheet (the yellow cardboard page inside the front cover of this book). You'll find a little blank for this information in the upper-left corner of your card, where it says "Your System version."

When you're finished with this little piece of homework, close the About This Computer window by clicking the little square in the upper-left corner — the Close box — to make it go away.

The main question is: Do you have something in the *Mac OS 8* family or the *System 7* family? The answer will make a big difference, both to your understanding of this book and to your ability to get dates at computer-club meetings.

All Macs made since 1991 come with System 7 or Mac OS 8; for the rest of this book, I'll assume that you have one of those versions. If your Mac is *really* old, and you have System 6, I respectfully refer you to the original *Macs For Dummies* (the first edition), deep in your library's sub-basement.

Double-clicking in theory and practice

All right, back to the lesson in progress. Make sure your hard-drive window is open.

So far, all of your work in the Finder (the desktop) has involved moving the mouse around. But your keyboard is useful, too. For example, do you see the System Folder? Even if you don't, here's a quick way to find it: Quickly type *SY* on your keyboard.

Presto, the Mac finds the System Folder (which happens to be the first thing that begins with those letters) and highlights it, in effect dropping it in front of you, wagging its tail.

Now try pressing the arrow keys on your keyboard — right, left, up, down. The Mac highlights neighboring icons as you do so.

Suppose you want to see what's in the System Folder. Of course, using your newfound noun-verb method, you could (1) click the System Folder to select it and then (2) choose Open from the File menu.

But that's the sissy way. Try this power shortcut: Point to the System Folder icon so that the tip of the arrow cursor is squarely inside the picture of the folder. Keeping the mouse still, click twice in rapid succession. With stunning originality, the Committee for the Invention of Computer Terminology calls this advanced computing technique *double-clicking*.

If all went well, your double-click opened a new window, showing you the contents of the System Folder. (If it didn't work, you probably need to keep the mouse still or double-click faster.)

Remember this juicy golden rule: *Double-click means "open."*

In your Mac life, you'll be asked (or tempted) to click many an item on-screen: buttons that say "OK"; tools that look like paintbrushes; all manner of multiple-choice buttons. In every one of these cases, you're supposed to click *once.*

The only time you ever *double*-click something is when you want to *open* it. Got it?

Multiple windows

Now you should have two windows open on the screen: the hard-disk window and the System Folder window. (The System Folder window may be covering the first one; they're like overlapping pieces of paper on a desk.)

Try this: Click the title bar of the System Folder window (just *one* click). Drag the title bar downward until you can see the hard-drive window behind it, as shown here:

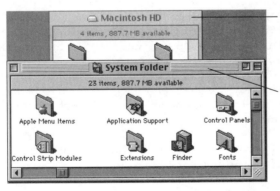

You can tell that this window is in back, because its title bar is solid light gray. Just click anywhere in the window to bring it to the front.

You know that this window is the top window, because its title bar is striped.

Take a stress-free moment to experiment with these two windows: Click the back one to bring it forward; then click the one that was in front to bring it to the front again.

Using a list view

There's one more aspect of windows that will probably make Type A personalities wriggle with delight. Up 'til now, you've been viewing the contents of your disk as a bunch of icons. Nice, but wouldn't it be neat to see things alphabetically?

1. **Make sure the System Folder is the active window (the one in front; "A." in the following figure).**

   We're going to use the System Folder because it's got a lot of stuff in it.

   Next, you're going to use a menu. Remember how to choose a menu command? Point to the menu's name and hold down the mouse button.

2. **Locate the View menu at the top of the screen. From it, choose "by Name" or "as List." (See "B." in the following picture.)**

   Suddenly, the big icons are replaced by a neat alphabetical list of the window's contents (labeled here as "C.").

A. 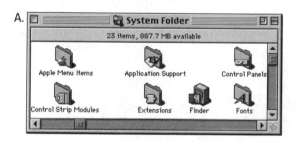   B.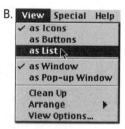

C.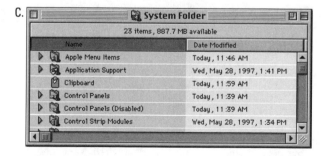

Invasion of the little triangles

When you view a window's contents in a list, each folder *within* the window is marked by a tiny triangle. The triangle points to the right.

You can open one of these folders-within-the-folder in the usual way, if you wish — by double-clicking. But it's much more satisfying for neat freaks to click the *triangle* instead. In the following figure, the before-and-after view of the Control Panels folder (inside the System Folder) shows how much more organized you can be.

When you click the triangle, in other words, your window contents look like an outline. The contents of that subfolder are indented. To "collapse," or close, the folder, click the downward-pointing triangle.

One more trick: See the words Name, Date Modified, and so on (at the top of the window)? Click any of these words. Instantly the Mac re-sorts everything in the window, based on the word you clicked. Example: click Size, if it's visible, and you'll see the largest files listed first.

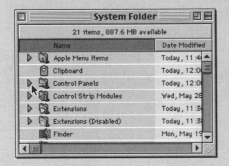

The easiest homework you've ever had

To reinforce your budding mouse skills, here's a pathetically easy assignment: Try out your Mac's silent but friendly Information Desk — its built-in help center. To visit it, look for a little question-mark menu (System 7.5 through 7.6) or a Help menu (Mac OS 8 or later) at the top of your screen:

System 7 through 7.6:

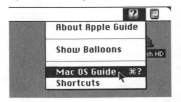

Mac OS 8 and later:

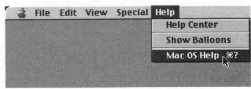

Help in System 7 through 8.1

When you choose Help or Macintosh Guide from this menu, up pops a handy welcome screen. Click the Topics button to see a list of common "How do I . . . ?" questions about common tasks (like printing and using disks) and definitions.

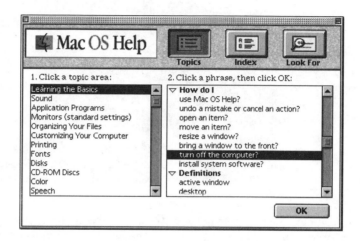

If you now double-click a question shown on the right side, the Mac will actually walk you through the steps for achieving whatever-it-is you're trying to do. All you have to do is follow the steps described in the little help window. When you've completed each step, click the right-arrow button on the screen to see the next step.

When you're supposed to use the mouse, a big fat red ghostly magic marker draws a circle around whatever you're supposed to manipulate. And if you ever get confused by even these patient instructions, you can click the "Huh?" button for an even more basic explanation. It's all pretty wonderful. More of life's institutions should have "Huh?" buttons.

Help in Mac OS 8.5 and later

In its effort to make the Help feature more helpful, Apple Computer over-hauled the guts of this feature when it wrote Mac OS 8.5. When you choose Mac OS Help from the Help menu, you get a window that looks more like this:

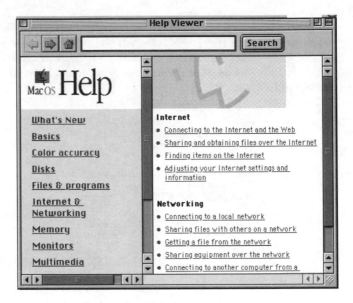

You can use this new help center in two ways. First, you can type a help topic into the blank at the top of the window (such as *naming files* or *dialing the Internet*) — and then click the Search button. If you're having a good night, the window will then show you a list of help pages that might contain the answer you're looking for; click the name of the topic that seems to hold some promise.

Second, you can click your way through this little help program. In the previous illustration, see all the topics written in blue underlined type?

Of course not. This is a black-and-white book. How silly of me.

But on your *screen*, all those underlined phrases show up in blue lettering. That blueness, and that underlining, means *click me to jump to a different page.* By clicking on successive blue underlined phrases, you can often home in on the precise Help article you're interested in.

Pit stop

Shut the Mac down now, if you want (flip back a few pages to the section "Shutting down" for complete instructions). Chapter $1\frac{1}{2}$ is something of a chalk-talk to help you understand what's really happening inside the computer's puny brain.

Chapter 1½

High-Tech Made Easy

● ●

In This Chapter

▶ How disks and memory work

▶ A floppy disk is neither floppy nor a disk. Discuss.

▶ Making the distinction between floppy and hard disks

▶ Why you'll never lose work to a computer glitch

▶ What to remember about memory

● ●

How a Mac Works

I'm a little worried about sticking this chapter so close to the front of the book. Plenty of people firmly believe that the Mac has a personality — that when something goes wrong, the Mac is being cranky; and when a funny message appears on the screen, the Mac is being friendly. Don't let the following discussion of cold, metal, impersonal circuitry ruin that image for you; the Mac *does* have a personality, no matter what the wireheads say.

For the first time, you're going to have to roll up your brain's sleeves and chew on some actual computer jargon. Don't worry — you'll feel coolly professional and in control by the time it's over. Besides, it's a short chapter.

Storing things with floppy disks

Human beings, for the most part, store information in one of two places. Either we retain something in our memory — or, if it's too much to remember, we write it down on the back of an envelope.

Computers work pretty much the same way (except they're not quite as handy with envelopes). They can either store what they know in their relatively pea-brained *memory,* which I'll cover in a moment, or they can write it down. A computer writes stuff down on computer disks.

The most common kind of disk is the floppy disk. Ironically, the Mac's floppy disks aren't floppy, and they're not disks. They're actually hard plastic squares, 3½ inches on a side.

Inside the protective hard shell, though, there's a circle of the same shiny brown stuff that cassette tapes are made of. (I suppose that means a floppy disk *is* really in there.) Anyway, instead of recording a James Taylor song or a Bruce Willis movie, as audio or videotapes would do, the computer records your documents: notes for your novel, your latest financial figures, or a fan letter to Hootie & the Blowfish.

Floppy disks come in several capacities, but even the largest one holds only about 1,000 pages' worth of data. That may seem like a lot, but that's just text. Pictures, for instance, take up much more space; that same floppy disk can probably only hold one or two color pictures. You can see, then, that floppies aren't very handy for storing *lots* of information. That's why they're has-beens, their careers fading faster than David Caruso's after leaving *NYPD Blue*. Current Mac models (including iMacs), in fact, can't even accept floppy disks, unless you buy an add-on floppy drive.

Conceptualizing the hard disk

Every Mac has an even better storage device built inside it — a *hard disk*. The concept of a hard disk confuses people because it's hidden inside the Mac's case. Since you can't see it or touch it, it's sort of conceptual — like beta-carotene or God, I guess. But it's there, spinning quietly away, and a hefty chunk of your Mac's purchase price paid for it.

Hard disks differ from floppy disks in a few critical ways. A hard disk delivers information to the computer's brain about 20 times faster, holds about 2,000 times more, and costs about 400 times as much. (Floppies are dirt cheap.)

Why all this talk of disks? Because a hard disk is where your life's work is going to live when the computer is shut off. You will, like it or not, become intensely interested in the overall health of your computer's hard disk.

Understanding memory

Okay. Now we get to the good stuff: how a computer really works. I know you'd just as soon not know what's going on in there, but this is mental broccoli: It's good for you, and later in life, you'll be glad you were forced to digest it. If, at this point, your brain is beginning to hemorrhage, skip this section and find serenity in Chapter 2.

There's actually a significant difference between a *Mac's* memory and *your* memory (besides the fact that yours is probably much more interesting). When the Mac is turned off at night, it forgets *everything*. It becomes a dumb, metal-and-plastic doorstop. That's because a computer's memory, just like yours, is kept alive by electrical impulses. When you turn off a Mac, the electricity stops.

Therefore, each time you turn on a Mac, it has to re-learn everything it ever knew, including the fact that it's a computer, what kind of computer it is, how to display text, how many days until your warranty expires, and so on. Now we arrive at the purpose of those disks I've been droning on about; that's where the computer's knowledge lives when the juice is off. Without a disk, the Mac is like someone with a completely hollow skull (and we've all met *that* type). If you're ever unlucky enough to experience a broken hard drive, you'll see how exciting a Mac can be without any disks: It shows a completely gray screen with a small blinking question mark in the middle. (I've met a few people like *that,* too.)

 When you turn on the Mac, there's whirring and blinking. The hard disk inside begins to spin. When it hits about 4,500 rpm, the Mac starts reading the hard disk — it "plays" the disk like a CD player. It finds out: "Hey, I'm a Mac! And this is how I display text!" and so on. The Mac is reading the disk and copying everything it reads into *memory.* (That's why the computer takes a minute or so to start up.)

Memory is really neat. After something's in memory, it's instantaneously available to the computer. The Mac no longer has to read the disk to learn something. Memory is also expensive (at least compared to disks); memory is a bunch of complicated circuits etched onto a piece of silicon the size of a piece of Trident by people in white lab coats.

Because it's more expensive, Macs have far less memory than disk space. For example, even if your hard disk holds every issue of *National Geographic* ever published, you're probably only going to *read* one article at a time. So the Mac reads "The Nocturnal Nubian Gnat: Nature's Tiniest Vampire" from your hard disk, loads it into memory, and displays it on the screen. So it doesn't matter that your Mac's memory doesn't hold as much as your entire hard disk; the hard disk is used for *long-term, permanent* storage of *lots* of things, and memory is used for *temporary* storage while you work on *one thing at a time.*

Who's Meg?

 You often hear computer jocks talk about megs. Only rarely are they referring to Meg Ryan and Meg Tilly. Meg is short for *megabyte.* So is the abbreviation MB. (*Mega* = 1,000,000 and *byte* = an iota of information so small it can only specify a single letter of the alphabet.)

What's highly confusing to most beginners is that memory (fast, expensive, temporary) and hard-disk space (permanent, slower) are measured in the *same units:* megabytes. A typical new Mac has 16 or 32 megs of memory (silicon chips), but 2,000 or 4,000 megs of hard-disk space (spinning platters).

(*Free bonus fact:* If a hard drive's size reaches 1,000 megs, it gets a new measurement name — its size is said to be one *gigabyte*. The abbreviation for one gigabyte is 1GB. Computer nerds sometimes use shorthand for this measurement — "My Mac's hard drive has eight gigs" — which absolutely bewilders jazz-club musicians.)

With these vital facts in mind, see if you can answer the following paradoxical dinner party question:

"How many megs does your Macintosh have?"

The novice's answer: "Um . . . say, have you tried those little cocktail weenies?"

The partly-initiated's reply: "I . . . I think 250?"

The truly enlightened response: "What do you mean, how many megs? Are you referring to *memory* or to *hard-disk storage space?* Here, have a cocktail weenie."

Understanding RAM

Let's add another term to your quickly growing nerd vocabulary list. It pains me to teach you this word, because it's one of those really meaningless terms that was invented purely to intimidate people. Trouble is, you're going to hear it a lot. You may as well be prepared.

It's RAM. You pronounce it like the sheep. RAM is memory. A typical Mac has 16, 32, or 64 megs of RAM (in other words, of memory).

Incidentally, this might be a good time to find out how much RAM *you* have. Here's how to find out.

Turn on your Mac.

Remember the menu? The fruit in the upper-left corner of the screen? Pull down that menu as you did in Chapter 1. Once again, slide the pointer down until About This Computer turns black, and then release the mouse button.

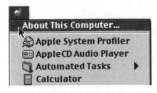

A window appears.

The number labeled Built-in Memory (which I've circled in the preceding picture) is how much actual RAM your Mac has. It's probably some multiple of eight. Older Macs probably have less; new ones have more. (Similarly, the number labeled Total Memory may be higher, thanks to tricks like RAM Doubler and virtual memory, which are explained in painstaking detail in Chapter 15.)

In any case, your Mac's RAM endowment is a statistic you'll enjoy reviewing again and again. Therefore, take this opportunity to write this number onto your yellow cardboard Cheat Sheet at the front of the book. There's a little blank for this information, near where you wrote your System-software version.

Putting it all together

Now that you know where a computer's information lives, let me take you on a tour of the computer's guts. Let's get into our little imaginary Disney World tram. Keep hands and feet inside the car at all times.

Why they call it RAM

You know what an *acronym* is, right? It's a bunch of initials, like M.A.D.D. or SALT Treaty . . . or RAM.

When the Committee for Arbitrary Acronyms (the CAA) ratified the abbreviation RAM, it probably stood for Random Abbreviation for Memory. Today, it supposedly stands for Random Access Memory.

Whatever *that* means.

When you turn on the Mac, as noted earlier, the hard disk spins, and the Mac copies certain critical information into its memory. So far, the Mac only knows that it's a computer. It doesn't know anything else that's stored on your hard disk. It doesn't know about Nocturnal Nubian Gnats, or your new screenplay, or how much you owe on your credit card — yet.

To get any practical work done, you now have to transfer the article (or screenplay, or spreadsheet) into memory; in Macintosh terminology, you have to *open a file*. In Chapter 2, you'll find out how easy and idiot-proof this is. Anyway, after you open a file, it appears on the screen. (It's *in memory* now.)

While your document is on the screen, you can make changes to it. This, of course, is why you bought a computer in the first place. You can delete a sentence from your novel or move a steamy scene to a different chapter (the term for this process is *word processing*). If you're working on your finances, you can add a couple of zeros to your checking-account balance (the term for this process is *wishful thinking*). All without any eraser crumbs or whiteout.

Perceptive readers who haven't already gotten bored and gone off to watch TV will recognize that you're making all these changes to what's in *memory*. The more you change the screenplay that's up on the screen, the more it's different from that *permanent* copy that's still on your disk, safe and sound.

At this point, you're actually in a pretty precarious position. Remember that memory is sustained by electricity. In other words, if your 4-year-old mistakes the Mac's power cord for a handy suckable plaything and jerks it out of the wall, then the electricity stops, the screen goes blank, and all the changes you've made disappear forever. You're left with the original copy on the disk, of course, but any work you've done on it vanishes, along with anything else in the Mac's memory.

However, every Mac program has a simple command, called Save, that saves your work back onto the hard disk. That is, the computer *updates* the original copy that's still on the hard disk, and you're safe. Even if a sun storm wipes out all power plants in the Northern Hemisphere and your Mac goes dark, your novel or letter or spreadsheet is safe on the disk. Most people use the Save command every five or ten minutes so that their work is always up to date and preserved on the disk. (You'll learn how to use the Save command in Chapter 4.)

"I lost all my work!"

So that you'll quit worrying about it, the precariousness of memory accounts for the horror stories you sometimes hear from people who claim that they lost their work to a computer. "I was on volume Y of the encyclopedia I've been writing," they'll say, "and I lost all of it because of a computer glitch!"

Now you can cry crocodile tears and then skip back to your office with a smirk. *You* know what happened. They probably worked for hours with some document on the screen but forgot to use the Save command. Then the unthinkable happened — someone tripped on the power cord — and sure enough, all the changes they'd made got wiped out. A simple Save command would have stored everything neatly on the hard disk.

Top Ten Differences between Memory and a Hard Disk

May you never confuse memory with a hard disk again.

1. You usually buy memory 16 or 32 megs at a time. Hard disks come in sizes like 2 gigs, 4 gigs, and on up. (A *gigabyte* is 1,000 *megabytes.*)

2. Memory comes on a little minicircuit board. A hard disk is a plastic- or metal-cased box with cables hanging out of it.

3. You can install memory only inside the computer (something you usually hire a local guru to do). A hard disk may be either inside the Mac (an *internal* drive) or a separate box you plug into the back (an *external* drive).

4. Memory delivers information to the Mac's brain almost instantly. The hard disk sometimes seems to take forever.

5. Some disks are removable. When one fills up, you can insert a different one. (Some examples: floppy disks, Zip disks, and SuperDisk disks.) Removing RAM is a more serious proposition, generally involving a knowledgeable geek's assistance.

6. Not every computer on earth has a hard disk. (The earliest Macs used nothing but floppy disks, and pocket organizers like the PalmPilot, Sharp Wizard, and Casio Boss have no disks at all.) But every computer ever made has memory.

7. If you listen carefully, you can hear when the Mac is reading information off a hard disk; it makes tiny frantic scraping noises. You can't tell when the Mac is getting information from RAM.

8. As a very general rule, RAM costs about $12 per meg, and hard drive space averages about 15 cents per meg.

9. Memory's contents disappear when you turn off the computer. A disk's contents stay there until you deliberately throw them away.

10. To find out how much *hard-disk space* you have left, you look at the top of a window on your desktop, like this:

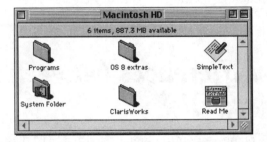

But to see how much *RAM* you have left, you have to choose About This Computer from your menu to get the window shown a few pages back.

The number where it says Largest Unused Block is roughly how much RAM you're not using at the moment. Details in Chapter 15.

Chapter 2

Doing Windows, Getting Floppy

● ●

In This Chapter

▶ All about windows, folders, and icons

▶ Learning keyboard shortcuts

▶ Working with floppy disks

▶ Tips on using windows and floppy disks to raise your social status

● ●

Becoming Manipulative

All the clicking and dragging and window-shoving you learned in Chapter 1 is, in fact, leading up to something useful.

Foldermania

I've said that your hard disk is like the world's biggest filing cabinet. It's where you store all your stuff. But a filing cabinet without filing *folders* would be about as convenient to handle as an egg without a shell.

The folders on the Mac screen don't occupy any space on your hard drive. They're electronic fictions whose sole purpose is to help you organize your stuff.

Mr. Folder

The Mac provides an infinite supply of folders. Want a folder? Do this:

From the File menu, choose New Folder.

Ooh, tricky, this machine! A new folder appears. Note that the Mac gracefully proposes "untitled folder" as its name. (Gotta call it *something,* I suppose.)

Notice something else, though: the name is *highlighted* (black). Remember our earlier lesson? Highlighted = selected = ready for you to *do* something. When *text* is highlighted, the Mac is ready for you to *replace* it with anything you type. In other words, you don't even have to backspace over the text. Just type away.

1. **Type** *USA Folder.* **Press the Return key.**

   The Return key tells the Mac that your naming spurt is over.

   Now, to see how folders work, create another one.

2. **From the File menu, once again choose New Folder.**

   Another new folder appears, once more waiting for a title.

3. **Type** *Ohio.* **Press Return.**

You're going to create one more empty folder. But by this time, your wrist is probably weary from the forlorn trek back and forth to the File menu. Don't you wish you could make a folder faster?

You can.

Keyboard shortcuts

Pull down the File menu, but don't select any of the commands in it yet. See those weird notations to the right of some commands?

Get used to 'em. They're *keyboard shortcuts,* and they appear in almost every menu you'll ever see. Keyboard shortcuts let you select certain menu items without using the mouse. (Although the menu shows capital letters, don't use the Shift key when the shortcut is, for example, ⌘-N.)

Unimportant sidebar about other menu symbols

Besides the little keyboard-shortcut symbols at the right side of a menu, you'll occasionally run into a little downward-pointing arrow, like this:

That arrow tells you that the menu is so long, it doesn't even fit on the screen. The arrow is implying that still more commands are in the menu that you're not seeing. To get to those additional commands, carefully roll the pointer down the menu all the way to that down-pointing triangle. Don't let the sudden jumping scare you: The menu commands will jump upward, bringing the hidden ones into view.

And then there are the little black triangles pointing to the *right* (left side of the illustration). These triangles indicate that, when selected, the menu command won't do anything except offer you several *other* commands, which pop out to the side (at right in the figure):

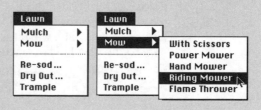

Some people love keyboard shortcuts, claiming that if you're in a hurry, pressing keys is faster than using the mouse. Other people hate keyboard shortcuts, pointing out that using the mouse doesn't require any memorization. In either case, here's how keyboard shortcuts work.

When you type on a typewriter, you press the Shift key to make a capital letter, right? They call the Shift key a *modifier key* because it turns ordinary, well-behaved citizen keys like 3 and 4 into madcap symbols like # and $. Welcome to the world of computers, where everything is four times more complicated. Instead of having only *one* modifier key, the Mac has *four* of them! Look down next to your spacebar. There they are: In addition to the Shift key, one says Option, one says Ctrl, and another has a little ⌘ symbol on it.

It's that little cloverleaf — the *command key* — whose symbol appears in the File menu. Next to the New Folder command, you see ⌘-N. That means:

1. **While pressing the ⌘ key, press the N key. Then release everything.**

    Bam! You've got yourself another folder.

2. **Type *Michigan* and press Return.**

    You've just named your third folder. So why have you been wasting a perfectly good afternoon (or whatever it is in your time zone) making empty folders? So you can pretend you're getting organized.

3. **Drag the Ohio folder on top of the USA Folder.**

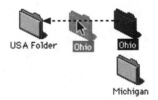

USA Folder   Ohio   Ohio

Michigan

    Make sure that the tip of the arrow actually hits the center of the USA Folder so that the folder becomes highlighted. The instant it turns black, let go of the Ohio folder — and watch it disappear into the USA Folder. (If your aim wasn't good, you'll now see the Ohio folder sitting *next* to the USA Folder; try the last step again.)

4. **Put the Michigan folder into the USA Folder in the same way — by dragging it on top of the USA Folder.**

    As far as you know, though, those state folders have *disappeared.* How can you trust me that they're now neatly filed away?

5. **Double-click the USA Folder.**

    Yep. Opens right up into a window, and there are your two darling states, nestled sweetly where they belong.

God never closes a window

When you opened the USA folder, did you notice how its icon changed texture? After you double-clicked it, the icon turned dark and sort of grainy.

It's *supposed* to do that. When you double-click any icon to make its window appear, the icon itself turns into a grainy silhouette. That's your visual clue that it's been opened.

The icon won't collapse back into its normal, more attractive state until you close the corresponding window. (Can't find it? Then double-click the already-opened icon *again*. Its window will pop to the fore.)

If you were to double-click one of the *state* folders, you'd open *another* window. (Having a million windows open at once is nothing to be afraid of. If you're a neatness freak, you might feel threatened, but closing them is easy enough — remember the close box in the upper-left corner of each one?)

Okay, so how do you get these inner folders *out* again? Do you have to drag them individually? That would certainly be a bummer if you had all 50 folders in the USA Folder.

Turns out there are several ways to select more than one icon at a time.

6. **Click above and to the left of the Ohio folder (Step 1 below). Without releasing the mouse, drag down and to the right so that you enclose both folders with a dotted rectangle (Steps 2 and 3).**

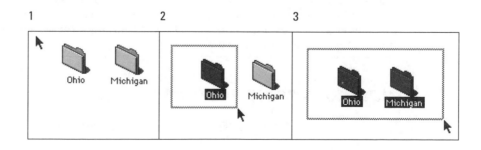

Bonus technique for extra credit

The method of selecting several icons by dragging a rectangle around them is fine if all the icons are next to each other. But how would you select only the icons that begin with the letter A in this picture?

The power-user's secret: Click each icon *while pressing the Shift key*. As long as you're pressing Shift, you continually add additional, non-adjacent icons to the selection. (And if you Shift-click one by accident, you can *deselect* it by Shift-clicking *again*. Try it!)

You can't very well enclose each A by dragging the mouse — you'd also get all the *other* icons within the same rectangle.

Release the mouse button when you've got both icons enclosed.

Now that you have several folders selected, you can move them en masse to another location.

7. Drag the Ohio folder outside of the USA Folder window.

The Michigan folder goes along for the ride.

This was a somewhat unproductive exercise, of course, because we were only working with empty folders. It gets much more exciting when you start working with your own documents. All these techniques work equally well with folders and with documents.

How to trash something

Here's one more icon-manipulation trick you'll probably find valuable.

1. Close the USA Folder by clicking its close box.

2. Drag the folder on top of the Trash can in the lower-right corner of the screen.

Don't let go until the Trash can actually turns black (when the tip of the arrow cursor is upon it). When you do let go, notice how the Trash can bulges or overflows, a subtle reinforcement of how important it thinks your stuff is.

Anyway, that's how you throw things out on the Mac: Just drag them on top of the Trash can. (In Mac OS 8 and later, there's even a keystroke for this: Highlight an icon and then press ⌘-Delete. The chosen icon goes flying into the Trash as though it's just been drop-kicked.)

What's really hilarious is how hard Apple made it for you to get rid of something. Just putting something into the Trash doesn't actually get rid of it; technically, you've really only put it into the Oblivion Waiting Room. It'll sit there forever, in an overflowing trash can. If you needed to rescue something, you could just double-click the Trash can to open its window; then you could drag whatever-it-was right back onto the screen.

So if putting something into the Trash doesn't really delete it, how *do* you really delete it? You choose Empty Trash from the Special menu.

But even *then* your stuff isn't really gone; you get a message like this:

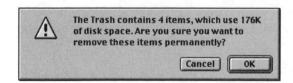

Click OK, and your file is finally gone.

Actually, don't tell anybody, but *even after* you've emptied the Trash, your file *still* isn't really gone forever. Programs like Norton Utilities can unerase a file that's been trashed, as long as you haven't used your Mac much since you threw away the file. That's useful to remember in case (1) you ever trash something by mistake, or (2) you're a spy.

Now you can understand why you never hear Macintosh owners complain of having thrown away some important document by accident — the Mac won't *let* you get rid of anything without fighting your way through four layers of warnings and red tape.

Pretty cool computer, huh?

Fun with Floppies

For our next trick, you're going to need a floppy disk. If you didn't buy a box of blank disks with your Mac, you're going to need some eventually. Call up Mac Warehouse and order some. They're cheap and you'll have them by tomorrow morning. (Phone number is in the Resource Resource at the back of the book.)

Or, if you're one of the 348 billion lucky souls who've landed on America Online's mailing list, you've probably been getting *free* floppy disks from them every week. Feel free to erase the extras and use them as blanks.

And what if you have an iMac, a blue Power Mac, or another model that doesn't have a built-in slot for floppy disks? Either buy an add-on floppy-disk drive, or just read along and nod knowingly.

How to insert a floppy disk

Take your first disk. Hold it flat. You're going to slip it into the Mac *metal side* first, *label side* up.

Put the floppy disk into the *disk drive slot,* which is the thin horizontal slit on the front of your Mac (or the side of some PowerBooks). Keep pushing the disk in until the Mac gulps it in with a satisfying *kachunk.*

If it's a brand new disk, or not a Mac disk, you'll probably see this message:

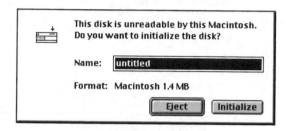

Go ahead. Click Initialize. (If you're given a choice of *how* to erase this disk, you generally want the "Macintosh 1.4MB" option. If you're going to be handing this disk to somebody who has to use a Windows or DOS-based computer, choose the DOS option, if it's there.)

You're then asked to name the disk; type a name, click OK, and then wait about 45 seconds while the Mac prepares the disk for its new life as your data receptacle.

If it's *not* a new disk — for example, if you're using one of the disks that came with your Mac — the floppy-disk icon shows up on the right side, just beneath your hard-disk icon:

To see what's on the disk, double-click the icon. As you've no doubt tired of hearing repeated, a *double-click* on a disk icon *opens* its contents window.

How to copy stuff onto a disk

This is important stuff: In your lifetime, you'll do a lot of copying from disks *to* your hard drive (such as when you buy a new program and want to put it on your hard drive). And if you're smart, you'll also do a lot of copying onto disks *from* your hard drive (such as when you make a backup copy of all your work, in preparation for the inevitable day when your hard disk calls in sick).

How not to erase a floppy

You know how an audiocassette has that small plastic tab, which you can pry out to prevent your little sister from accidentally recording over the tape? And you know how when you want to record over the cassette later, you have to put a piece of Scotch tape over the resulting hole? And you know how the Scotch tape comes off inside the machine, ruining your recording and your $300 stereo system?

Well, progress has marched on. A floppy has a "can't-erase-this-disk" tab, too. But on a disk, you don't actually have to pry out the tab; you can just slide it, like an On/Off switch, back and forth.

Check it out: In the corner of the disk, on the back, on the top left, there's a little square sliding tab. When you can see through the hole, you've *locked* the disk, and you can't erase it or trash any of its contents.

When you slide the tab so that it *covers* the hole, the disk is unlocked, and you can erase it, trash it, or copy new stuff onto it.

In that case, beware of little sisters.

Here's how you copy stuff onto a floppy disk. (If your Mac has another kind of removable storage disk, such as Zip, Jaz, or SuperDisk disks, you can follow the exact same steps. They hold many times more than floppy disks, but they otherwise behave exactly the same.)

We'll assume that you've already inserted a floppy disk.

1. **Double-click your hard-disk icon to open its window.**
2. **Drag the Ohio folder on top of the floppy-disk icon.**

That's it. On a Macintosh, making a copy of something is as easy as dragging it to the disk you want it copied onto. You can also drag something into the disk's *window* (instead of onto its *icon*).

How to copy something to your hard drive

Copying something *from* a floppy *to* your hard disk is equally easy. Open the floppy-disk window (by double-clicking the floppy-disk icon). Then drag whatever icons you want from the window onto the hard-disk icon (or into the hard-disk window).

For example, in the following illustration, two files are being copied from a floppy disk — not just into the hard-disk window, but into a *specific folder* on the hard disk:

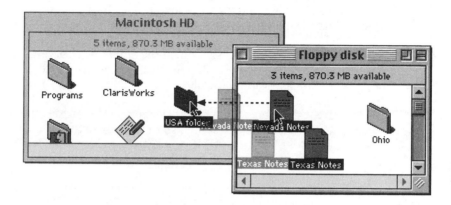

(This is also how you copy something from a CD-ROM disc, or a Zip disk, or any other kind of disk, onto your hard drive. See Chapter 18 for details on those contraptions, which are just like floppy disks, only bigger.)

You can make as many copies of a file as you want without ever experiencing a loss of quality. You're digital now, kids.

Disk info you can safely skip

Floppy disks through the ages have come in three different capacities, although all the disks look alike: the 400K, or *single-sided* disks, nearly extinct; 800K, or *double-sided* disks, still kicking around in veteran Mac fans' bottom drawers; and 1.4MB, or *high-density* disks, which is just about the only kind you encounter these days.

Actually, 1.4MB is a *lot* of storage for such a little disk — around 1400K, or 3.5 times as much as the original single-sided disks. High-density disks are marked with the letters CH, for some reason:

Well, okay, it's really supposed to be an upside-down *HD,* for high-density, but the logo designer had a bad night.

How to get a disk out again

Okay, so you've made a backup copy of your fourth-quarter report, or you've just copied a new program onto your hard disk. Now what? How do you get the disk out? And if you've inserted a CD-ROM disc into your Mac (see Chapter 18), how do you get *it* out again?

In Mac OS 8, just click the disk icon on the screen — and then, from the Special menu, choose Eject Disk. The disk — floppy, Zip, CD, whatever — pops out of the Mac automatically.

But in previous systems, the Eject Disk command spits out the disk — but leaves the disk's *icon* on the screen so that the Mac thinks it's still available. The minute you try to go on with your work, the Mac will start displaying messages demanding that you give the disk back to it. Totally annoying.

A much better way to get rid of the disk, in that case, is to select its icon (noun) and choose *Put Away* (verb) from the File menu. That makes the disk pop out, *and* its image disappears from the screen. (If you care, there's a keyboard shortcut for Put Away: ⌘-Y.)

But the funnest way to eject a disk or CD is to drag its icon *to the Trash can!* Yes, yes, I *know* it looks like you're erasing the entire disk. It looks that way to *every* first-time Mac user. But you're not — instead, the disk just pops out of the slot.

When the disk is too shy to come out

Every now and then, you'll be stuck with a floppy disk or CD-ROM disc that won't come out of the drive, even if you've tried the usual ways of ejecting it.

In that case, turn the Mac off. While pressing the mouse button down continuously, turn it on again. Keep the mouse button pressed until the Trash can appears.

And if *that* doesn't pop the disk out, straighten a paper clip. Push it slowly but firmly into the

tiny pinhole to the right of the drive slot. That'll shove out the disk or CD no matter *what*.

Unless, of course, you're like my client Elsie, who, after trying all of these steps, *still* couldn't get her floppy to pop out. I drove over to her house to help — and discovered why the floppy wasn't ejecting: It wasn't there! Her floppy drive was empty.

Top Ten Window, Disk, and Trash Tips

Staggering through the basics of using your Mac unattended is one thing. Shoving around those on-screen windows and icons with grace is quite another. Master the following, and then invite your friends over to watch some evening.

1. To rename an icon or disk, click carefully on its name. Wait for a second or so, until a rectangle appears around the name. That's your cue to type away, giving it a new name. Press Return when you're done.

2. Don't forget that you can look at a window's contents in a neat list (choose "as List" or "by Name" from the View menu). Once in a list view, when a folder is highlighted, you can press ⌘-→ to expand it (as though you'd clicked the triangle to view its contents) and ⌘-← to collapse it again.

3. Every time you choose Empty Trash from the Special menu, the Mac asks you if you're absolutely sure. If you'd prefer to simply vaporize the Trash contents without being asked for confirmation, select the Trash icon. From the File menu, choose Get Info, and then click the "Warn before emptying" checkbox so that the checkmark (or X) disappears.

4. If you have a very important document, you can prevent it from getting thrown away by accident. Click its icon. From the File menu, choose Get Info. Turn on the Locked checkbox. Now, even if you put it in the Trash and try to empty the Trash, the Mac will simply tell you that there's a locked item in the Trash, which it won't get rid of.

5. You already know how to copy a file from one disk to another. You can copy it on the *same* disk, too. Click the icon and choose Duplicate from the File menu.

   Or, while pressing the Option key, drag the icon into a new window or folder.

6. Isn't it frustrating to open a window that's too small to show you all of its contents?

   Of course, you could spend a weekend fussing with the scroll bars, trying to crank the other icons into view. Or, using error-and-trial, you could drag the lower-right handle (the resize box) to make the window bigger.

There's a much quicker solution. Click the *zoom box* in the upper-right corner of the window. The Mac automatically makes the window *exactly* large enough to show all of the icons.

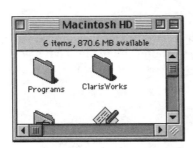
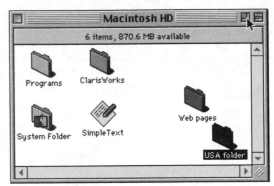

7. You don't have to be content to leave the Trash stranded way down there at the bottom of your screen. You can move it anywhere you want, just by dragging it.

   That's especially handy if you're lucky enough to have one of those screens the size of a Cineplex Odeon and don't feel like packing a week's worth of supplies every time you want to make a Journey to the Trash Corner.

8. In Mac OS 8 and later, a sneaky shortcut awaits. But it depends on your ability to locate the *Control* key (labeled Ctrl) at the lower corner of your keyboard. I'll wait right here until you've found it.

   Back so soon? Then try this: While pressing the Control key, point the cursor tip on an icon, disk, or the inside of a window. Keep the Control key pressed; if you now hold down the mouse button, a pop-up menu appears at your cursor tip, listing commands that pertain only to that icon, disk, or window.

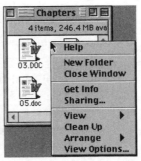

For example, if you Control-click a disk, you'll be offered commands like Eject, Help, and Open. If you Control-click an icon, you get commands like Get Info, Duplicate, and Move to Trash. And if you Control-click anywhere inside a window — but *not* directly on an icon — you're offered New Folder, Sort List, and Close Window. (The geek term for this phenomenon is *contextual menus* — because the menu is different depending on the context of your click.)

9. When your life overwhelms you with chaos and random events, at least your Mac can give you a sense of control and order.

If you have Mac OS 8 or later, try this little stunt. Open a window, such as your Macintosh HD window. From the View menu, choose "as Icons." Note how messy, crude, and slovenly your icons look!

Now, from the View menu, choose View Options. In the window that appears, click Keep arranged, like this:

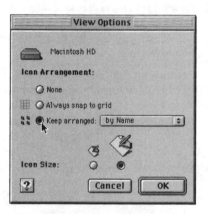

And then click OK. Now, no matter how many icons you add to this window, and no matter what size you make the window, your icons will always remain in neat alignment.

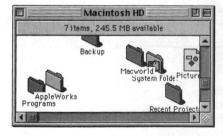
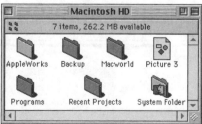

But what if your Mac doesn't have Mac OS 8 or later? (Consult the Cheat Sheet at the front of this book, where you were supposed to record this information.) You're not out of luck. You can achieve the same effect by pressing the Option key as you choose Clean Up by Name from the Special menu.

Once again, your icons snap into alignment — it's just that they don't *stay* that way, as they do in Mac OS 8. The minute you move an icon in or out of this window, it's back to chaos and randomness.

10. You don't have to eject disks and clean up your windows before you shut down the computer. Floppy disks pop out automatically, and the windows are right where you left them the next time you turn on the Mac.

The mystery of the reverse alphabet

It happens to everyone. It will happen to you. You wake up one morning, and all your files are listed in *reverse* alphabetical order.

Has the planet entered some kind of alternate dimension? No, nothing that exciting. Actually, you've accidentally clicked the *reverse-alphabetization button,* which appears in the upper-right corner of every list-view window, as highlighted here:

Reverse-alphabetization button

	Name	Date Modified	Size	K
▶	Help	6/3/98	79 MB	fo
▶	Extensions	Today	70.6 MB	fo
▶	Preferences	Today	16.2 MB	fo
▶	Appearance	6/3/98	15.6 MB	fo
	System	Yesterday	8.9 MB	s
▶	Apple Menu Items	6/3/98	8.6 MB	fo

System Folder
35 items, 1.4 GB available

Just click that doodad a second time to restore the sorting order you grew up with.

Chapter 3

Actually Accomplishing Something

● ●

In This Chapter

▶ What software is, for those who care

▶ Copying and pasting

▶ Desk accessories and the fruit-shaped menu they're listed in

▶ The pure, unalloyed joy of control panels

● ●

*T*he Mac is like a VCR. The disks you slide into the Mac are like the tapes you slip into your VCR. Without tapes (disks), the VCR (Mac) is worthless. But with tapes (disks), your VCR (Mac) can take on any personality.

A VCR might let you watch a Western one night, home movies another, and a *60 Minutes* exposé about a corrupt Good Humor man another night. In the same way, your Mac can be a typing instructor, a checkbook balancer, or a movie-editing machine, depending on the software you buy. Each piece of software — usually called a *program,* but sometimes known as an *application* — is like a different GameBoy cartridge: It makes the Mac look, feel, and behave differently. The average Mac user winds up using about six or seven different programs regularly.

Obsolescence Therapy

Your relationship with a software company doesn't end when you buy the program. First, the company provides a technical help staff for you to call when things get rocky. Some firms are great about this relationship — they give you a toll-free number that's answered immediately by a smart, helpful, customer-oriented technician. More often, though, sending out an SOS is a long-distance call . . . and a long-distance five- or ten-minute wait before somebody can help you. How can you find out how good a company's help line is? By asking around and reading the reviews in Mac magazines (such as *Macworld, MacHome Journal,* or *MacAddict*).

Like the computers themselves, software programs are continually being improved and enhanced by their manufacturers. Just as in owning a computer, owning a software program isn't a one-time cash outlay; each time the software company comes out with a new version of the program, you'll be offered the chance to get it for a small "upgrade fee" of $25 or $99, for example.

You'd think people would get fed up with this endless treadmill of expenses and just stick with the version they've got, refusing to upgrade to successive versions. Some manage it. Most people, however, succumb to the fear that somehow they'll be left behind by the march of technology, and wind up forking over the upgrade fees once a year or so. Let your budget and sense of independence be your guide.

Credit Card Workout #2: Buying Software

(Credit Card Workout #1, by the way, was buying the computer.)

The occasional Mac model, such as the iMac, comes with a handsome bonus gift of software preinstalled on the hard disk. If yours didn't, then until you go on another buying spree, you won't be able to do much more than admire the Mac's contribution to the décor.

Names and numbers

After you spend a while with Macs, you start to notice some peculiar naming conventions in software. First of all, all programmers must have broken space bars, because you never see spaces between words in the names of programs: PageMaker, WordPerfect, QuarkXPress, and even MyAdvanced-LabelMaker (I'm not making these up). Today, having a space in your title is like clipping your nails on the bus: It's simply not done.

You learn to tell how recent a program is by the version number after its name. What begins as BeeKeeper Version 1 becomes BeeKeeper 1.5 when its maker adds a spelling checker to the program, for example. Then the maker adds built-in help messages and calls the program BeeKeeper Pro 1.5.2. I don't know where the idea of multiple decimal points came from, but it's pretty dumb. It's only a matter of time before we'll start seeing ads for things like MacFish 2.4.9.6 and PageMan 3.6.5.4.2.1.

Oh, and when a program gets upgraded too many times, the company adds the word Pro to its name.

Of course, every Mac comes with *some* software. For example, each Mac comes with the System software (on a CD) that it needs for its own internal use. It comes with some miniprograms, like the Calculator and the Note Pad, called *desk accessories*. But none of this free software will make you very productive on the day you set up your computer.

Software, for the most part, is expensive. The most popular Mac word processing program, for example, is Microsoft Word, and it goes for about $300. If you plan to do number crunching, over 90 percent of Mac users use the spreadsheet Microsoft Excel (another $300). Want a database for handling order forms, tracking phone calls, and creating form letters? Check out the fantastic FileMaker Pro (around $200). (Try, *try* not to focus on the fact that what you *get* for that money is a 50 cent disk and a $3 manual.)

There are lower-priced alternatives, of course. For example, you can get a lot of power in the form of an *integrated* program like AppleWorks (formerly called ClarisWorks) — which comes already installed on some Mac models. For the cost of a single program, you get several programs mashed into one: word processor, database, spreadsheet, drawing program, and so on. (See Chapter 7, "A Whole Big Chapter on AppleWorks (ClarisWorks).")

In any case, you definitely need a word processor. Most people could use an address book program and a calendar/reminder program (or a combo address book/calendar program like Chronos Consultant). And then there are graphics: If you want to draw or paint, read Chapter 6 for some explanations and suggestions.

Where to get it

There are two places to buy software: via mail order and at a store. Unfortunately, as you'll quickly discover, today's computer stores generally offer a pathetically small selection of Macintosh software. On the other hand, mail-order companies offer thousands of choices, give much bigger discounts, take returns after you've opened the box, and don't charge sales tax. And, of course, you don't have to fire up the old Volvo. You get your stuff delivered to your door by the next day (the overnight shipping charge is usually $5 per order).

Check the Mac magazines like *Macworld* and *MacHome Journal* for more info on mail-order companies. They're called things like MacConnection, Mac Zone, and MacWarehouse. They all have toll-free phone numbers, and their catalogs and ads all appear in every single issue of those magazines. (Their numbers also appear in Appendix B, "The Resource Resource.") Overnight mail-order companies like these are truly one of the bright spots in the Mac world. You can call MacConnection, for example, until *2:45 a.m.* and get your new programs by midmorning (seven hours later). After being around them a while, you'll start to wish there were overnight mail-order grocery stores, gas stations, and dentists.

All right, maybe not dentists.

In the next chapter, you're going to do some word processing. That's what 90 percent of Mac users do the most of (when they're not hang gliding, housing the homeless, and saving the environment, I mean). I have no way of knowing what software, if any, you bought with your computer. Maybe you already have a word processing program, maybe not. (Look over your pile of boxes. If there's one that says Microsoft Word, Microsoft Office, WordPerfect, Nisus, or anything that ends with -*Write* or -*Works,* then you have a word processor.) If you don't have a word processor yet, call up a mail-order company and order one right now so that you'll be able to work with it tomorrow.

Until FedEx delivers your new software, however, let me show you some of the basic principles of using programs on the Mac. To make sure you've got the same thing on your screen that I do, we'll start off by using the built-in programs that came with your Mac.

Your very first software

There are several *menus* across the top of the screen (remember these?). As you get to know the Mac, you'll discover that their wording changes from program to program. Right now, they say, for example, File, Edit, View, and Special; in a word processor, they might say File, Edit, Font, Size, Format, and so on. The menu names (and the commands listed in those menus) are tailored to the function of the software.

El Cheapo software

Once you've read Chapter 12, and you've decided it might be fun to plug your Mac into the telephone line to dial up faraway computers, you may stumble onto another kind of software: *shareware*. These are programs written by individuals, not software companies, who make them freely available on the Internet. You can grab them, via telephone, and bring them to your own Mac. And get this: Only the *honor system,* for heaven's sake, compels you to pay the authors the $15 or $20 they're asking for.

Sure, shareware often has a homemade feel to it. On the other hand, some of it's really terrific. You can search for the kind of shareware program you want (and also for acres of sounds, pictures, clip art, and games) on America Online and on the Internet (such as at *www.shareware.com*).

There's one menu that's *always* on your screen, though: our friend the Apple menu (the at the left edge of the menu bar). Among other things, this menu provides immediate access to some useful miniprograms known as *desk accessories.* Desk accessories are surefire, nonthreatening, and fun — perfect for your first baby steps into the world of software.

Desk Accessories

Let's start simple. Move your cursor up to the menu and choose Calculator. The Calculator pops up in a tiny window of its own.

The Calculator

Using the mouse, you can click the little calculator buttons. The Mac gives you the correct mathematical answer, making you the owner of the world's biggest pocket calculator.

What's neat is that you can also type the keys on your *numeric keypad,* the block of number keys off to the right side of your keyboard. As you press these real keys, you can watch the on-screen keys in the Calculator window get punched accordingly. Try it out!

(Of course, most PowerBooks don't *have* a numeric keypad. Still, the numbers on the top row of regular alphabet keys work just as well.)

Take a moment to reinforce your love of windows: By dragging the *title bar* (where it says "Calculator"), move the Calculator window into a new position. If you were good and tired of looking at it, you could also make the Calculator go away by clicking its close box (in the upper-left corner, like on all windows).

But don't close the Calculator just yet. Leave it open on the screen.

The Note Pad

Now go to the menu again, and this time choose Note Pad. Instantly, the world's most frill-free word processor appears on the screen.

You'll learn more about word processing in the next section. For now, we're just going to do some informative goofing around. With the Note Pad open on your screen, type a math problem, like this:

37+8+19*3-100

(In the computer world, the asterisk * means "times," or multiply.) If you make a mistake, press the big Delete key at the upper-right corner of your keyboard. This means "Backspace."

Now, by dragging the Note Pad's title bar, move it so that you can see the Calculator window, too.

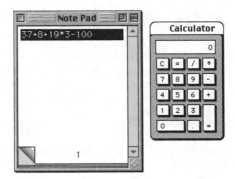

You're going to use two programs at once, making them cooperate with each other — one of the most remarkable features of the Mac.

Selecting text

This is about to get interesting.

Using the mouse, position the pointer at the left side of your equation (below, top). Press the button and drag, perfectly horizontally, to the right (middle). Release the mouse after you've highlighted the entire equation (bottom).

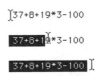

You've just *selected* some text. Remember in Chapter 1 when you *selected* an icon — and then used a menu command? Struggling, as always, to come up with a decent analogy, I likened this *select-then-operate* sequence to building a noun-verb sentence.

Secrets of the menu

The Calculator, along with other miniprograms like the Note Pad, Key Caps, and so on (all in the menu), is called a *desk accessory.* It's always available to you, no matter what Mac activity you're in.

One of the special features of the Mac, however, is that you can stick *anything you want* into that menu: full-fledged software applications, a disk icon, a folder, a document you work on a lot, a sound, and so on. (Some people wind up with *very* long menus.)

Want to know the secret of making your own menu? Check it out: Point to your hard-drive icon in the upper-right corner of the screen and double-click. Now double-click your System Folder icon. Inside *that,* you'll find a folder called Apple Menu Items. (Pretty cryptic, I know.)

Go ahead and drag any icon into this folder: another folder, a letter, your word processing program, whatever; instantly it appears in the menu for easy access.

(It's better still to put an *alias* of your icon in there, but Chapter 9, where aliases are explained, is still miles away.)

Well, it works just as well with text as it does with icons. You've now highlighted, or selected, some text. The Mac now knows what the noun is — what it's supposed to pay attention to. All you have to do is select a verb from one of the menus. And the verb du jour is *Copy.*

The cornerstone of human endeavor: Copy and Paste

Choose Copy from the Edit menu.

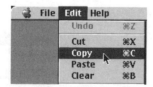

Thunder rolls, lightning flashes, the audience holds its breath . . . and absolutely nothing happens.

Behind the scenes, though, something awesomely useful occurred. The Mac looked at the selected equation and memorized it, socking it away into an invisible storage window called the *Clipboard.* The Clipboard is how you transfer stuff from one window into another and from one program into another. (Some programs even have a Show Clipboard command, in which case I take back the part about the Clipboard being invisible.)

Now then. You can't *see* the Clipboard at this point, but in a powerful act of faith, you put your trust in me and you believe that it contains the high-lighted material (the equation).

The Application menu

Do you see the tiny Note Pad icon at the right end of your menu bar? (If you have Mac OS 8.5 or later, it also *says* Note Pad, or whatever program you happen to be running.)

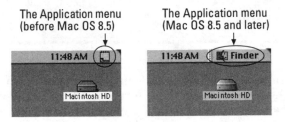

The Application menu
(before Mac OS 8.5)

The Application menu
(Mac OS 8.5 and later)

This icon actually represents a menu — the Application menu, of course. It lists all the programs you have running at once. At this moment, you have *three* programs running at once: the Note Pad, the Calculator, and the famous Finder (or desktop).

You multitasking maniac, you.

Choose Calculator from the Application menu.

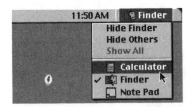

The Calculator window comes to the front, and the icon in the upper-right changes to look like a Calculator.

Those of you still awake will, of course, object to using the Application menu to bring the Calculator forward. You remember all too plainly from Chapter 1 that simply *clicking* in a window brings it to the front, which would have required less muscular effort.

Absolutely right! You may now advance to the semifinals. However, learning to use the Application menu was a good exercise. Many times in your upcoming life, the program in front will be covering up the *entire* screen. So *then* how will you bring another program forward, big shot? That's right. You won't be able to *see* any other windows, so you won't be able to click one to make it active. You'll have to use the Application menu.

In any case, the Calculator is now the active application. (*Active* just means it's in front.) Now then: Remember that intricate equation that's still on the Mac Clipboard? Instead of having to type an equation into the Calculator by punching keys, let's just paste it in.

1. **Press the Clear key (or the letter C key) on your Mac keyboard, or click the C button on the Calculator.**

   You just cleared the display. We wouldn't want your previous diddlings to interfere with this tightly controlled experiment.

2. **From the Edit menu, choose Paste. Watch the Calculator!**

If you looked in time, you saw the number keys flashing like Las Vegas at midnight. And with a triumphant modesty, the Mac displays the answer to your math problem. (It should be 92.)

Did you get what just happened? You typed out a math problem in a word processor (the Note Pad), copied it to the Clipboard, and pasted it into a number-cruncher (the Calculator). Much of the miracle of the Mac stems from its capability to mix and match information among multiple programs in this way.

It's a two-way street, too. You can paste this number back into the word processor.

1. **From the Edit menu, choose Copy.**

   But wait! Something was already on the Clipboard. Where is the Mac supposed to put this *new* copied info?

   On the Clipboard, of course. And whatever was there before (your equation) gets nuked. The Clipboard contains exactly one thing at a time — whatever you copied *most recently*.

2. **From the Application menu, choose Note Pad (or just click the Note Pad window).**

   The Note Pad is now the active application.

3. **Type this:**

   Dear son: You owe me $

   Stop after the $ sign. Move the mouse up to the Edit menu.

4. **From the Edit menu, choose Paste.**

   Bingo! The Mac pastes in the result from the Calculator (which it had ready on the Clipboard).

   Incidentally, whatever's on the Clipboard stays there until you copy something new or until you turn off the machine. In other words, you can paste it over and over again.

5. **For a second time, choose Paste from the Edit menu.**

   Another 92 pops into the window.

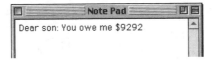

You don't have to use the menu to issue a command like Copy or Paste. If you wish, you can use a keyboard shortcut to do the same thing. You may remember having used the ⌘ key in Chapter 2 to issue commands without using the mouse.

And how are you supposed to remember which letter key corresponds to which command? Well, usually it's mnemonic: ⌘-P means Print, ⌘-O means Open, and so on. But you can cheat; try it right now. Pull down the Edit menu, but don't let go of the mouse button.

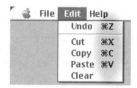

There's your crib sheet, carefully listed down the right side of the menu. Note that the keyboard shortcuts for all four of these important commands (Undo, Cut, Copy, Paste) are adjacent on the keyboard: Z, X, C, V.

C is Copy. And V, right next to it, is Paste. (I know, I know: Why doesn't *P* stand for Paste? Answer: Because *P* stands for Print! And anyway, V is right next to C-for-Copy, so it *kind of* makes sense.)

Let go of the mouse button and let's try it.

1. **While holding down the ⌘ key, type a V.**

   Bingo! Another copy of the Clipboard stuff (92) appears in your Note Pad. (In the future, I'll just refer to a keyboard shortcut like this as "⌘-V.")

2. **Press ⌘-V again.**

   Yep, that kid's debt is really piling up. He now owes you $92,929,292.

   But after all, he's your son. Why not just let him pay 1 percent down on the amount he owes you? In other words, why not *undo* that last 92 pasting?

3. **From the Edit menu, choose Undo.**

   The most recent thing you did — in this case, pasting the fourth 92 — gets undone.

Rewriting history is addicting, ain't it?

Remember, though, that Undo only reverses your *most recent* action. Suppose you (1) copy something, (2) paste it somewhere else, and then (3) type some more. If you choose Undo, only the typing will be undone (step 3), *not* the pasting (step 2).

Control Panels

There's one item in your menu that *isn't* a desk accessory. It says Control Panels, and all it does is open up your Control Panels folder. So what exactly is your Control Panels folder? It's a folder that lives inside your System Folder. It contains a bunch of icons, each of which controls some aspect of your Mac. Choose Control Panels from the menu to make this window appear:

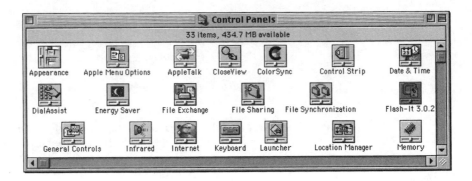

Everybody's got a slightly different set of control panels, so your screen may look different. In any case, I'll show you around one control panel; then you can take it from there.

1. **Quickly type *DA* on your keyboard.**

   Remember this handy trick? You can select one icon in a folder just by typing the first couple of letters of its name. In this case, you get the Date & Time icon.

2. **Double-click the Date & Time icon.**

   The Date & Time control-panel window opens. This is where you set the clock — as displayed, for example, at the top right of your screen. To change the time, click on a number, and then type the correct number.

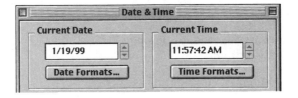

All right — close the Date & Time window by clicking the close box in the upper-left corner.

Top Ten Control Panel Explanations

Dozens of control panels are kicking around in your Control Panels folder. Here are a few national favorites. (Some have different names, depending on when you bought your Mac.) For much more detail about all the stuff in your System folder, see Chapter 8.

1. **Monitors & Sound** — lets you switch your monitor among various color settings (such as *grayscale,* like a black-and-white TV, or various degrees of richness of color).

2. **Mouse** — controls how sensitive the pointer movement is. Incidentally, the pointer on the screen *always* moves slowly when you move the mouse slowly. This control panel lets you adjust how quickly the arrow moves when you move the mouse *quickly.*

3. **Keyboard** — lets you decide whether holding down a key should type its letter repeatedly, like XXXXXXXXXXX, and how fast it repeats.

4. **Appearance** or **Color** — lets you decide what color "highlighting pen" you want to use whenever you drag the mouse across text. (Mac OS 8 and Mac OS 8.5 offer additional options in this control panel; see Chapter 9 for details.)

5. **Map** — tells what time it is anywhere in the world. Either click to specify a location, or type the name of a major city or country and click the Find button.

6. **Speech** — lets you choose a voice for the Mac to use when *talking to you* (see Chapter 20).

7. **File Exchange** or **PC Exchange** — lets your Mac use floppy disks from Windows computers.

8. **Energy Saver** — lets you establish automatic shutoff times (or automatic sleep times) for your Mac, in the name of saving electricity. For example, mine is set to go to sleep if I haven't used the computer in 30 minutes.

9. **General Controls** — offers a slew of handy customizing features: how fast your cursor blinks when you're word processing, whether or not you want your System folder protected against marauding children, and so on. Also holds the on/off switches for three of the Mac's most useful features: the Launcher (see Chapter 4), the Documents folder (Chapter 4 again), and self-hiding programs (see Chapter 8 under "General Controls").

10. **Desktop Pictures** or **Desktop Patterns** — lets you choose a new backdrop design for your desktop. The Teddy Bears design is a particular favorite of macho computer nerds everywhere.

To find a pattern you like, click the arrows at either end of the horizontal scroll bar. When you see one that catches your fancy, click the Set Desktop (or Set Desktop Pattern) button.

In Mac OS 8 and later (shown on the next page), there's an extra button called Desktop Picture. This button lets you fill your screen with one *big* picture of your choice, instead of small, *repeated* pictures like the teddy bears.

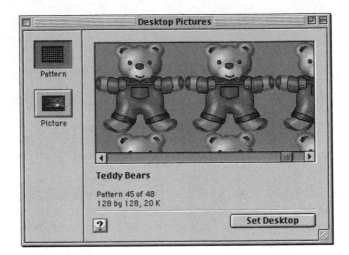

If you have Mac OS 8.5 or later, this entire feature has been assimilated into the Appearance control panel. There's no Desktop Pictures control panel at all. I mention that to save you the trip back to the computer store to return your Mac because you think you're missing components.

Chapter 4

Word Processing, Saving Files, and Finding Them Again

In This Chapter

▶ Unlearning years of typewriter lessons

▶ Copying and pasting

▶ How to save your files so that they're not lost forever

▶ You — yes, you — the desktop publisher

*L*et's not kid ourselves. Yeah, I know, you're gonna use your Macintosh to do photo retouching, to conquer the Internet, to compose symphonies. But no matter who you are, what you'll probably do the *most* of is good old *word processing*.

But just because everybody does it doesn't mean word processing isn't the single most magical, amazing, time-saving invention since the microwave dinner. Master word processing, and you've essentially mastered your computer.

Your Very First Bestseller

If you have a word processing program, install it onto your hard disk now, if you haven't already done so. You'll find the instructions at the beginning of the program's manual; see Chapter 19 for some hints on installing software.

Find the program's icon on your hard disk. It may be inside a folder, which you can open by double-clicking. It may also be staring you in the face, in the form of a big fat Launcher button (see the sidebar called "All about big fat Launcher buttons").

In any case, after you find the word processing program icon, double-click it; you'll be presented, after a moment, with a blank white screen. (If you have AppleWorks or ClarisWorks, the program starts by asking you what kind of work you want to do; click Word Processing and click OK.)

All about big fat Launcher buttons

Do you recognize this thing?

On some Macs, this special window — called the Launcher — has been floating on your desktop since the day you first turned it on. If you don't see it, you can make it appear by choosing Launcher from the Control Panels command of your menu.

The Launcher is supposed to make getting into your programs easier. Studies showed that *double-clicking* an icon, as you've been thus far instructed, was beyond the technical abilities of some people. Thus the Launcher was born, where a *single* click on any icon launches (opens) a program.

The rules for using the Launcher are simple:

1. To switch to another "page" (window-full) of icons, click one of the wide text buttons at the top of the window — Applications, for example.

2. If there's some program on the Launcher window that you don't really use, you can get rid of it. While pressing the Option key, drag that sucker right to the Trash. (You aren't trashing the *actual* program, wherever it may reside on your computer. You're just getting its *icon* off the Launcher window.)

3. If there's some program — or document, or folder — whose icon *isn't* on the Launcher window but should be, simply drag its icon into the Launcher window and release. A copy of that icon appears automatically, ready for subsequent one-click launching.

4. If you'd rather not have the Launcher window confronting you at all every morning, choose Control Panels from the menu. Double-click the control panel called General Controls. Click the option called "Show Launcher at system startup" to turn it off.

If you don't have a word processor yet, you can use the super-budget word processor that comes with every Mac, the Note Pad; choose its name from the menu.

Top three rules of word processing

The first rules of typing on a computer are going to be tough to learn, especially if you've been typing for years. But they're crucial:

> ✔ **Don't press the Return key at the end of each line.** I'm dead serious here. When you type your way to the end of a line, the next word will automatically jump down to the next line. If you press Return in the middle of a sentence, you'll mess everything up.

✔ **Put only one space after a period.** From now on, everything you write will come out looking like it was professionally published, instead of being cranked out on some noisy Selectric with a bad ribbon. A quick glance at any published book, magazine, or newspaper will make you realize that the two-spaces-after-a-period thing is strictly for typewriters.

✔ **Don't use the L key to make the number 1.** Your Mac, unlike the typewriter you may have grown up with, actually has a key dedicated to making the number 1. If you use a lowercase L instead, the 1 will look funny, and your spelling checker will choke on it every time.

If those statements give you uncontrollable muscular facial spasms, I don't blame you. After all, I'm telling you to do things that you were explicitly taught *not* to do by that high-school typing teacher with the horn-rimmed glasses.

There are a few other rules, too, but breaking them isn't serious enough to get you fired. So let's dig in. Make sure you have a blank piece of electronic typing paper open in front of you — a new, untitled word processing screen.

The excitement begins

You should see a short, blinking, vertical line at the beginning of the typing area. They call this the *insertion point*. It shows you where the letters will appear when you start to type.

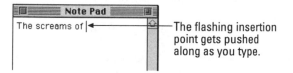

The flashing insertion point gets pushed along as you type.

Type the upcoming passage. If you make a typo, press Delete, just like Backspace on a typewriter. *Don't* press Return when you get to the edge of the window. Just keep typing, and the Mac will create a second line for you. Believe. *Believe.*

> *The screams of the lions burst Rod's eardrums as the motorboat, out of control, exploded through the froth.*

See how the words automatically wrapped around to the second line? They call this feature, with astonishing originality, *word wrap*.

But suppose, as your novel is going to press, you decide that this sleepy passage really needs some spicing up. You decide to insert the word *speeding* before the word *motorboat*.

The point of no returns

Why aren't you supposed to hit Return at the end of each line?

First time in print! An actual example of the kind of mess you can get into by pressing Return after each line of text.

At left: the original passage. Suppose you decide to remove Paulson's title, "Chief Executive Officer," since everybody already knows what kind of guy he is. But suppose you'd been foolish enough to press Return after each line of text; if you remove those three highlighted words, the word *Paulson* flops back to the left side of the line, but the rest of the sentence stays where it is, looking dumb (right).

On the other hand, if you *hadn't* put Returns into your text, you'd get the figure below, where everything looks peachy.

Remember the blinking cursor — the insertion point? It's on the screen even now, blinking calmly away at the end of the sentence. If you want to insert text, you have to move the insertion point.

You can move the insertion point in two ways. First, try pressing the arrow keys on your keyboard. You can see that the up- and down-arrow keys move the insertion point from line to line, and the right- and left-arrow keys move the insertion point across the line. Practice moving the insertion point by pressing the arrow keys.

If the passage you want to edit is far away, though (on another page, for example), using the arrow keys to move the cursor is inefficient. Your fingers would be bloody stumps by the time you finished. Instead, use the mouse:

1. **Using the mouse, move the cursor (which, when it's near text, looks like this I) just before the word *motorboat*. Click the mouse.**

   The I-beam changes to the insertion point.

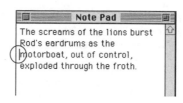

```
┌─────────────────────────────────┐
│ ▣         Note Pad          ▣ │
├─────────────────────────────────┤
│ The screams of the lions burst  ⇧
│ Rod's eardrums as the           │
│ ⊖motorboat, out of control,     │
│  exploded through the froth.    │
│                                 │
│                                 │
└─────────────────────────────────┘
```

This is as confusing as word processing ever gets — there are *two* little cursors, right? There's the blinking insertion point, and there's this one |, which is called an *I-beam* cursor.

In fact, the two little cursors are quite different. The blinking insertion point is only a *marker,* not a pointer. It always shows you where the next typing will appear. The I-beam, on the other hand, is how you *move* the insertion point; when you click with the I-beam, you set down the insertion point.

In other words, editing stuff you've already typed, on the Macintosh, is a matter of *click, then type.*

2. **Type the word** *speeding.*

   The insertion point does its deed, and the Mac makes room on the line for the new word. A word or two probably got pushed onto the next line. Isn't word wrap wondrous?

Editing for the linguistically blessed

So much for *inserting* text: You click the mouse (to show the Mac *where*) and then type away. But what if you need to delete a bunch of text? What if you decide to *cut out* the first half of our sample text?

Well, unless you typed the challenging excerpt with no errors, you already know one way to erase text — by pressing the Delete key. Delete takes out one letter at a time, just to the left of the insertion point.

Deleting one letter at a time isn't much help in this situation, though. Suppose you decide to take out the first part of the sentence. It wouldn't be horribly efficient to backspace over the entire passage just so you could work on the beginning.

No, instead you need a way to edit any part of your work, at any time, without disturbing the stuff you want to leave. Once again, the Macintosh method, noun-then-verb, saves the day. Try this:

1. **Using the mouse, position the I-beam cursor at the beginning of the sentence.**

   This takes a steady hand; stay calm.

2. **Click *just* to the left of the first word and keep the mouse button pressed down. Drag the I-beam cursor — *perfectly horizontally,* if possible — to the end of the word *as.***

   As you drag, the text gets highlighted, or *selected.* You've done this once before, in your copy-and-paste lesson.

   The screams of the lions burst Rod's eardrums as the speeding motorboat, out of control, exploded through the froth.

   If you accidentally drag up or down into the next line of text, the highlighting jumps to include a big chunk of that additional line. Don't panic; without releasing the mouse button, simply move the cursor back onto the original line you were selecting. This time, try to drag more horizontally.

If you're especially clever and forward-thinking, you'll have selected the blank space *after* the word *as,* as well. Take a look at the previous illustration.

All right, in typical Mac syntax, you've just specified *what* you want to edit by selecting it (and making it turn black to show it's selected). Now for the verb:

1. **Press the Delete key.**

   Bam! The selected text is gone. The sentence looks pretty odd, though, since it doesn't begin with a capital letter.

2. **Using the mouse, position the cursor just before (or after) the letter *t* that begins the sentence. Drag the cursor sideways across the letter so that it's highlighted.**

   the speeding motorboat, out of control, exploded through the froth.

   Here comes another ground rule of word processing. See how you've just selected, or highlighted, the letter *t?* The idea here is to capitalize it. Of course, using the methods for wiping out (and inserting) text that you learned earlier, you could simply remove the *t* and type a *T.* But since you've selected the *t* by dragging through it, replacing it is much easier:

3. **Type a capital *T.***

The selected text gets replaced by the new stuff you type. That, in fact, is the fourth ground rule: *Selected text gets replaced by the new stuff you type.* As your Macintosh life proceeds, keep that handy fact in mind; it can save you a lot of backspacing. In fact, you can select 40 pages of text so that it's all highlighted and then type *one single letter* to replace all of it. Or you could *select* only one letter but replace it with 40 pages of typing.

Take a moment now for some unsupervised free play. Try clicking anywhere in the text (to plant the insertion point). Try dragging through some text: If you drag perfectly horizontally, you select text just on one line (below, left). If you drag diagonally, you get everything between your cursor and the original click (below, right).

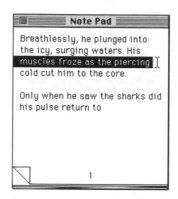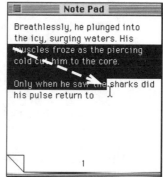

You *deselect* (or, equally poetically, unhighlight) text by clicking the mouse. Anywhere at all (within the typing area).

Here's about the most fabulous word processing shortcut ever devised: Try pointing to a word and then double-clicking the mouse! You've easily selected *exactly* that word without having to do any dragging.

As you experiment, do anything you want with any combination of drags, clicks, double-clicks, and menu selections. It's nice to know — and you might want to prepare a fine mahogany wall plaque to this effect — that *nothing you do using the mouse or keyboard can physically harm the computer.* Oh, sure, it's possible to erase a disk or wreck one of your documents or something, but none of that requires a visit to a repair shop. You can't *break* the computer by playing around.

Puff, the Magic Drag-n-Drop

You kids today, with your long music and loud hair! You don't know how lucky you are! Why, when I was your age, if I wanted to rearrange a couple of words, I'd have to *copy and paste them!*

But not anymore. Nowadays, you can move text around on the screen just by *pointing* to it! This profoundly handy feature is known as Macintosh drag-and-drop.

Unfortunately, drag-and-drop doesn't work in every program, but it works in most of the biggies: the Note Pad; AppleWorks; ClarisWorks (version 4.0v4 or later); Microsoft Word (5.0 or later); WordPerfect (3.5 or later); SimpleText; America Online (3.0 or later); FileMaker; Mariner Write; Nisus Writer (5.0 or later); and so on.

1. **Launch a program that offers drag-and-drop.**

   If you're panicking, remember that the good ol' Note Pad offers this feature. Choose its name from the menu, if you like.

2. **Type up two phrases, as shown here:**

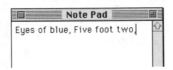

3. **Highlight _Eyes of blue._**

   You've done this before: Position the insertion-point cursor just to the left of the word Eyes, and _carefully_ slide directly to the right, highlighting the sentence (below, left).

4. **Let go of the mouse. Now position the arrow cursor right smack in the middle of the blackened phrase — hold down the mouse button — and _drag_ the arrow to the end of the line (above, right).**

   When your arrow is correctly positioned at the end of the line, you'll see the new insertion point appear there.

5. **Release the mouse!**

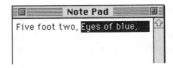

   As you can see, you've just _dragged_ the first phrase into position after the second phrase! Cole Porter would be very grateful for your correcting his lyrics.

A word processing rule-ette

You know, by now, that your mouse pointer looks like this — I — whenever it's near text. And you know, by now, that you use this cursor to *click* wherever you want to type next.

But suppose you want to add some words way down the page, like this:

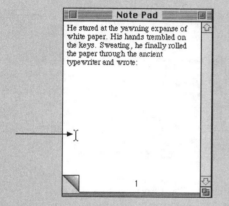

You'll discover pretty quickly that the Mac won't let you type there. The rule is: You can click your cursor anywhere on the page *that already has typing on it.* But if you try to click down *below,* in the white space, you're out of luck; the blinking insertion-point cursor simply

jumps back up to the end of what you've already typed. In its ornery way, the Mac enforces its own rule of writing: No jumping ahead, bub.

Of course, you *can* skip down the page if you want some words to appear there. But you have to *type your way* down the page first. That's why God invented the Return key. Press it over and over again until your little insertion-point cursor is blinking merrily away at the bottom of the page — or wherever you tell it to go — and *now* start typing.

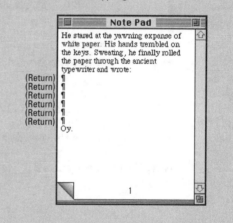

But wait — there's more! Once you've mastered the art of dragging text around your screen, the sky's the limit! To wit:

> ✔ If you press the *Option* key while you drag some highlighted text, instead of *moving* that phrase, you actually make a *copy* of it, as shown here.

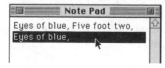

✔ You can actually drag text *clear out of the window* and into another program — for example, from the Note Pad into a waiting ClarisWorks window. (This trick and the next work in Microsoft Word 98 and Excel 98, but not in previous versions of those programs.)

✔ You can also drag text clear out of the window and *onto the desktop.* When you release the mouse, you'll see that your little drag-and-dropped blurb has turned into a *text clipping,* as shown here:

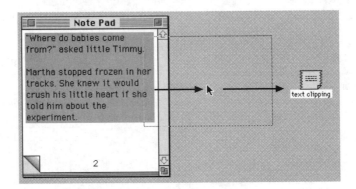

Next time you need that blob of text, you can point to the text clipping and drag it back into your word processing program, and presto! — the text appears there, exactly as though you'd typed it again.

Now if they'd only work it out so we could edit our *printouts* using drag-and-drop. . . .

Form and Format

For the rest of this lesson, you're going to need a real word processing program. Sorry, kids: The Note Pad will only get you so far in life. (If you're on a tight budget, you're welcome to use SimpleText for this exercise; you'll probably find SimpleText in your Apple Extras or Applications folder.)

One of the most important differences between a typewriter and its replacement — the computer — is the sequence of events. When you use a typewriter, you set up all the formatting characteristics *before* you type: the margins, the tab stops, and (for typewriters with interchangeable type heads) the type style.

But the whole point of a word processor is that you can change anything at *any* time. Many people type the text of an entire letter (or proposal or memo) into the Mac and *then* format it. When you use a typewriter, you might discover, after typing the entire first page, that it's *slightly* too long to fit, and your signature will have to sit awkwardly on a page by itself. With a Mac, you'd see the problem and nudge the text a little bit higher on the page to compensate.

Word processing has other great advantages: no crossouts; easy corrections that involve no whiteout and no retyping; a permanent record of your correspondence that's electronic, not paper, and so it's always easy to find; a selection of striking typefaces — at any size; paste-in graphics; and so on. I think it's safe to say that once you try processing words, you'll never look back.

The return of Return

With all the subtlety of a Mack truck, I've taught you that you're forbidden to use the Return key *at the end of a line*. Still, that rectangular Return key on your keyboard *is* important. You press Return at the end of a *paragraph,* and only there.

To the computer, the Return key works just like a letter key — it inserts a *Return character* into the text. It's just like rolling the paper in a typewriter forward by one notch. Hit Return twice, and you leave a blank line.

The point of Return, then, is to move text higher or lower on the page. Check out this example, for instance.

Return characters move text down on the page. So, if you want to move text up on the page, drag through the blank space so that it's highlighted (above left); of course, what you've really done is select the usually invisible Return characters. If you delete them, the text slides up the page (right).

Combine this knowledge with your advanced degree in Inserting Text (remember? you *click, then type*), and you can see how you'd make more space between paragraphs or push all the text of a letter down on the page.

Appealing characters

Another big-time difference between word processing and typing is all the great *character formatting* you can do. You can make any piece of text **bold,** *italic,* underlined, all of the above, and more. You also get a selection of great-looking typefaces — only a few of which look like a typewriter. By combining all these styles and fonts randomly, you can make any document look absolutely hideous.

Here's the scheme for changing some text to one of those character formats: noun-verb. Sound familiar? Go for it:

1. **Select some text by dragging through it.**

   Remember, you can select a single word by double-clicking it; to select a bunch of text, drag the cursor through it so that it turns black. You've just identified *what* you want to change.

   Each word processor keeps its Bold, Italic, and Underline commands in its own specially named menu; it may be called Font, or Style, or Format. Drag your cursor through each menu name, reading the commands on each menu as it drops down, until you see the character formats like bold and italic.

   (In Microsoft programs, the Bold, Italic, and Underline commands may not be in a menu at all. Instead, you may have little buttons labeled **B**, *I*, or U at the top of your screen.)

2. **From the Font menu (or Format menu, or whatever it's called in your program), choose Bold.**

   (Or click the B button on your screen, if you have one.) You've just specified *how* you want to affect the selected text.

You can apply several of these formats to the same text, too, although you won't win any awards for typographical excellence. Try changing the typeface, also; the various fonts are called things like Chicago, Geneva, Times, and so on. Changing fonts works the same way: Select text and then choose the font.

And sizes — same deal: Select some text and then choose a type size from your word processor's menu. (Again, the name of the menu may vary. But for specifics on Microsoft Word and AppleWorks/ClarisWorks, see Chapters 6 and 7.) The font sizes are measured in points, of which there are 72 per inch. Works out nicely, too — a typical Mac monitor has 72 *screen* dots per inch, meaning that 12-point type on the screen really is 12-point.

Before you know it, you'll have whipped your document into mighty handsome shape.

Formatting paragraphs

Whereas type styles and sizes can be applied to any amount of text, even a single letter, *paragraph formatting* affects a whole paragraph at once. Usually these styles are easy to apply. To select a paragraph, you don't have to highlight all the text in it. Instead, you can just click *once,* anywhere, within a paragraph to plant the insertion point. Then, as before, choose the menu command that you want to apply to that entire paragraph.

This figure shows some of the different options every word processor provides for paragraph formatting — left-justified, right-justified, fully justified, and centered. (SimpleText, the Discount Word Processor, doesn't have this kind of paragraph-formatting command. That's why it's Simple.)

The efficiency zealot's guide to power typing

Because you *can* format text after you've typed it doesn't mean you *have* to. Most power-users get used to the keyboard shortcuts for the common style changes, like bold and italic. They're pretty easy to remember: In nearly every word processing program, you get bold by pressing ⌘-B and italic with ⌘-I.

What's handy is that you can hit this key combo just *before* you type the word. For example, without ever taking your hands off the keyboard, you could type the following:

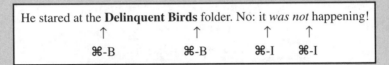

In other words, you hit ⌘-B once to turn bold *on* for the next burst of typing, and ⌘-B again to turn it off — all without ever having to use a menu.

Her heart pounding, she looked toward the door. It swung open with a creak. The stench hit her first—an acrid, rotting swamp smell. She covered her mouth with the blood-soaked handkerchief and stepped backward, her naked back pressed hard against the fourposter.

Left justified

Her heart pounding, she looked toward the door. It swung open with a creak. The stench hit her first—an acrid, rotting swamp smell. She covered her mouth with the blood-soaked handkerchief and stepped backward, her naked back pressed hard against the fourposter.

Fully justified

Her heart pounding, she looked toward the door. It swung open with a creak. The stench hit her first—an acrid, rotting swamp smell. She covered her mouth with the blood-soaked handkerchief and stepped backward, her naked back pressed hard against the fourposter.

Right justified

Her heart pounding, she looked toward the door. It swung open with a creak. The stench hit her first—an acrid, rotting swamp smell. She covered her mouth with the blood-soaked handkerchief and stepped backward, her naked back pressed hard against the fourposter.

Centered

You can control paragraphs in other ways, too. Remember in high school when you were supposed to turn in a 20-page paper, and you'd try to pad your much-too-short assignment by making it two-and-a-half spaced? Well, if you'd had a Mac, you could have been much more sneaky about it. You can make your word processed document single-spaced, double-spaced, quadruple-spaced, or any itty-bitty fraction thereof. You can even control how tightly together the letters are placed, making it easy to stretch or compress your writing into more or fewer pages.

Take this opportunity to toy with your word processor. Go ahead, really muck things up. Make it look like a ransom note with a million different type styles and sizes. Then, when you've got a real masterpiece on the screen, read on.

Working with Documents

It might terrify you — and it should — to find out that you've been working on an imaginary document. It's only being preserved by a thin thread of streaming electrical current. It doesn't exist yet, to be perfectly accurate, except in your Mac's *memory*.

You may recall from the notes you took on Chapter 1¹/₂ that memory is fleeting. (Specifically, I mean *computer* memory, but if you find a more universal truth in my words, interpret away.) In fact, the memory is wiped away when you turn the Mac off — or when your coworker's trip over the power cord turns it off *for* you. At that moment, anything that exists on the screen is gone forever.

Therefore, almost every program has a Save command. It's always in the File menu, and its keyboard shortcut is always ⌘-S.

When you save your work, the Mac transfers it from transient, fleeting, electronic memory onto the good, solid, permanent disk. There your work will remain, safely saved. It will still be there tomorrow. It will still be there next week. It will still be there ten years from now, when your computer is so obsolete it's valuable again.

Therefore, let's try an experiment with your ransom note document on the screen. From the File menu, choose Save.

Uh-oh. Something weird just happened: The Mac presented you with a box full of options. It's called a *dialog box,* because the computer needs to have a little chat with you before proceeding.

Note from the Confusion Editor: The dialog box that just appeared probably looks like this:

What you see when you save a file before Mac OS 8.5

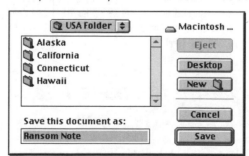

But if you have Mac OS 8.5 or later (see Chapter 1), you may see the redesigned version of this dialog box, which looks like this:

What you see when you save a file in some Mac OS 8.5 programs:

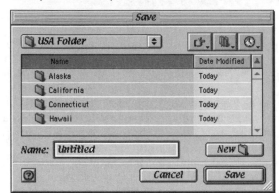

As you can see, the old and the new dialog boxes are essentially alike; I'll show you pictures of the newer style for the rest of this discussion so that the book feels modern and with-it. Thanks for playing along.

Anyway. When you see this box, what the Mac mainly wants to know is: "Under what name would you like me to file this precious document, Masssssster?"

And how do you know this? Because in the blank where it says "Save as," a proposed title is highlighted (selected already). And what do you know about highlighted text? *Anything you start typing will instantly replace it.*

The Mac, in its cute, limited way, is trying to tell you that it needs you to type a title. Go ahead, do it: Type *Ransom Note.*

At this point, you could just click the Save button. The Mac would take everything in perilous, fleeting memory and transfer it to the staid, safe hard disk, where it would remain until you're ready to work on it some more.

However, a bunch of other stuff lurks in this dialog box. Especially since this is the Numero Uno source of confusion to beginners, I think a tour of the Save File box is in order.

Navigating the Save File (and Open File) box

You've already learned about the way your computer organizes files: with folders and with folders *in* folders. Remember this little exercise where you put state-named folders inside the USA Folder?

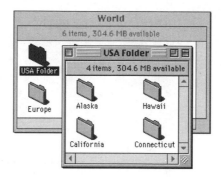

Well, all the complicated-looking stuff in the Save File box is a miniature version of that same folder-filing system. Suppose you see this when you're trying to save your file:

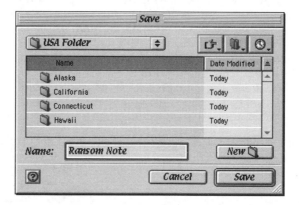

Look at the open-folder "menu" (in a rectangle above the list). It tells you that you're viewing the contents of the USA Folder. In other words, if you click the Save button, you'll file your new Ransom Note document in the USA Folder, mixed in among the state folders.

But suppose you want to file the Ransom Note document in one of the state folders. You already know how you open a folder — by double-clicking it — so you'd point to Alaska, for example, and double-click.

Now the open-folder "menu" above the list says *Alaska,* and you can see the stuff inside the Alaska folder. Some names are dimmed because they're all *documents;* the only things whose names are black in this dialog box are folders. (The Mac wants to know where you want to put your new document.

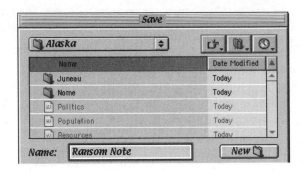

Because you can't very well store one document inside *another* document, the names are grayed out and unavailable, and only the folder names are black and available.)

Okay. So now you're viewing the contents of the Alaska folder. What if you change your mind? What if you decide that the ransom note should really go in the World folder — the one that *contains* the USA Folder?

You must retrace your steps. That's what the little folder menu is all about (the folder icon is in front of the word *Alaska*). They call this doohickey a *pop-up menu:* It's a menu, but it's not at the top of the screen. The small black triangles beside the name Alaska tells you: "Click me!"

Sure enough, when you click the word Alaska (above, left), you see the list of all the nested folders you had to travel through to get here (above, right). This is where things get a little weird: The list is *upside-down* from the path you took!

In other words, if you were in the Finder instead of in this Save File dialog box, you started at the Desktop level (colored background). You'd have double-clicked the hard-disk icon (usually called Macintosh HD) to open its window. Then you'd have double-clicked the World folder to open that, and the USA folder inside of *that,* and finally the Alaska folder. If you look at the preceding menu picture, you'll see that, sure enough, your entire folder path is listed. You can view the entire hierarchy of folders — as long as you get used to the fact that the list is upside-down, and the outer levels (the hard disk and the Desktop) are listed at the bottom.

Therefore, if you wanted to file the ransom note in the World folder (next figure, right), you'd simply slide down the pop-up menu list and choose World (next figure, left).

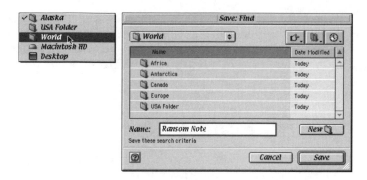

Then, at long last, when you're viewing the contents of the folder you want to save the file in, you can click the Save button.

For the purposes of following along with this exercise, double-click a folder — any folder — to store your file in. And then click Save.

Your file gets snugly tucked away into the folder whose contents you're viewing. Want proof, O Cynic? All you have to do is choose Finder from the Application menu. Remember, the Application menu is the icon at the upper-right side of the screen. It lists all the programs that are running at once.

When you choose Finder, our friends the folders, windows, and Trash can pop up. If you wanted to make sure your file really exists, and it really got put where you wanted it, you could now double-click your way through folders until you found it. In our example, your ransom note would be in the World folder:

Why are we kicking this absolutely deceased horse? Because the same folder-navigation scheme (where you see an upside-down list of nested folders) is used for *retrieving* files you've already created. You need to know how to climb up and down your folder tree, as you'll see in a moment, if you ever want to see your files again.

Closing a file, with a sigh

You've created a ransom note. It's got all kinds of text and formatting. You've saved it onto the disk so that it'll be there tomorrow. In a moment, you'll get a chance to prove it to yourself.

Click the close box in the upper-left corner of the window. Once.

In the Mac's universal language of love, clicking the small square up there means *close the window,* as you'll recall. If all went well, the window disappears.

How to find out what's going on

This gets sort of metaphysical. Hold on to your brain.

Just because you closed your *document* doesn't mean you've left the *program.* In fact, if you pull down the Application menu at the right side of the screen, you'll see that the word processing program is, in fact, still running. (It's the one with a checkmark beside it; your word processing program may be different.)

You could bring the Finder to the front by choosing its name from the Application menu — without exiting the word processor. They both can be running at the same time, but only one can be in front.

In fact, that's the amazing thing about the Mac. You can have a bunch of programs all open and running at once. The more memory your Mac has, the more programs you can run simultaneously.

What gets confusing is that one program (say, your word processor) may be active, but you'll *think* you're in the Finder. After all, you'll see your familiar icons, Trash, folders, and so on. You have to understand that all this is simply *shining through* the emptiness left by your word processor, which has no windows open at the moment. If a window *were* open, it would cover up the desktop behind it.

Right now, for instance, I realize that it's hard for you to believe that you're using a word processor, when there are no words on the screen. But you have several clues as to what program you're using:

Worrywarts' corner

From the way I've described the terrifyingly delicate condition of a document that's on the screen (that you haven't saved to disk yet) — that is, precariously close to oblivion, kept alive only by electric current — you might think that closing a window is a dangerous act. After all, what if you forgot to save some work? Wouldn't closing the window mean losing that critical memo?

Not really — if you try to close a document, the Mac won't *let* you proceed until it asks you if you're *sure* you want to lose all the work you've done. It will say something like:

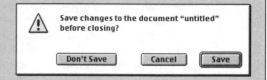

Click Save if you do want to save your work. Click Don't Save if you were only goofing around and don't want to preserve your labors.

Click Cancel if you change your mind completely about closing the document and want to keep working on it.

CLUE #1: The first command in the Apple menu always identifies the program you're in.

CLUE #2: The menu titles are different in each program.

CLUE #3: In Mac OS 8.5 and later, the program you're in is named here.

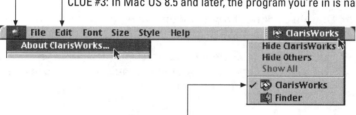

CLUE #4: The checkmark in the Application menu indicates the program you're in.

For the moment, I want you to stay in your word processing program.

Getting It All Back Again

Okay. You've typed a ransom note. Using the Save command, you turned that typing on your screen into an icon on your hard disk. Now it's time for a concept break.

Crazy relationships: Parents and kids

Two kinds of files are lying on your hard disk right now: *programs* (sometimes called *applications*) and *documents*. A program never changes; it's like a Cuisinart on your kitchen counter, sitting there day after day. Documents are what you *create* with a program — they're the coleslaw, crushed nuts, and guacamole dip that come out of the Cuisinart. You pay money to buy a program. Once you own it, you can create as many documents as you want, for free.

For example, you could use the Word Proc-S-R program (top of preceding figure) to create all the different word processing documents below it and thousands more like them. If you love analogies as much as I do, you can think of the application as the mommy and the documents as the kiddies.

Here's what their family relationships are like:

- ✔ Double-click the *program* icon when you want to open a brand new, untitled, clean-slate document.

- ✔ Double-click a *document* icon to open that document. Unbeknownst to you, double-clicking a document simultaneously opens the program you used to create the document.

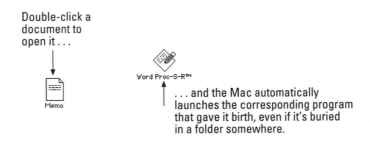

Fetch: How to retrieve a document

Let's pretend it's tomorrow. Yawn, stretch, fluff your hair (if any). You find out that the person you've kidnapped actually comes from a wealthy Rhode Island family, and so you can demand much more ransom money. Fortunately, you created your ransom note on the Mac, so you don't have to retype anything; you can just change the amount you're demanding and print it out again.

But if you've been following the steps in this chapter, then there's *no* document on the screen. You're still *in* your word processing program, though (or should be; look for the check mark in the Application menu). So how do you get your ransom note file back?

Like this:

1. **From the File menu, choose Open.**

   A dialog box appears. You probably remember dialog boxes — in fact, you probably remember this one. It looks just like the Save dialog box, where you were asked to give your document a title. This one, navigationally speaking, works exactly the same way, whether you have the old-style box:

   Double-click a folder to see what's in it.

   Use this pop-up menu to see what folder this folder is inside of.

   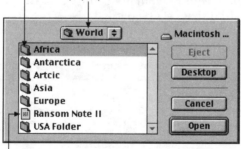

   You can tell that this is a document because its icon isn't a folder. You can open it by double-clicking its name.

   — or the Mac OS 8.5-and-later box:

In Mac OS 8.5 and later, you can also click a "flippy triangle" to see what's inside a folder. (The contents are indented to help you figure out what's inside of what.)

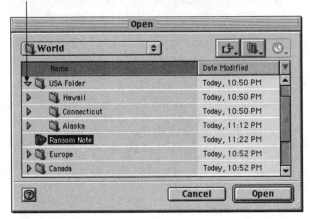

Unfortunately for my efforts to make this as instructional as possible, if you've been following these steps, your ransom note is staring you in the face right now. It's in whichever folder you saved it into. The Mac is nice that way — it remembers the most recent folder you stashed something in and shows you that location the next time you try to save or open something.

If you want to emerge from this experience a better person, pretend you can't find your ransom note. Pull down the pop-up menu and jump to your hard-disk level (below, left). Now the display changes to show you the contents of your hard disk (below, right).

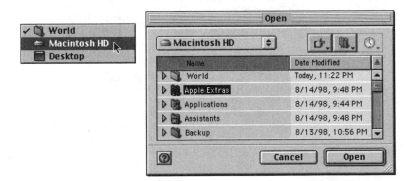

And from here, you know how to get back into the World folder, don't you? Correct — double-click the World folder, and you're right back where you started.

2. **Double-click the ransom note.**

    This is what you've been working up to all this time. The ransom note appears on your screen in its entirety. Now, at last, you can edit it to your heart's content.

Save Me Again!

To continue this experiment, make some changes to your document. Once again, you have to worry about the fact that your precious work only exists in a fragile world of bouncing electrons. Once again, turning the Mac off right now means you'll lose the *new* work you've done. (The original ransom note, without changes, is still safe on your disk.)

Therefore, you have to use that trusty Save command each time you make changes that are worth keeping. (For you desk potatoes out there, remember that ⌘-S is the keyboard shortcut, which saves you an exhausting trip to the menu.) The Save dialog box will *not* appear on the screen each time you use the Save command (as it did the first time). Only the very first time you save a document does the Mac ask for a title (and a folder location).

As mentioned in Chapter 1½, you've probably heard horror stories about people who've lost hours of work when some glitch made their computers crash. Well, usually it's their own darned fault for ignoring the two most important rules of computing:

> **Rule 1. Save your work often.**
>
> **Rule 2. See Rule 1.**

"Often" may mean every five minutes. It may mean after every paragraph. The point is to do it a lot. Get to know that ⌘-S shortcut, and type it reflexively after every tiny burst of inspiration.

Learning to be a quitter

Now you know how to start a new document, edit it, save it onto the disk, reopen it later, and save your additional changes. You know how to launch (open, or run) a program — by double-clicking its icon. But now you have to learn to get out of a program when you're finished for the day. It's not terribly difficult:

Choose Quit from the File menu.

Two easy ways to avoid losing stuff

This business about the "Save Where?" dialog box is, as anybody will tell you, the most confusing thing about the Mac. After years of experience, a few professional beginners have adopted one of the following cheats — and they never lose another file.

Cheat 1:

Whenever you save a file, and you're faced with the Save dialog box, *click the Desktop button first.* Only then should you click the Save button.

Go ahead, ask it. "What's the point?"

Easy: When you're done working for the day, and you return to the desktop, you won't have to wonder what folder your document's icon fell into. Your new file will be sitting right there, *on the desktop,* in plain sight.

At this point, it's child's play to drag the icon into the folder you *want* it in.

Cheat 2:

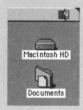

So many people complained that they couldn't find documents that they had saved that Apple invented the Documents folder. On older Macs, it sits on your desktop (as shown at left).

On recent models, the Documents folder appears in your hard-drive window instead. Furthermore, it doesn't show up there until the first time you actually save a document.

To make yours appear, choose Control Panels from your menu. Double-click General Controls. In the lower-right corner of the resulting window, select Documents folder (to turn it on) or one of the other choices (to turn it off). Close all the windows you've just opened.

From now on, every time you save a file — or try to open one — you'll always be shown the contents of the Documents folder:

Documents ⬍	⬜ Macintosh ...
📄 Dogs	Eject
📄 Emeralds	Desktop
📄 Fish	New
📄 Gold	
Save this document as:	Cancel
Goats	Save

The contents of this special magnet folder will be in your face at all times. You'll never wonder where some file went — it'll always be right in your Documents folder.

If the word processor was the only program you were running, then you return to the Finder. If you were running some other programs, then you just drop down into the next program. It's as though the programs are stacked on top of each other; take away the top one, and you drop into the next one down.

The other most important computer rule

Duty compels me to keep this chapter going just long enough to preach one other famous word of advice to you: Back up.

To *back up*, or to *make a backup*, means to make a safety copy of your work.

When you're in the Finder, the documents you've worked on appear as icons on the hard disk. Your hard disk is like a giant-sized floppy disk. Like any of us, these disks occasionally have bad hair days, go through moody spells, or die. On days like those, you'll wish you had made a *copy* of the stuff on the hard disk, so your life won't grind to a halt while the hard disk is being repaired.

The idiot-proof guide to backing up

Put a blank floppy disk in the disk drive. If it's a brand new disk, you'll be asked to *initialize* it (prepare it for use by a Mac); do it.

(If you have an iMac or other current model, you'll quickly discover you *can't* insert a floppy disk — there's nowhere to insert one. If you're truly adventurous, you could back up your work by *e-mailing it to yourself,* in effect using cyberspace as a giant backup disk. If you're not quite that avant-garde, you'll have to buy an external floppy-disk drive or Zip drive. [A Zip disk looks like a thick floppy disk — but it holds 70 times as much as a floppy. If your Mac is floppyless, be sure to buy the special *USB* version of the Zip drive.])

Now select the icons of the documents you want to back up. Drag them, together or one by one, onto the floppy disk (or Zip, or SuperDisk disk) icon. If the disk fills up, insert another one and continue. Label the disks *Backup* (and note the date). Keep them away from magnets and telephones.

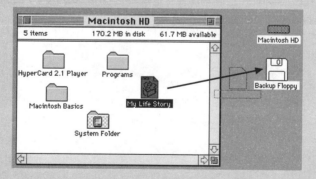

If this starts to get tedious, buy a backup *program,* which essentially backs up automatically. Speed Doubler and Retrospect are some popular backup programs. Your Mac may even have come with File Synchronization (in your Control Panels folder), which can back up important folders on your hard drive automatically.

You know the cruel gods that make it rain when you forget your umbrella? Those same deities have equal powers over your hard disk, and an equal taste for irony. That is, if you don't back up, your hard disk will *certainly* croak. On the other hand, if you back up your work at the end of every day or every week, nothing will ever go wrong with your hard disk, and you'll mumble to yourself that you're wasting your time.

Life's just like that.

When What Was Found Is Now Lost

Okay. You've practiced saving and retrieving files. You've dog-eared critical pages of this chapter — heck, you've torn out all the pages and taped them to the walls. Yet still it happens: You can't find some file you were working on.

This is nothing to be ashamed of! Thousands of people lose files every day. But through the intervention of caring self-help groups, they often go on to lead productive, "normal" lives.

Here's what to do: Sit up straight, think positive thoughts, and press ⌘-F. (Or do it the long way: Choose Find, or Sherlock, from your menu.)

On the screen, you see the Find box: your personal electronic butler who's prepared to spend the next few seconds rummaging through the attics, garages, and basement of your Mac. (This illustration is what Mac OS 8.5's Find program looks like; the window is simpler in previous versions.)

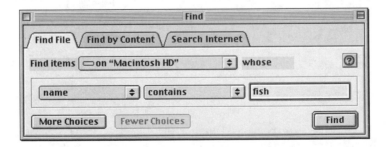

Type a few letters of the missing file's name. (Capitals don't matter, but spaces do!) Then click the Find button (or press Return).

A new window appears, listing everything on your hard drive whose name contains what you looked for. At this point, you can perform any of the following stunts:

Double-click an icon to open it. Or drag it someplace — onto the desktop, maybe, or even directly to the Trash. To open the window a file's in, click the icon and press ⌘-E.

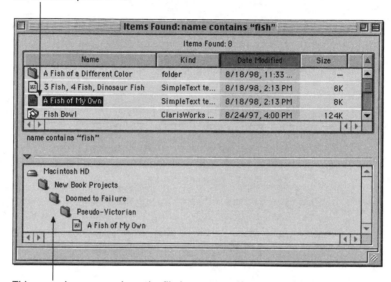

This area shows you where the file is, no matter how many folders deep it's buried. You can double-click a folder, too, to open it.

When you're finished playing with the Find File thing, choose Quit from its File menu (or press ⌘-Q).

Top Ten Word Processing Tips

1. Select a word by double-clicking — and then, if you keep the mouse down on the second click and drag sideways, you select additional text in complete one-word increments.

2. Never, never, never line up text using the space bar. It may have worked in the typewriter days, but not any more. For example, you may get things lined up like this on the screen:

   1963   1992   2001
   Born   Elected President Graduated college

Yet, sure as death or taxes, you'll get this when you print:

1963	**1992**	**2001**
Born	Elected President	Graduated college

So instead of using spaces to line up columns, use *tab stops* instead. Learn how your word processor does tabs and use 'em! (There's a scintillating lesson on just this topic in *MORE Macs For Dummies,* this book's equally instructive sequel.)

3. You can select all the text in your document at once by using the Select All command (to change the font for the whole thing, for example). Its keyboard equivalent is almost always ⌘-A.

4. Aesthetics Rule of Thumb: Don't use more than two fonts within a document. (Bold, italic, and normal versions of a font only count as one.) Talk about ransom notes!

5. Don't use underlining for emphasis. You're a typesetter now, babe. You've got *italics!* Underlining is a cop-out for typewriter people.

6. The box in the scroll bar at the right side of the window tells you, at a glance, where you are in your document:

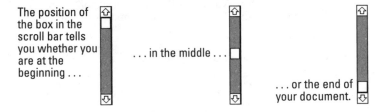

The position of the box in the scroll bar tells you whether you are at the beginning . . .

. . . in the middle . . .

. . . or the end of your document.

By dragging that box, you can jump anywhere in the document.

You can move around in two other ways:

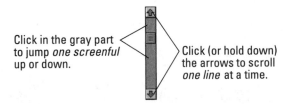

Click in the gray part to jump *one screenful* up or down.

Click (or hold down) the arrows to scroll *one line* at a time.

This would be the logical place, by the way, for me to mention the bizarre feature of Mac OS 8.5 and later known as *double-headed scroll-bar arrows.* To turn on this option, you open your Appearance control panel, click Options, and turn on the "Smart Scrolling" option.

Mac OS 8.5 and later: Super-Find!

In the illustration of the Find window a couple pages back, you may have noticed two other interesting-looking places to click: a tab that says Find by Content and one that says Search Internet.

See, the trouble with the traditional Find command is that it searches only the *names* of your files. If you wrote a 253-page thesis on Wombat Worship Societies, but you accidentally *named* that file "Gift Ideas for Marge," you could search for "Wombat" from now until doomsday without turning up the file.

It would be different, however, if the Find command were smart enough to search for words *inside* your documents. That's exactly what the Find by Content thing does (in Mac OS 8.5 and later).

But before you can use this feature, the Mac must be allowed to create its own private card-catalog of your hard drive. This process is called *indexing* — spending a couple of hours analyzing every single document you've got. To make this happen, click the Index Volumes button, click the name of your hard drive, click Create Index, and then go out to see a nice long movie (such as *Titanic II: The Return*). (If you're *really* into your Mac, you could teach yourself to use the Schedule button, which makes your Mac do this kind of thing in the middle of the night, unattended.)

When it's over, you'll be able to use the Find by Content thing to look for words inside your files. (You'll need to let the Mac update that index from time to time to keep it current; fortunately, each index-updating takes only 10 minutes or so.)

The final tab of the Find program, Search Internet, isn't nearly as complicated. It does require, however, that you have an Internet account (see Chapter 11). Once you're hooked up, you can type something into this Find blank, wait a few minutes, and be shown a list of every World Wide Web page that matches your search request. Not bad for a hunk of software, eh?

The result looks like this, with *both* scroll-bar arrows at *one end* of your scroll bar:

The idea, of course, is to help out people whose screens are so enormous, they'd have to pack a lunch before setting out for one window corner or another. With double-headed scroll arrows, they have both their scroll-up and scroll-down arrows in the same place.

But frankly, I find the whole affair so confusing and weird-looking, I'm not even gonna bring it up.

7. You've already learned how to *copy* some text to the Clipboard, ready to paste into another place. Another useful technique is to *cut* text to the Clipboard. Cut works just like Copy, except it snips the selected text out of the original document. (Cut-and-paste is how you *move* text from one place to another.)

8. It's considered uncouth to use "straight quotes" and 'straight apostrophes.' They hearken back to the days of yore (the days of your typewriter, that is). Instead, use "curly double quotes" and 'curly single quotes' like these. (See the difference?)

   You can produce curly double quotes by pressing Option-[(left bracket) and Shift-Option-[for the left and right ones, respectively. The single quotes (or apostrophes) are Option-] (right bracket) and Shift-Option-], for the left and right single quotes, respectively.

   But good heavens — who can remember all that? That's why every word processor (AppleWorks, ClarisWorks, Word, and so on) has an *automatic* curly quote feature, which is a much better solution.

   (On the other hand, don't type curly quotes into an e-mail message; they come out as bizarre little boxes and random letters at the other end. That's because the antiquated equipment that runs the Internet can't understand anything but the old-fashioned straight quotes.)

9. If there's an element you want to appear at the top of every page, like the page number, or the date, or *The Mister Rogers Story, Part VII: The Early Years,* don't try to type it onto each page. Not only is that a waste of effort, but the minute you add or delete text from somewhere else, this top-of-the-page information will become *middle*-of-the-page information.

   Instead, use your word processor's *running header* feature — it's a little window into which you can type whatever you want. The program automatically displays this info at the top of each page, no matter how much text you add or take away. (There's also such a thing as a *running footer,* which appears at the *bottom* of the page, as well as a *running politician,* which you want to avoid at all costs.)

10. You know how to select one word (double-click it). You know how to select a line (drag horizontally). You know how to select a block of text (drag diagonally through it). By now, you're probably about to reach Selection-Method Overload.

    But none of those techniques will help when you want to select a *lot* of text. What if you want to change the font size for *ten pages'* worth? Don't tell me you're going to sit there dragging the cursor through 117 screens of text.

    Instead, try this two-part tip. First, click at the *beginning* of the stuff you want to highlight so that the insertion point is blinking there. Now scroll to the *end* of what you want to highlight. Hold down the *Shift key* with one hand, and click the mouse with the other. Magically, everything between your original click and your Shift-click gets highlighted!

Chapter 5

A Quiet Talk about Printers, Printing, and Fonts

- -

- -

I hope you're seated for this chapter. In fact, I hope you're leaning way back with your feet up and a daiquiri in your hand.

Few topics are more confusing and jargon-filled than printers and fonts, and how to get the best of the latter from the former. After dropping $1,000 on a laser printer, some people still get jaggedy, irregular type in their printouts. Others aren't able to print at all — they get error messages.

It's time to make some sense of it all. If possible.

Credit Card Workout #3: A Printer Primer

You, gentle reader, are fortunate that you waited until now to get into the Mac. You completely missed the era of *dot-matrix* printers, whose printouts were so jagged that they looked like Dante's *Inferno* written in Braille.

Today, your printer choices fall into two categories: *laser printers* and *inkjet printers*.

Inkjets: StyleWriters, DeskWriters, and Epsons

The least expensive kind of printer is called an *inkjet*. Before it got out of the printer business, Apple made inkjet printers called StyleWriters. Today, Hewlett-Packard (HP) makes a line called DeskWriters; and Epson makes some terrific color-printing models known as the Stylus Color series.

Inkjet printouts are so good they almost match a laser printer's. The printers are small, lightweight, and almost silent. You can feed all kinds of nonliving things through them: tagboard, envelopes, sheet metal, whatever. And they cost less than $300, even for ones that can print in color. (If you have a color inkjet, and you want to print out photographs, you can buy fancy shiny paper for this — correction: *expensive* fancy shiny paper — that make the printouts look almost like actual photos.)

So what's the catch? Well, they're inkjet printers. They work by spraying a mist of ink. Therefore, the printing isn't laser-crisp if your stationery is even slightly absorbent, and you have to replace the ink cartridges fairly often. Note, too, that inkjet-printed pages smear if they ever get the least bit damp, making them poor candidates for use during yacht races.

Still, inkjet printers are so compact, quiet, and inexpensive that they're hard to resist, especially if you want to print in color.

Laser printers

If you can afford to pay something like $900 for a printer, some real magic awaits you: *PostScript laser printers*. Don't worry about the word *PostScript* for now. Just look for the word PostScript in the printer's description, as though it's some kind of seal of approval.

Tales of dpi

Why have America's scientific geniuses invented all these different kinds of printers?

In a word, they're on a quest for higher *dpi*. That stands for "dots per inch," and it measures the quality of a printout. We're talking about *tiny* dots, mind you — there are about 100 of them clumped together to form the period at the end of this sentence. Clearly, the more of these dots there are per inch, the sharper quality your printouts will have.

A typical inkjet printer, such as a DeskWriter, sprays 360 or even 720 dpi onto your paper. Old laser printers manage 300 dpi, and today's generally do 600 dpi. Those Epson color inkjet printers, if you use the expensive glossy paper, actually manage 1,440 dpi. Photos printed by a 1,440 dpi printer *look* like photos, let me tell you.

Pretty good, you say? Yeah, well, so's yer ol' man — this book was printed on a *2,400* dpi professional printer!

A PostScript printer, like HP's LaserJet and DeskJet series or Apple's discontinued (but ubiquitous) LaserWriters, can print any text, in any style, at any size, and at any angle, and everything looks terrific. PostScript laser printers can also print phenomenal-looking graphics, like all the diagrams in Macintosh magazines and the weather maps in *USA Today*. They're quick, quiet, and hassle-free; most can print envelopes, mailing labels, and paper up to legal-size (but not tagboard). They're also much bigger and bulkier than inkjets.

Remember the old saying, "Freedom of the press is guaranteed only to those who own one"? Well, the combination of a Mac and a laser printer is what put the Mac on the map because it turns anybody into a self-publisher. If you can afford a PostScript printer, get it. If you're a small-time operation — a home business, for example — get the cheapest PostScript laser printer you can find. Almost all laser printers between $800 and $1,400 have exactly the same quality printouts.

Just remember that laser printers, while superior to inkjets for *black-and-white* quality, aren't what to buy if you want color. Sure, you can *buy* a color laser printer — for several thousand dollars — but the printouts aren't even as realistic as color *inkjet* printers' printouts.

How to Print

I'm going to assume that you've happily purchased a printer. If it's already hooked up, and you've made some successful printouts already, fast-forward to the end of this section.

Plugging in an inkjet

If you bought a DeskWriter or other inkjet, a cable (printer-to-Mac) probably came with the printer. There's only one possible place to plug the cable into the printer. If you have an iMac or another recent model, plug the other end into one of your USB (skinny rectangular) jacks. On older Mac models, plug into the little round jack with a printer icon.

Plug your printer here

Of course, you also need to plug your new appliance into the wall.

Plugging in a laser printer

If you bought a laser printer, believe it or not, you probably did *not* get a cable with it. Like anything precious in the computer jungle, it'll take some bushwhacking through the technical underbrush to get at the explanation.

When Apple invented the LaserWriter — the very first PostScript laser printer — they charitably recognized that not every company could afford a $7,000 printer to sit beside each desk. They had a great idea, though: Invent a system where several Macs could all plug into the *same* printer.

Ladies and gentlemen, I hereby introduce you to the word *network*.

If you have an iMac, blue Power Mac, or other recent model, your network wiring is called *Ethernet.* For an explanation of hooking up your Mac to an Ethernet-ready laser printer, see *MORE Macs For Dummies;* for now, suffice it to say that you'll probably have to buy a $50 Ethernet *hub* box, a couple of cables, and the time of a local guru.

If you have an older Mac, one with a round printer port, you need to buy a couple of *PhoneNet connectors.*

A PhoneNet connector

What's great about PhoneNet-type connectors is that you string ordinary *telephone wire* between them. If you decide to move your printer into the next room, no big deal — just buy a longer piece of phone wire from Radio Shack.

Plug one PhoneNet connector into the back of the printer and the other into your Mac's printer jack. Then connect the connectors with a piece of phone wire.

The Chooser: Where Mac meets printer

The hardest part of printing on a Mac comes at the very beginning — an unfortunate fact for the novice who simply wants to get going. You have to take this step no matter what brand or kind of printer you've just connected, or you won't be able to print a thing.

When you first plug a printer into the Mac, it's not smart enough to notice that it's got a new friend; you have to *tell* it. Therefore, after the Mac is connected to the printer, turn on both machines. Now choose Chooser from the ⬛ menu. It looks something like this:

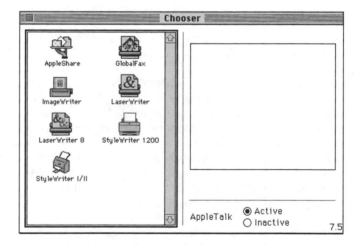

The icons that appear in the left half of the window depend on which *printer drivers* are in your System Folder. A printer driver is a little piece of software that teaches the Mac how to communicate with a specific printer. Its name and its icon match the printer itself, as you can tell, sort of, from the preceding figure.

If you see a printer driver icon in the Chooser window that matches your printer, you're in luck! Click it.

If you have a laser printer, click your model's icon. If you don't see your specific model named, try the LaserWriter 8 icon. Either way, if your printer is turned on, you should see its actual name show up in the *right* side of the Chooser window, as shown here; click the printer's name.

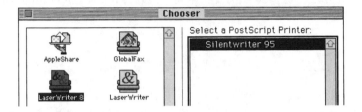

If, on the other hand, you have an inkjet printer, you'll see a choice of jacks. If you plugged yours into the printer jack as instructed above, click (obviously) the printer icon.

Good going! Everything's coming up roses. If the names of *several* printers show up on the right, then you're either part of an office network with several printers, or you're an unexpectedly wealthy individual. Congratulations. Click the one you want to print on.

If you click the driver icon, but your printer's name doesn't show up in the right side of the window, see Chapter 15.

Anyway, once you click a printer driver icon, a couple of things happen. If you're selecting a laser printer, you may be told to turn on *AppleTalk*. AppleTalk is the networking feature, in which your Mac constantly sends little messages out that telephone wire to see if any other Mac is trying to strike up a conversation — remember that if you have a laser printer, you're supposedly part of a network. So make sure the little AppleTalk setting (in the lower-right corner of the dialog box) is Active if you have a laser printer. Conversely, make sure AppleTalk is *inactive* if you have an inkjet printer plugged into your Mac's printer jack.

When you close the Chooser, you get a soon-to-be-annoying alert message. It tells you (as if you didn't know) that you've just changed to a new printer. Just ignore it and click OK.

You've just introduced the Mac to its new printer. All of this is a one-time operation, by the way. Unless you have to switch printers or something, you'll never have to touch the Chooser again.

Background printing

In the Dark Ages of the 1980s, when you printed something, the printer's soul took over your Mac's body. You couldn't type, you couldn't work, you couldn't do anything but stare at the sign on the screen that said "Now printing." It was a dark and stormy era, a time of wild and rampant coffee breaks. Only when the paper came out of the printer were you allowed to use your computer again.

Since then, some clever engineer at Apple figured out how to allow *background printing*. When you use this handy feature, the Mac sends all the printing information, at a million miles per hour, into a *file* on your hard disk. It then immediately returns its attention to you and your personal needs.

Then, quietly, behind the scenes, the Mac shoots a little bit of that file to your printer at a time. It all happens during the microseconds between your keystrokes and mouse clicks, making it seem as though the Mac is printing in the background. In time, the printer receives all the information it needs to print, the paper comes gliding out, and you've been able to keep working the whole time.

In practice, there are a few chilly background printing realities to consider. First, a document takes much *longer* to print in the background than it would if the Mac devoted all of its brain power to printing. Similarly, making your Mac concentrate on two things at once also bogs down what *you're* doing; while something's being printed in the background, you can outtype your word processor, windows seem to take longer to open, and so on.

Turning Background Printing on and off is easy. When the Print dialog box appears (see the next page), click the General pop-up menu; choose Background Printing. You'll see the On/Off buttons.

I mention this tidbit so that you'll remember it when you're in a serious hurry for a printout. When it's 1:55 p.m. and the meeting is at 2:00. Or you're leaving the house anyway and want to make sure your printout is ready when you get back. In all of these cases, it would be wise to turn *off* background printing to ensure that you get your printout as fast as possible.

After all that: How you actually print

Suppose that your printer is finally plugged in and, via the Chooser, has been introduced to the Mac. The moment has arrived: You'd actually like to *print* the thing.

From the File menu, choose Print. A dialog box appears; it looks different depending on your printer, but the one pictured here is typical of what you see if you have a laser printer:

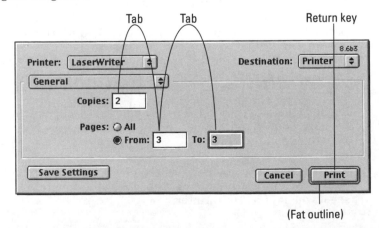

For 95 percent of your life's printouts, you'll completely ignore the choices in this box and simply click the Print button.

For the other 5 percent of the time, the main thing you do in this dialog box is tell the Mac which pages of your document you want it to print. If you just want page 1, type *1* into *both* the From and To boxes. If you want page 2 to the end, type *2* into the From box and leave the To box empty.

Specify how many copies you want by clicking and typing a number in the Copies box.

Using the Tab key in dialog boxes

Now would be a good time, I suppose, to mention what the Tab key does in dialog boxes. Suppose you want to print *two* copies of page 3. Instead of using the mouse to click in each number box on the screen, you can just press Tab to jump from box to box.

Therefore, you'd just type *2* (in the Copies box); press Tab, type *3* (in the From box); press Tab, type *3* again (in the To box). And the mouse just sits there gathering dust.

Anyway, after you're done filling out the options in this box, you can either click the Print button *or* press the Return key. (Pressing Return is always the same as clicking the outlined button.) The Mac should whir for a moment, and pretty soon the printout will come slithering out of your printer.

A shortcut for multiple-printer owners

As often happens in democracies, the rich sometimes carry special influence. In the case of the Mac, the early 1990s saw the uprising of the powerful People With More Than One Printer lobby (the PWMTOP, as it's known in insider circles). These people resented having to lumber off to the Chooser each time they wanted to redirect their printouts from one printer to another. They asked Apple to come up with some easier method of switching.

Beginning with System 7.6, Apple complied. If you have this system version or something later, you may have noticed an icon that matches your printer sitting out *on the desktop,* as shown below.

To create more of these, the PWMTOP members simply select corresponding icons in the Chooser; each time they do so, another printer's icon shows up on the desktop. Thereafter, these lucky folk can direct a printout to a particular printer just by dragging the document's icon onto the appropriate printer icon, like this:

If, on the other hand, you use only *one* printer, this desktop printing thing is a waste of your memory, disk space, and screen space. Here's how you can turn it off:

1. From the menu, choose Control Panels.

2. Double-click the one called Extensions Manager. (If you see something called Conflict Catcher or Now Startup Manager, open that instead.)

   You should now see a list of a million computer-looking control panels and *extensions,* as they're called. (More about these in Chapter 15.) Click all the ones with the word *Desktop Printing* or *Desktop Printer* in them to turn them off (so that they're no longer highlighted or checked off).

3. Restart your Mac. Now you can throw away any printer icons that still appear on your desktop (which now probably have a big X through them).

Now *that's* what I call a grass-roots campaign against the rich!

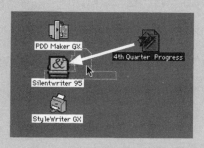

This handy shortcut — using the Tab key to move around the blanks, and pressing the Return key to "click" the OK or Print button — works in *any* Mac dialog box. In fact, any time you ever see a button with a black or double-thickness outline, as shown in the preceding illustration, you can press the Return key instead of using the mouse.

Canceling printing

If you want to interrupt the printing process, ⌘-period does the trick — that is, while pressing the ⌘ key, type a period. Several times, actually. Even then, your printer will take a moment (or page) or two to respond.

Where the Fonts Are

Your Mac comes with a juicy selection of available typefaces. Just check the Font menu of your friendly neighborhood word processor, and you'll see what I mean. Whatever the tone of the document you're writing — serious, fancy, loony — you'll find a typeface that suits you.

So where do you get additional fonts? The universal response to that kind of question is, of course, *buy* them.

Those on a budget, however, can still get tons of great fonts. Call up your local user group and pay about $5 for a disk full of new fonts. Or if you have a modem (described in Chapter 11), you can dial up America Online or the Internet and help yourself to as many fonts as your typographical taste buds can tolerate. (On America Online, use keyword *filesearch;* on the Internet, try *www.shareware.com*; either way, search the resulting page for "fonts.")

How to install a font

Quit all your programs (if you're running any) before trying this.

Drag the font-file icon (shaped like a suitcase) on top of the System Folder icon. (Do *not* drag it into the open System Folder *window*. Do not drag it to the Trash can. Do not collect $200.) You'll see a message alerting you that the Mac is going to install the font for you. Just smile, wave, and click OK.

System Folder   Yer Basic Font Suitcase   Yer Basic Font Suitcase

The only sidebar about user groups

Just in case the term "user group" caught you by surprise, here's the lowdown.

There are hundreds of these things — Macintosh User Groups, or MUGs. They go by names like LAMUG, NYMUG, and THUG (for the LA, NY, and The Hudson organizations, respectively). Each is a teeming hotbed of Mac enthusiasts of all different levels. They usually meet monthly, crank out a newsletter a month, and charge low annual dues. Each is also a dandy place to get your questions answered, your purchases previewed, and your social cravings slaked.

To find out which group is closest to you and your Mac, call Apple's user-group hot line at 800-538-9696.

How to remove a font

Open your System Folder and then open the Fonts folder therein. You'll now see a list of your fonts in a window as shown here:

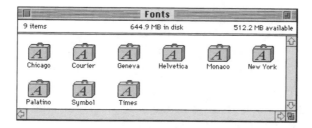

To see what a font looks like, double-click its suitcase icon. You'll get a window showing the individual font sizes, like Times 10 and Times 18; double-click one. A little window opens, displaying a few words to live by (such as: "Cozy lummox gives smart squid who asks for job pen"), displayed in the font you're investigating.

To remove a font, just drag it — or its entire suitcase — out of the window. Put it onto the desktop. Or put it into some other folder — or right into the Trash can.

Top Ten Free Fun Font Factoids

1. Every Mac comes installed with Times, Helvetica, Courier (which looks like an electric typewriter), Symbol (a bunch of Greek symbols), New York, Palatino, Chicago (the font used for menu names), Geneva (the font

used for icon names in the Finder), and Monaco (looks ugly on-screen but looks okay when printed). The Mac won't let you remove the last three; it uses them for various things on the screen.

Starting with Mac OS 8.5, you get a few extra ones (Gadget, Textile, Sand, and so on). Revel in your newfound font freedom.

2. There are two kinds of people: those who place everything into two categories, and those who don't. Among fonts, there are two basic types: *proportional* fonts, where every letter gets exactly as much width as it needs, and *monospaced* fonts, where every letter is exactly the same width, as on a typewriter. What you're reading now is a proportional font; notice that a W is much wider than an I.

Your Mac comes with two monospaced fonts: Courier and Monaco. All the others are proportional.

And who the heck cares? You will — the moment somebody sends you, perhaps by e-mail, some text that's supposed to line up, but doesn't. For example, this table that arrived by e-mail:

```
From:     IntenseDude
To:       pogue@aol.com

Hello, David! Here are the prices you asked about:

Item              Features            Price
----              --------            -----
Seinfeld Statuette      Removable hairpiece       $25.00
Baywatch digital watch  Surfboard sweep-second hand $34.50
"60 Minutes" bowtie     Mike Wallace autograph    $65.75
E.R. BandAid Pak™       100 per box               $ 9.85
```

All you have to do is highlight this text and change it to, say, Monaco, and everything looks good again!

```
From:     IntenseDude
To:       pogue@aol.com

Hello, David! Here are the prices you asked about:

Item                    Features                    Price
----                    --------                    -----
Seinfeld Statuette      Removable hairpiece         $25.00
Baywatch digital watch  Surfboard sweep-second hand $34.50
"60 Minutes" bowtie     Mike Wallace autograph      $65.75
E.R. BandAid Pak™       100 per box                 $ 9.85
```

3. Ten font families are built into most PostScript laser printers: Times, Helvetica, Helvetica Narrow, Avant Garde, Palatino, Bookman, New Century Schoolbook, Symbol, Zapf Chancery, and Zapf Dingbats.

(Although *Oblique* and *Demi* may sound like part of a sleazy trapeze act, they are in fact the trendy words for *Italic* and *Bold,* respectively.)

Times Roman
Times Bold
Times Italic
Times Bold Italic

Avant Garde Roman
Avant Garde Demi
Avant Garde Italic
Avant Garde Demi Italic

Bookman Roman
Bookman Demi
Bookman Italic
Bookman Demi Italic

New Century Schoolbook
  Roman
New Century Schoolbook
  Bold
New Century Schoolbook
  Italic
New Century Schoolbook
  Bold Italic

Palatino Roman
Palatino Bold
Palatino Italic
Palatino Bold Italic

Courier Roman
Courier Bold
Courier Italic
Courier Bold Italic

Helvetica Roman
Helvetica Bold
Helvetica Oblique
Helvetica Bold Oblique

Helvetica Narrow Roman
Helvetica Narrow Bold
Helvetica Narrow Oblique
Helvetica Narrow Bold Oblique

Zapf Chancery

Σψμβολ (Symbol)

✹❂✽ ✤✣✳❂❂ (Zapf Dingbats)

Any PostScript font that doesn't appear on this list has to be *downloaded* (transferred) to the printer each time you turn on the printer and try to print. As such, they're called *downloadable* fonts.

Downloadable fonts impact your life in several ways. First, you have to buy them. Second, documents that use downloadable fonts take more time to print; the Mac has to teach the printer what each character looks like.

4. From the File menu, choose Page Setup. The Page Setup dialog box offers a handful of useful options — whether you want the paper to print lengthwise or the short way, for example, or how much you want your document enlarged or reduced.

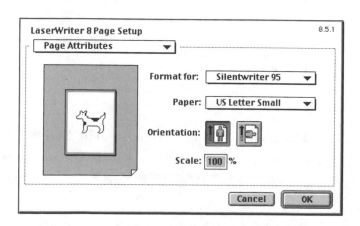

The Dogcow

No Mac book would be complete without at least a passing acknowledgment of the Dogcow. To see him, choose Page Setup from the File menu — or check out the picture of the Page Setup dialog box in item 4 of this chapter's Top Ten list.

His name, need I point out, stems from the fact that nobody can precisely figure out what kind of animal he is. In the inner sanctum of Apple Computer Corporation, it is said that, late at night, you can hear the sound made by the Dogcow: Moof!

The Paper pop-up menu near the middle, however, offers one of the most useful controls. If yours says "US Letter Small," your laser printer leaves a half-inch margin all the way around the page, chopping off any part of your printout that extends into it. If that bothers you, choose US Letter from that pop-up menu (and to make your change permanent, hold down Option as you click OK). From now on, your laser can print to within a quarter-inch of the edge of the paper.

5. Suppose that you select some text and make it bold. Then you try to print, but the text keeps coming out as *non*bold on the printed page.

   The problem is that some PostScript typefaces, notably Zapf Chancery, *don't have* a bold version. (Zapf Chancery doesn't even have an italic style because it's already sort of italic.)

6. If you've got Mac OS 8.5 or later, you've got the slickest font trick yet at your disposal. It goes like this:

   From your menu, choose Control Panels. Double-click the one called Appearance, and click the tab that says Fonts. Turn on the option called "Smooth all fonts on screen."

   Now revisit your word processor (or any other program, for that matter). Notice that the edges of your typed letters are drawn with softer and smoother edges, making your entire computer look as though it's an elegantly designed ad.

Before	After
The Staten Island Fairy	**The Staten Island Fairy**
A true story in nine chapters	*A true story in nine chapters*
Once upon a time there was a water sprite named Tia. She lived in New York, near the harbor where	Once upon a time there was a water sprite named Tia. She lived in New York, near the harbor where

7. In AppleWorks, ClarisWorks, Word 98, and some other word processing programs, you can actually see the names of the fonts in your font menu *in* those typefaces, like this:

```
┌─────────────────────────────────┐
│ Font                            │
│ Arial                           │
│ Arial MT Condensed Light        │
│ Arial Narrow                    │
│ Arial Rounded MT Bold           │
│ Avant Garde                     │
│ Bauhaus 93                      │
│ Bodoni MT Ultra Bold            │
│ Book Antiqua                    │
│ Bookman                         │
│ Bookman Old Style               │
│ Bookman Old Style Bold          │
└─────────────────────────────────┘
```

Problem is, how are you supposed to read the names of *symbol fonts* — fonts where every "letter" is actually a symbol or little picture (such as Zapf Dingbats)? Easy. Hold down the Shift key as you pull down the Font menu. Now every font *doesn't* show up in its own typeface — they're all in the usual menu font now.

8. When you first buy your laser printer, you may have noticed (and sworn at) the fact that it spits out a "startup page" every time you turn it on. This startup page contains a host of extremely unimportant information, like the number of pages you've printed in the printer's lifetime (including the useless startup page in your hand). Meanwhile, the Brazilian rain forests keep getting smaller.

   You can tell the printer not to waste that paper and ink, if you want. Use the little program called Desktop Printer Utility, Apple Printer Utility, or LaserWriter Utility. (In the halls of Apple, they play this fun game every year called "Rename that program!") It's on the CD that came with your Mac.

   Double-click this Utility program's icon, and choose Start Page Options from the Utilities menu. Click Off, and savor the fact that you made the world a better place for your grandchildren.

9. Want to look good the next time you're hanging out with a bunch of type geeks? Then learn to bandy about the terms *serif* (pronounced SAIR-iff) and *sans serif* (SANNZ sair-iff).

   A serif is the little protruding line built onto the edges of the letters in certain typefaces. In the *serif font* pictured in the top example here, I've drawn little circles around some of the serifs:

Terrif serifs
Sans-serif

A *sans serif* font, on the other hand, has no little protuberances, as you can see by their absence in the little square (in the lower example above). Times, Palatino, and the font you're reading are all serif fonts. Helvetica, Geneva, and the headlines in most newspapers are sans serif fonts. And that information, plus 32 cents (as of this writing), will buy you a first-class U.S. postage stamp.

10. This one's techy, but it's good.

   When the Mac prints, it matches the placement of each word *exactly* according to its position on the screen. Trouble is, the Mac's screen resolution isn't that good — it's only 72 dots per inch instead of 300 or 600 dpi (the usual for printers). As a result, you sometimes get weird spacing between words, especially between **boldface** words (see the bottom-left printout below).

   The solution: When you print, turn on the Fractional Character Widths feature. This makes words look a little bit cramped on the screen (top right in the figure below), but makes your printouts look *awesomely* professional (bottom right).

	Fractional Widths OFF	Fractional Widths ON
On the screen:	**Bullwinkle's Little Secret**	**Bullwinkle's Little Secret**
In the printout:	**Bullwinkle's Little Secret**	**Bullwinkle's Little Secret**

   So how do you find this magical feature? In WordPerfect and Word 5, it's in the Page Setup box (File menu). In Word 6, it's in the Options box (Tools menu); click the Print tab. In Word 98, choose Preferences from the Tools menu and click the Print tab. In AppleWorks/ClarisWorks, Fractional Widths is one of the Preferences (Edit menu). Try keeping it off when you're typing and on when you print.

Part II
Increasing Your Coolness Quotient

The 5th Wave By Rich Tennant

"WELL, RIGHT OFF, THE RESPONSE TIME SEEMS A BIT SLOW."

In this part . . .

Either you've faithfully plowed through the personality-enriching material so far, nursing your inner child (the one that always wanted to use a computer), and are now ready for more . . .

. . . or you've just skipped over a lot of stuff to get here. Either way, you won't be disappointed: the mind-blowing Faking Your Way Through the Top Ten Programs will be your survival guide for maintaining status in the office, and the chapter about your System Folder will help you reach a peaceful oneness with your Mac's operating system.

Chapter 6

Faking Your Way Through the Top Ten Programs

In This Chapter

▶ Faking your way through word/page processing programs like Microsoft Word

▶ Faking your way through famous number/data crunchers like Excel, Quicken, and FileMaker

▶ Faking your way through graphics programs like ClarisWorks

*T*his chapter is a survival guide for stranded-on-a-desert-island, filling-in-for-Mr.-Big, my-son's-at-school-but-I-need-to-print-out-something, the-computer-just-arrived-but-the-board-meeting-is-in-two-hours, in-a-computer-store-to-try-something-but-don't-know-how-it-works situations.

Macintosh users are notorious for not reading their software manuals. They're actually belligerently *proud* of the fact that they never read manuals. Of course, two years down the line, one user will look at another user's techniques and intone, astounded, "I never knew it could do *that!*"

You're welcome to join this cult of instant gratification, with this chapter as your guide — but at least read the manual for your word processor (or whatever program you spend the most time in).

The one thing this chapter *isn't* for is to help you use an illegal copy of one of these programs. Humor me on this; living near New York City is dangerous enough without worrying that some scary-looking goons in trench coats and dark glasses are gonna show up at my door accusing me of encouraging software piracy.

Why There Are Only Seven Programs in This Chapter

The *name* of this chapter makes reference to "the top 10 programs," yet this chapter contains writeups of only seven such programs.

Let me explain: You know how the phone company is running out of phone numbers, so they're frantically sitting around a table somewhere making up weird new area codes like 007 and 456?

That's what happened here. The ClarisWorks, Netscape Navigator, and Internet Explorer sections just got so darned big that they wound up getting their own chapters elsewhere in this book. And somehow "Faking Your Way Through the Top Seven Programs" doesn't have quite the same ring to it as "Top Ten." So I left the title and moved the chapters.

Will you forgive me?

Drawing Programs (ClarisDraw, ClarisWorks, & Co.)

Drawing programs are everywhere. MacDraw, ClarisDraw, Canvas, drafting programs, and the Drawing window of AppleWorks/ClarisWorks are all drawing programs. So are the graphics tools in FileMaker, Microsoft Word, Excel, and PowerPoint. In all of these programs, you'll find pretty much the same set of tools working pretty much the same way.

But as much as "drawing programs" sounds like they'd be the same things as *painting* programs, they're not.

Paint versus draw

Painting programs create art called *bitmapped* graphics. When you lay down some "paint," it's stored as a bunch of dots. You can erase the dots, but you can't change the original shape you painted — a circle, say, or a letter of the alphabet — because the Mac no longer thinks of them as a circle or a letter. It just thinks of them as a bunch of painted little dots. The advantage: You have control over each individual dot, and you have dot-manipulation tools like the Spray Can. In the next figure, note (1) the speckled effect, and (2) the fact that you can drag a chunk of circle out of the original collection of dots:

Drawing programs, on the other hand, create *object-oriented* graphics. When you draw a circle, the Mac doesn't store it as a map of black dots. It remembers that you drew a circle of a fixed shading and size. That means that you could never speckle it, and you could certainly never erase (or remove) a chunk of it.

But the advantage of drawing programs is that, later, you can return to that circle and move it by dragging it. Or you can overlap another object on top of it — and later change your mind. Or you can change a circle's shading long after you drew it. Or, as shown in the next figure, you can tug a circle's handles to stretch it.

Drawing programs print out with much sharper quality than painting programs.

Drawing concepts

The palette in all of these drawing programs contains the same basic tools. These tools are *incredibly* common; they even crop up in all kinds of *non*-art programs. For example, you use these same techniques to add graphic elements to your Web page (in Web-page-making software), to create movie credits in Adobe Premiere, to design mailing labels in FileMaker, to add "On vacation!" banners across the calendar squares of Now Up-to-Date, to fiddle with charts and graphs in Excel, and so on.

Here's the *Reader's Digest* condensed version:

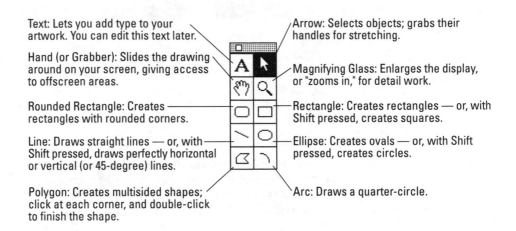

Text: Lets you add type to your artwork. You can edit this text later.

Hand (or Grabber): Slides the drawing around on your screen, giving access to offscreen areas.

Rounded Rectangle: Creates rectangles with rounded corners.

Line: Draws straight lines — or, with Shift pressed, draws perfectly horizontal or vertical (or 45-degree) lines.

Polygon: Creates multisided shapes; click at each corner, and double-click to finish the shape.

Arrow: Selects objects; grabs their handles for stretching.

Magnifying Glass: Enlarges the display, or "zooms in," for detail work.

Rectangle: Creates rectangles — or, with Shift pressed, creates squares.

Ellipse: Creates ovals — or, with Shift pressed, creates circles.

Arc: Draws a quarter-circle.

Each program has a few goodies of its own, too, but these basics are always included.

To draw something, click the tool (and release the button), move to a blank part of the screen where you want to place the object, hold down the mouse button, and drag. When you let go, you'll see the new line or shape enclosed by small, black, square *handles*. Using the Arrow Tool, you can drag these handles to stretch or resize the object you just drew. Or click in the middle of it to drag the object to a new location.

Or just click an object to make its handles show. After handles appear — letting you know that the object is selected — you can use the menus to change the object's appearance. For example, suppose you draw a thin line (next illustration, left). While it's selected, you can choose a new line thickness (below, middle) from the line thickness palette (every program has one). The result: The same line has a different thickness (below, right).

Using the palette of colors (or of patterns), you can change the color (or pattern) that fills the inside of a shape the same way: Select and then apply.

Actually, you'll generally find *two* different pop-up controls: one for the *outside* of a shape and another for the *inside*. In the picture below, from a ClarisWorks-type program, you can see these two separate sets of controls. The top row, marked by the little pouring-paint-button icon, has three pop-up buttons that control the *inside* of the selected rectangle — the three buttons change the color, pattern, and *gradient* (shifting-color fill), respectively. The bottom row, marked by the pen icon, has three pop-up buttons that control the *outline* of the rectangle — these three buttons change the color, pattern, and line thickness, respectively.

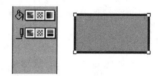

The power of Shift

When you press the Shift key while you draw something, the Mac constrains the movement of your mouse to flat or symmetrical movements. For instance, press Shift when you draw a line, and the line will be perfectly horizontal, vertical, or 45-degree diagonal. Press Shift while you draw a rectangle, and it will be a perfect square. And so on.

Selecting and grouping multiple objects

In the Finder, after you click one icon, you can select additional icons by Shift-clicking them (that is, clicking them while pressing the Shift key). In a word processor, if you have selected a word, you can extend the selection by Shift-clicking some place later in the paragraph.

Yes, indeed, Mr. Watson, there is a pattern here. This Shift-click-to-extend-a-selection deal is a common Mac technique. Same thing in drawing programs: Click to select one object, Shift-click to select others.

After you've got a bunch of objects selected, you can *group* them — combine them into a single new object — using (what else?) the Group command. You can even group groups. You may want to group objects in this way just to make sure their alignment to each other doesn't get disturbed.

Handiest yet, you can *un*group a group, or even ungroup a grouped group of groups. (I'll give you a moment to work on that.) Drawing programs ungroup objects in the same order in which they were grouped. So imagine that you group objects A and B together, and then group object C to the first group. The first time you use the Ungroup command, you'll wind up with the A/B group and the C object loose; apply Ungroup a second time to split up A and B.

Text FX

One of the nicest things about drawing programs is that text is text, and text it remains. Text in a *painting* program, on the other hand, turns into a text-shaped collection of painted *dots* instantly. You can't edit the text or change the font or correct a typo after you finish typing. And the printout looks exactly as jagged as it does on the screen:

A Green Onion

In a drawing program, though, because the Mac still thinks of text as text (and not dots), it prints out at full text sharpness:

A Green Onion

Furthermore, in a drawing program, each piece of text remains editable inside its little boundary rectangle. You can change the font or the size of the text or the dimensions of this rectangle at any time. For example, if you notice a typo (in the top part of the following figure), just click the text object with the appropriate text tool selected, click the problem text, and edit away (bottom of the following figure):

Carefull typeing

Careful **typing** I

After you create a text block, you can paste it into a word processor and drag those little corner boxes. The word processor thinks it's just a plain old graphic and proceeds to squish it any way you like. The result is fantastic text effects you couldn't create in a word processor alone:

A Green Onion

A Green Onion

Beyond these concepts, a drawing program really doesn't require a degree in rocket science. I now release you to your creative juices.

Painting Programs (Photoshop, ClarisWorks Again)

About a dozen of these programs roam the earth. Pro-level photo-editing programs like Photoshop, Painter, Dabbler, and Color It are painting programs. Even AppleWorks (formerly ClarisWorks) has a painting window. Most painting programs work alike — only the frills differ from program to program.

They're called *painting* programs because they produce *bitmapped* artwork. (For a discussion of what that means, see "Paint versus draw," earlier in this chapter.) Printouts from bitmapped programs tend to be a little bit jagged, since the Mac is reproducing the Mac screen when it prints out.

There's not much mystical hidden knowledge to be unearthed in paint programs. Once you've used a tool, you've pretty much mastered it for life. Here, then, is a typical tool palette. You click a tool (and release), move the cursor to the page, and then drag across your white screen. With this guide — and the all-important Undo command in the Edit menu — you're well on your way to the world's toniest art galleries.

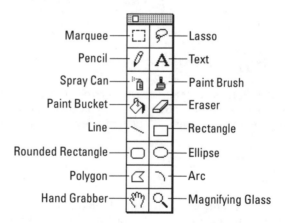

Marquee	Lasso
Pencil	Text
Spray Can	Paint Brush
Paint Bucket	Eraser
Line	Rectangle
Rounded Rectangle	Ellipse
Polygon	Arc
Hand Grabber	Magnifying Glass

Marquee and Lasso

These tools don't create any marks on the artwork. Instead, they're *selection* tools. They draw a dotted, shimmering line as you drag the mouse; you're creating an enclosure. Anything within the enclosure — the selected area — will be affected by your next move. For example, you can click within the selection to drag that chunk into a new position. Or press the Delete key to erase it. You can also apply special effects to the selected region, such as Invert (which swaps white areas for black, and vice versa) and, in some programs, Blur or Sharpen.

The Marquee and Lasso differ in two important ways. The Marquee always creates rectangular selected areas, including whatever white space is inside the rectangle. In the following illustration, you can see that when you drag a rectangular selection on top of a dark object (left), the white part of the selection remains opaque (right):

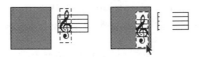

The Lasso, on the other hand, requires you to draw a circle all the way around the image you're trying to select. When you let go of the mouse, the dotted line snaps inward like a rubber band, enclosing only black regions of your artwork (below, left). Therefore, when the selected part is dragged on top of a dark object, the latter shows through the former (below, right):

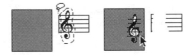

Pencil

The Pencil is pretty tame. Drag across the white area to draw a one-dot-thick line. There's only one trick to it. If you begin your line by clicking in a dark spot, the line you draw will be white, even if you cross over into a white area.

Text

Not much to this tool: Click in a blank area and start typing. While you're typing, you can press Delete (or Backspace) to fix a typo; in some programs, you can even use the mouse to drag through stretches of text for editing. But beware! The instant you click the mouse outside of the text box, your text freezes into a noneditable clump of dots (yes, a bitmap).

Spray Can

Painting at its finest. Drag the Spray Can across the painting area to create a fine mist of dots, just like an airbrush or spray paint can. Dawdle over an area to make it darker; hurry across the screen for a lighter mist. The color (or pattern) of the spray is whatever color (or pattern) you've selected from the color (or pattern) pop-up menu. For post-pubescent thrills, try drawing a subway car and then spray paint your name across it.

Eraser

Pretty basic. Drag across dark areas to erase them. Don't forget to zoom in (enlarge the screen image, using the Magnifying Glass) for detail work. For more mature thrills, draw your ex-spouse on the screen and then erase his/her head.

Line

Choose a line thickness (there's usually a pop-up menu for this purpose) before you draw. Then drag to create a straight line. If you want a perfectly horizontal, vertical, or 45-degree line, press Shift while you drag. Some programs also let you specify the line's color or pattern.

Rectangle, Ellipse, Polygon, and Arc

These shape tools pretty much work alike: You drag diagonally to produce the shape. (The Polygon tool works differently — click once for each corner point of your multisided shape; then double-click to finish the shape.)

In any case, you can usually control both the color (or pattern) of the *interior* of the shape as well as that of the *outline* of the shape by using pop-up color (or pattern) menus (see "Drawing Programs," earlier in this chapter, for an example). The Line Thickness pop-up menu governs the thickness of the outline. As before, the Shift key is the great constrainer: Press it to create a perfect square (with the Rectangle tool), circle (with the Ellipse tool), and so on.

Hand Grabber

Depending on the size of your monitor, you may not be able to see your entire artistic masterpiece at once. You can always use the scroll bars to slide your image up or down on your screen. But the Hand Grabber is much more direct — just drag in the direction you want to shift the painting.

Magnifying Glass

Click this tool; then click the painting to zoom in and/or enlarge the display for detail work. Of course, you're not actually making anything bigger (in terms of its printout); you're really just magnifying the screen image to get more control over those pesky dots. Keep zooming in until you get an idea of how those little dots make up your painting. You can then use the Pencil or another tool to continue painting.

To zoom out again or return to normal size, you usually press Option while clicking the painting.

Microsoft Word 98

Q: Where does an 800-pound gorilla sit?

A: Anywhere it wants.

Refer to this age-old discourse the next time somebody asks you why Microsoft Word, a program with numerous flaws and irritations, is the best-selling Macintosh program of all time. Microsoft is a gargantuan software company in Washington state. They sell so much software that the founder/owner (Bill Gates) is the richest man in America. Probably because of Microsoft's huge presence in the IBM-PC world, it's the 800-pound gorilla in the Mac world, too.

Of course, Microsoft Word isn't bad. In fact, it's got some truly wonderful features, one of which is that almost everybody uses it. That means that when you send your file to friends, you usually don't have to worry whether or not they've got the software needed to read it.

Anyway, you've already absorbed most of the basics of word processing (in Chapter 4). Word has a few fancy features worth learning, though (and does some basic things in interesting ways).

Incidentally: Word 98 is a lot better than its mutant predecessor, Word 6. If you're still using Word 6 or even Word 5.1, try to dig up a copy of *Macs For Dummies,* 5th Edition, where those programs are covered with characteristic poignancy.

Views

To start a new document, double-click the Microsoft Word icon. (*Hint:* Never move the Microsoft Word icon from its Microsoft Office 98 folder; if you do, it will politely decline to operate. If you really want to put the Word icon somewhere else on your hard drive, make an *alias* of it, as described in Chapter 9, and move *that*.)

A Microsoft joke that says a lot

How many Microsoft software programmers does it take to change a light bulb? None. They just declare darkness to be the standard.

You arrive at a blank screen. Go ahead and start typing your Oscar-winning screenplay. Use the usual word processing techniques (Delete to backspace, drag through text to select it, don't press Return at the end of each line, and so on) to whip it into shape.

You'll discover, though, that your piece of paper appears to be endless, as though it's delivered on a never-ending roll of Bounty. That's because you're in Normal view, where you never see a page end. (The end of a page is symbolized by a thin dotted line, but you sort of have to watch for it.) In Normal view, you don't get to see page-related elements like page numbers, either. They're hidden until you go to another view.

If you want to see a more accurate display of what you'll get when you print, choose Page Layout from the View menu. Things start to bog down in Page Layout view — that is, it takes longer to scroll around and visit different corners of your document. But you clearly see where each page ends, and you get to see things like page numbers and multiple columns.

Page break

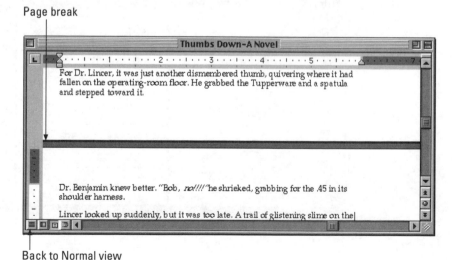

Back to Normal view

The View menu also contains commands for Online Layout view, which just makes the page narrower so that your text looks more like a magazine article; Outline view, a bizarre realm where you can rearrange your headings by dragging them; and Master Document, which only one person in America understands, and he's out of town until the 25th.

Finally, there's Print Preview, an absolutely vital and useful view. (Just to make sure the program isn't too easy to use, they've put the Print Preview command in the *File* menu, not the View menu with the other views.) In Print Preview you get to see the entire page — in fact, two side-by-side pages — no matter what size monitor you have.

To change the margins

Print Preview also provides the easiest way to adjust the margins. See the rulers at the top and left edges of the page? Position your cursor *carefully* over the spot where the white and dark gray strips of the ruler meet. Wait for the arrow cursor to change its shape into a double-headed arrow — and then drag to change the margins. (Remember that you're adjusting the margins for *all* the pages when you do this.)

Drag to change the page margins (only when cursor is a double-headed arrow)

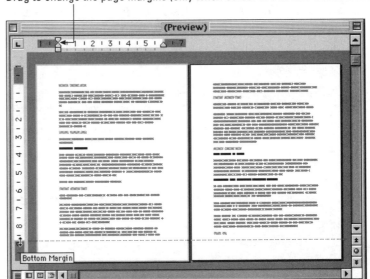

You can also, by the way, change the margins by choosing Document from the Format menu. A dialog box appears into which you can specify what you want for the top, bottom, left, and right margins. Specifying margins by typing numbers isn't as much fun as dragging the margins manually, but it does leave less margin for error.

(Dear Editor: That's the dumbest pun in the whole book. Let's make sure it gets taken out before the book is actually published, OK? Love, David.)

Invasion of the toolbar people

Toolbars are strips of icon buttons, each of which does exactly the same thing as one of the menu commands. When you first install Word 98, you get these two toolbars (called, respectively, the Standard and Formatting toolbars). Here are what a few of the most useful buttons do:

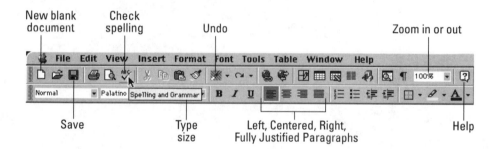

For the most part, the Standard toolbar controls the *program* (like opening, saving, and printing your work), and the Formatting toolbar controls *formatting* — the size of type, the style (bold or italic), the font, and so on. To do formatting, you *first* have to select some text you've already typed, by dragging through it.

If you ask me, the most useful settings are the B, I, and U buttons in the middle (for Bold, Italic, and Underline). You can glance at them and know immediately what formatting the next letters you type will have. The font and size controls (toward the left side) are useful, too, after you figure out that you have to click the downward-pointing triangle to change the setting.

Formatting paragraphs

In the middle of the Formatting strip are icons that make changes to an entire paragraph at a time — and remember, a "paragraph" is anything you've typed that ends with a Return. Before you can use the ruler, you must first *select the paragraphs you want to change!*

Nine out of ten novices surveyed find this concept hard to get used to. If you want to make one paragraph centered, just click anywhere in it so that the insertion point is blinking within it, and then click the Centered icon in the middle of the Formatting toolbar. If you want to affect several paragraphs but not the whole memo, drag through them before clicking on the toolbar.

The point is to remember the Macintosh mantra: Select, then apply. Select, then apply. Select, then apply. . . .

Toolbar bedtime

Fortunately, you can summon toolbars that pertain to every conceivable word processing task. Unfortunately, turning on a lot of them has one small downside: It doesn't leave you any room to *type*.

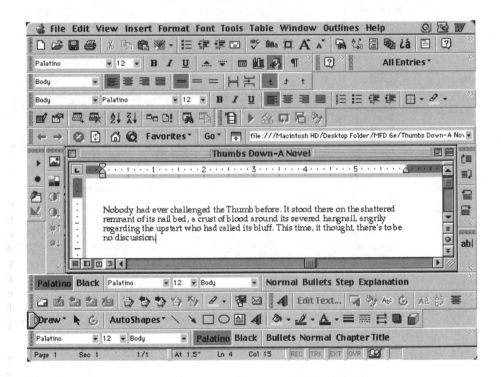

 Fortunately, you don't have to have these things cluttering up your screen. In fact, you can make them come and go as your whims dictate. The scheme for doing so is pretty simple: From the View menu, from the Toolbars sub-menu, choose the name of the toolbar you want to disappear (if it has a checkmark) or reappear (if it doesn't).

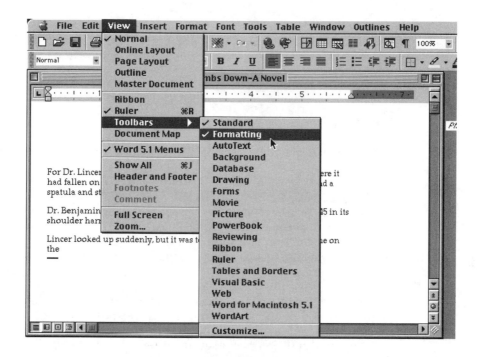

A palette for every palate

Q: When is a toolbar not a toolbar?

A: When it's a palette.

Look at one of the toolbar illustrations in this chapter. See the tiny dotted grip-strip at the left edge of each toolbar? Put your cursor on it and drag downward. Before your eyes, that horizontal icon strip morphs into a rectangle that you can drag anywhere on the screen. You've just turned the toolbar into a *palette.* All the buttons work as they always did — but now you can put them in a more convenient place. (To turn a palette *back* into a toolbar, drag it close to any edge of the screen — again, using its dotted grip-strip as a handle — until it clicks into its new, strip-like shape.)

Palettizing your toolbars has a certain logic, by the way. Unless you're some kind of technological weirdo, your screen is wider than it is tall. Therefore, horizontal toolbars are the worst possible use of your extra screen space; they eat into the vertical space that your document otherwise *could* be using. Meanwhile, there's a blank, empty area of screen off to the right of your document that's humming softly to itself, twiddling its thumb.

By putting your icon buttons (on palettes) off to the right of your work window, you can reclaim some of the vertical space, making your work window taller.

Don't let your self-esteem take a hit if you decide to turn off all of the tool-bars. Thousands of people have *all* of these strips turned off. Without these strips, using Word is almost exactly like using a typewriter, and that's 100 percent okay.

Be careful on the strip

And here you thought we'd finished talking about all Word's strips. No such luck.

Word's most hazardous feature, as far as you, Most Honorable Newcomer, are concerned, is its *selection bar*. This is a very, very skinny, invisible stripe up the left side of the window. You'll know when your cursor has inadvert-ently wandered in there because your arrow pointer will suddenly start pointing to the *right* instead of left. (This narrow vertical slice is in every version of Word.)

You may find this impossible to believe, but Word's left-margin strip was not, in fact, designed out of pure foaming malice toward new Mac users. It's actually supposed to make editing your work easier by providing some text-selecting shortcuts. Here are a few favorites.

Shortcut 1: Select one line of text by clicking in the selection strip.

> Lisa choked back the sobs as the explosions shook the earth around her.
> "Harry...oh, my poor Harry," she moaned.
> How could it have happened? A moment
> ago she'd walked into the lab with an armload
> of sweet-smelling roses. Then, within seconds,
> the pulverizing blows of the hammering bomb
> shattered her world.

Shortcut 2: To select a paragraph instantly, double-click in the selection strip. (Or triple-click anywhere inside a paragraph.)

> Lisa choked back the sobs as the explosions shook the earth around her.
> "Harry...oh, my poor Harry," she moaned.

Shortcut 3: To select the entire document, triple-click in the selection strip. (Do this when you want to change the font for the entire memo, for example.)

> Lisa choked back the sobs as the explosions shook the earth around her.
> "Harry...oh, my poor Harry," she moaned.
> How could it have happened? A moment
> ago she'd walked into the lab with an armload
> of sweet-smelling roses. Then, within seconds,
> the pulverizing blows of the hammering bomb
> shattered her world.

Moving text by dragging it

One of the coolest features in Word is "drag-and-drop" text manipulation. You can highlight some text and simply drag it into a new position without doing the tawdry Cut-and-Paste routine. (If this all sounds familiar, it's probably because you read about *Macintosh* drag-and-drop in Chapter 4.) As in AppleWorks, ClarisWorks, and most other law-abiding programs, Word 98 lets you even drag text completely out of the window and onto your desktop, where it becomes an icon called a *clipping file,* suitable for dragging back *into* any drag-and-droppable program.

And if Word's drag-and-drop deal doesn't work at all for you, some vandal probably turned this feature off. Choose Preferences from the Tools menu, click the Edit tab, and turn it back on.

Checking your spelling, grammar, and vocabulary

Word 98 has this funny quirk of checking your spelling and grammar *all the time.* The instant you type a boo-boo, Word lets you know with a colored, wavy underline.

You could, of course, rely on your years of schooling, experience, and quiet can-do attitude to correct such mistakes yourself. Or you could take the easy way out: While pressing the Control key, click (and hold the mouse button down) on the wavy-underlined word. A special pop-up menu appears, sprouting directly out of your cursor, offering — get this — suggestions for correcting the misspelled word! (You can also spell check your entire document by choosing Spelling from the Tools menu.)

> Nobody had ever seen anything quite like Tara. Half womon, half ferret, she dominated the room like Tom Cruise at a cheerleader's conv
>
> | woman |
> | women |
> | **Ignore All** |
> | **Add** |
> | **AutoCorrect** ▶ |
> | ✓ **Spelling...** |

If the wavy line is green, Word is suggesting that your *grammar* could stand improvement; its suggestions (when you Control-click the sentence) aren't always terrific improvements over your original, but they're sometimes worth considering.

And speaking of Control-clicking: That same trick works on words that *aren't* underlined. The resulting pop-up menu shows a Synonyms command that actually lists synonyms for the word you clicked — the perfect cheat for the vocabularically impaired.

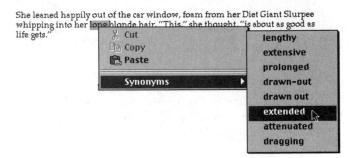

Killing the "Choose a template" box

One of Word's most annoying tics is that whenever you want a new document, it presents you with a stupid list window offering you such preformatted layouts as Thesis, Weekly Time Sheet, and Brochures 1 and 2. Well, that's terrific — too bad for the 98 percent of us who just want to type up a gosh-darned letter.

Fortunately, you can eliminate this annoying obstacle to getting on with your work day. Instead of choosing New from the File menu, just press ⌘-N — instant blank document.

Single-spaced or double?

If you wonder why millions of Mac fans quietly grumble about Microsoft's mediocrity, here's a classic example: There's no easy way to change your document from single-spaced to double-spaced.

Anyway, here's what you have to do: From the Format menu, choose Paragraph. In the dialog box that appears, click Indents and Spacing. You should now see the tiny pop-up menu that lets you control spacing — not just Single and Double, but even "1.5 lines" or any number of lines you type into the box.

Page numbering

To add page numbers to your document, choose Page Numbers from the Insert menu. A neat little dialog box appears, where you can specify where you want the page number to appear: top, bottom, left, or right — and whether you want a number to appear on page 1.

How to kill superfluous commands

Unless you're trying to crank out the next Sears catalog on your iMac or something, chances are good you won't be needing indexing, auto-hyphenation, and other abstruse options in Word.

Removing a command you never use is incredibly easy. While pressing ⌘ and Option together, press the minus (hyphen) key. Your cursor turns into a big fat minus sign! Handle your mouse with care, now — it's a loaded weapon. Any menu command you touch will disappear from the menu.

Here's a partial listing of the commands I nuked from my Word 98 menus. Depending on how far you intend to let Word take you, you may want to augment this list (or leave some of these alone):

- **File menu:** Open Web Page, Save as HTML, Versions, Properties
- **Edit menu:** Paste Special, Go To, Publishing, Links, Object
- **View menu:** Master Document, Online Layout
- **Insert menu:** Frame, Field, Caption, Cross-Reference, Index and Tables, Text Box, Movie, Frame, Object, Hyperlink
- **Format menu:** Drop Cap, Style Gallery, Text Direction, Background, Object
- **Tools menu:** Language, Merge Document, Protect Document, Revisions, Macro, Templates and Add-Ins
- **Table menu:** Almost everything

And, by the way, you're not removing these commands from the *program* — you're simply removing them from the menu listings. If you ever want to restore Word's menus to their original condition, choose Customize from the Tools menu. In the dialog box that appears, scroll down, click Menu Bar, then click Reset. (And when Word asks if you're sure, click OK.)

Getting help — and goofy animations

This crash course in Word 98 has been brought to you by People With Very Little Spare Time. But if you're going to get into Word's more advanced features — you know, putting boxes around paragraphs, automatic indexing, outlining, making tables — you'll need to consult Word 98's manual. It's electronic, built right into the program, saving you years' worth of paper cuts. From the Help menu, choose Microsoft Word Help. If he's not already on your screen, the little dancing Mac (known as Max) appears in his little movie window, like this:

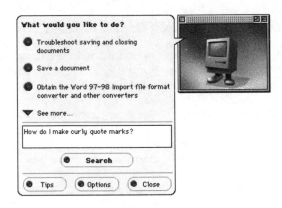

Into the little Search blank, type whatever you'd like help with (such as "margins" or "green text") or even a question (such as "How do I make an outline?"). Then click Search. After a moment, you'll be shown a list of help topics; click one to read all about it. Word's not always brilliant at providing answers — but every now and then, it'll surprise you.

And speaking of Max the animated doodad: Public opinion is evenly divided on this little guy. Half the world thinks he's kinda cute; the other half considers taking a sledge hammer to their screens.

If he bugs you, click the tiny close box in the upper-left corner of his window, and watch him wave goodbye forever. If he charms you, hold down the Control key, click his window, and choose Animate! from the pop-up menu that appears. Each time you do so, Max will perform another little stunt for you, such as dismantling himself, putting on glasses, going to sleep, and so on.

Who *said* computers don't make us more productive?

Quicken

Here it is, kids — one of the best designed, best known, best loved programs on the planet. Microsoft *never* could have come up with this one.

Quicken, of course, is the ultimate checkbook program. Of course, calling Quicken a checkbook program is slightly understating the case, like calling AT&T a phone company or calling O.J. Simpson a former football player. As you'll discover, Quicken can really be the cornerstone of your entire bank account, credit card, tax, investment, and otherwise financial empire.

The category concept

When you first launch Quicken, it asks you to name the file you're keeping all of your financial info in. In the same dialog box where you type a name, Quicken makes you choose a set of *categories* before you do anything else — either Home or Business. When it's time to do your taxes; when you want to see where your money's going; when you want to plan ahead for next year; in all of these cases, Quicken can show you a snapshot of your current financial status, organized, as always, by *category*. It's a great system.

Pick Home, Business, or both to start you off, depending on how you're going to be using Quicken, to get past the opening screen or two. (You can always make up your own categories later.)

When you arrive at this screen, grab your bank-account statement.

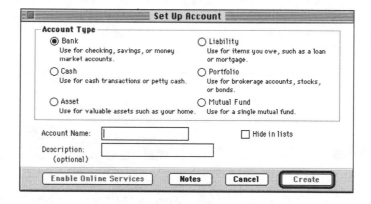

Fill in what you want to call this account. *Money-Grubbing Corporate Bank Vermin* is fine, except that it won't fit. *Savings* or *Checking* is a more common title.

The Register

At last you're permitted to see the Face of Quicken: the Register window.

Type in the opening balance — in other words, the ending amount on your last bank statement.

Checking: Register							
Date	Number	Payee/Category/Memo		Payment	Clr	Deposit	Balance
3/20/99	*Num*	Opening Balance		*Payment*	✓	5,000.00	5,000.00
		[Checking]	*Memo*	Split		Shortcuts ▼	
3/20/99							

| Record | Restore | Sort by: Date ▼ | Balance Today: | $5,000.00 |
| | | | Balance 3/20/99: | $5,000.00 |

Type in the date and final amount of your last bank statement, as shown above.

This register window may look like any normal Mac window, but that's like saying that a jalapeño looks like any normal salad component. There are a thousand handi-features™ to make typing in information fast and easy. To wit:

✔ **Change the date by pressing the + and – keys on your keyboard.**

Date	Number	Payee or Description	
		Category	Memo
▶ 6/7/98		Opening Balance	
		[CitiBank Chk ▼]	

Most of The Quicken Experience involves recording money you've spent and money you've made. The first stage of each typing binge is to set the date. Just click the date, and then make the date advance or retreat by using + and – ; the longer you hold down the key, the faster the number changes.

Neater yet — after you've clicked the Date blank, you can also type *t* for today's date, *m* or *h* for the beginning or ending date of the **month**, or *y* or *r* for the beginning or ending date of the **year**. Isn't that adorable?

✔ **Press Tab to jump from column to column.**

Press *Shift*-Tab to jump *backwards* through the blanks. You can get by for months without ever needing the mouse.

✔ **Don't bother tabbing to the cents place; just hit the decimal.** When you're typing in a dollar amount, leave off the $ sign and just type a decimal point (period) in the usual place. Quicken's smart enough to put the dollars and cents on opposite sides of the dividing line.

✔ **If Quicken recognizes something you're typing, it'll finish the phrase for you.** You do *not* have to type *Metropolitan Light, Power, and Water Authority of Northern California* every time you cut a check for utilities. By the time you've typed *Metrop,* Quicken will have filled in the rest of the payee for you (assuming you've ever typed it before).

If Quicken guesses *wrong,* just keep typing. Quicken will remove its guess.

✔ **After entering a transaction, press Return.** Quicken sets you up with a new blank line, ready to receive the next scrap from your envelope of receipts. Oh, yeah — it also does all the math for you and updates the bottom line at the bottom of the window.

Just another $10,000 day

Now that you've got your register set up, the rest of Quicken is simplicity itself. Suppose you made a bank deposit today — your weekly paycheck plus the first installment from a lottery you won. (I like to use examples that everyone can relate to.)

Click in the bottom row of the ledger, which is blank. (There's *always* one blank line at the bottom of the register. If you don't see it, maybe you need to scroll down using the scroll bar at the right side.) Use the + and – keys, naturally, to adjust the date (or type *t* for today).

Tab.

Then type a description of today's event — in this case, *Paycheck and Lottery #1.*

Tab.

Now type in the *total* amount of your bank deposit, paycheck plus prize money. If this weren't a dual-source deposit, you'd be done — but you're not. Here's where it gets really neat.

See the little *Split* button in the Payment column? (In Quicken version 6 and earlier, it's a Splits button at the middle bottom of the window.) Click it. A stack of sub-blanks appears, in which you can break down your total transaction amount, as shown here:

When you click the Split button, this sub-list appears.

```
┌────────────────────────── Checking: Register ──────────────────────┐
│ Date  │Number│  Payee/Category/Memo  │Payment│Clr│Deposit│ Balance │
│3/20/99│ Num  │Paycheck and Lottery #1│Payment│   │10,000.49│        │
│       │ ▼    │              Memo     │ Split │   │Shortcuts▼│        │
│          Category        │     Memo        │    Amount             │
│    Salary                │includes year-end bonus│    0.49 ▲        │
│                      ▼   │                 │  10,000.00            │
│                          │                 │                ▼      │
│        [Close Split]  [Clear Split]  [Adjust Total]                │
│  [Record]   [Restore]      Sort by: Date ▼   Balance Today: $5,000.00│
│                                              Balance 3/20/99: $5,000.00│
└──────────────────────────────────────────────────────────────────┘
```

The Category must be on the Category list — generic labels like Tax, Auto, or Insurance.

The Memo can be anything you want.

You've got to choose a category for this part of the split. For the paycheck, no sweat — it would be Salary. If you type the letters *Sa,* Quicken will recognize where you're headed, and it will fill in the rest of the word. (Alternatively, you can press ⌘-L, for *list,* to see Quicken's complete list of categories. You can double-click anything on that list to make it fill in the Category blank here. Or, if you have Quicken 98 or later, you could also choose a category name from the pop-up menu — the tiny black down-pointing triangle at the right edge of the Category blank.)

Tab.

Then type in, for the paycheck, a memo. Anything you want. Or nothing.

Tab.

Now enter the amount of the paycheck. In this case, you work as a tollbooth operator for a remote and impoverished township in a debt-ridden South American country, so you only make 49¢ per week. Type *.49.*

Tab.

Creating a new category

Now you're supposed to enter the category for your lottery money. Yet oddly enough, Quicken doesn't come with a Lottery Winnings category. You're going to have to make it up.

Suppose you decide to call this category *Prizes.* Type that, then press Tab — and Quicken will tell you that you've colored outside of the lines.

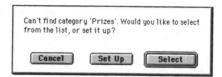

Fortunately, Quicken also offers you the easy way out. Click Set Up. Now you can create your new financial category.

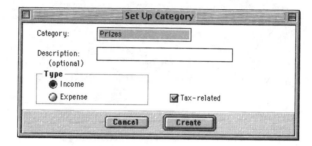

When coming up with a name for your new category, think general. Think tax time. Don't create a category called *Beige leatherette camera case, that one with the tassels.* Instead, the IRS would probably be content to see *Equipment* or something.

In the case of the lottery winnings, be sure to specify the Type — Income — and that, God knows, it's tax-related. In other words, this little baby is definitely going to find a place on your 1040 form. Groceries, on the other hand, will not.

Click Create. You return to your entry, where Prizes is now accepted as a legit category name. Tab over to the Memo blank, type something like *First installment,* and you're done. Quicken has already entered $10,000 into the Amount blank to make the split amounts match the grand total.

To close up the Split window, click the *left* side of the Split icon (or press ⌘-E).

More typical examples

Another great candidate for the Split window: credit-card payments. Suppose you write a check to pay this month's credit-card bill. (Most people have a separate Checking account, which you can create by choosing New Account from the File menu.)

Choose Write Checks from the Activities menu. You get this representation of America's most recognized piece of paper:

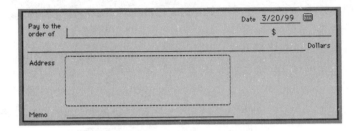

Start typing the payee's name. As you know by now, if Quicken recognizes the name, the program will complete the typing for you.

Tab.

Type in the amount.

This time when you press Tab, you get to see one of the slickest features ever. If you typed in $432.45, Quicken writes out, in longhand English, *Four hundred thirty-two and 45/100* on the second line.

Tab your way into the Address box and type the mailing address (press *Return* after each line, *not* Tab). Then Tab to the Memo blank and type your account number. And *now* (egg roll, please) — choose Memorize from the Edit menu. From now on, when you start to make a check out to *Citib,* Quicken will fill in the payee name *and* the address *and* the account number!

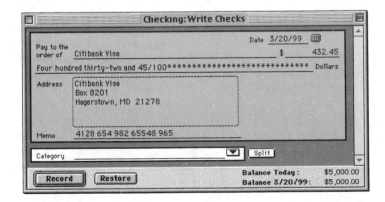

Before you hit Return (or click Record), it's a good idea to note what this credit-card payment *covers*. Just as you did before, click the Split button at the bottom of the check window. Now your expenditures are logged safely in case of disaster (such as fire, flood, or April 15).

The category payoff

The point of all this categorizing, of course, comes at year-end (or any other occasion where a financial snapshot is required). Quicken does some amazing number crunching.

At tax time, for example, choose Reports from the Reports & Graphs command in the Activities menu. Double-click, say, Category Summary. Plug in the year's starting and ending dates; instantly you've got a detailed breakdown to hand your tax guy (or yourself, as the case may be). The graphs are equally impressive (choose Graphs from the Reports & Graphs command).

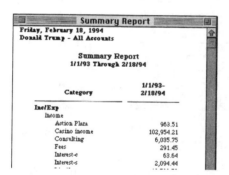

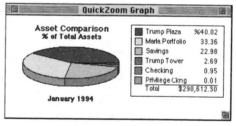

Reconciling for the non-accountant

Yeah, Quicken's great, it's fast and easy, it's dirt cheap to buy, yadda yadda yadda. But none of that puts it in the Hall of Greats. No, the real plum is the reconciling feature. You're entitled not to believe me, but you'll actually come to look *forward* to curling up with Quicken and your bank statement each month.

Like many of us out in America Land, there was a time when I, too, occasionally failed to compare my checkbook with the bank statement each month. But trusting the bank's computers can be dangerous; they *do* make mistakes. In my six years of using Quicken, I've caught my bank with its computerized hands in my tiller twice — $45 the first time, $200 the second!

Anyway, here's how reconciling works. With your bank statement in front of you, choose Reconcile from the Activities menu. Fill in the closing balance from the bank statement; fill in any interest your money earned, too, as well as any finance charges those filthy usurers charged you.

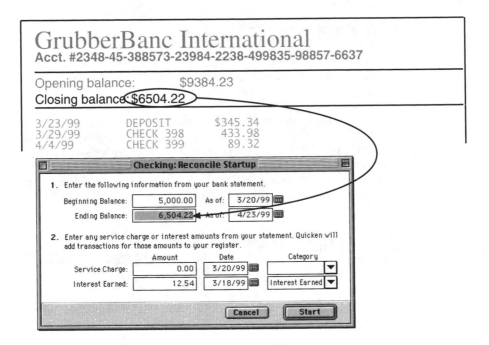

Click OK. Now the fun begins.

Read down the transactions listed on your bank statement. Each time you find one that matches a listing in Quicken's Reconcile window, click it in the Reconcile window, so that a checkmark appears. Keep going until you've accounted for everything on the statement.

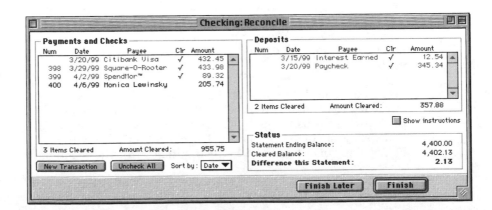

If Quicken shows extra items

Almost always, Quicken will show transactions that your bank statement doesn't. That's normal. It means that your life didn't stop on the 15th of the month (or whenever the bank's cutoff date for your statement was). The items you're seeing are transactions you've made since the day the statement was printed and mailed.

If the statement has extra items

But what if the bank lists some deposit or payment that Quicken doesn't know about? In most cases — forgive me — this is your mistake; you probably forgot to record something in Quicken. (Or, as they say in the biz, PBKC: *problem between keyboard and chair*).

On the other hand, as I've noted, once in a blue moon, you'll catch a genuine bank mistake.

If you note discrepancies as you go, use one of these two techniques:

> ✔ **Double-click any transaction listed in Quicken's Reconcile window.** You'll be teleported directly to the Register entry for that item, so you can read the description and try to get more information. For example, if you have two different entries for "New co-op in St. Thomas," then odds are pretty good you entered it twice. Unless you truly did buy two, delete one of them (use Delete Transaction in the Edit menu).
>
> ✔ **Pull the Register window to the front.** If you discover a transaction on the statement that you forgot to plug into Quicken during the month, click the New Transaction button and type it in. Then return to the Reconcile window and click it off.

What's *supposed* to happen is that the line called Difference This Statement (see the previous illustration) winds up at zero. If it does, click OK and bask in the warm sunny feeling of Quicken's little congratulatory message.

If the Difference This Statement doesn't come out to zero, you can either squirm for another 20 minutes trying to find out why your computer doesn't match the bank's, or you can take the fatalistic approach and click the OK button.

In that event, Quicken will create a new entry in your register called, ahem, Balance Adjustment. Try, *try* not to think of it as shouting in huge capital letters, *"This is where you screwed up, you numerically incompetent clod!"* every time you look at it for the rest of your life.

In my experience, by the way, the temptation to simply accept the discrepancy is much greater when it's in your favor.

Excel 98

Microsoft Excel is the best-selling Macintosh spreadsheet program. Well, "best-selling" is about the understatement of the decade. (A recent Excel ad headline said, "99 out of 100 spreadsheet users use Excel. What are we doing wrong?")

If you're not familiar with a *spreadsheet,* get psyched — even if you only use 1 percent of its features, Excel can really be a godsend. It's for math, finances, figuring out which of two mortgage plans is more favorable in the long run, charting the growth of your basement gambling operation, and other number-crunchy stuff.

Starting up

Double-click the Excel icon. A blank spreadsheet appears on your screen. It's a bunch of rows and columns, like a ledger book. The columns have letters, and the rows are numbered. Each little rectangular cell is called, well, a cell. It's referred to by its letter and number: A1, for example.

To type a number into a cell, click the cell with the mouse and begin typing. Unless your version of Excel is very old, you can do your typing (and editing) in the cell itself, but notice that all the action is duplicated in the editing strip at the top of the window. When you're done typing or editing, press Enter.

Formatting numbers and text

As you enter numbers, don't bother to format them with dollar signs, decimal points, and all that jazz. Formatting can be applied later. For instance, you could enter the following numbers, each of which has a different number of decimal places (below, left). Now drag vertically through them with the pointer (below, right).

645		645
213.5		213.5
645.88		645.88
987.556		987.556

By now you can probably say it in your sleep: in the world of Mac, you select something first and then act on it . . . *Select, then apply.* . . . After the numbers are selected, you can format them all with dollar amounts in one fell swoop. See the little dollar-sign button on the lower toolbar at the top of the screen? (If you don't, open the View menu, choose Toolbars, and choose Formatting from the submenu.) Click that $ icon.

Instantly, Excel formats all the selected numbers as dollar amounts. Note how it adds zeros (or rounds off excess decimal places) as necessary.

Spreading the sheet

Now it gets good. If you've been fooling around so far, erase everything you've done. Drag the cursor diagonally through whatever you've typed and then choose Clear from the Edit menu (and All from the submenu). We're gonna start you off fresh-like.

Click in cell B3 (that's column B, row 3; a spreadsheet is like a good game of Battleship). Type in *1969.*

To jump into the next cell to the right, press Tab. Or press the right-arrow key. (You move to the *left* by pressing *Shift*-Tab, or the left-arrow key.) In any case, enter *1979.* Repeat until you've filled in the years as shown below.

You move *down* a row by pressing Return or the down-arrow key. Shift-Return moves you up a row, and so does the up-arrow key. (There's a certain twisted logic to this, isn't there?)

You can also jump to any cell by clicking in it, of course. Now then: Go wild. With these navigational commands under your belt, type in the text and numbers as shown below. (Frankly, it doesn't make any difference *what* numbers you type. I made them all up anyway.)

	A	B	C	D	E	F
1						
2						
3		1969	1979	1989	1999	
4	Quarter 1	1234	2345	4567	7899	
5	Quarter 2	3123	2396	3556	3488	
6	Quarter 3	120	1589	6455	122	
7	Quarter 4	2000	3225	5353	8441	
8						
9	TOTALS:					
10						
11						
12						

Sample — Sheet1 / Sheet2 / Sheet3

Want to make the top row boldface, as shown in the preceding figure? Drag the cursor through the years. Now click the B button on the toolbar at the top of the screen. If you haven't guessed, **B** means **Bold,** and *I* means *Italic.* (And I mean italic!)

Creating automatically calculating cells

Here comes the juicy part. Click in the Totals row, under the 1969 column of numbers. Click the funny Σ button on the top toolbar, as shown here:

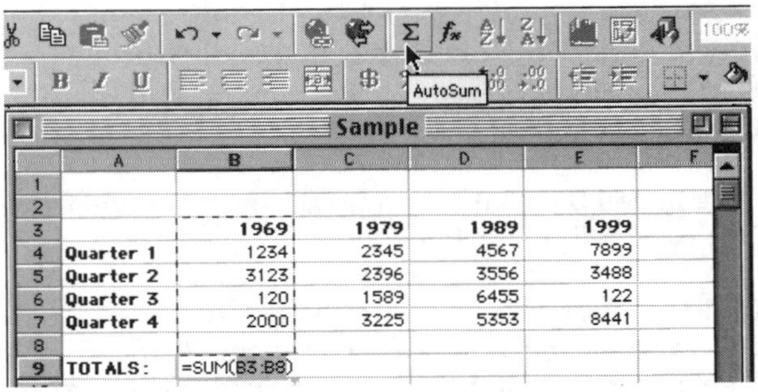

That's the Sum button, and it's some button.

In the formula bar at the top of the screen, you'll see that Excel has entered "=SUM(B3:B8)."

In English, the program is trying to say: "The number I'll enter into the cell you clicked (Total) is going to be the sum of . . . well, I suppose you mean the numbers directly *above* the cell you clicked — cells B3 down to B8." Isn't it smart to guess what you mean?

Well, smart, but not quite smart enough — because you *don't* want the number 1969 included in the total! So you can override Excel's guess by showing it which numbers you *do* want totaled . . . by dragging through them. Try it. While the dotted-line rectangle is still twinkling, drag vertically through the four cells *below* 1969. Then press Enter.

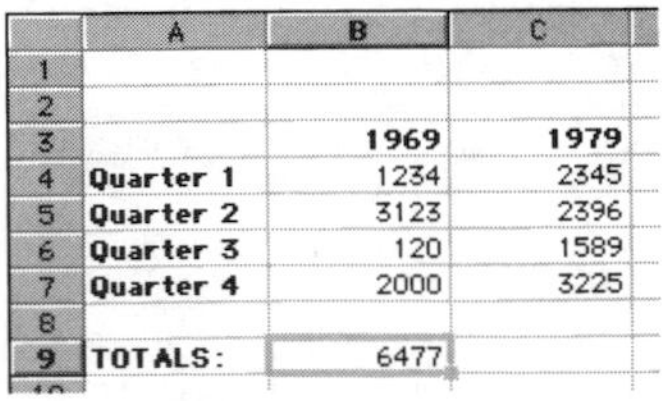

Neat, huh? Excel automatically totals the four numbers you selected. But that's only the half of it. Now click one of the cells below the 1969 heading — and *change the number*. That's right, type a totally different number. (And press Enter when you're done typing. You always have to press Enter to tell Excel you're done working in a cell.) Voilà — the total *changes* automatically!

This is the origin of the phrase "What-if scenario." You can sit here all day, fiddling with the numbers in the 1969 column. As soon as you change a number and press Enter, the total updates itself. That's why it's so easy to compute a mortgage at 10 percent for five years and see if it's better than one at 8 percent for seven years (or whatever).

Fill right, feel right

Now then. You have three other columns to contend with. Do you have to redo the Σ business each time? Nope. You've already explained to Excel how the Total row should work: It should add up the four numbers above it, *not* including the year at the top of the column.

So you could just take that magic total cell (B9 in the preceding picture) and *copy* it into the three cells to its right. Excel is smart enough to add up the right numbers in each column (no, it won't put the *1969* total into each cell).

Of course, you could use the regular Copy and Paste commands — but that's too tedious. Use the Fill Right command instead. Drag through the Totals row, starting with the 1969 total and extending through the three other years' total cells.

Then press ⌘-R — or do it the long way: From the Edit menu, choose Fill, and choose Right right from its submenu. Bingo! Excel intelligently copies the *formula* from the first cell into the other cells, totaling each column automatically. You may as well know that there's also a Fill Down command, used when you want to copy a formula to a series of cells *below* the one that contains it.

From here to infinity

Using the standard math symbols (+, -, / for division, and * for multiplication), you can build much more complicated auto-calculating cells than the simple SUM function described in "Creating automatically calculating cells." For example, you can use nested parentheses and the whole works. To make a cell calculate how many hours there are in ten years, for example, you'd click on it. Then you'd type **=(24*365)*10** and press Enter. The formula always has to begin with the equal sign, but otherwise your equations can be as complicated as you want.

You can have formula cells that work with numbers from *other* formula cells, too — in the example above, you could create a Grand Total cell that would sum up the 1969, 1979, 1989, and 1999 totals automatically. There are even a few dozen more complex formula elements — financial, statistical, math, and time functions — listed in the Paste Function command (Edit menu), if you're into that kinky stuff.

Making a chart

There are a zillion options for charting, too, but here's the quick-and-dirty approach.

Drag through the table you created earlier — just the data part, not the totals in the bottom row. After this section is highlighted, click the Chart Wizard button on the ribbon, as shown here:

	A	B	C	D	E	F
1						
2						
3		1969	1979	1989	1999	
4	Quarter 1	1234	2345	4567	7899	
5	Quarter 2	3123	2396	3556	3488	
6	Quarter 3	120	1589	6455	122	
7	Quarter 4	2000	3225	5353	8441	
8						
9	TOTALS:	6477	9555	19931	19950	

Now a dialog box appears, filled with amazing-looking examples of every kind of chart you've ever seen: bar, pie, line, area, Perot, and so on. Click the kind you want. In fact, you could spend several more hours here, tweaking every little chart option — but for this example, simply clicking the Finish button is enough.

When the dialog box disappears, a charming little chart pops up. (If it's charmingly covering up your numbers, hold down the cursor inside an empty part of the graph and drag it into a new position.) Double-click an individual bar (or other piece of the chart) to adjust the colors and styles for that element.

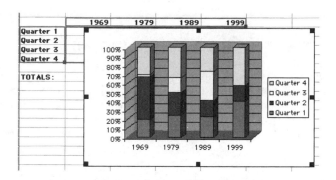

Excel also has outlining, drawing tools, macros, a database function, and probably a convenient toaster-oven . . . but this was supposed to be a crash course. If you want those frills, you'll have to actually put your nose in the manual.

FileMaker Pro

FileMaker is the king, queen, and princess of *database* programs. A database is just what it sounds like: a base of data — a pile of it, if you will — that you can view in a million different ways. It's perfect for lists, CD collections, invoices, catalogs, and so on.

Stop me if you've heard this one. Suppose you have a mailing list, and you want to know how many people in Zip code 44122 have last names beginning with M. Or you have a list of 2,000 books and want to sort them by author's name or print a list only showing hardcover volumes, or find out the publisher of a book of which you know only one word of the title. For all these tasks, a database is the way to go.

The really far-out feature of FileMaker is that you can set up several different views of the information. Suppose you have a mailing list for a party. You could set up your Data Entry view with great big 18-point bold type, which makes it easier for you to type in those names without your glasses. You'd also want a Mailing Label layout, though, which neatly arranges the addresses side-by-side across the page, in a much smaller type size, so that you can print and mail the invitations. Yet a third layout could be the Name-Tag view; it would place only the person's name (and not the address) in a cute font, preceded by the words "Hello! My name is." Using these different layouts — of the same information — really lets you put the data to work without having to do any retyping.

No Save command!?

Why the heck do you have to name your file *before* you type any information into it? Isn't that exactly opposite from the way most programs work, where you type some stuff and then choose Save (and give the file a name)?

Yup.

In FileMaker, though, you'll actually come to like this feature — the program saves your data *automatically*, without your having to remember. The result: Your data is always up to date, even when something goes wrong.

Step 1: Starting a file

Double-click the FileMaker icon. A dialog box appears, where you're either supposed to open an existing data file or create a new one; click New. In the next dialog box, type a name for your file and click New again.

Before you know it, a *really* complex-looking dialog box appears. Brace yourself for a couple more terms.

As you design your database, you'll be creating two units of information. First of all, there are the individual blanks: the name, the Zip code, and the state. These are called *fields*. (The International Council of Nerds evidently felt that calling them *blanks* wouldn't have confused people enough.)

A set of fields constitutes one *record*. A record might be a complete name-street-city-state-Zip set for a mailing list; if there are three people's addresses, there are three records in the database. Still with us?

Okay then. In the dialog box now staring you in the face, you're being asked to create the *fields* (the blanks). First type the name of the field; it might be First Name or Last Name or Street or Account Number or Date or Eyebrow Thickness or whatever. Now tell FileMaker what *kind* of data is going to be in this blank, as shown in the following table.

If you select this data type . . .	. . . then this happens.
Text	You can enter any kind of typed data.
Number	FileMaker won't let you type letters of the alphabet — only digits.
Date, Time	Dates or times in any format.

If you select this data type . . .	. . . then this happens.
Container	This kind of blank holds pictures, movies, sounds, and other things that can't be typed.
Calculation	You can't paste or type anything. FileMaker fills in this field automatically by performing math on other fields, like adding the Amount and Tax fields.
Summary	You can't paste or type anything. FileMaker fills in this field automatically by performing math on other fields, like adding them, counting them, or giving you a running total.
Global	If there's some particular piece of information that's going to remain the same all the time, you can put it here. Used primarily for creating complicated formulas and automated data-crunching. See your cheerful neighborhood consultant.

For each field you'll want on the screen, then, type a name and select a data type, and click Create. Repeat for the other fields. (If you want FileMaker to automatically enter data, like today's date, then click Options just after creating a field.)

Anyway, after you're done defining every blank you'll want to use, click Done. You've just finished step 1.

Step 2: Data entry

At this point, you can start typing away to input data. The rules are simple: It's just like a word processor, so you use the Delete key to backspace over a typo, cut, copy, and paste selected text, and so on. To advance to the next field, press Tab. To jump back to the previous field, press Shift-Tab. To create a new, blank record (for a new person's address, say), choose New Record from the Edit menu. (Again, for a complete illustrated tour of this process, see the ClarisWorks chapter coming up.)

A calculated maneuver

If you created a Calculation field, a dialog box appears as soon as you click Create. In this box, you can build the equation you want FileMaker to use. The equation usually involves other fields — which are listed at the upper left — combined with the +, -, / (divided by), and * (times) symbols. For example, if you're crazy enough to live in New York City, you would define the Sales Tax field as Purchase Amount * 1.0825 (8.25 percent is the sales tax rate).

As you create more records, the little open book icon at the upper left will indicate that it has more and more "pages," each of which is a record. This little diagram shows the four ways you can navigate your pile of data.

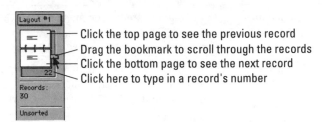

Click the top page to see the previous record
Drag the bookmark to scroll through the records
Click the bottom page to see the next record
Click here to type in a record's number

If your goal in reading this section is to perform the joyous task of *entering* data, this may be all the info you'll need. Put down this book and get busy. If, on the other hand, you want to create a database of your own, or if you're supposed to modify an existing database, you may want to learn step 3.

Step 3: Designing a layout

When you first create a new FileMaker file and define some fields, the program creates a simple default arrangement of the blanks so that you can type in some data. The default arrangement looks like this:

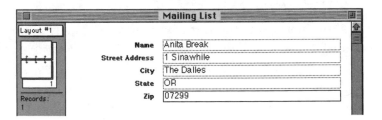

But suppose you want those same fields arranged in a more mailing-labelish layout, like this:

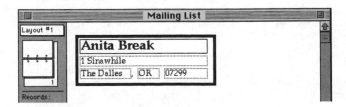

To accomplish this, you must enter the Layout Zone. Choose Layout from the Mode menu. You enter a view that looks a lot like MacDraw (or any other drawing program). And, in fact, all the tools (line, rectangle, blah, blah, blah) work exactly as they do in a drawing program (see "Drawing programs" at the beginning of this chapter).

So click the Arrow Tool. Drag the fields around (make sure you can tell the difference between a field and its label, which you may or may not want to appear on the screen). Or click a field and then change its type style from the Format menu.

Since you can have as many different arrangements of your information as you want, use this pop-up menu to select the Layout you want to edit.

These are field labels. They don't have to appear in a layout if you don't want them to.

These boxes represent the fields themselves. To resize one, click and then drag a corner handle. To move a field, drag it by its center.

If you want to see more than one record at a time (when you're in data entry mode), drag the little Body tag upward until it's just below your fields, choose Browse from the Mode menu, and then choose View as List from the Select menu.

Remember, too, that you can *delete* a field from a particular layout. For example, if you're creating "Hello! My name is" stickers, you certainly don't need each person's phone number to appear on his or her badge (unless it's *that* kind of party). So you can delete the phone number field from the layout; you do *not* lose any data you've typed in. The phone number field still *exists* — just not in this layout. Using the New Layout command in the Edit (or Mode) menu, you can create another layout . . . and another . . . and so on, until you've had your fill of data rearrangement.

When you're finished designing layouts, return to data entry mode by choosing Browse from the Select (or Mode) menu.

Finding

Once you've got some data typed in, you can manipulate it in all kinds of fun and exciting ways. Choose Find from the Mode menu to get what appears to be a blank layout. Type what you're looking for into the appropriate blanks. For example, if you're trying to find everybody who lives in Zip code 90210, you'd fill out the Find dialog box this way:

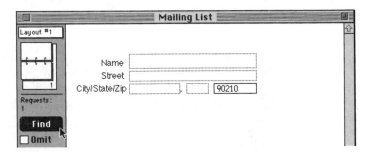

Then click the Find button. After about one second, you'll be returned to Browse (data entry) view, where you'll see the results of your search. This is important — FileMaker is *hiding* the records that *didn't* match your search requirements. You haven't lost them; they're just out of sight until you choose Find All from the Select menu. You can prove this to yourself by consulting the little book at the left side of the screen. It will say "Records: 194, Found: 22." That means FileMaker still knows there are 194 addresses in your mailing list, but only 22 have Zip code 90210 (and they're all attractive teenage models on a major TV show).

Sorting

To sort your records, choose Sort from the Mode menu. FileMaker needs to know how you want to sort your records: by first name, Zip code, nose length, or what? On the left side, you see a list of all the fields in your database; just double-click the one you want to sort by. If you want to sort by last name and then sort by first name *within* each common last name, double-click First Name. Finally, click Sort.

(Sorting is the one major drag with FileMaker, by the way. As you're about to discover, FileMaker doesn't *keep* your stuff in the sorted order! Every time you add a record or search for something, all your records jump back into the order in which you first entered them! You have to use the Sort command over again every time you want things sorted again.)

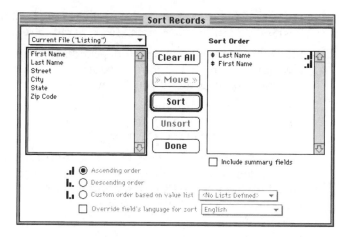

Other steps

FileMaker can do a million other cool things. For example, it can look up a piece of info (like a phone number) from *another* FileMaker file and copy it into the appropriate place in *this* file. In fact, today's FileMaker is, as they say, *relational.* Instead of just looking up a piece of information from another file, you can actually put particular fields in more than one FileMaker file — change somebody's phone number on his order blank, and your mailing-list file is automatically updated. Really neat; really complicated.

FileMaker also has a powerful Scripts command, which performs a series of steps automatically. In other words, you can make the program find all names added since last week, sort them by last name, switch to the Mailing Label layout, and print them — all with a single command from the Scripts menu. These rarefied pleasures are not, however, for the unenlightened. Grab whichever is closest — the manual or your resident computer guru person.

Top Ten Programs Not in the Top Ten

For your shopping pleasure and entertainment: a double handful of neat programs that are often discussed at techno-savvy cocktail parties. ("Hi there, baby. Want to come up and see my FreeHand printouts?")

Plug alert: If these additional programs interest you, then so might *MORE Macs For Dummies;* its "Faking Your Way Through Eight More Programs" covers many of them.

1. **FreeHand** or **Illustrator.** Primo, powerful, professional, pricey PostScript graphics programs. Be prepared to read the manual.

2. **Photoshop.** ClarisWorks's painting window on steroids. A stunning, pro-level photo painting program, capable of fantastic transparency effects or undetectably painting your in-laws right out of the family portrait.

3. **Eudora Planner.** An address-book/calendar program. Stores your names, addresses, e-mail addresses, appointments, and even dials the phone for you. Similarly: Chronos Consultant.

4. **Microsoft PowerPoint.** It's called *presentation software.* Lets you quickly and easily assemble slide shows — graphs, bullet charts, colorful diagrams — with a choice of many rich, unified color schemes. Print the slides onto slides or transparencies, or use the Mac itself to give a slide show.

5. **PageMaker** or **QuarkXPress.** These are what's known as *page-layout* programs — something like a cross between a word processor and a graphics program. They're designed to let you design flyers, newsletters, magazines, and so on, complete with photos, boxed mini-articles, headlines, and so on.

6. **Kid Pix.** Mind-blowing, colorful, audio-equipped version of a painting program. Designed for kids but equally addictive for adults. The drippy paintbrush runs, the eraser makes scritch-scratch sounds, and when you want to start over, the Dynamite Tool blows up your artwork.

7. **Myst** and its sequel, **Riven.** Reason enough to justify the invention of the CD-ROM player (which you need for these CDs). Spectacular visual treats, and darned addictive wordless mysteries.

8. **Claris Emailer.** If you use America Online or the Internet primarily for e-mail, this program is a godsend. In the middle of the night (or in the middle of whatever part of the day you specify), it quietly dials up your account, fetches all the waiting messages, and hangs up, offering you a neat list of all the messages. You can answer them at your leisure, without being online; at its *next* dialing time, it'll send your replies, and the cycle begins again. Makes organizing and filing your e-mail a million times easier, and can even act as an e-mail answering machine while you're away. (Eudora and Outlook Express are similar, but can't get your mail from America Online — only from the Internet itself.)

9. **InfoGenie.** A sizzlingly fast Rolodex program. Can pull up one person's card out of 2,000 in less than half a second. Can even dial the phone if you have a modem. Easier to use than a hairbrush.

10. **Premiere.** For high-horsepower Macs. This is the program for making your own digital QuickTime movies right on the screen. And what's QuickTime? Like the man said: digital movies right on the screen. See Chapter 20.

Chapter 7

A Whole Big Chapter on AppleWorks (ClarisWorks)

- -

In This Chapter

▶ Tooling around in the world's most multitalented software

▶ Nonchalantly combining text, graphics, and database information

▶ Going beyond the call of duty: slide shows, press releases, and company

- -

ClarisWorks — recently renamed AppleWorks, but most people know it as ClarisWorks, so in this chapter I'll still call it ClarisWorks, because saying "ClarisWorks/AppleWorks" three times per paragraph would drive you quietly postal — is Swiss Army Knife software. Just look at all you get, even if you don't know what they are yet: a word processor, a database, and a spreadsheet. Now how much would you pay? But wait: You also get a graphics program that can even serve as a basic page-layout system. And if you order now, you even get a little telecommunications program — absolutely free!

All of these modules are neatly bundled into a single integrated program. You can write a letter and put a graphic in it, or design a flyer that has a little spreadsheet in it, and so on. This chapter will be worth reading even if you don't own this particular software, because ClarisWorks works exactly like most other Mac programs.

Launching ClarisWorks

Double-click the ClarisWorks icon.

After the Claris logo disappears, you're asked to decide what you want to accomplish. Because you'll face this decision every time you use this program, a rundown may be in order here. (In this chapter, you'll see pictures of AppleWorks/ClarisWorks 5.0, but every version looks pretty much the same.)

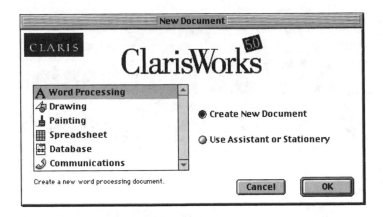

Word Processing: You know what a word processing document is: something you type. A memo, a novel, a ransom note.

Drawing: This is a *drawing program* (see "Drawing programs" in the previous chapter). In this kind of document, you toy around with lines, shapes, and colors to produce such important visuals as logos, maps, and Hangman diagrams.

Painting: This is a painting window (see "Painting programs" in the previous chapter). *Painting* is another way of making graphics. But unlike the Drawing mode, where you can only create distinct circles, lines, and squares, the Painting tools let you create shading, freeform spatters, and much more textured artwork.

Spreadsheet: A computerized ledger sheet, almost exactly like Excel (also in the previous chapter). Crunches numbers: calculates your car's mileage per gallon, your bank account, how much of the phone bill your teenage daughter owes, that kind of thing.

Database: An electronic index-card file, very much like FileMaker (see the previous chapter). You type in your lists — household expenditures; record collections; subscriber list to *Regis & Kathie Lee!* magazine — and the program sorts them, prints them, finds certain pieces of info instantly, and so on.

Communications: You need this kind of program if you want to use your modem for dialing up local "electronic bulletin boards" (a rapidly fading memory, thanks to the much zestier Internet) and hacking your grades on the school's computer. (You *don't* use this program to dial up America Online or the Internet. See Chapter 11.)

To make ClarisWorks strut its stuff, I'll show you how to create a thank-you letter. But not just any thank-you letter — this is going to be the world's most beautiful and personalized *form letter*. You're going to merge a list of addresses into a piece of mail, creating what appear to be individually composed letters; thus, the technoid term for what you're about to do is *mail merge*.

Yeah, yeah, I hear ya: Form letters aren't exactly what you bought a computer to do. Follow along anyway. This exercise will take you through most of ClarisWorks, and you'll brush up against some features that *will* be useful to you.

Your first database

Suppose you just got married. You were showered with lovely gifts. And now it's your task to write a charming thank-you note to each of your gift givers. You'll begin by typing a list of the gift givers. The ideal software for organizing this kind of information is a *database*.

Therefore, double-click the word Database, shown on the facing page.

Don't be alarmed. The screen that now appears may look complicated, but it's actually not so bad — it simply wants to know what *blanks* you'll be wanting to fill in for each person in your list (name, address, gift type, and so on).

```
┌──────────────────────────────────────────────────────────┐
│                    Define Database Fields                 │
├──────────────────────────────────────────────────────────┤
│  Field Name:                    Field Type:               │
│  ┌────────────────────────────────────────────────────┐  │
│  │                                                  ▲ │  │
│  │                                                    │  │
│  │                                                    │  │
│  │                                                    │  │
│  │                                                  ▼ │  │
│  └────────────────────────────────────────────────────┘  │
│                                                            │
│  Field Name:  │First Name      │   Field Type: │Text ▼│   │
│  ┌──────────┐   ┌──────────┐   ┌──────────┐  ┌──────────┐ │
│  │  Create  │   │  Modify  │   │  Delete  │  │ Options…│ │
│  └──────────┘   └──────────┘   └──────────┘  └──────────┘ │
│  ┌─┐  Type a field name and click Create, or select a field, make changes, and  ┌──────────┐ │
│  │?│  then click Modify.                                      │   Done   │ │
│  └─┘                                                     └──────────┘ │
└──────────────────────────────────────────────────────────┘
```

You're about to type names for these blanks (which the program calls *fields*). As always, if you make a typo, just press the Delete key to backspace over it. Here we go:

1. **Type *First Name*. Press the Return key.**

   Pressing Return is the same as clicking the Create button.

2. **Type *Last Name*. Press Return.**

3. **Type *Address*. Press Return.**

   See how you're building a list?

4. **Type *Gift*. Press Return.**

5. **Type *Adjective*. Press Return.**

   In this blank, you'll eventually type a word that describes the glorious present this person gave you.

6. **Finally, type *Part of House*. (You'll see why in a moment). Press Return.**

   Your masterpiece should look something like this:

   Define Database Fields

Field Name:	Field Type:
First Name	Text
Last Name	Text
Address	Text
Gift	Text
Adjective	Text
Part of House	Text

   Field Name: **Part of House**   Field Type: **Text ▼**

   [Create]   [Modify]   [Delete]   [Options...]

   [?] Select a field and click Options to change attributes, or change the name or field type and then click Modify.   [Done]

   ---

7. **Click the Done button in the lower-right corner.**

   The dialog box goes away.

When you see what you've created, things should make a little bit more sense. You've just created the blanks (oh, all right, *fields*) to be filled in for each person in your list.

First Name	
Last Name	
Address	
Gift	
Adjective	
Part of House	

Data entry time

This is important: To fill in the fields of a database (like this one), just type normally. To advance from one field to the next — from "First Name" to "Last Name," for example — *press the Tab key.* Do not press the Return key, as every instinct in your body will be screaming to do. You'll discover why in a moment. (You can also move to a new field by clicking in it, but the Tab key is quicker.)

So here goes:

1. **Make sure you can see a dotted-line rectangle for each field, like the ones in the preceding figure. If not, press the Tab key.**

   The little blinking cursor should be in the "First Name" blank. (If it's not, click there.)

2. **Type *Josephine*. Press the Tab key to jump to the "Last Name" field.**

First Name	Josephine
Last Name	
Address	
Gift	

3. **Type *Flombébé*. (See "Accent heaven" on the next page to see how you make those cool little accents.) Again, press Tab.**

   Now you're in the Address blank.

4. **Type *200 West 15th Street*. Ready to find out what the Return key does?**

   Go ahead: Now press Return. Note that you don't advance to the next blank; instead, the program thoughtfully makes this box bigger, so there's room for another line of address.

First Name	Josephine
Last Name	Flombébé
Address	200 West 15th Street
Gift	New York, NY 10010
Adjective	
Part of	

If you ever hit Return by *mistake,* intending to jump to the next blank (but just making this blank bigger), press the Delete key.

Accent heaven

Ah, mais oui, mon ami. C'est vrai, c'est la vie, c'est le résumé.

I know what you're thinking: What a smooth, sophisticated guy to be able to speak French like that! Thank you.

But you're also thinking: How did he get those cool accent marks? Very easily — and you, having been smart enough to choose a Mac over all its inferior competitors, can do it, too.

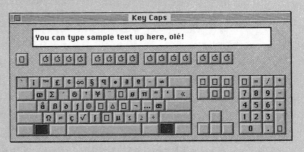

The Mac has a ton of these special characters. Look at your keyboard — I bet you don't see © or ™, or •, or ¢, or any other useful symbols Mac people use all the time. That's because they're hidden. The secret that unlocks them is ... the Option key.

It works like the Shift key: While pressing Option, you type a key. Here are some popular ones:

To get this ...	Press Option and type this ...
©	g
™	2
ç	c
¢	4
i	1
£	3
•	8
®	r
†	t

Anyway, the Mac has dozens of these things. What's nice to know is that you have a complete built-in cheat sheet that shows their locations on the keyboard. It's the Key Caps desk accessory, which is in your menu.

Open it up and take a look. Now try pressing the Option key.

So that's where all those little critters live!

Anyway, there's one more wrinkle to all this. A few symbols, called *diacritical marks* (that's not a computer term, it's a proofreading one, I think) can be placed over any letter. They include the markings over this ü, this é, this è, and so förth. Since the Mac doesn't know ahead of time which vowel you're going to type, creating these marks is a two-step process:

1. While pressing Option, type the key as shown here:

To get this ...	Press Option and type this ...
é	e
ü	u
è	`
ñ	n
î	i

When you do this, nothing will happen. In other words, no marking appears on the screen — until you do step 2.

2. Type the letter you want to appear under the diacritical marking.

Only now does the entire thing — letter and marking — appear on the screen. So if you think about it, typing the six-letter word résumé requires eight keystrokes. *C'est formidable, ça!*

5. **Go ahead and type *New York, NY 10010*. Then press Tab.**

   And don't worry that the second line of the address immediately gets hidden. The information you typed is still there.

6. **Type *acrylic sofa cover* (and press Tab); *practical* (and press Tab); *living room* (and stop).**

You've just filled in the information for your first gift sender. So that this won't take all day, let's pretend that it was what they call an *intimate* wedding, and you only received gifts from three people.

But let's see, we need a new set of fields, don't we? Come to think of it, wouldn't life be sweeter if there were a computer *term* for "set of fields"? By gumbo, there is! A set of fields is called a *record*.

I wouldn't bother with that term if it didn't crop up in the next instructions.

1. **From the Edit menu, choose New Record.**

   A new record ("set of fields") appears, and you're ready to type the second person's information.

2. **Type anything you want, or copy the example below, but remember to press Tab at the end of each piece of information.**

   (Oh, and if you want a second line for the address, press Return. Make up a town and state; you're a creative soul.)

First Name	Ginnie
Last Name	May
Address	42 Pocono La.
Gift	air conditioner w/ remote
Adjective	high-tech
Part of	bedroom

3. **Once again, choose New Record from the Edit menu. Type a third set of information, perhaps along these lines:**

First Name	Suzie
Last Name	Khiou
Address	1 Doormouse Ave.
Gift	Harley
Adjective	expensive
Part of	garage

Fabulous! You're really cooking now.

4. **As a final wise step, choose Save from the File menu. Type** *Gift List* **as the name of your database.**

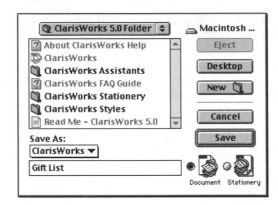

5. **Click Save to preserve your database on the hard disk.**

You've just created your first database. Having gone through the tedium of typing in each little scrap of information the way the Mac wants it, you can now perform some stunts with it that'd make your grandparents' jaws drop. You can ask the Mac to show you only the names of your friends whose last names begin with Z. Or only those who live in Texas. Or only those whose gifts you've categorized as *fabulous*.

For instructions on finding, showing these lists, and sorting your database, read the section on FileMaker in Chapter 6.

Forming the form letter

Next, you're going to write the thank-you note. At each place where you want to use somebody's name (or other gift-related information), you'll ask ClarisWorks to slap in the appropriate info.

1. **Choose New from the File menu.**

Once again, you're asked to choose the kind of document you want.

2. **Double-click Word Processing.**

Now you get a sparkling new sheet of electronic typing paper.

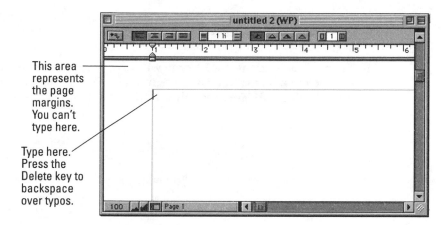

This area represents the page margins. You can't type here.

Type here. Press the Delete key to backspace over typos.

If you'd rather think of the margins as a metaphysical concept (instead of staring at a big fat empty strip all the way around your page), you can hide it easily enough. Choose Document from the Format menu. A dialog box appears; click the Show Margins checkbox to deselect it. And then click OK. Now your whole screen is filled with typeable area.

Now then — on with the form letter. You'll start the letter with the address, of course. Yet the address will be different on each letter! This is where mail-merging is handy.

3. From the File menu, choose Mail Merge.

When the little window appears, you'll see your database name, "Gift List," prominently displayed.

4. Double-click Gift List to tell ClarisWorks that it's the database you want to work with.

Now a strange-looking window appears:

In the scrolling list you see the *field names* from your database. Here's how it works.

5. Point to First Name and double-click.

See what happened? The program popped a placeholder for the First Name right into your letter. When you print, instead of *<<First Name>>*, it will say *Josephine*.

6. **Type a space. In the Mail Merge window, point to *Last Name* and double-click. Press Return to begin a new line of the address; then point to the Mail Merge window again and double-click *Address*.**

Before you continue typing, you may want to drag the little Mail Merge window off to the right of your screen as best you can. (To move the window, drag its title bar.) You're going to want to see both it and your typing simultaneously.

7. **Press Return a couple of times. Type *Dear*, followed by a space.**

8. **Point to the words *First Name* in the Mail Merge window, as you did a moment ago. Double-click. Type a comma.**

Your letter should look something like this:

«First Name» «Last Name»
«Address»

Dear «First Name»,

9. **This is where it gets good. Press Return a couple of times. Type *I nearly cried when I unwrapped the incredible*, followed by a space.**

10. **Double-click the word *Gift* in the Mail Merge window.**

11. **Continue typing: *you gave me for my wedding. It is far and away the most* (and now double-click Adjective in the Mail Merge window) *gift I will ever receive.***

«First Name» «Last Name»
«Address»

Dear «First Name»,

I nearly cried when I unwrapped the incredible «Gift» you gave me for my wedding. It is far and away the most «Adjective» gift I will ever receive.

Are you getting the hang of this? At each place where you want ClarisWorks to substitute a piece of information from your Gift List database, you insert a little <<placeholder>>.

To see the last field name, Part of House, you may have to use the Mail Merge window's scroll bar. Then finish the letter as follows.

12. Type *It will look sensational in the* (double-click Part of House in the Mail Merge window) *of our new home.*

13. Press the Return key twice and finish up like this: *I had to write this personal note to you and you alone, so you'd know how much I treasure your gift above all the others. Love, Marge.*

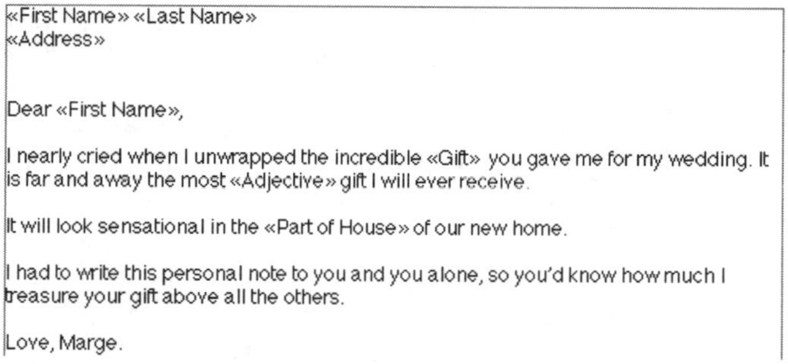

```
«First Name» «Last Name»
«Address»


Dear «First Name»,

I nearly cried when I unwrapped the incredible «Gift» you gave me for my wedding. It
is far and away the most «Adjective» gift I will ever receive.

It will look sensational in the «Part of House» of our new home.

I had to write this personal note to you and you alone, so you'd know how much I
treasure your gift above all the others.

Love, Marge.
```

Miss Manners would go instantly bald in horror if she thought you were about to send out a letter that says *Dear First Name.* But through the miracle of computers, when these letters are printed, it'll be impossible to tell that each one wasn't typed separately.

Save from the File menu. Type *Thank-you letter* and click Save.

The graphics zone: Designing a letterhead

You can read a lot more about graphics programs in the previous chapter. But just to show you how you can tie everything together, let's whip up a quick letterhead in the Graphics module.

Choose New from the File menu. Our friend, the New Document dialog box, appears. This time you should double-click the Drawing button.

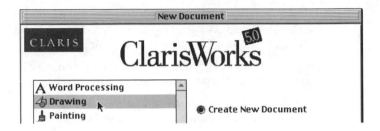

ClarisWorks shows you its drawing window. The grid of dotted lines is there to give things a nice architectural look; it won't appear in the finished printout.

See the tool icons on the left side of your screen? They're pretty much covered in the section on drawing programs in the preceding chapter. Now then:

1. **Click the Text tool — it looks like a letter A — and release the mouse button. Move your cursor onto the drawing area and drag across the screen, as shown here:**

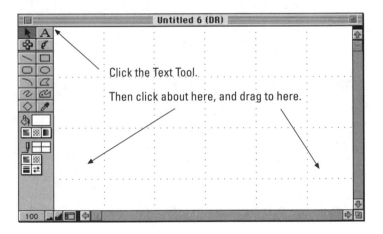

2. **Use the Font menu; choose Times. Use the Size menu; choose 24 Point.**

3. **Type three spaces and then a long dash. (To make a long dash, hold down the Shift and Option keys, and type a hyphen.) Type** *A Very Personal Note.* **Type another long dash and then three more spaces.**

—A Very Personal Note—

4. **Press the Enter key so that handles appear around your text. Using the Alignment submenu of the Format menu, choose Center.**

Finally, you'll add that elegant white-lettering-against-black look that shows up on so many corporate annual reports. At the left side of your screen, there's a set of odd-looking icons. Find the one immediately below the tiny pouring paint can icon, as shown by the arrow in this illustration (left):

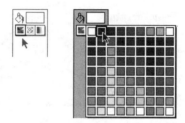

This icon is actually a pop-out palette.

5. **Click the paint-can icon, but keep the mouse button pressed so that the palette appears (previous figure, right). Drag carefully to the right until the pointer is on the solid black square, as shown. Release the mouse.**

You've just used the Fill palette to color in the entire text block with black. Which is just great, except that now the text is a solid black rectangle! To fix the problem, you need to make the text *white*.

6. **From the Text Color submenu of the Format menu, choose White. Ta-da!**

—A Very Personal Note—

You used a ClarisWorks Graphics window to make manipulating your text easier. Of course, while you're in the graphics mode, you could actually do some graphics . . . you could use any of the other drawing tools to dress up your logo. You could draw a box around this letterhead. You could rotate the whole thing 90 degrees. You could make all kinds of insane diagonal stripes across it. You could choose, from the File menu, Library — and select any of the "libraries" full of ready-to-use graphics (flags, stars, flowers, and so on), worthy of dragging into your drawing as an aid to the artistically challenged.

Keep those creative possibilities in mind when it comes time to design your real letterhead.

For control freaks only: The View buttons

Before you leave the drawing window, cast your eyes upon the lower-left corner of the screen. There you'll find this odd-looking array of controls:

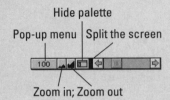

Hide palette

Pop-up menu | Split the screen

Zoom in; Zoom out

As you can tell, AppleWorks/ClarisWorks makes blowing up your work extremely easy. (Obviously, I mean *magnifying* it; *destroying* it is up to you.) A quick click on either of those little mountain buttons makes the artwork smaller or larger. Or jump directly to a more convenient degree of magnification by using the percentage pop-up menu (where it says 100 in the figure to the left). You're not changing the actual printed size — only how it's displayed on the screen.

The return of Copy and Paste

All that remains is for you to slap this letterhead into your mail-merge letter.

1. **Using the Arrow tool, click your letterhead. From the Edit menu, choose Copy.**

2. **Now you have to return to your word processing document. Here's a quick way to pull it to the front: From the Window menu, choose Thank-You Letter (WP).**

   (WP stands for Word Processing document, DB stands for Database, DR stands for Drawing, and PT stands for Painting.)

   Your letter springs to the fore.

3. **From the Format menu, choose Insert Header.**

   (A *header* is an area at the top of every page, above whatever text you've typed. In this case, it looks like an empty text area.)

4. **From the Edit menu, choose Paste.**

   Et voilà . . . your graphic pops neatly into the header.

You've actually done it: combined a database, a word processor, and a drawing program in a single project! For a real kick, click the Print Merge button. It's on the little floating mail merge window-ette that should still be on the screen. Watch how the program automatically replaces actual names for the <<placeholders>> on the screen.

Other Cool Stuff ClarisWorks Does

The little form-letter thank-you note example was only one example of ClarisWorks's power. It left plenty of features unexplored, however.

A little paint

If you've been following along, you haven't yet tried the Painting window. By this time, I trust you know how to get there: Choose New from the File menu and then double-click the Painting button.

Suddenly, you're in a pixel-blitzing wonderland, where you can create all kinds of "painted" artwork. As you discovered when reading Chapter 6, this kind of artwork has pros and cons. The pro is that you can change the color of *every single dot* on the screen (instead of just drawing circles, lines, and rectangles, which is all you can do in the Drawing window). The con is that you can't move or resize something in a painting after you've laid down the "paint" (which you *can* do in the Drawing window).

A little slide show

One of the strangest and most delicious things people do with a Macintosh is make slide shows. These can be self-running (a new "slide" every four seconds, say). They can be controlled by you (a new slide every time you click the mouse button). Most of all, they can be really impressive-looking to your friends.

You're in for another *Macs For Dummies* Bargain-Hunter's Paradise, by the way. Plenty of businesspeople spring $300 to buy a program that does nothing but slide shows. (They have a $300 word for it, too: "presentation software.") You, of course, get one in ClarisWorks at no extra charge.

If you have ClarisWorks 4 or later, making a slide show is particularly easy, because you can use the idiot-proof Assistant feature. Choose New from the File menu; select "Use Assistant or Stationery"; double-click the Assistant called Presentation. Now ClarisWorks asks you a series of questions, such as what kind of message you want to present, what style of slide background you want, and so on.

When you're finished answering, you've got a terrific-looking slide show on the screen. Use the scroll bars to move among the slides, changing the (forgive the term) dummy text on each slide to say what you want it to say.

Other Assistants

While we're on the topic of Assistants, remember that ClarisWorks beats the pants off most other programs when it comes to creating certificates, press releases, address books, to-do lists, and so on. The key, after choosing New from the File menu, is to select the "Use Assistant or Stationery" checkbox, as shown here:

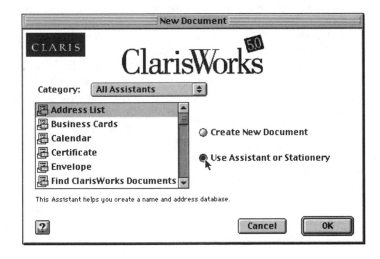

Experiment with the pop-up menu at the top of this screen; some of the most useful ready-made documents (which they call *stationery*) are hiding in here.

Chapter 8

System Folder: Trash Barge of the Macintosh

- -

In This Chapter

▶ What the System Folder is for

▶ Just enough verbiage on System 7.5, Mac OS 8, Mac OS 8.5, and so on

▶ What junk you can throw out of your System Folder

- -

*T*here it sits. Only one folder on your hard drive looks like it — or acts like it. It's the System Folder, which holds software that the Mac needs for itself. Every Mac has a System Folder. (Correction: Every *functioning* Mac has one.) Yours probably looks like any other folder, except that it's called System Folder and its icon has a tiny, special logo in the middle:

In System 7 through
System 7.6:

System Folder

In Mac OS 8 and later:

System Folder

Someday you, like millions of Mac users before you, will attempt to open the System Folder. You'll discover that it's absolutely *crawling* with files, overrun with zillions of little icons you've never seen before, teeming like so many roaches under the floorboards.

You're perfectly entitled to exclaim, "Jeez, what *is* all this stuff?!" And, before having read Chapter 1¹/₂, you might also have exclaimed, like many Mac beginners before you: "For the love o' Mike, all those files are gonna *use up all my memory!*"

Naturally, you now realize the foolishness of this comment. Data resting comfortably on your hard drive doesn't use up *any* memory. It *does,* however, take up *disk space.* Furthermore, each item in your Control Panels and Extensions folders makes your Mac take longer to start up in the morning — and increases the likelihood of system crashes. As you can read in Part IV, a Mac with few extensions is a healthy, happy, crash-free Mac.

For these reasons, I'm going to show you exactly how much of the System Folder clutter you can safely throw away. A huge percentage of this clutter is designed for such special purposes as connecting Macs to an office network, opening files from Windows computers, and doing other things *most* Mac fans don't bother with.

You should also know about the System Folder because it's the nerve center of your whole Mac . . . the heart . . . the brain . . . the headquarters. A Mac without a System Folder is like a car without an engine. A house without a roof. *Terminator* without Arnold.

Battle of the Systems

Back in Chapter 1, I hinted that your Mac may be outfitted with a special feature called Mac OS 8 or even Mac OS 8.5. And instead of explaining what that meant, I muttered something along the lines of "Tell you later." Before we get busy with our System Folder trash-fest, we need to get this explanation over with.

You know how General Motors comes out with a new model of each of its cars every year? Apple does the same thing: It keeps making minor changes to its computers, trying to make them better (and provide more incentive to buy them).

In 1991, Apple came out with a version of the System Folder contents called System 7. In '94, we had System 7.5. And then in 1997, Mac OS 8 appeared. In 1998/1999, Apple topped itself by releasing Mac OS 8.5 and then 8.6.

And in 1999, we'll supposedly witness the dawn of an even more major overhaul, called Mac OS X (that's "O. S. ten," not "O. S. Ex") that's so wonderful we'll all fall into an ecstatic trance, sell our homes, and move to California.

Anyway, it's easy to tell which System you have. In Chapter 1, you used the About This Computer command in the menu to find out. But I'm here to offer an insider's tip: Look in the upper-right corner of the screen. Do you see this icon ⁇? If so, you have System 7-point-something. If the upper-right of your screen contains a more mod-looking question mark — like this — then you have the even more trendy System 7.5 or System 7.6. And if you have no question mark menu at *all,* but instead you have a menu called Help, you're using Mac OS 8 or later.

Names and numbers

When people say "System 7" or "Mac OS 8," they're not being terribly specific. Apple keeps making little changes. Each time, they rename the thing by changing the digits after the decimal point. First there was System 7.0. Then they made a few touch-ups and called it System 7.0.1. They then made some more improvements and dubbed the result System 7.1, and so on.

When I was your age, we were taught: one decimal point per number. Anyway, if you ignore the second decimal point, you can pretty much figure out which System version is more recent. For example, 7.01 is a smaller number than 7.1, so it's therefore earlier.

Finally, there's *x*. You'll sometimes hear computer people say that something won't work if you have Mac OS 8.*x*. That's shorthand. It means "Mac OS 8, Mac OS 8.1, Mac OS 8.5, or Mac OS 8-point-anything." As opposed, naturally, to System 6.*x* or 7.*x*.

Anyway, for your purposes, here's the scheme behind the numbering. When only the *second* decimal-point number changes, such a tiny number tweak generally signifies that the new version offers no *new* features. Instead, it's probably only a cleaned-up (less bug-ridden) version, or else it's just been updated to be a little faster. Almost always, you should get this kind of update (it's usually free, if you have a modem, from America Online or the Internet at *www.apple.com*) and install it right away.

Then there are the meatier upgrades, where the number next to the first decimal point changes (from 7.6 to 8.0, for example, or from Mac OS 8 to 8.5). This kind of overhaul introduces more wrinkles into your life than the Double-Decimal Update — but probably a lot of neat new features, too.

This kind of upgrade affects your life more dramatically for another reason, too: You have to *pay* for these babies.

I bring all this up because in the following trash-fest of your System Folder, I'll be listing the components of *all* System versions, 7.5 and later. You won't have *everything* named in this chapter — and now you know why.

System-Folder Trash-O-Rama

Who else would be utterly mad enough to say the following in public? *Half the stuff in your System Folder is worthless.* It's designed for power-users, or people in big corporate networks, or superweenie jet-propulsion scientists and their Mensa-qualifying 8-year-old offspring. Meanwhile, these files are taking up room on your hard drive.

Do it right now: Double-click your System Folder to open it. (Your System Folder is in your main hard-drive window.) Now click the zoom box, the tiny square in the top-right corner of the System Folder window (the *inner* top-right corner, if you have Mac OS 8-point-something), so you can see as much of the System Folder contents as possible. As a matter of fact, move your mouse up to the View menu and choose "by Name" or "as List." That should put everything into a neat list.

Just *look* at all that junk! *You* sure as heck didn't put it there — what's it *doing* there?

Here's a wonderful, worth-the-price-of-the-book-right-there list of everything in your typical System Folder, item by item. I'll tell you which of these things you can safely trash.

Don't have a cow about throwing things away, either. This is not like cleaning your attic, where if you toss that box of your drawings from elementary school, you've wounded your inner child forever. No, *this* stuff you can always get back again if you need it. It's all on the system-software CD-ROM that came with your Mac.

As a bonus, as you go along, I'll try to point out some handy little treasures you didn't know you had. (Jeez, this is getting to be more like an attic-cleaning with every passing moment.)

The Apple Menu Items folder

Let's start with the stuff in the Apple Menu Items folder, which is, alphabetically speaking, the first thing in your System Folder. You'll recall that anything in this folder also appears in the menu at the left side of your screen.

This is really a two-for-one discussion: Most of the Apple menu items are also desk accessories like the ones you worked with in Chapter 3. So now you'll get to find out what exactly those things in your menu are . . . acquire a deep and abiding appreciation of their importance and value . . . and *then* throw them away.

AppleCD Audio Player — It has Play, Stop, and Rewind controls for playing regular *music* compact discs on your CD-ROM drive.

Apple System Profiler — A neat little program that gives all kinds of mind-numbing technical details about your Mac. *You'll* probably never use it. But someday, when you're calling Apple in a desperate froth about some problem you're having, they may well ask you to consult the System Profiler to answer a couple of questions.

Apple Video Player — Certain Mac models have VCR-style jacks on the back panel. They let you plug in your camcorder, turning your home movies into digital movies on the Mac (see Chapter 20). If your Mac is one of the lucky models thus blessed, Apple Video Player is the program you use to record, and play back, your movies. Otherwise, toss this.

Automated Tasks — Automated Tasks isn't a program at all. It's merely an alias, dropped by Apple into your menu for convenience. It lists several handy *AppleScripts* — mini-programs, each of which performs one simple timesaving step when opened. For example, **Add Alias to Apple Menu** puts an alias of a selected icon into your menu. Most of the others, such as Share a Folder and Start File Sharing, have to do with networking.

Calculator and **Note Pad** — You already know about these desk accessories (see Chapter 3). Leave them for now.

Chooser — You *definitely* need this, as you can find out in Chapter 5.

Connect To... — In Mac OS 8 and 8.1, this tiny program-ette brings up a simple dialog box into which you can type an Internet or Web address. When you click Connect, your Mac dials and connects to that address, launching your e-mail program or Web browser. (See Chapter 11 for more on Internet connections. This little program is for people who have direct Internet accounts, not America Online.)

Enter an Internet address (URL) to connect to:

    http://www.aardvarklovers.com

[Cancel] [Connect]

Control Panels — This folder is simply a shortcut (an *alias*) to opening your real Control Panels folder. More on control panels later in this chapter.

Desktop Printers — If you own only one printer, throw this away. (See the sidebar "A shortcut for multiple-printer owners" in Chapter 5.)

Favorites — This command gives you quick access to files or folders you use a lot. See "Special folders in Mac OS 8.5 and later," later in this chapter.

Find or **Find File** — A turbocharged file-finding feature. Worth its weight in the precious metal of your choice. Just type in what you're looking for, and the Mac finds it . . . *fast*. (See the end of Chapter 4 for a complete demonstration.)

Guard this desk accessory with your life; even when you grow up to be a great big computer guru, you will *still* forget where you stored a file now and then. (The Find command in the File menu, by the way, brings up the exact same feature.)

Graphing Calculator — Puts fancy moving 3-D graphs on your screen, so you can show your friends how high-tech and brilliant you've become. And if you're into math, it's actually pretty darned good at graphing little equations like $y = x - 1$.

Internet Access — This set of handy Net-related commands includes:

✔ **Browse the Internet** — This command launches your Web browser program, such as Netscape Navigator or Internet Explorer. And it opens to your preferred home page. (You use the Internet control panel to choose both which browser you prefer and which home page you like, as described later in this chapter.)

✔ **Connect To** — See "Connect To," earlier in this list.

✔ **Disconnect** — Hangs up your modem's phone line after you've been using the Internet (see Chapter 11).

✔ **Internet Setup Assistant** — Walk through this series of screens while your Internet access company's tech-help agent is on the phone with you, and you'll save yourself a lot of grief in establishing an Internet account for the first time. (See Chapter 11 for details.)

✔ **Mail** — This command launches your e-mail program. (Applies to people with direct Internet accounts, not America Online.)

Jigsaw Puzzle — Highly silly desk accessory whose Novelty-Wear-Off Quotient is about five minutes. Upon reaching the sixth minute, trash it.

Key Caps — Another desk accessory. It helps you find out which combinations of keys you're supposed to press when you want to type wacky symbols like ¢ or ¥ or © (see details in Chapter 7).

Network Browser — For people in an office with multiple Macs networked together. If that means you, use this program as a map of the whole network. If that doesn't mean you, throw this thing out. (See *MORE Macs For Dummies* for details on networking.)

Recent Documents, Recent anything — A very handy shortcut! These submenus list the last few documents, applications (programs), and *servers* (other Macs in your office) you've had open, so that you can get to them again conveniently. (If you're not on a network, you can do without Recent Servers. Open your Apple Menu Items control panel and put a zero where it says Servers; the Servers item will disappear from your menu.)

Remote Access Status — This handy Mac OS 8.5 mini-program offers Connect and Disconnect buttons to help you get on and off the Internet (assuming you've signed up for a direct Internet account, as described in Chapter 11). And while you're connected, this window shows how long you've been tying up the phone.

Scrapbook — This desk accessory is worth keeping. Using Copy and Paste, you can put pictures, sounds, movie clips, or blocks of text into it for later use. For example, after you spend three weekends designing an absolutely gorgeous logo for yourself, paste it into the Scrapbook. Thereafter, whenever you need that logo again, open the Scrapbook and copy it, so that it'll be ready to paste into your memo or package design.

SimpleSound — A mini-program that lets you record sounds (if your Mac has a mike). See Chapter 9 for details.

Stickies — How did we *live* before Stickies? Sheer, purest genius. Stickies are electronic Post-It notes. That's all. Just choose New Note from the File menu, jot down what you want, and maybe pick a new pastel hue from the Color menu.

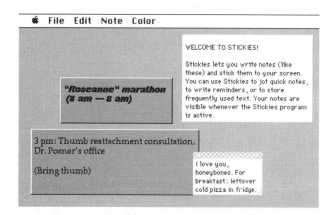

When you try to close Stickies (by choosing Quit from the File menu), you'll be asked nicely if you want the Stickies to reappear each time you turn on the Mac. Say yes, and you'll never forget another dog-grooming appointment.

• **Shut Down** — This command (in System 7.5 through 7.6) is the same as the usual Shut Down command. Why a duplicate here in the menu? So that you can get to it without having to quit whatever program you're using at the time. Saves a step when dinner's ready.

The Contextual Menu Items folder

You can read about the fascinating *contextual pop-up menu* feature (of Mac OS 8 and later) in Chapter 9. For now, know ye that this feature provides shortcut menus when you click things (like icons and windows) while pressing the Control key.

It's technically possible to *add more* commands to these Control-key pop-up menus, and many Web-surfing power-users do. If you become one of that special breed, this folder is where you put the additional commands (in the form of special icons).

The Control Strip Modules folder

You can read about the Control Strip in "The Control Panels folder" section to follow. There, you'll learn that the Control Strip is an ever-present floating strip of tiles that offer quick access to Mac settings (such as the speaker volume). This folder is where those tiles are stored.

The Control Panels folder

Control Panels is another folder inside your System Folder. As you can read in Chapter 3, a control panel is a tiny miniprogram that changes some aspect of the Mac's behavior.

Appearance (in Mac OS 8 and 8.1) — Offers two satisfying tweaks for the interior designer in you. The Color option lets you change the highlight colors for subtle aspects of your Mac's screen display (scroll bars, "now copying" progress graphs, highlighted text, and so on). The Options option gives you a choice of two typefaces to be used in menus, among other things.

Appearance (in Mac OS 8.5) — *This* beefy Appearance control panel is not to be confused with its spindly predecessor from Mac OS 8. With *this* control panel, you can do far more than meekly change the font used in your menu; now you can change the look and feel of your Mac in much more radical ways. For example:

✔ **Appearance** — These options let you choose a highlighting-pen color (for use when you drag your mouse across some text) and an accent color (for scroll bars, progress bars, and other tinted on-screen accessories).

✔ **Fonts** — Click the Fonts tab to view three pop-up menus that let you change the typefaces your Mac uses for menus, labels, and lists.

Note especially the option called "Smooth all fonts on screen." When you turn it on, the edges of your on-screen type gets softer and smoother (or *antialiased,* as the geeks would say). See the Top 10 list at the end of Chapter 5 for an illustration.

✔ **Desktop picture** — By clicking the Desktop "tab," you can choose a photo or pattern with which to plaster the backdrop of your screen. (See "Desktop Pictures" later in this chapter.)

✔ **Sounds** — If you click the Sound tab and choose Platinum from the pop-up menu, you get crisp, cheerful little sound effects as you do anything on your Mac, like using scroll bars, menus, icons, the Trash, windows, disks, or almost anything else that requires mouse manipulation. (Health warning: Don't turn on sounds when using your Mac at the public library, at international chess matches, or during microsurgery on a relative.)

✔ **Scroll bars** — If you've forgotten that *scroll bars* are the strips at the bottom and right edges of windows that you use to move around in a window, review Chapter 1. Anyway, the new, steroid-enhanced Appearance control panel offers a fascinating new option (on the Options tab) called Smart Scrolling. It moves both scroll-bar arrows to one end of the scroll bar, as shown at the end of Chapter 4.

That option also makes the *scroll box* (the square handle you drag) larger or smaller to reflect the amount of the document that's visible in the window. That is, if the scroll bar handle is one-third the height of the scroll bar, you're seeing one-third of the document in your document window.

✔ **Themes** — After you've visited all of the various tabs (Appearance, Desktop, Fonts, Sound, and Options) to get the Mac behaving just the way you like it, you can preserve the particular combination of settings you've just established as a *Theme*.

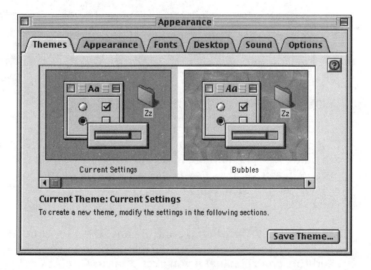

To do so, click the Themes tab, where you'll see a new entry called Current Settings. Click the Save Themes button, give your new "theme" a name, and call it a day. From now on, you can jump to your newly established theme (or any of the predefined ones) by clicking it whenever you feel the need for a change of scene.

Apple Menu Options — This little gizmo provides the submenus in your menu, so that you can (for example) open a specific control panel from the Control Panels command. It also creates, in your menu, folders that track the last bunch of documents and programs you used, which is handy.

AppleTalk — An important item *if* you're on a network. It's part of Open Transport, described later. It lets you specify *how* your Mac is connected to other Macs (or laser printers); with Ethernet cables, LocalTalk wires, using the iMac's infrared transmitter, and so on. (See *MORE Macs For Dummies* if you have the least interest in hooking your Mac up to other Macs.)

At Ease Setup — Remember all that talk of folders, windows, and disks that you slogged through in the beginning chapters of this book? It must've made your head spin at first. Now imagine that you're a 6-year-old, and you'll understand why Apple invented At Ease: a sweet little program that *covers up* all that stuff you've spent so much time and effort learning. (You can buy At Ease; it also came preinstalled with some older Mac models.) In fact, the entire Finder (the desktop) gets hidden when At Ease is running. Instead, you (or your young companion) see this when using the Mac:

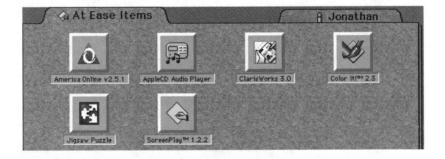

This screen shows all the *programs* you've set up for this individual; click the name "tab" (Jonathan, in this picture) to view all the *documents* that person has created since At Ease was installed. You can open any icon with a *single* mouse click, not a double-click. You hear a cool clicky sound when you click.

Anyway, the At Ease Setup control panel lets you choose which icons you want on your big fat At Ease tablecloth. If you use At Ease, take note: You need this control panel if you ever want to turn At Ease off!

ATM — Adobe Type Manager, which makes typefaces look smoother.

AutoRemounter — Useful only for connecting Macs together — in this case, a PowerBook and a regular Mac. (It automatically reconnects the two whenever you wake a sleeping PowerBook.) If you have neither PowerBook nor network, send it Trashward.

CloseView — Magnifies the screen if you have trouble seeing. The area of enlargement follows your little pointer around, which takes some getting used to. If your eyesight is fine, out it goes.

Color — (pre-Mac OS 8) Lets you choose what shade you want to use when you highlight some text.

ColorSync, ColorSync Profile — Software that tries to make colors consistent among scanners, monitors, and color printers. If you don't print in color and don't have a scanner, out this goes.

Control Strip — All this control panel does is hide or show the *Control Strip*. Trouble is, nobody ever bothers to explain the Control Strip to the average Mac fan — but it's a terrific time-saver that's worth meeting.

The Control Strip starts out as a tiny gray tab hugging the edge of your screen, like this:

Click that little tab (and let go) to make the Control Strip stretch out to its full length, like a python sunning itself on the beach. Here's what some of the typical tiles do (your assortment may be slightly different):

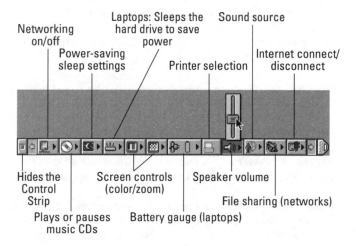

Each tile, as you can see by the Sound Volume example in the picture, is a little pop-up menu; click a tile to view a menu of choices. You can muddle through life without ever using the Control Strip, of course — most of the tiles' functions are duplicated by the various gizmos in your Control Panels folder. But the Control Strip lets you adjust these settings much more conveniently.

But that's not all. I tell ya, this thing's got more secrets than David Copperfield. If you click the little end tab, the Strip collapses so that *only* the tab appears, at the very edge of your screen. Another click expands it again. You can also shrink the Control Strip to any length by tugging — *dragging* — its little end tab.

Furthermore, if you press the Option key, you can drag the entire strip *up or down* the side of your screen, or across to the opposite edge. (You can't drag the Strip to the middle of the screen, however; it must hug the right or left side.) The Option key has another handy effect on the Control Strip: If you drag one of the little tiles while pressing Option, you can slide that tile horizontally to a new position.

If there's a tile you find yourself never using, feel free to get rid of it. *If you have Mac OS 8.5 or later:* While pressing the Option key, drag the tile to the Trash. *If you have something earlier:* Open your hard drive; open your System Folder; open your Control Strip Modules folder. Trash the icon that corresponds to the one you never use.

Date & Time — Lets you set the Mac's clock and date. Also controls whether the time appears at the top of your screen. And if you have Mac OS 8.5 or later — and an Internet account — you can even make your Mac set its *own* clock by dialing into some high-tech atomic clock out in cyberspace somewhere. Now *that's* progress.

Desktop Patterns — (System 7.5 through 7.6) Lets you choose a fancier backdrop pattern for your computer.

Desktop Pictures — (Mac OS 8 and 8.1) Just like Desktop Patterns, but has an added feature: It lets you select a graphics file, a single big picture or photo, to plaster across your desktop (instead of a tiled repeating *little* picture). (See "Looks Are Everything" in Chapter 9 for a dramatic illustration.)

Dial Assist — Lets you create and store complicated dialing instructions for making calls with your modem. Unless you work at a company where somebody has told you otherwise, throw this away.

Easy Access — For people who have difficulty using a mouse or typing with both hands. If you're coordinated and two-handed, throw this thing away.

Editor Setup — The command center for OpenDoc, a wizzy new technology that never caught on. Toss this baby, baby.

Energy Saver — Turns the Mac off (or puts it to "sleep") after you haven't used it for, say, half an hour, to save electricity. Pretty useful, really. On PowerBook models sold in 1998 and later, it also lets you determine how quickly the computer gets sluggish and dim when you're not using it (in an effort to save battery power).

Extensions Manager — Here's how it works. As the Mac is starting up, press and hold your space bar. Eventually, you'll be shown a list of almost *everything* listed in this chapter — all the control panels and extensions. By clicking their names, you can decide which of them you'd like to use during the work session that's about to begin. If you're a pack rat, for example, you could simply turn off the ones you don't need instead of throwing them away. *Great* for troubleshooting (see Chapter 16).

File Exchange — This little Mac OS 8.5-and-later doodad gives your Mac two magical powers. First, you can insert a disk from DOS or Windows computers into your Mac and see its icon appear on the desktop, just like a Mac disk. And not just floppies — Windows-formatted SyQuests, Zip disks, and other removable disks can also appear on your desktop. (Whether your programs can open the files *on* those disks is a topic for this book's sequel — but at least you'll be able to see their icons.)

Second, File Exchange performs the highly technical stunt formerly handled by its predecessor, Mac OS Easy Open (described later in this chapter): When you try to double-click a file of unknown parentage — something sent to you via e-mail, for example — File Exchange shows you a list of programs capable of opening it and asks which one you'd like to use. In other words, File Exchange is occasionally useful.

File Sharing — The central control for *file sharing* (making your Mac's hard-drive contents available to other people on your office's network). If your Mac isn't on an office network, toss this sucker.

File Sharing Monitor — Yet another control panel involved in hooking Macs together into a network. If you have no plans to plug your Mac into somebody else's, throw this away.

File Synchronization — This fascinating doodad is, in effect, a backup program. It's designed to make the contents of one folder on your hard drive up-to-date with another folder (usually on a different disk or Mac).

For example, many people keep all their important work in a Documents folder (see the upcoming sidebar "Secrets of the General Controls"). You could use File Synchronization to back up that Documents folder onto, say, a Zip disk automatically. (See Chapter 18 for more on Zip disks.)

Here's how you set it up: Launch the File Synchronization program. Indicate the two folders you'd like kept up-to-date with each other by simply dragging them one at a time directly onto the pictures of folders in the File Synchronization program's window, like this:

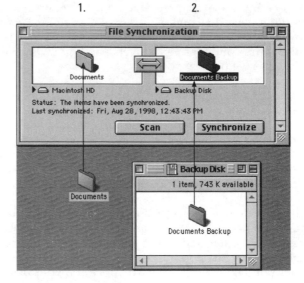

From now on, whenever you open this control panel and click Synchronize, the Mac analyzes each folder and makes them match, copying the most recent files to each, as necessary. (Another neat trick: If you have a PowerBook laptop, you can set up File Synchronization to bring key folders up-to-date with your laptop *before* a trip, and then to bring the main Mac's folders up-to-date *after* the trip.)

I realize that's a lot of ink to describe one little control panel. But the day your hard drive croaks and only your backup Zip disk saves you from aging 10 years on the spot, you'll thank me.

General Controls — A useful control panel. Sets your cursor-blinking speed, whether you want System Folder Protection turned on (it prevents marauding preteens from dragging anything out of your System Folder), and so on. And have you ever noticed how, after a system crash and you turn the Mac on again, a message scolds you for not having shut down the machine correctly (as though it's *your* fault)? Turn off the "Warn me if computer was shut down improperly" checkbox if you'd prefer the Mac not to rub it in your face.

General Controls also offers two *killer* useful features for beginners. Details in the "Secrets of the General Controls" sidebar.

Infrared — The front panel of an iMac, or the back panel of a PowerBook laptop, contains a dark red plastic transmitter. It makes possible a glitzy feature: Aim two such transmitters at each other, and you can send files back and forth over an invisible, through-the-air network. This little control panel lets you choose which of two through-the-air languages will be spoken (the unhelpfully named *IRTalk* and *IrDA*). It also serves as a status panel, letting you know when it perceives any other infrared Macs within shooting distance. (Requires the IrDALib and IrLanScannerPPC files in your Extensions folder, described later in this chapter.) See Chapter 20 for instructions.

Internet — Shortly after you start hooking up to the Internet (see Chapter 11), you'll discover why only 35 percent of Americans are online: There are just too many technical codes to type in when setting up an online account. In *each one* of your Internet programs (your Web browser, your e-mail program, and so on), you have to type your name, address, e-mail address, SMTP codes, social security number, junior-high math teacher's nickname, and so on.

The Internet control panel provides a central place to type in every conceivable shred of Internet-related information — right down to the signature at the bottom of your e-mails — *once*. Thereafter, each of your Internet-related programs can refer to *that* information (instead of making you retype it).

For example, in Netscape Navigator (see Chapter 12), choose Preferences from the Edit menu. Click the Identity icon, and you'll see the "Use Internet Config" checkbox. (The name of that checkbox means "Use the info I typed into the Internet control panel," in case you were wondering.) Netscape Navigator then fills in all the necessary blanks for you, based on your Internet control panel information.

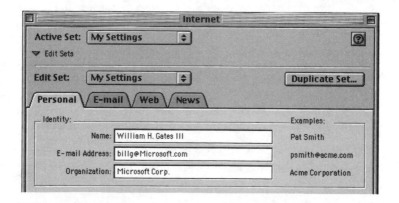

Keyboard — Use this control panel to change how a key behaves when you keep it pressed. Does a held-down key start repeating like thisssssssssss? And how fast?

Many first-time Mac users fare better if they turn the repeating-key feature off. That way, if a book happens to lean on the spacebar while you're on the phone for 20 minutes, you won't hang up to find 536 pages of blank space in the letter you were working on.

Secrets of the General Controls

For many people, the purchase of a Mac is a primal attempt to get their lives, so full of traffic and turbulent relationships and scraps of paper, into some kind of order.

Little do they know what awaits them on the typical Mac: Their important documents get every bit as lost as their paper-based counterparts once did. Even the great Mac gurus of our time have, at one time or another, saved some document created on the Mac — and then found themselves unable to find it again because it got arbitrarily stashed in some hidden folder somewhere.

Enter the Documents folder — one of the features you can turn on in the General Controls panel. See its icon in the picture below? As you work with your Mac and create different documents, the Mac housekeeps for you by storing them *all* in this folder automatically. See page 88 for details on the Documents folder and how to make it appear.

In theory, you'll never lose anything again; everything you do will always be in one place. (That feature makes backing up your work simple, too; you now have only one folder to copy to a different disk.)

The other great feature of General Controls is what I call self-hiding programs. To explain, let me show you what life is like on a regular Mac:

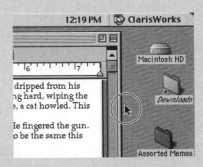

There's actually a significant problem with this setup. A beginner — and we were all beginners once — might, in reaching for the scroll bar, accidentally click outside the word processor window. Immediately, the desktop (Finder) jumps to the front, showing files and folders, and the word processor window gets shoved to the back, apparently vanishing, causing (in the beginner) distress, unhappiness, and occasionally hair loss.

Now then, suppose you open General Controls and turn *off* the "Show Desktop when in background" option. When you open a document *now*, the world of the Finder (icons, windows) *disappears,* as shown below. *Now,* if you click outside the word processor window, absolutely nothing happens. In fact, you *can't* return to the desktop without choosing Finder from the application menu in the upper-right corner of your screen.

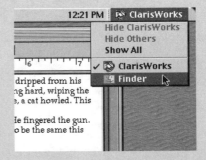

Oh, and on recent Macs, this control panel also lets you change your keyboard's personality, making it type the correct funny symbols corresponding to Swedish, Italian, Dutch, and any of 18 other languages. People who can fluently speak 21 languages find this a handy feature, although they annoy the heck out of the rest of us.

If you couldn't care less about repeating-key rates or ünûsúâl symbøls, throw this one away.

Labels — *Labels* are a way to categorize your files. You just highlight an icon and choose a label, such as "In Progress," from the Label menu. (If you have System 7-point-something, you have a Label menu at the top of the screen. If you have Mac OS 8-point-something, the Label command is hidden in the File menu. Check it out.)

Labels are a wonderful, ingenious, fascinating concept. Almost nobody uses them.

Use this control panel, Labels, to change *what* you want your seven available labels to be. (At this moment, my labels are: In Progress; Late; Very Late; Past Due; Deadline Hell; Hysterical Editors; and Time-Killing Games.)

If you don't use labels, which is probably the case, it's fine to chuck this. (If you have Mac OS 8 or later, you don't even have this control panel. Instead, you have a Preferences command in your Edit menu, which serves the same function.)

Launcher — What the Launcher *is:* a control panel, just like the others described in this chapter. What it *does* is display a handy, in-your-face window containing jumbo icons for the programs and files you intend to use the most often. For details, see "All about big fat Launcher buttons" in Chapter 4.

You can move, resize, or close the Launcher window just as you would any window (Chapter 1). Once closed, it will reappear if you choose Launcher from your list of control panels (from the menu, for example).

Location Manager — This clever but complex program was originally designed for PowerBooks. It was inspired by a breakthrough concept: that laptops are likely to be *moved around*. Using this control panel, you can change a slew of settings — the time zone, local Internet access phone number, speaker volume, and so on — with a single click of the mouse.

Figuring out how to use Location Manager is roughly as easy as solving the Pythagorean Theorem or whether the 32-ounce ketchup at $1.59 is cheaper than the 20-ounce at $1.05. If you're genuinely interested, open Location Manager, choose Apple Location Manager Help from the Help menu, and get somebody to read you what it says.

Mac OS Easy Open (or **Macintosh Easy Open**) — If there's one thing that frustrates novices and old Mac salts alike, it's seeing that infernal "Application not found" message when you double-click an icon. With this control panel installed, when you double-click an icon, you don't get an error message — you get a dialog box that lists the programs you own that *can* open the mystery file.

MacLinkPlus Setup — Designed primarily to open Windows-computer files when you double-click them, translating them into a Macintosh format. If you don't work with files from a DOS computer, out this goes, along with everything else in your System Folder called MacLink.

MacTCP — If you're not on a network and don't use the Internet, throw this out. Also throw it out if you have the control panel called TCP/IP, described later, which makes this one obsolete. See Chapter 11 for more on the Internet.

Map — This control panel is primarily useful for people who do business with different geographical locations. You type a major city's name and click Find, and the Map shows you where that city is. It also tells you how far away it is, and what the time difference is. (Want to see Apple's sense of humor at work? Type *MID* and press Return . . .)

Memory — As the French say, *Ne trashez pas!* You'll need this one. Details on memory, and Memory, in Chapter 15.

Modem — This simple control panel is where you specify the exact brand and model of the modem your Mac has. Pick the wrong one, and your ability to explore the Internet, send faxes, and attain Nirvana will be extremely limited. (If you don't see your model listed here, contact the modem's manufacturer and ask where you can get the necessary *modem script.*)

Monitors & Sound — Use this control panel to switch between different color settings for your monitor (such as colors, grays, or black-and-white) — and different *resolutions* (degrees of magnification for the whole screen).

The Mac that's always in color

If you experimented with the Monitors & Sound control panel just now, you may have discovered an unsettling fact: On any recent Macintosh model, *black-and-white* isn't among your Monitors color-setting options. Apple apparently discovered that it could save money this way. Somehow.

Anyway, if your model is affected, you can't do much except enjoy full color forever.

The Alerts portion of this control panel lets you choose which irritating sound effect you want to squawk at you when you make a mistake. And the Sound portion lets you specify what you want the Mac to listen to when recording or playing sounds: a microphone (if you have one), your built-in CD-ROM drive, and so on.

Mouse — Try this: Move the mouse very slowly across three inches of desk space. The arrow moves three inches. But now *jerk* the mouse across the same three inches. Now the cursor flies across your entire monitor!

The Mouse control panel lets you adjust how much of this speed-exaggeration you'll get when you move the mouse. It also lets you decide how fast two clicks must be to count as a double-click.

Network — Used to switch between different kinds of networks, such as Ethernet and LocalTalk (whatever *they* are). Replaced by the AppleTalk control panel in recent Macs.

Numbers — For non-Americans. Lets you change the way the Mac punctuates numbers. For example, the French use periods in large numbers instead of commas. You'd say, "Bonjour! You owe moi $1.000.000, Monsieur." If you're satisfied with the American way of doing things, throw this away.

Password Security — This control panel protects PowerBooks from unauthorized snooping by requiring a password each time you turn on (or, if you so choose, wake up) the laptop. Moreover, when you type your password, you see only bullets (•••••) appearing in the Password blank, so that the guy in the next airplane seat can't learn your password by looking over your shoulder.

Helpful hint: Don't forget the password. If you do, your only options are to (a) take your PowerBook, complete with purchase receipt, to an Apple service center, where they have the special tools needed to bypass the security, or (b) use your PowerBook as a windshield scraper.

PC Exchange — Lets you shove Windows-computer disks into your Mac. If you only work with Macs, and don't anticipate needing to show off your Mac's versatility for your IBM buddies, send this baby Trashward.

PC Setup — Useful only if you paid an extra $400 for your Mac to get a so-called DOS Compatibility Card, meaning you can run DOS or Windows programs on your Mac. Use this control panel to change a bunch of weird-looking options only a DOS person could understand.

PowerBook — Controls how quickly your pre-1998 laptop Mac goes to "sleep" to conserve battery juice. Naturally, if you don't have a PowerBook, it's Trash Time. (See Chapter 10 for more on PowerBooks.)

PowerBook SCSI Disk Mode — If your Mac library is complete enough to include *Macworld Mac Secrets,* also published by IDG Books, you can read all about connecting a PowerBook laptop to a desk Mac via a special, $45, fat, high-speed *SCSI cable.* If you have no intention of buying that cable or transferring files in this way, you have no need for this little program.

PowerBook Setup — Lets you schedule a time for your PowerBook to wake up by itself. Why? You tell me.

PowerTalk anything — Unless somebody in your office specifically told you to leave it, discard this slow, memory-hogging, extremely complicated networking software.

PPP — If you've signed up for an Internet account (see Chapter 11), this is the important control panel that stores your name, password, and local phone number for dialing into the Internet. (In Mac OS 8.5, and on the iMac, renamed *Remote Access.*)

QuickTime Settings — You can read all about QuickTime in the "Extensions" section later in the chapter. This control panel lets you make various settings pertaining to playing music CDs and Mac CD-ROMs. You'll never need any of them except one: If you turn off the AutoPlay CD-ROM option, your Mac is protected against the nasty AutoStart virus (see Chapter 15).

RAM Doubler — A program (didn't come with the Mac; you bought it) that makes your Mac think it has much more memory than it actually does, for the purpose of letting you run more programs without quitting. Details in Chapter 15.

Remote Access — If you've got an iMac or Mac OS 8.5 (or later), this control panel is where you specify your Internet name, password, and local phone number. No Internet account? Toss it.

Sharing Setup, Users & Groups — More control panels used only for networking. Throw them away unless you want to connect to other Macs over the office network.

Sound — Lets you adjust the volume of your speaker. Also lets you choose from among several equally uncouth sound effects for use as your error beep (what the Mac does when you make a mistake); see Chapter 9 for a quick tour. (Modern Macs have the Monitors & Sound control panel instead.)

Speech or **Speech Setup** — Extremely cool for at least 15 minutes. Lets your Mac read, out loud, what you have typed. Details in Chapter 20.

Speed Doubler — A program purchased by you or somebody you love that speeds up your Mac in a few subtle ways: Empties the Trash faster, makes copies faster, and so on.

Startup Disk — You'd use this if you had *more than one* hard drive connected to your Mac. You have one hard drive inside the Mac. Some people purchase another one, or a removable-cartridge thing like a Zip drive, that plugs into the back. Startup Disk lets you choose *which* hard drive's System Folder you want to run the show when you next turn on the computer. If the hard drive in your Mac is your only hard drive, toss Startup Disk.

TCP/IP — If you've signed up for an Internet account (see Chapter 11), this control panel stores the complex numbers that identify the company you've signed up with.

Text — Mr. Pointless. Would let you choose a language software kit other than English for your computer — if you had any installed. You don't. Throw this away.

Trackpad — On trackpad-equipped laptops, this works just like the Mouse control panel (described earlier) . . . except, of course, it adjusts the trackpad sensitivity, not the mouse's. Also lets you decide whether taps on the *trackpad* should be interpreted as mouse-button clicks; see Chapter 10 for details and an illustration.

Views — (pre-Mac OS 8) When I showed my grandfather my PowerBook, one thing bothered him: The icons' names were too small to read. So I opened up the Views control panel, typed a new point size, and handed the Mac back to him. He loved it.

He did remind me, however, that when he was growing up, they didn't even have *electricity.*

Web Sharing — (Mac OS 8 and later) This control panel is primarily of interest to networked companies; it lets you make a particular folder on your hard drive available to anyone who dials into your Mac. If you don't have an office guru who explains how to use this, throw it away.

WindowShade — (System 7.5 through 7.6) Just when you'd gotten used to thinking of *menus* as behaving like window shades, now *windows* snap up like window shades. After you've opened up this control panel and turned it on, you can *double-click a window's title bar* to unclutter your screen. Double-click the floating title bar — all that remains — to re-expand the window.

So how come this control panel isn't in Mac OS 8? Because this feature is now built into *every* window, courtesy of the new little upper-right-corner doodad you can click (see Chapter 2).

The Extensions folder

An *extension* is a little program that runs automatically when you turn on the Mac. It usually adds some little feature to your Mac that you want available at all times: a screen saver, for example, that automatically blanks your screen after a few minutes of inactivity on your part.

Extensions aren't the only thing in your Extensions folder, however — oooooh, no; that would be far too logical. The Extensions folder also contains something called *shared libraries,* which are little blobs of computer instructions that your various programs call on when necessary. (Any file ending with *Lib* is one of these shared libraries. So don't go to a party and pronounce it "Open Transport Libb." It's "lybe," short for *library.*) Anyway, shared libraries are far less annoying than actual extensions, which make your Mac take longer to start up, use up memory, and contribute to freezes and crashes. Shared libraries don't do any of that.

AOL Link, AOL Scheduler — The Link one is required if you want to use America Online 3.0 or later. The Scheduler one isn't as critical; it's useful only if you want your Mac to dial America Online automatically in the middle of the night, unattended.

Appearance Extension — (Mac OS 8 or 8.1) Performs the magic dictated by the Appearance control panel, described in the Control Panels section of this chapter. Whatever you do, don't move this extension! Your Mac won't start up without it.

Apple Built-In Ethernet or **Apple Enet** — Lets your Mac connect to Ethernet networks. If you're not on an office network, toss these.

Apple CD-ROM or **Apple CD/DVD Driver, Foreign File Access, anything-Access** — Why does Apple's CD-ROM player need so many little extensions? Heaven knows. All I know is that you need these if you have a CD-ROM drive.

Apple Color SW anything — Software to make your Color StyleWriter printer work. If you don't have one, throw these away.

Apple Guide, anything-Guide — Remember, from Chapter 1, the electronic help desk called Apple Guide, in which you're given step-by-step on-screen instructions for doing something? These are the files that contain all the instructions. If you use the Apple Guide feature, leave these here. If you don't, you can save a lot of disk space by tossing anything with the word Guide in it.

Apple IX3D anything — Power Macs of the 1997/1998 era included fancy accelerated graphics circuitry that let the computer draw pictures on the screen faster. These files are the required software. Leave 'em be.

Apple Modem Tool, anything-Tool — These are all plug-in items for use with modem software. If you don't use a modem, out they go.

AppleScript, Finder Scripting Extension, anything-Script — All components of a very technical feature intended for the kind of person who wouldn't be caught dead reading this book. However, even if you don't use these yourself, some of the Mac's best features depend on these extensions, so leave them in place.

AppleShare, File Sharing Extension, Network Extension, Network — Still more doodads for networking Macs together. If you're not on a network, out they go.

Application Switcher — This extension is responsible for the Amazing Tear-Off Applications Palette of Mac OS 8.5 and later, as described in Chapter 9. It also lets you switch from one open program to the next by pressing ⌘-Tab. Try it — you'll like it!

Assistant Toolbox — Only for PowerBooks. Lets you control certain functions from the keyboard: ⌘-Shift–zero puts your laptop to sleep, and ⌘-Shift-Control–zero makes your hard drive stop spinning. In general, it's for power-geeks only. (Built into System 7.6 and later.)

ATI anything — These five or six files are required for certain ATI graphics boards (which come built into many Power Macs). Leave them alone.

Caps Lock — Only for PowerBooks. Because the Caps Lock key on certain models doesn't light up or stay down when you press it, this little extension puts an up-arrow symbol on your menu bar when Caps Lock is engaged. That way, you know when you're about to inadvertently type 46 pages in all caps.

Clipping Extension — This is the magic software responsible for a nifty feature called Macintosh Drag & Drop, the word processing shortcut described in Chapter 4's "Puff, the Magic Drag-N-Drop" section.

Color Picker — The Color Picker is that dialog box that shows a big color wheel, allowing you to choose a particular color. It appears, for example, when you're in the Labels control panel (or, in Mac OS 8 and later, the Edit menu's Preferences command) and you click a label color to change it. This extension adds a More Choices button to that dialog box, allowing you to choose some super-techie options. Trash it.

Color SW anything — Still more software to make your Color StyleWriter printer work. If you don't have one, throw these away.

ColorSync — See "ColorSync" in the Control Panels listing.

Contextual Menu Extension — (Mac OS 8 or later) Brings you the magical pop-up menus that appear when you hold down the Control key and click something. See Chapter 9 for the gory details.

Control Strip Extension — Starting in Mac OS 8.5, the Control Strip (described earlier in this chapter) is easy to modify. You can drag new tiles directly onto it (to install them) or Option-drag them to the Trash (to uninstall them). This extension makes it all possible.

Default Calibrator — This extension adjusts your Apple monitor at startup to ensure that it's colorifically perfect. If, by some fluke, you don't work in the professional color printing industry, toss this one.

Demo click&drag, Demo anything — Only PowerBook laptops come with these files, which are actually little movies. They're designed to be used exclusively by, of all things, the Apple Guide system. Why are they parked in the Extensions folder? Well, as my mother used to say: Why is the sky blue?

Desktop Printing anything — For people whose Macs are attached to *multiple* printers. Adds printer icons to your desktop, so that you can decide which one should print your latest masterpiece (see Chapter 5 for details). If you have but one printer, throw *all* of this out and have a happy life.

DNSPlugin — No joke: Apple describes this as an extension that "allows your computer to receive listings of network objects from DNS directory services." Turns out there's no such thing. Throw this away.

EM Extension — Another piece of Extensions Manager, described under "In your Control Panels folder," earlier in this chapter.

Energy Saver extension — Does the actual starting up and shutting down you've specified in the Energy Saver control panel (see "Energy Saver," earlier in this chapter).

Ethernet anything — More stuff for connecting your Mac to an office network or laser printer.

File Sync Extension — Required for the File Synchronization control panel, described earlier in this chapter.

Find, FindByContent, FBC Indexing Scheduler — These extensions make possible the Find By Content feature, which lets you search for words *inside* your files (when you can't remember what name you gave some file). For details, read the sidebar "Mac OS 8.5 and later: Super-Find!" in Chapter 4.

Find File Extension — Comes with System 7.5 through 7.6.1. You want it; trust me. It's responsible for bringing up that wonderful Find File feature described near the beginning of this endless chapter.

Folder Actions — For programmers only. Out it goes.

Graphics Accelerator — Makes your Mac repaint the screen faster. Works only on recent Power Macs.

IceTEe — If you use the Internet, this little gizmo is worth having. It adds to *all* your programs an advanced, but timesaving, feature: When you ⌘-click the text of any Web-page address, wherever it shows up (in your word processor, in an e-mail, or wherever), your Mac dials the Internet and shows you that Web page. Similarly, you can ⌘-click an e-mail address to open a new, blank, preaddressed e-mail in your favorite e-mail program.

Indeo Video, Intel Raw Video — If you use Microsoft Internet Explorer (see Chapter 12), these extensions got dumped into your System folder. They let your Mac see movies (which, presumably, you find on the Web) that have been prepared in Windows format (AVI).

IIci/IIsi Monitors, anything-Monitors — These extensions add a couple of technical monitor-configuration options that you can't even see unless you open your Monitors control panel and click the Options button. Throw these away except the one that describes your Mac model.

Internet Access — If you have Mac OS 8 or 8.1, you need this shared library to dial into the Internet. Otherwise, not.

Internet Config Extension — This extension goes with the Internet control panel, described earlier in this chapter. (It also goes with the Internet control panel's predecessor, called Internet Config.) If you're *not* using the Internet, toss it.

Iomega driver — Lets your Mac work with Zip and Jaz drives. If you didn't buy one, out these go.

IrDALib, IrLanScannerPPC, IR-anything — Lets PowerBooks beam files to each other through the air, using their built-in infrared lenses. If that's not something you do, these aren't files you need.

jgdw.ppc — Installed by Microsoft Internet Explorer. I haven't the faintest idea what it does.

Kodak Precision CP-anything — A color-management system a lot like ColorSync, described earlier. Dumped into your System folder by PageMaker, CorelDraw, Canvas, and other graphics programs.

LaserWriter, StyleWriter, anything-Writer — Recognize these names? They're various printers made by Apple. You only need one of them — the one that matches your printer. Throw away all the others. (More on printers in Chapter 5.)

Location Manager-anything — See "Location Manager," earlier in this chapter.

MacinTalk anything — Lets your Mac *speak*. See Chapter 20.

Microsoft Dialog Library, Microsoft-anything — Unfortunately, you're stuck with all of this System Folder crud if you hope to make Microsoft programs work.

Modem Scripts — Before you go online (either with America Online or an Internet account), you're supposed to tell the Mac what kind of modem you own. You choose your model from a really long list. For every corresponding modem name, a file sits here in your Modem Scripts folder.

You should feel absolutely great about taking 10 minutes right now to *throw away* every modem-model file except the one you actually own. You'll save RAM, hard-disk space, and time when you launch your modem programs.

MRJ Libraries — This folder (which stands for Macintosh Runtime for Java) contains the software necessary for your Mac to run Java programs — that is, animated ads and little games that you find on Web pages as you surf the Internet. You be the judge.

Multiprocessing — (Mac OS 8 and later) It's the latest rage: Sticking *more than one* processor chip into a single computer for added speed. If you're one of the 11 people who have such a Mac, hang on to this.

ObjectSupportLib, AppleScript Lib, anything-Lib — For pre-Mac OS 8 Power Macs only; some kind of deep-seated, high-tech data-sharing technology you're not supposed to know about. Leave these alone.

OpenDoc Libraries — Throw this out; OpenDoc is dead.

Open TPT anything — This super-techie collection of System Folder lint (known as Open Transport technology) makes your Mac capable of connecting to the Internet, a network, or America Online.

PC Card anything — These files let your PowerBook laptop recognize *PC cards* (those little credit-card size modems), as described in Chapter 15.

PowerBook 3400/G3 anything — These files let your laptop talk to its own built-in networking/modem circuitry.

PowerBook ZoomedVideo — Throw this away unless you remember spending several hundred dollars on a *zoomed video card* (which lets you watch live video via cable) for your PowerBook.

PowerTalk anything — Throw this all away; PowerTalk is another abandoned Apple technology.

Printer Descriptions — This folder contains one little file for each individual printer model. Open this folder and discard the icons for any printers you don't use.

PrintMonitor — The genie that grants the miracle of background printing, a concept you probably don't understand unless you've read Chapter 5.

Printer Share — Lets you share one StyleWriter among several networked Macs. No network? Toss this baby.

QTVR anything, QuickTime VR — *QuickTime VR* is a special kind of digital photo. If you drag your cursor around in the picture, you change the camera angle, so that you can look all around you. You don't run across VR (virtual-reality) "movies" very often — but when you do, these doodads make them possible.

QuickDraw 3D-anything — QD3D stands for *QuickDraw 3D*. This assortment of a half-dozen extensions lets your Mac show, create, and accelerate 3D graphics. Unfortunately, you need special programs and special add-on circuit boards to take advantage of it. For most people, the Trash is the correct location for all this gunk.

QuickDraw GX anything — Lose 'em. Yet another dead technology.

QuickTime-anything — You need these little jobbers if you plan to use (or are using) digital movies on the Mac. You know, little flicks that play inside a Triscuit-sized window right on your screen, complete with sound (see Chapter 20). The QuickTime extension (and accompanying files) make those movies possible; many CD-ROM discs require this item. If you're not a Hollywood wannabe, and don't use CD-ROMs, then save yourself the memory and disk space and send this one to the cutting room floor.

Serial (Built-in) — Still more Open Transport crud (see "Open TPT anything").

Shared Library anything — You need these to manage your *shared libraries,* described at the beginning of this section.

Shortcuts — Another piece of Macintosh Guide (see "Apple Guide" at the beginning of this extensions listing).

SLPPlugin — Exactly like the delightful DNSPlugin described earlier in this section.

SOMobjects for Mac OS — Yet another shared library, as discussed at the beginning of this section. This one is required to make Mac OS 8-and-later's *contextual menus* work (see Chapter 9).

Sound Manager — For sound recording and playback. Leave it for now.

Speech Manager, Voices — For speech recognition and text-reading-out-loud, as described in Chapter 15. If you aren't regularly talking or listening to your Mac — besides just arguing with it — out these go.

System AV — Required by the Monitors & Sound control panel, described earlier in this chapter.

Text Encoding Converter — All computers understand A through Z, but the wackier symbols (such as curly quotes, foreign diacritical markings, and so on) are internally summoned differently on each type of computer. Ever get an e-mail in which all the apostrophes appear as capital U's? Or in which all the quote marks have turned into weird boxes? Now you know the problem.

The Text Encoding Converter is designed to translate other computers' wacky alphabet references into the Mac's system, so that fewer nutty boxes and U's show up in your e-mail. Leave this in place.

Time Synchronizer — The Date & Time control panel (in Mac OS 8.5 and later) can set your Mac's clock *automatically* by dialing into the Internet. This extension makes that feature possible.

UDF Volume Access — Lets your Mac talk to *DVD discs* (which are like CDs, but hold 14 times as much). If you remember paying $400 to have a DVD drive added to your Mac, keep this; otherwise not. ("Volume," in this case, doesn't mean "loudness"; it refers to a *disk.*)

Video Startup — This extension is required by Apple Video Player, described at the beginning of this chapter.

XTND Power Enabler — Given unto you, most likely, by a Claris program (such as ClarisWorks). It lets your Claris program open (and create) documents from rival word processors.

WorldScript Power Adapter — Makes word processing on a Power Macintosh slightly faster. Leave it.

The Fonts folder

This folder contains your fonts. (Did you guess?) See Chapter 5 for a detailed explanation of all this junk.

The Launcher Items folder

The purpose of this folder is to let you specify what jumbo icons you want to appear in your Launcher window, the Mac's one-click program-launching bay. See "Launcher" earlier in this chapter.

The Preferences folder

The Preferences folder is filled with information, and *none* of it's for you.

Every single file in this folder was put there by *another* piece of software. Let's say you change a setting in your word processor: You always want it to make your typing double-spaced, for example. Well, where do you suppose the computer stores your new setting? It jots it down in a *preferences file.* And this prefs file lives — wild guess — in the Preferences folder.

Prefs files are famous for frustrating beginners. Because they're for use by your programs, and not by you, virtually every one of them gives you a rude error message if you try to double-click it. You simply can't open a Prefs file; only your software can.

You really can only do one good thing with the Preferences files: throw them away. That is, throw away any that belong to programs you no longer use.

Special folders in Mac OS 8.5 and later

In its noble (but hopeless) quest to neaten up your System Folder, Apple continues to introduce new holding-tank folders. In Mac OS 8.5, for example, these additional System Folder folders debuted:

- **The Application Support folder:** If the various Mac software companies wind up complying with Apple's request, they'll dump all their programs' associated crud — dictionary files, file-conversion stuff, and so on — into this folder.

- **ColorSync Profiles:** As you can read earlier in this chapter, ColorSync is a software scheme for ensuring that scanners, screens, and color printers all agree on what, for example, "red" is. This folder contains individual color-description lists for every model of Apple scanner, monitor, and printer. If color consistency is important to you, use the ColorSync control panel to specify which models you own.

- **The Favorites folder:** "Favorites" means "icons I'd like quick access to from now on." To create a Favorite, click it and choose Add to Favorites from the File menu. It instantly appears in your Favorites command (in the ⌘ menu), as shown here:

1. Choose Add to Favorites . . .

2. . . . and from now on, your favorite icons are available from the Apple menu.

 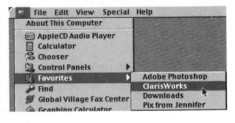

Behind the scenes, the Mac has simply placed an *alias* of that icon into the Favorites folder. (See Chapter 9 for a description of aliases.) In other words, to remove something from the Favorites menu, remove it from this folder.

- **The Help folder:** Apple puts its own help files (which create what you see when you use the Apple Guide feature, for example) into this folder. Other software companies may follow suit.

✔ **The Internet Search Sites folder:** Mac OS 8.5's Find command is capable of searching the entire, vast Internet, not just your puny little hard drive. The files in this folder each teach the Find command how to talk to a different World Wide Web search page. (See Chapter 4 for more on using Find, and Chapter 12 for more on Web search pages.)

✔ **The Scripts Folder:** A place for programmers to stash their stuff.

Loose in the System Folder

Clipboard — Every time you use the Cut or Copy command in a program, the Mac, according to what you read earlier, socks the selected material away on an invisible Clipboard. Well, guess what: It's not actually invisible. Technically speaking, that info you copied has to be put *somewhere*. This is where: in the Clipboard file.

Little-known fact: You can double-click the Clipboard file to open a window that shows the last thing you cut or copied. (Another little-known fact: The last swallow of a can of soda is 69 percent saliva.)

Extensions (Disabled) — This explanation is tricky and techie, but I'll do my best. Remember Extensions Manager, described under "In your Control Panels folder" earlier in this chapter? It lets you turn extensions or control panels on and off. When you click some extension's name to switch it off for the day, Extensions Manager doesn't *delete* that extension; behind the scenes, it just *moves* it into this Extensions (Disabled) folder. When the Mac next starts up, it only "loads" the extensions that are in the actual Extensions folder.

To turn that particular extension on again, you can, of course, use Extensions Manager again — but you could also, in a pinch, move the file manually back into the regular Extensions folder. (Rival programs, like Conflict Catcher, work the same way.)

And if you turn off a *control panel,* sure enough, it winds up in a folder called **Control Panels (Disabled).**

Finder — This is the most important program on your Mac. Without it, a System Folder is just a folder, and your Mac won't even turn on. The Finder file is responsible for creating your basic desktop: the Trash, your disk icon, windows, and so on.

System — This is *also* the most important file on your Mac. It contains all kinds of other info necessary for the computer to run: reams and reams of instructions for the computer's own use. Without a System file, the Mac won't even turn on, either.

anything-Enabler — If you *have* an Enabler in your System folder, then it, too, is the most important file on the Mac, critical to the Mac's being able to work at all. However, not every Mac has one of these. If you have one, don't touch it.

Desktop Printers — The icons for your various printers (*if* you have more than one). See the sidebar called "A shortcut for multiple-printer owners" in Chapter 5.

Scrapbook file, Note Pad file — When you paste something into the Scrapbook or Note Pad desk accessories, behind the scenes, the Mac actually stores it in these files.

Mac OS ROM — Got an iMac? Then you've got this file. Whatever you do, don't fold, move, spindle, or mutilate it. It contains the iMac's brains. Throw it away, and you've got yourself a see-through, $1,300 doorstop. (Fortunately, a *clean install,* described in Chapter 16, can bring a thus-crippled iMac back to life.)

Startup Items, Shutdown Items — Fascinating, Captain. Anything you put into the Startup Items folder (a program, a document, a sound, a folder) gets opened with a mysterious automatic double-click whenever you turn on the Mac. If you don't do anything but word process, for example, drag the icon of your word processor into this folder. Thereafter, every time you power up for the day, your word processing program will be on the screen awaiting your brilliance.

The Shutdown Items folder is the same deal, except anything in *here* gets run automatically when you *shut down* the computer. Automatic-backup programs come to mind. A sound that says "Th-th-th-th-th-that's all, folks!" also comes to mind.

Part III
Toward a New, Nerdier You

The 5th Wave   By Rich Tennant

"Well, the first day wasn't bad—I lost the Finder, copied a file into the Trash, and sat on my mouse."

In this part . . .

There comes a time in everyone's life when just turning
the computer on and off no longer brings the surge
of excitement it once did. Now it's time to maneuver this
baby to the autobahn, open 'er up, and see what she can do.

That's why the next two chapters move beyond the
desperate, what-am-I-doing? basics and show you some of
the more rarified talents of your machine.

Chapter 9

Putting the Mouse to the Metal

. . . .

In This Chapter

▶ Forbidden secrets of the Option key

▶ Duplicating, finding, and splitting the personality of icons

▶ Vandalizing your own Mac, without spray paint or a sledge hammer

▶ Wizzy new window stunts in Mac OS 8 and 8.5

. . . .

This chapter is about honing your basic skills. It's about becoming more efficient in the way you work — shortcuts, hidden secrets, and slick tricks to astonish your friends. And it's about turning the basic Mac that *millions* of people have into one that's unmistakably yours.

Maybe it'd be better if I avoided the term that's about to apply to you . . . *power user.* Maybe those words will strike fear once again into your soul. But even if you started *out* as a Mac virgin, either leery or outright petrified about the alien technology before you, by now you've almost completely mastered the Mac. The only tidbits left to explore are the ones normally classified as — yes — *power-user secrets!*

The Efficiency Nut's Guide to the Option Key

Yeah, yeah, everybody knows that you can close a window by clicking its close box. But you didn't fork over good money for this book to learn something that's on page 1 of the Mac manual.

No, these tips are much choicer. They show you how to unlock the power of that most overlooked of keys, the Option key. It's been placed closer to you than any letter key on the keyboard — and that's no accident.

Closing all windows at once

Suppose you've opened a gaggle of folders and their windows are lying open all over the screen. And suppose that the niggling neatness ethic instilled in you by your mother compels you to clean up a bit.

You could, of course, click the close box of each window, one at a time. But it's far faster to click only *one* window's close box while pressing the Option key. Bam, bam, bam — they all close automatically, one after another.

Windows and folders: Tunnel vision

When you're trying to find a document icon that's inside a folder inside a folder inside a folder, it's hard to avoid having COWS (Cluttered, Overlapping Windows Syndrome). By the time you finally arrive at the darned icon, your screen is filled with windows.

If you press Option while double-clicking each nested folder, though, the Mac will neatly close the *previous* window before opening the next one. Criminy — this computer even *cleans up* after you!

In the following figure, you could press Option while double-clicking the Oregon folder (left); the USA folder that contains it would automatically close as the new window opened (right):

Okay. So here we are in the Oregon folder. What if we want to backtrack and go back to the USA folder (or the World folder)? A little-known trick lets you jump to the folder that *contains* it: Press the ⌘ key and click the window's title!

Chapter 9: Putting the Mouse to the Metal

In the preceding figure, you ⌘-click the word Oregon at the top of the window. Now you slide down the pop-up menu that lists the nested folders from innermost to outermost. Let go when you reach the folder you want (below, left); the Mac opens the folder you selected (below, right):

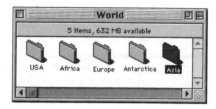

And, logically enough, if you press ⌘ *and* Option as you choose the new folder name, you'll simultaneously close the original nested window.

The silence of the Trash

Let's review: You drag an icon on top of the Trash can and the icon disappears. The Trash can bulges or overflows. You smile gently at the zaniness of it all. Then you choose Empty Trash from the Special menu, and a little message appears on the screen, saying something like:

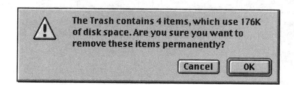

That's all very well and good, but busy Americans concerned with increasing their productivity may not always have time for such trivial information. Therefore, if you want to dump the trash, but you *don't* want that message to appear, press Mr. Option Key while you choose Empty Trash. (Option is also the key for emptying the trash when the Mac tells you something is "locked" in the Trash can.)

'Smatterafact, you can shut up the Trash's warning permanently, if you're so inclined. Click the Trash can. From the File menu, choose Get Info. Turn off "Warn before emptying." What an improvement!

Multitasking methods

As you discovered early on, the Mac lets you run more than one program simultaneously. (Remember when you tried some tricks with both the Note Pad and the Calculator open on the screen at once?) You can switch from one program to another by choosing the program's name from the Application menu at the top right of your screen, marked by the icon of whichever program is currently in front.

We haven't yet examined the other commands in this menu, such as Hide Others and Show All. These are anti-COWS commands that help keep your screen neat and clean. For example, suppose you're trying to use the Calculator, but so many other programs are running that your eyes cross:

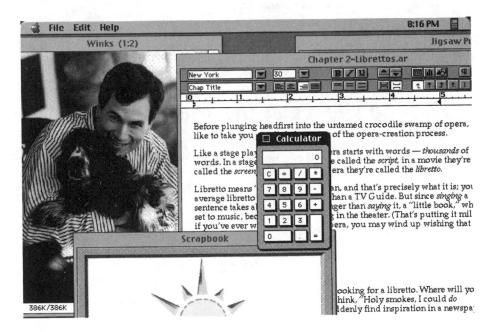

By choosing Hide Others from the Application menu, all windows that belong to other programs disappear, leaving the frontmost window all by itself:

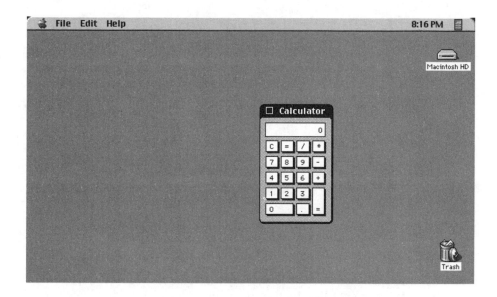

The other programs *are still running,* and they *do* still exist. But their windows are now hidden. You can verify this by checking the Application menu, where you'll see that their icons appear dimmed.

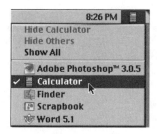

So how does the Option key play into all this? When you switch from one program to another, you can make the program you're *leaving* hide itself automatically. Just press Option while choosing the new program's name (or clicking in its window). That way you always keep nonessential programs hidden.

And if you've got Mac OS 8.5, you can even press Option as you click different tiles on your *application switcher palette* (described at the end of this chapter). Once again, the program you were just *in* gets hidden as you switch to the next program.

Making an instant document copy

In most Mac graphics programs, the Option key has a profound effect on a selected graphic item: It peels off a copy of the selected graphic as you drag the mouse. For example, the left eye (right) is selected and then Option-dragged to the right:

You can accomplish essentially the same thing in the Finder, making duplicates of your files instead of eyeballs. Normally, when you drag an icon from one folder to another *on the same disk,* of course, you simply *move* that icon. But if you press Option while dragging an icon to a new folder (or to the Desktop — the colored background), the Mac places a *copy* of the file in the new folder and leaves the original where it was, as shown here:

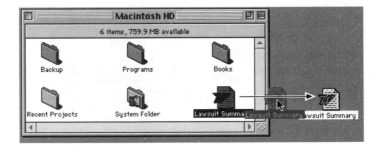

Funny little hidden Option-key stunts

Those wily Apple guys! The sneaky programmers! The funsters in Apple Land have buried all kinds of amusing little surprises in the control panels and other places. Try these:

- The weird little Map control panel lets you find any major city by latitude and longitude, and tells you the time zone difference. If you hold down Option as you open the Map control panel, the map appears at double size.

✔ Speaking of the weird little Map, if you press Option and repeatedly click the Find button, you'll get to view every city or location in the Map's secret database! Around the world in 80 clicks.

✔ When you're in the Finder, the first item under the menu normally says About This Computer. Choose it to view some critical specifications about your machine — how much memory it has, for example. But if you press *Option* while choosing it, the command changes to say About the Finder — and shows you a pleasant Silicon Valley scene. Wait long enough, and you'll see some scrolling credits.

Buried Treasures

Did you enjoy those obscure, useless Option key tricks? Then you'll really love these equally scintillating techniques, not one of which requires the Option key.

Make an alias of a file

The File menu has a command called Make Alias. Although you might expect this command to generate names like One-Eyed Jake or "Teeth" McGuire, the term *alias* in the Macintosh world represents something slightly different — a duplicate of a file's *icon* (but not a duplicate of the file itself). You can identify the alias icon because its name is in italics, as shown here. (In Mac OS 8.5, a tiny arrow icon appears on the alias, too.)

Downloads

Downloads alias

What's neat about aliases is that, when you double-click an alias icon, the Mac opens the *original* file. If you're a true '90s kinda person, you might think of the alias as a beeper — when you call the *alias,* the *actual* file responds.

So who on earth would need a feature like this? Well, there's more to the story. An alias, for one thing, only requires a tiny amount of disk space (a couple of K) — so it's not the same as making an actual copy of the full-sized, original file. (And you can make as many aliases of a file as you want.) Therefore, making an alias of something you use frequently is an excellent time-saver — it keeps the alias icon readily accessible, even if the real file is buried somewhere four folders deep.

Another very common trick: Place an alias of a program, or a document, into your menu, where you don't have to open *any* folders to get at it.

Here's the drill:

1. **Click the real icon once.**

2. **From the File menu, choose Make Alias.**

3. **Open your System Folder.**

4. **Drag the alias into the folder called Apple Menu Items (within the System Folder).**

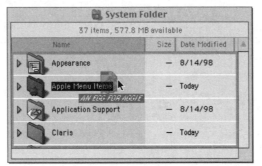

5. **Now look in your menu.**

Sure enough — there's your file! Choose it from the menu to open the original file.

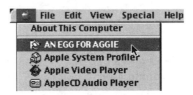

And yet, because you used an alias, the *real* file can be anywhere on your hard disk or on a different disk. You can move the real file from folder to folder or even rename it, and the alias still opens it properly.

Trash, aliases, and a word of caution

When you trash an alias, you're only deleting the alias. The original file is still on your disk. If you delete the *original* file, however, the alias icons will remain uselessly on your disk, rebels without a cause, babies without a mother, days without sunshine. When you double-click an alias whose original file is gone, you'll just get an error message. (In Mac OS 8.5, the error message offers you the chance to attach this orphaned alias to a *different* "real" file — but the original file is still gone forever.)

Likewise, if you copy your inauguration speech file's *alias* to a floppy disk, thinking that you'll just print it out when you get to Washington, think again. You've just copied the alias, but you *don't* actually have any text. That's all in the original file, still at home on your hard disk.

The L.L. Screen catalog

Every now and then, you might find it useful to create a list of files or folders on your disk. But it's hardly worth your time to go to the Finder, look at the first file's name, switch to your word processor and type it, and then repeat with the second file. Here's a much faster way:

1. **Select the files whose names you want to copy.**

   You might want to use the Select All command in the Edit menu, at which point you can press the Shift key and click "off" the items you don't want.

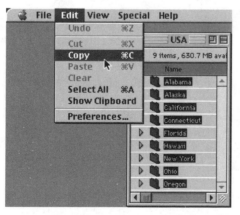 

2. **From the Edit menu, choose Copy (above, left).**

3. **Launch your word processor (or even the Note Pad under the menu) and choose Paste from the Edit menu. Presto: a neatly typed list of file names (above, right)!**

(P.S. — If your Mac has something before Mac OS 8, the list can't be a terrifically long one; the Mac copies only 256 characters of text at a time. In that case, you can always repeat the process.)

Have it your way — at Icon King

You don't have to accept those boring old icons for files, programs, and folders. If you want anything done around the Mac, heaven knows, you've got to do it yourself.

1. **Go into ClarisWorks (the painting window) or Photoshop, or Kid Pix, or some other program that lets you paint stuff. Make a funny little picture.**

   And I mean *little* — remember, you're drawing a replacement icon for some hapless file. Like this guy here, for example:

2. **Copy your creation to the Clipboard.**

3. **Go to the Finder and click the file whose icon you want to replace.**

4. **From the File menu, choose Get Info, so that the Get Info box appears.**

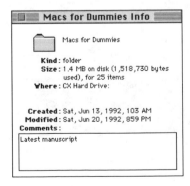

5. **See the folder icon in the upper left? Click that sucker — a[
   paste away!**

From now on, that little picture is the new icon for the file (or folder, or disk). To restore the original icon, repeat the Get Info business, but this time, after you click the icon, press the Delete key.

Taking a picture of the screen

In this book, you've probably noticed a number of pictures that illustrate objects on the Mac screen. Now I'll show you how to take your own snapshots of the screen.

It involves pressing three keys simultaneously: Command (⌘), Shift, and 3. You hear a satisfying *kachunk!* camera-shutter sound. After a moment, a new file appears in your hard disk window, called Picture 1. (If you take another shot, it'll be called Picture 2, and so on.)

If you double-click this Picture file, it opens in SimpleText (which came with your Mac). Once SimpleText opens, you'll see that you've successfully captured your screen image.

The ⌘-Shift-3 keystroke captures the *entire screen*. If you have System 7.6 or later, though, you can *specify* which part of the screen you want — press ⌘-Shift-4 instead, and your cursor will turn into a tiny cross. Drag this cross diagonally across the piece of screen you want; you'll hear the camera-shutter snap when you let go. In fact, while we're on a roll, here's one more: If your Caps Lock key is down when you press ⌘-Shift-4, your cursor turns into a bullseye, which you can now click on a window or a dialog box to capture only that rectangle.

Just say no

There's a wonderful keyboard shortcut that means *no* in Mac language. It could mean *No, I changed my mind about printing* (or copying or launching a program); *stop right now.* It could mean *No, I didn't mean to bring up this dialog box; make it go away.* Or: *No, I don't want to broadcast my personal diary over worldwide e-mail!* Best of all, it can mean *Stop asking for that disk! I've already taken it out of your slot! Be gone!*

And that magic keystroke is ⌘-period (.).

When you begin to print your Transcripts of Congress, 1952–1998, and you discover — after only two pages have printed — that you accidentally spelled it "Transcripts of Congrotesque" on every page, ⌘-period will prevent the remaining 14 million pages from printing. Because the Mac has probably already sent the next couple of pages to the printer, the response won't be immediate — but it will be light-years quicker than waiting for Congress.

Or let's say you double-click an icon by mistake. If you press ⌘-period right away, you can halt the launching and return to the Finder. And if the Mac keeps saying, "Please insert the disk: Purple Puppychow" (or whatever your floppy disk was called), you can tell it to shut up by doing that ⌘-period thing over and over again until the Mac settles down with a whimper. Show it who's boss.

Colorizing and Other Acts of Vandalism

The great thing about the Mac is that it's not some stamped-out clone made in Korea. It's one of a kind — or it will be after we get through with it. These tips illustrate some of the ways you can make the Mac match your personality, sensibility, or décor.

Color-coding your icons

Here's a pretty neat colorization feature that hardly anyone uses, but is still worth knowing about: color-coding. All you do is select an icon or a whole passel of them (below, left), and choose a color from a menu.

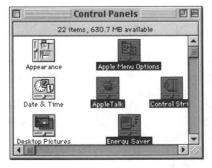
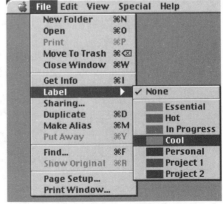

In Mac OS 8 or later, the color choices are hidden in the File menu, as shown above, right. In previous systems, the color choices are in the Label menu at the top of your screen.

Two questions, then: (1) How do you change the colors and labels into something more useful, and (2) what's the point?

Well, most people never bother with labeling their icons. You could argue, though, that it makes life more convenient since you can use the Find command to search for a file that has a certain label. You might give one label to everything related to, say, a certain book project — "Saddam Hussein: The Sensitive Side" — and then when it's time to back up your work, use the Find command to round up all files with the Hussein label, so that you can copy them all at once. (Or, when the project is over, you could happily *delete* them all at once.)

Anyway, if you *do* want to use this feature, you'll probably want to change the labels Apple suggests (Essential, Hot, In Progress, and so on) to something more useful. Here's how:

- ✔ **Mac OS 8 and later:** From the Edit menu, choose Preferences.
- ✔ **Previous system versions:** From the menu, choose Control Panels. When the Control Panels window appears, double-click Labels.

Either way, you'll see a list of the label choices, something like this:

![Preferences dialog box showing Font for views: Geneva 9; Simple Finder checkbox with "Provides only the essential features and commands"; Spring-loaded folders checkbox with "Delay before opening" slider (Short, Medium, Long); Grid Spacing with Tight (more items) and Wide (neater arrangement) options; Labels: OPRAH, Interviews, Geraldo's Comments, The Diet, The Diet Part XVI, Personal, Not yet backed up]

To change the wording of a label (remember, you're actually changing the wording of the Label *menu*), just double-click a label and type in something new. To change the color, click the color swatch; a dialog box appears where you can select a new color by clicking.

Views and window preferences

One famous aspect of the Mac is the degree to which you can tailor it to your tastes. You can make it look user-chummy and kid-friendly, or you can make it look high-tech and intimidating.

For starters, you can change the typeface used to display the names of your icons. If your vision is going — or you're trying to demonstrate the Mac to a crowd — make the font huge. If you want to make your icons as high as possible per square inch, pick a tiny, compact type style.

Once again, the steps differ depending on your Mac's system-software version:

 ✔ **Mac OS 8.5:** Open your Appearance control panel. Click the Fonts tab.

 ✔ **Mac OS 8 and 8.1:** From the Edit menu, choose Preferences.

 ✔ **Previous system versions:** Choose Control Panels from the ✿ menu. When the Control Panels window appears, double-click Views.

The window that appears is the control freak's best friend. Now you should be looking at font and size controls — something like this:

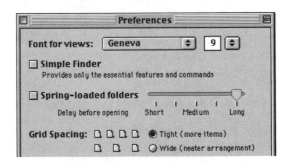

If you've got Mac OS 8.5 or later, you get three pop-up menus, including ones that control the fonts for your menus and your icons:

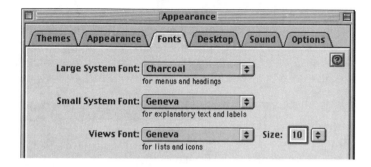

Go wild with these options. A couple of possibilities are shown here:

 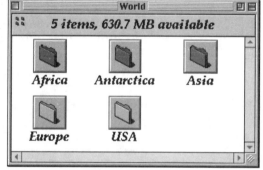

You might notice that the "look" in the second example is strikingly idiot-proof: big bold icons. If you could actually click the page of this book, you'd furthermore discover that *one* click on each of these "button" icons opens it, instead of the usual two.

That window got that way only after judicious tweaking — somebody chose the *as Buttons* command from the View menu.

U R A recording studio

The iMac, all PowerBook laptops, and many Mac monitors have a microphone built right into the screen. And for any Mac, you can buy an Apple microphone for about $20. It's not exactly the same one Madonna licks in her videos, but it's good enough for what we're about to do. And that is to change the little beep/ding sound the Mac makes (when you make a mistake) into some other sound, like "Oops!" or a game-show buzzer or a burp or something.

Here's how it works, once you've hooked up your mike:

1. **From the menu, choose SimpleSound.**

   You get something like this:

2. **Click the Add button. Now you see this:**

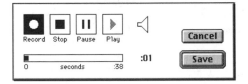

3. **To record, just click Record and speak into the microphone.**

   Be ready to click Stop when you're done, or else you'll accidentally include a bunch of silence and fumbling at the end of your sound.

You can play back your new sound in a plethora of ways. You could, mnemonically enough, click the Play button. Then again, you could click Save and give the sound a title, so that you'll be able to preserve it for your grandchildren. When you return to the list of sounds in the Sound control panel, click your new sound's name to play it. If you leave it selected in the list, though, you've just selected it to be your new error beep.

A sound-playing fact for the detail-obsessed

Here's a way to play a sound that doesn't even involve opening a control panel. If you're a double-clicking kinda person, open your System Folder and then double-click the System *file*. It opens into a window showing all your fonts and all your sounds. Just double-click any sound's icon to hear it played.

How to adjust your Mac's speaker volume

While we're on the subject of sound, now would be as good a time as any to show you how to adjust your Mac's sound volume.

The easy way, of course, is to use the Control Strip, described and illustrated in Chapter 8.

The macho way (*translation:* long way) is to choose Control Panels from your menu. Open the one called Monitors & Sound. You'll see the master volume sliders for all the various sound-makers attached to your Mac:

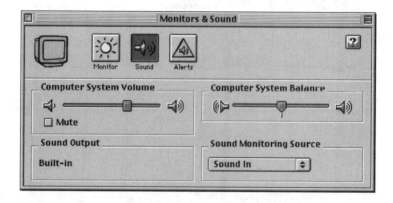

This is also, by the way, where to tell the Mac *what* it should be recording: the sounds from your microphone, for example, or the sounds from a music CD you've put into your CD drive. Use the Sound Input pop-up menu to switch between them.

If your older Mac doesn't have a Monitors & Sound control panel, then it *does* have a Sound control panel. If you choose Volumes from the pop-up menu, you'll be shown a new window, where the overall Mac speaker's volume slider appears. Adjust away!

Private Pages for People with Mac OS 8.x

After participating in the Information Age for about ten minutes, you notice something funny about software: It gets *replaced* all the time. Suddenly your mailbox is full of come-on postcards urging you to junk the $499 software you bought *last* year and spend $99 to replace it with a bigger, better, upgraded version *this* year.

Buying into these upgrades is optional, of course — even when the software being upgraded is the System Folder, the very software that runs your Mac. But such upgrades to the *operating system* (or OS) are worth paying attention to, because every now and then Apple comes up with something great.

This section is all about the cool new things you can do *only* if your Mac has Mac OS 8.0, Mac OS 8.1, or Mac OS 8.5 installed. (The phrase "Mac OS 8.*x*" is nerd shorthand for "Mac OS 8-point-anything.") Quick way to tell if you have such an OS: Does the word Help appear as a menu title at the top of your screen? If so, you've got Mac OS 8 or later.

Meet Mr. Window

In Mac OS 8, Apple blessed your icons, windows, and menus with 3-D surfaces, sleek gray-tinted lines, and a general Martha Stewart overhaul. And the Trash . . . oh, what a cute little Trash!

The most noticeable improvement to the way things work, though, is *windows,* those rectangular, name-at-the-top views into your stuff. How do we love them? Let us count the ways:

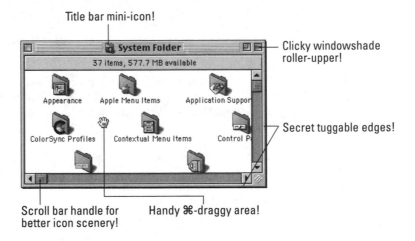

Title bar mini-icon!

Clicky windowshade roller-upper!

Secret tuggable edges!

Scroll bar handle for better icon scenery!

Handy ⌘-draggy area!

Now, since I'm not exactly sure that "Secret tuggable edges" and "Clicky windowshade roller-upper" are the actual official computer terms for these features, let me explain:

✔ **Secret tuggable edges:** In the olden days, you could move a window around the screen only by clicking on its striped *title bar*. In Mac OS 8 and later, however, you can actually hold your mouse button down on the thickened edges of each window — and move the window by dragging.

✔ **Clicky windowshade roller-upper:** Click this tiny square in the upper-right of any window to make the window itself *disappear* — all except the striped title bar. The effect is like the Cheshire cat in *Alice in Wonderland* disappearing completely except for his smile, except that this is actually *useful.* By judiciously clicking the clicky windowshade roller-uppers, you can hide and unhide a bunch of windows with aplomb, easily burrowing your way around without losing sight of the big picture.

✔ **Scroll bar handle for better icon scenery:** You may remember from Chapter 1 that the little square box inside a scroll bar lets you view what's hidden in a window — what's above or below what you're seeing, for example. (Man, I sure *hope* you remember — otherwise, you've been using your Mac all this time without ever writing a memo taller than three inches.)

In the magical world of Mac OS 8-and-later, if you drag this handle slowly, you actually *see* the icons moving by, so you're much less likely to overshoot.

✔ **Handy ⌘-draggy area:** If you have Mac OS 8.5 or later, you don't need no steenkin' scroll bars. You can move around inside a window just by holding down the ⌘ key while dragging anywhere inside.

For the first time in Macintosh history, in other words, you can actually shift your view in a window *diagonally* (instead of having to use one scroll bar at a time).

✔ **Title-bar mini-icon:** While we're talking about new doodads in Mac OS 8.5, check this out: See the tiny folder icon in the title bar (at upper left in the previous picture)? It's a *handle.* You can use it to drag the open window to another place, such as your backup disk or (in the case of perfectionist computer-book authors) directly to the trash.

✔ **Rearrangy columns 'n' things:** Another useful Mac OS 8.5 feature: When you're looking at a window in a list view, you can make the columns of information bigger or smaller by dragging the tiny divider lines indicated by A in this picture:

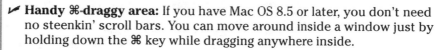

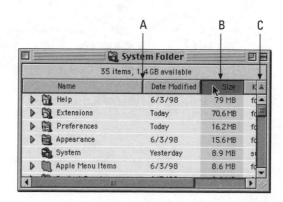

In fact, you can even *rearrange* the columns — putting the Kind column before the Size one, if that suits you — just by dragging the column headings around, such as B in the preceding picture.

Okay, while we're engaged in dead-horse beating, one more thing: You can click the tiny pyramid (marked C) to reverse the sorting order — from Z to A, for example, instead of A to Z.

Now we can all get a good night's sleep.

Poppin' fresh windows

Windows do something else funky in Mac OS 8, too: They *pop*. If you drag a window to the very bottom of the screen, something bizarre happens:

Drag to the bottom of the screen . . .

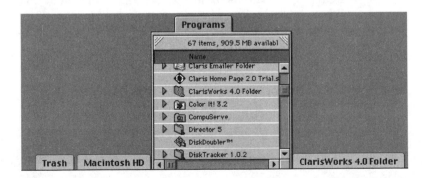

. . . and the window turns into a tab.

Sure enough, your little *window* turns into a *tab*. If you click this tab, the window shoots up like a strawberry Pop-Tart; click the tab on top again, and it crumbles back down into its former tab position. The point of this is that you can turn *several* windows that you use a lot into bottom-feeding tabs, like this:

. . . and rapidly switch among them just by clicking tabs. (You don't have to collapse one popped-up windowette before popping up the next — the Mac automatically closes one when you click the next tab.) Try setting up frequently accessed windows this way, such as your Programs, Launcher, and Documents folders.

Oh, by the way: To turn a bottom-hugging tab *back* into a full-fledged window, just tug its tab way high up into the middle of the screen. No problem.

Looks are everything

In the earliest days of computer technology (that is, before July 1997), you could make a few feeble attempts at changing the way your Mac looked. You could, for example, make Teddy Bears your desktop pattern.

But Mac OS 8 says: "Teddy Bears? — *Hah!*" Using the new Desktop Pictures control panel in Mac OS 8, or the Appearance control panel in Mac OS 8.5, you can fill your desktop with not just a repeating pattern, but a *full-screen* picture file!

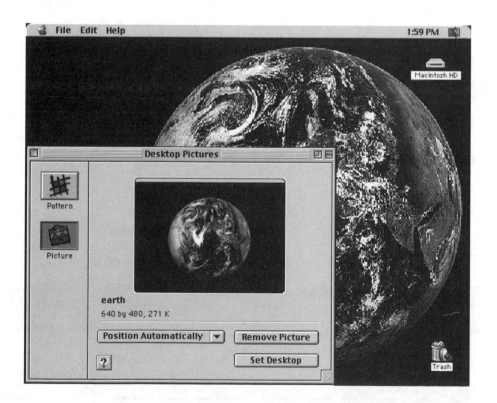

To do so in Mac OS 8.5, open the Appearance control panel, click the Desktop tab, and click the Select Picture button. To do it in Mac OS 8 or 8.1, open the Desktop Pictures control panel, click the button that says Picture and click the Select Picture button.

Either way, you're now asked to locate the graphic file you want to use as a backdrop. As for *getting* such a picture file, well, that's pretty much up to you. But America Online and the Internet are *teeming* with great pictures, from Planet Earth to Bo Derek. It's also easy enough to make your own, using (a) ClarisWorks or Photoshop, (b) a digital camera like those described in Chapter 18, or (c) a scanner, also described in Chapter 18.

Stay-open menus

As I hinted in Chapter 1, if you click the title of a menu (like File, Edit, View, or Special) in Mac OS 8.*x*, the menu drops down — and *stays* down, even if you take your finger off the mouse button for a moment to scratch your head. At this point, you can click a menu item to choose it, or click anywhere else on the screen to close the menu, or just wait about 15 seconds for the menu to roll itself back up. (Pop-up menus in dialog boxes work this way, too.)

This feature is especially great for PowerBook users; if you've ever tried to pull open a menu in a cab driving over Manhattan potholes at 75 mph while keeping the mouse button pressed and manipulating the cursor using a *trackpad,* you know exactly what I'm talking about.

The secret keystrokes of OS 8

Sure, there are loads of new gizmos in Mac OS 8: Control-key menus, ambidextrous windows, yadda yadda yadda. But some of the features speed freaks wind up using the most aren't even visible on the screen: They're *keystrokes* that do things.

For example: Want to trash an icon? Click it and then press ⌘-Delete (the Delete key in the upper-right of the keyboard). The highlighted icon immediately disappears, only to reappear in the Trash can. (Make no mistake: ⌘-Delete doesn't *delete* anything. It merely *moves* it into the Trash. Nothing's gone from the Trash until you choose Empty Trash from the Special menu.)

A couple other new keystrokes: If you click an *alias* (an icon whose name appears in *italics,* as described earlier in this chapter), you can press ⌘-R to jump to the original icon from which this alias was made.

And if you press the ⌘ and Option keys while dragging an icon out of its window, you *create* a new alias of it. The beauty part: The new alias doesn't even have the word *alias* on the end, like aliases made using the Make Alias command (in the File menu). Progress!

Handy desktop featurettes

Apple's overhaul of the Finder goes beyond pure windows and pure looks. A few of the improvements are actually *useful.* For example:

✔ **Spring-loaded folders:** For years, people wanting to move an icon into a folder that's inside a folder that's inside *another* folder had to cancel all their meetings for the day and lock the door. They'd have to open the first folder into a window; open the folder inside it; drag the icon into place; then close all the windows they've opened in the process.

In Mac OS 8-point-anything, however, you can simply drag an icon onto a folder (below, left) — *don't let go!* — and it will open *automatically* into a window (below, right).

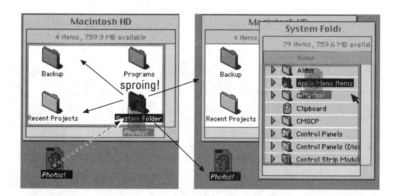

Now you can drag that icon on top of the *next* folder, and it, too, will spring open — *don't let go!* — so that you can drop it on its final, target folder destination.

Now let go. All the intermediate windows that opened on your journey snap shut automatically. Using this technique, you can actually place an icon into a folder within a folder within a folder — with a single drag.

✔ **Simple Finder:** This option is for people who sink into trembling hysteria by the presence of too many menus. It gives you (or children, or first-timers) a streamlined, simpler Finder with menus greatly shortened to bare technophobe-friendly essentials, like Empty Trash and Shut Down. (No aliases, labels, sleep, or other extraneous commands.)

To try out this Simple Mac view, choose the Preferences command from the Edit menu; in the dialog box that appears, turn on Simple Finder. (Turn it off again the same way.)

✔ **Simple Buttons:** New in the View menu is the Buttons command. When you invoke this setting, instead of viewing the window's contents as a list or as a bunch of double-clickable icons, you get *jumbo* icons — that launch when you click *once*. This option, too, makes great training wheels for the very young or very new at this.

The Program Switcher

Mac OS 8.5's upper-right corner is more informative than any other upper-right corner on earth. It now shows you the name of the program you're using at the moment — a blessing for the easily confused.

That upper-right corner is still a menu, however, listing all the programs you're running at the moment (the *Application menu,* as it's called). But in Mac OS 8.5 and later, the Application menu has a new talent: If you drag down the Application menu past the bottom, you *tear it off* (below, left):

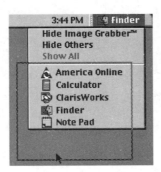

The menu turns into a small floating rectangle that lists your running programs (above, right); just click a program's name to switch to it.

And if you find this floating palette too wide for your tastes, click carefully just inside the right end of one of its buttons, as shown above — and drag to the left. You've just made the entire palette skinnier.

Isn't technology wonderful?

Chapter 10
The PowerBook Survival Guide

*I*t's a little bit mind-blowing that PowerBooks today have just as much computer horsepower as the most hulking desktop models. Apple makes almost no compromises: the speed, storage capacity, memory, screen size, and back-panel jacks on a PowerBook are almost exactly the same as those on regular Macs — but they're crammed into a book-size case that weighs eight pounds and conceals dirt.

PowerBook Care and Feeding

In fact, working on a PowerBook is so much like working on a desktop Mac that a separate chapter is almost unnecessary. *Almost.* But a few weirdnesses remain, largely pertaining to this diminutive Mac's screen, battery, and portable nature.

Sleep is good. We like sleep.

Do you have a PowerBook? Don't tell me you shut it down at the end of each day!

Yes, alas, thousands of people shut their PowerBooks off unnecessarily each day or — horrors! — even more than once a day. Don't do it!

Instead, put your PowerBook to *sleep* — that is, choose Sleep from the Special menu when you finish using the machine. Or, if yours was made in 1996 or later, just *close the lid*. The thing instantly blinks off.

Sleep is almost like Off. You're not running down the battery; nothing moves; all is calm, all is dark. But the advantages of letting a sleeping PowerBook lie are considerable. For example, when you want to use it again, you can just *touch any key* to wake it up. And when the thing wakes up, it doesn't go through the usual 45-minute "Welcome to Macintosh" startup process — instead, it takes you instantly right back to whatever you were doing. If you were typing up a letter, you wake up to your half-finished letter, still on-screen. Great timesavings.

You don't have to shut your PowerBook down for travel, either. The only time you need the Shut Down command is when you'll be storing the PowerBook for more than a couple of weeks. (You also have to shut it down whenever you plan to attach any major equipment to it, such as a scanner or a monitor. Most smaller attachments — printers, modems, a microphone, speakers, a keyboard, a mouse, a removable CD-ROM or floppy drive, and so on — can be attached when the machine is sleeping.)

Battery positives and negatives

Of course, it's perfectly possible to work for years on your PowerBook with its power cord firmly attached to a wall outlet, happily ignoring its capacity for running on battery power. Plenty of people do just that — people who bought a PowerBook for its compact size, not because they travel on airplanes a lot.

And that's perfectly okay. In fact, keeping your PowerBook plugged in whenever possible is a great idea.

But if you *do* plan to use your PowerBook in the back seats of taxis, in hot-air balloons, and on Grand Canyon promontories, you'll be running on battery power. In that case, every time you move the mouse or type something, you wince, wondering if you just unnecessarily sped closer to your battery charge's demise. It's a strange feeling, running a Mac on battery juice; in no other circumstance do you feel time's winged hoofbeats beating so loudly at your back. *(Is that your best simile? — Ed.) (Keep out of this. — Auth.)*

At the end of this chapter, you'll find out how to milk the most minutes from each charge. Frankly, though, if you find yourself going crazy worrying over your battery, spending the $90 for a second battery might be a worthwhile expenditure.

Aside from making it last longer, here are some fun and interesting battery facts to help you better understand your little square gray electrovoltaic friend:

✔ Your battery is recharging whenever the PowerBook is plugged in.

✔ No laptop computer battery ever lasts even close to the number of hours advertised. Not Macs, not IBMs, not any. You'll be lucky to get 90 minutes out of the standard "three-hour" battery. It's a fact of life. Or advertising. Or something.

✔ Even when your PowerBook is sleeping or completely off, your battery is still slowly being drained. That's why you may return to your PowerBook, which had had a full battery, after a couple weeks away, only to find the battery half empty. No big deal.

✔ PowerBooks make especially good use of the clever little onscreen gizmo known as *the Control Strip*. You can read more about it in Chapter 8. For the purposes of our battery discussion, however, notice the little battery gas-tank gauge that's part of the Control Strip. While wildly inaccurate, this little gauge is the best indicator you've got as to how much longer you can work on your current battery charge.

✔ Running out of battery juice at 39,000 feet with six hours to go before Paris may be inconvenient, but it really doesn't endanger whatever you've been working on. You get two or three warnings — increasingly urgent messages on the screen — stretching over a 15-minute period. And then the PowerBook goes to sleep. (It actually says, "Good night!" Isn't that adorable?)

Even if you hadn't saved your work, whatever is in memory is completely safe for another week or so, even after the PowerBook has gone to sleep. Just plug your PowerBook in at the next opportunity, wake it up, save your masterpiece, and go see the Eiffel Tower.

✔ PowerBook batteries are good for about 500 chargings. That, as well as common sense, should be your cue to use the PowerBook plugged into the wall whenever possible. You'll know when it's time to retire a battery when it just won't hold a charge anymore. At that point, unless you've got some psychotic grudge against the neighborhood raccoons, don't chuck this lethal chunk of toxic chemicals into the garbage. Instead, return it to an Apple dealer, who will send it back to Apple's battery-recycling program.

Trackpad Proficiency Drill

A PowerBook works great with a mouse — when you're home at your desk. Finding a place to lay down your mouse pad can be a challenge, however, when you're using your PowerBook in a telephone booth or while whitewater rafting.

That's why PowerBooks come with a *trackpad,* the flat plastic square between you and the keyboard, across which you run your fingers to simulate mousing. You need to know just a few fun factoids about the two-inch Teflon square that's about to become your best friend:

✔ When you first buy your PowerBook, all you can do with your trackpad is slide the arrow cursor around the screen. But the trackpads on all modern PowerBooks actually offer many additional features — if you know how to unlock them!

The secret is the control panel called Trackpad (get to it by choosing Control Panels from your menu). It offers three more trackpad features worth trying out (click each checkbox to turn the feature on).

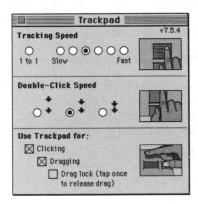

Clicking means that you can tap the trackpad surface itself (instead of clicking the big thumb button) to "click the mouse button," and even double-click on the pad to "double-click." Dragging lets you "drag the mouse" by tapping down-up-down (and moving your finger once it's down for the second time); you can even continue a long drag by lifting your finger between scoots.

And then there's Drag lock, by far the most useful option, since it helps with pulling down menus and moving icons around (which is difficult to do if you're working while, say, riding a camel). When this third checkbox option is on, you can double-click the trackpad — but if you begin moving your finger after the *second* click, the Mac won't "release the mouse button" when you lift your finger — even if you lift it *forever.* You must tap the trackpad again to release the drag lock.

No doubt about it, some people loathe these newfangled behaviors, preferring to do all their clicking, dragging, and drag-locking by pressing the big plastic clicker below the trackpad. But give them a try, in the name of becoming a more skilled PowerBooker.

The one extended-warranty deal that's not a scam

Just a word of advice about Apple's extended-warranty program, known as AppleCare. In general, as with those ridiculous $600-a-year service contracts they try to sell you with your $250 television, I don't believe that these contracts ever pay off. Macs in general are built like bricks.

It's different with PowerBooks. You carry them around, you put them to sleep and wake them up, attach and unattach equipment constantly, shove them into overhead racks, and set down your orange-juice glass on them. With this kind of treatment, *you* would be more prone to failure, too. In short, getting AppleCare for a PowerBook is an excellent investment.

✔ PowerBooks show up in a lot of big movies (*Independence Day, Mission: Impossible, Deep Impact,* and so on). Can you spot the whopping implausibility?

No, no, not that Tom Cruise gets safely off an exploding helicopter chasing a bullet train at 160 miles per hour. No, I'm referring to the fact that *the trackpad doesn't work if you're nervous.* If your hands are damp, sweaty, or lotioned in any way, the electronic sensors inside the pad get confused. Yet even as aliens were blowing up Los Angeles, Jeff Goldblum seemed to have no problem operating his laptop.

Personally, that glaring gaffe ruined the movie for me.

Anyway, several easy solutions await. For example, if you've just washed your hands and are in a hurry to use the PowerBook, you can put a piece of paper (such as a Post-It note) over the trackpad as a temporary measure.

✔ Here's a tip for leaping into the corners of your screen. Try moving your finger a short distance across the pad in the direction of the corner you seek — and then tap the pad with the *next* finger, an inch or so from where your first finger was moving. You've just fooled the thing into thinking that your finger covered the distance between the fingers instantaneously, and it teleports the pointer directly to the corner of your screen.

Of course, many a newcomer discovers this shortcut *accidentally:* If a second finger bumps the pad as the first finger is trying to do the cursor-moving, the cursor shoots away across the screen just at the critical moment.

Have Laptop, Might Travel

Okay. You've figured out how to work your laptop. Now you want to show it off — somewhere other than your living room. Who can blame you? A few pointers, if I may.

X-ray machines and you

Airport X-ray machines can't hurt your PowerBook.

Airport X-ray machines can't hurt your PowerBook.

Airport X-ray machines can't hurt your PowerBook.

Okay?

Desperate for a fix

Now look, I don't want to get angry letters from spouses and significant others, blaming me for converting their beloveds into power-nerd hermits. What I'm about to tell you should be socked away in the back of your mind and used only in emergencies.

The tip is about airplanes and airports. You know that PowerBooks and airplanes were made for each other. What you may not know is what to do when the dreaded "Your screen has been dimmed" message pops up, warning you that you have only a few minutes of battery power remaining, while you're in the middle of a brainstorm.

First of all, you can find publicly available power outlets at every gate of every airport (and at every bus and train station, too). The outlets are there, actually, for the benefit of the cleaning staff's vacuum cleaners; as such, the outlets are sometimes concealed on the side of a pillar. Unfortunately, the outlets are *never* convenient to a seat, so if your Mac habit is stronger than your pride, you'll have to sit on the floor.

What's more, when you run out of juice *on the plane,* let me call to your attention the electric-razor outlet in the bathroom of almost every plane in America. You feel like an absolute idiot, of course, wedged in there on that toilet with your adapter cord snaking up to the plug above the doll-size sink while your laptop recharges.

Well, that's what I've been *told,* anyway. Naturally, *I* would never do anything that pathetic.

Insta-Printer

Okay, so you bought the PowerBook. But what do you print on? Painful experience has demonstrated that few airlines accept a 45-pound laser printer as carry-on.

There *are* portable printers, of course; they're generally expensive, fragile, and slow. But here's a better idea: Get a fax modem for your PowerBook, if it doesn't already have one. (Most recent PowerBook models have a little slot in the side into which you can stick a "PC-card" modem — a modem the size of a credit card.) Thus equipped, just *fax* whatever-it-is that you want to print *to yourself.* For example, fax it from the PowerBook, while sitting in your hotel room, to the same hotel's front desk. Ingenious, fast, and free.

No need to thank me.

The one real jack

Most modern-day PowerBooks have a jack on the back called Printer/Modem. Where most Macs have *two* jacks — one each for printer and modem — the laptop has but one.

So how does the PowerBook know which personality (modem port or printer port) its sole jack is going to take at any given moment? The secret control is the Chooser, which you can find in your menu. Open it. You'll see, in the lower-right, the controls to make *AppleTalk* active or inactive.

When AppleTalk is *active,* you can (a) use a laser printer or (b) connect to a network. For all other purposes, including (1) printing on a StyleWriter or other inkjet, (2) connecting MIDI, digital cameras, a modem, or any other modem-port attachables described in Chapter 18, turn AppleTalk *off.*

Top Tips for Maximizing Battery Power

Many new PowerBook owners are devastated to find that instead of getting "two to three" hours of life out of each freshly charged battery, they get only 90 minutes or so. These tricks can help.

1. The lighting for the screen uses up *half* the power. The more you turn brightness down, the longer your battery lasts. (The backlight control is a physical push-button affair on the dark gray plastic "frame" around your laptop's screen.)

2. Remember reading about the memory effect earlier in this chapter? Or did you *forget?* (Get it?)

Anyway, as observed earlier, this fairly rare event can easily explain a low-capacity PowerBook battery. Try the empty/recharge routine.

3. Another enormous battery-drainer is your hard drive. Keeping those platters spinning at 4,500 rpm would drain my battery, too.

   It might seem silly to suggest that you try to avoid making your hard drive spin, but actually it's possible. First, visit your PowerBook or Energy Saver control panel and set the slider to Better Conservation. This setting makes your hard drive stop spinning sooner when it isn't really needed. Second, avoid Microsoft programs, which make your hard drive spin constantly.

   Finally, if you have the Control Strip, as described earlier, you can actually force your hard drive to stop spinning — on cue. To do so, place the cursor on the hard-disk icon, and choose Spin Down Hard Disk.

   Suppose, for example, that you've been merrily typing away into ClarisWorks for 20 minutes. The hard drive has been peacefully still. But now you want to *save* your work. The drive spins into action, and your file is saved.

   Now, as far as you're concerned, the drive's work is done. But if left to its own devices, the drive would continue to spin needlessly for another 15 minutes (or whatever period you've specified using the PowerBook control panel). That's 15 minutes of hard-drive juice you can save yourself by shutting the thing up, via the Control Strip, soon thereafter.

4. Every little appliance you attach *to* the PowerBook takes little sips from each battery charge. That especially includes external monitors, the built-in CD-ROM, keyboards, and mouse. And the speaker — if you're *really* fanatical about saving juice, turn off the PowerBook's speaker (use the Sound control panel or the Control Strip's volume control, and set the thing to zero).

5. Turn off AppleTalk — an incredible power drain that saps a half-hour of life from your battery. To do so, use either the Control Strip or the Chooser (in the menu). Select AppleTalk Inactive.

6. If you're not going to use the machine, even for five minutes, put it to sleep. (Choose Sleep from the Special menu, or use the little Zzzzzzz icon on the Control Strip, or just close the lid.)

7. Virtual memory (a techie feature described in Chapter 15) is supposed to be turned *on* on any Macs that have so-called PowerPC chips inside — which includes all PowerBooks made since 1996.

   But because virtual memory uses the hard drive a lot, it uses up lots of battery juice. What's a laptop-toter to do?

   If the answer is worth $50 to you, buy RAM Doubler. It offers the same benefits of virtual memory without making the hard drive spin — ideal, in other words, for PowerBooks.

   (No, this is not a paid endorsement for RAM Doubler. In fact, nobody's ever even *tried* to bribe me. What am I doing wrong?)

Part IV
The Internet Defanged

The 5th Wave   **By Rich Tennant**

TOM'S COMPANY OCCASIONALLY CONDUCTED SPOT CHECKS TO MAKE SURE THE EMPLOYEES WEREN'T SNEAKING THEIR MACINTOSHS INTO THE OFFICE.

Pencil box,...Rolodex,... large glowing chef's hat, nope, no Macintosh here.

In this part . . .

1 know, I know: if you hear *one more person* start droning on about the Internet, the Web, or the Information Superhighway, you'll tie them to a chair to watch 18 hours of the Home Shopping Network.

Actually, though, despite the overwhelming abundance of ridiculous, time-wasting chaff in cyberspace, there's also a lot of useful stuff, plus Dilbert cartoons for free. Here's how to go get it.

Chapter 11

Faking Your Way onto America Online and the Internet

*I*f you haven't heard of America Online or the Internet by now, you must've spent the last ten years in some Antarctic iceberg cave. These days, you can't make a move without seeing an e-mail address on someone's business card, a World Wide Web address (like *www.moneygrub.com)* on a magazine ad, or the glazed raccoon look of the all-night Internetter on a friend's face.

Going online gains you endless acres of features: the ability to send e-mail, instantly and for free, to anyone else who's online; incredible savings when you buy stuff (there's no middleman!); vast amounts of reading and research material (*Time* magazine, *The New York Times,* and so on, *free*); discussion bulletin boards on 20,000 topics (left-handed banjo-playing nuns, unite!); live, typed "chat rooms" that bring you together with similarly bored people from all over the world; and much more.

Before you begin this adventure, though, a grave warning: Going online is every bit as addictive as heroin, crack, or Presidential sex scandals, but even more dangerous. As you explore this endless, yawning new world, filled with surprises at every turn, you're likely to lose track of things — such as time, sleep, and your family. Take it slow, take it in small chunks, and use these services always in moderation.

Above all, remember that the Internet wasn't designed by Apple. It existed long before the Macintosh. It was invented by a bunch of military scientists in the '60s whose idea of a good conversation was debating things like *TCP/IP, FTP,* and *ftp.ucs.ubc.ca.* As a result, going online is all quite a bit more complicated and awkward than everyday Mac activities.

In other words, if you can't figure out what's going on, *it's not your fault.*

First, the Modem

To connect your Mac to your phone line, you need a *modem*. These little electronic boxes are priced according to their speed. Most people these days buy 56-mph models — that's what comes built into the iMac and some PowerBook laptops. (Technically, modem speeds are measured in *Kbps,* but I always say *mph* so people know what I'm talking about.) You can find fantastic deals on the older 28.8- and 33.6-mph models, but they're slow enough to drive you crazy if you plan to spend much time on the World Wide Web, described in the next chapter.

If you didn't get a modem with your computer, my suggestion, as always, is to buy it by mail order (see Appendix B for some hints on where to buy).

Now then: When the Mac makes a call, it dials the phone many times faster than, say, a teenager, but ties up the phone line just as effectively. When your Mac is using the modem, nobody else can use the phone.

Therefore, you need to figure out how you're going to plug in your modem:

✔ **Share a single line with the modem.** Most modems have two little jacks on the back: one for your telephone and one for a wire to the phone jack on the wall. This arrangement lets you talk on the telephone whenever you aren't using the modem, and vice versa.

✔ **Install a second phone line.** This is clearly the power user's method: give the modem a phone line unto itself. Pros: (1) Your main family phone number is no longer tied up every time your modem dials up the latest sports scores. (2) You can talk to a human on one line while you're modeming on the other. (3) If you're in an office with one of those PBX or Merlin-type multiline telephone systems, you have to install a new, separate jack for the modem *anyway.*

Cons: (1) This option is expensive; (2) it involves calling up the phone company, which is about as much fun as eating sand; and (3) you run a greater risk of becoming a serious modem nerd.

America Online or Direct to the Internet?

When it comes to visiting the vast, seething world of cyberspace, you have two on-ramps. You can become an America Online member, or you can sign up for a direct Internet account from any of 500 Internet-access companies (MCI, AT&T, MindSpring, EarthLink, and so on). The geeks call Internet-access companies *ISPs,* short for *Internet Service Providers.*

The birth of the Confusion Superhighway

The Internet began as a gigantic communications network for the U.S. military. The idea was to build a vast web of computer connections all over the country, so that if an enemy bomb destroyed one city, the government's electronic messages could still reach their destinations. (Gee, *that's* reassuring. Yeah, okay, New York is in cinders — but hey!, at least the company picnic memo got delivered.) As a result, you might send an e-mail message to your next-door neighbor — but it might reach him only after traveling from your Macintosh to Omaha, bouncing down to Orlando, returning to Toronto, and finally reaching the house next door.

There's no central location for the Internet; it's everywhere and nowhere. Nobody can control it; nobody even knows how many computers are connected to it. It's impossible to measure and impossible to control — which is why American teenagers love it, and governments try to ban it.

Anyway, when the U.S. government threw open the Internet to the public, it triggered an incredible explosion of interest, commerce, and nauseating buzzwords like *information superhighway*. There's a lot of useful stuff out on the Internet — and, as a pure time-killer, there's nothing like it. But there's also a lot of chaff to wade through. Let this chapter and the next be your guides to finding your way.

I find the term Internet Service Provider — let alone *ISP* — pretentious and overly nerdy, like calling a pilot an "Aerodynamic Services Provider." Unfortunately, you can't crack open a magazine or visit a computer club without hearing people talk about ISPs. ("My ISP only charges $18 a month!" "Really? Maybe I'll change ISPs then.") So, with your permission, I'll refer to the companies who rent you time on the Internet *ISPs,* just like everyone else does.

In this chapter, I'll show you both methods of getting online. Each route has significant pros and cons, however, which you'll find in the following table. Photocopy, distribute to your family members, and discuss over dinner.

America Online	*Internet Service Provider (ISP)*
$22 per month, unlimited access	Usually $20 per month, unlimited access
Frequent busy signals between 6 p.m. and midnight	Busy signals are rare
Hangs up on you after several minutes of your not doing anything	Doesn't hang up on you
Long hold times for help, but fairly Macintosh-savvy agents are available	Help agents are sometimes clueless about the Mac

(continued)

America Online	Internet Service Provider (ISP)
The one program on your hard drive — the America Online and program — does everything: e-mail, World Wide Web surfing, chat rooms	You need a separate program for each Internet feature: e-mail, Web surfing, and so on
Generally safe for kids; no pornography on America Online itself	Adult supervision required
Very simple, sometimes frustrating; the geeks look down on people with AOL accounts	More complex, less limiting; nerds admire you for having a "real" Internet account

America Online (often called AOL) is an *online service.* That is, its offerings are hand-selected by the company's steering committee and sanitized for your protection. Contrast with the Internet itself, where the offerings constantly change, nobody's in charge, and it's every Mac for itself.

Going onto AOL is like going to a grocery store, where every product is neatly organized, packaged, and labeled. Going onto the Internet, by contrast, is like going to a huge farmer's market that fills a football stadium, filled with whichever vendors happened to show up with their pickup trucks. At the farmer's market, wonderful bargains may await — but it's hard to find anything particular, some of the produce may be rancid, and there's no clerk to ask for help.

On the other hand, don't forget that America Online *also* gives you the actual Internet, *in addition* to its own hand-picked goodies. That is, the AOL grocery store has a back door into the farmer's market. But parents, don't freak out: America Online offers extensive, easy-to-use features for blocking the raunchy stuff so that your kids don't see it.

AOL, the CyberGrocery

Today's Macs come with the America Online (AOL) dialing software already on the hard disk. Skip the next paragraph.

If the AOL software *isn't* on your Mac already, you'll need a free AOL starter disk. Now, most Americans have already received enough of these starter disks in the mail to tile a small bathroom. But if, by some freak of the U.S. Postal System, you don't have one, call 800-827-6364 to request it.

How to connect to it

After you've installed America Online onto your hard drive, you'll see an America Online folder. Inside this folder is the America Online *program* whose icon you double-click to get started.

The first time you double-click this icon, you'll be guided through a series of setup steps. You'll be asked:

✔ For your name, address, and credit-card number. Remember, though, that you get 100 hours of time online (during the first month) for free. Cancel within the first month, and your card is never charged.

✔ To choose a local *access number* from a list (and a backup number). Fortunately, AOL has worked out a clever scheme that lets you, as one of 90 percent of Americans living near metropolitan centers, make a *local* call to America Online. Somehow, this system carries your call all the way to Virginia for free. (That's where the actual gigantic AOL computers live.)

✔ To make up a "screen name" and a password.

The *screen name* can be ten letters long, but you can't use punctuation. You can use a variation of your name (A Lincoln, MTMoore, Mr Rourke) or some clever CB radio-type handle (FoxyBabe, Ski Jock, NoLifeGuy). Do understand, however, that America Online has over *12 million* members, and *each* of them (including you) can choose up to five different names, one for each family member. In other words, you can pretty much bet that names like Helen, Hotshot, and Mac Guy were claimed some time in the Mesozoic Era.

If you pick a name that someone has already claimed, the program will make you keep trying until you come up with a name that hasn't been used before.

When all of this setup information is complete, your modem begins screaming and making a hideous racket, and you see an America Online logo screen that says things like "Checking Password."

Your password is checked to make sure you're not some high-school hoodlum trying to break into America Online's computers. Finally, if everything goes well, you're brought to this screen:

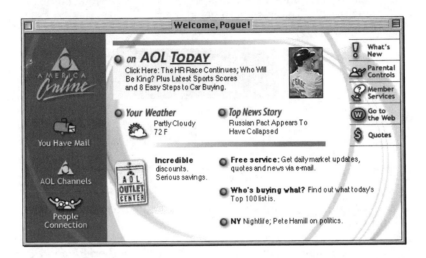

You also get to hear a recording of the famous Mr. Cheerful, the man who says "Welcome!" as though you're *just* the person he's been waiting for all day. If you've got e-mail waiting, he also says "You've got mail!," which he's *really* happy about. (To read the mail, click the "You Have Mail" icon.)

Exploring by icon

America Online, you'll quickly discover, is a collection of hundreds of individual screens, each of which represents a different service or company. Each day, several of them (one of which is always News) are advertised on the welcome screen. To jump directly to the advertised feature, click the corresponding icon.

On AOL, you don't always have to *double-click* to open icons, as you've learned to do on the Mac in general. Sometimes it's once, sometimes it's twice . . . come to think of it, just double-click all the time. An extra click won't hurt anything.

The broader America Online table of contents, however, appears when you click the AOL Channels button on the opening screen (older AOL versions look different):

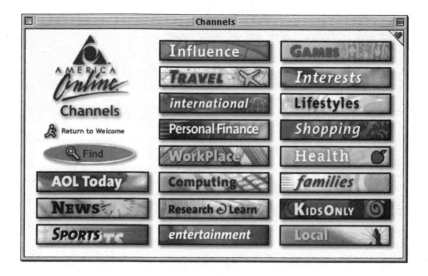

Each of these buttons takes you to yet another screen, where you can visit related services. For example:

- ✔ The *Research & Learn* (called Reference Desk in some versions) button lets you consult a dictionary, a national phone book, or a choice of encyclopedias.

- ✔ You can get actual, updated-hourly headlines and news articles — plus sports, weather, entertainment, and so on — by clicking the *News* button.

- ✔ The *Personal Finance* page is stock-market city: You can check quotes, actually buy and sell, get mutual-fund stats, read tax and investing advice, and so on.

- ✔ Another one of those "You can do *that* online?" features: If you click the *Travel* button, you can actually look up plane fares and even make reservations.

Navigating by keyword

If you poked around enough, clicking icons and opening screen after screen, you'd eventually uncover everything America Online has to offer. In the meantime, however, you'd run up your phone bill, develop mouse elbow, and watch four presidential administrations pass.

A much faster navigational trick is the *keyword* feature. A keyword is like an elevator button that takes you directly to any of the hundreds of features on AOL, making no stops along the way.

To use a keyword in America Online version 3 or earlier, choose Keyword from the Go To menu or press ⌘-K. You get this box:

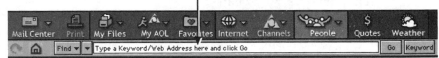

```
┌──────────────────────── Keyword ────────────────────────┐
│                                                          │
│  Keyword                                                 │
│  Type an AOL Keyword or Web address in the input box, then click Go.  │
│                                                          │
│  Enter word(s):     │books                          │   │
│                                                          │
│        [    Go    ]    [  Keyword List  ]    [  Help  ]  │
│                                                          │
└──────────────────────────────────────────────────────────┘
```

Type the name of your destination into the blank and press Return.

In America Online 4, just type the keyword of your choice directly into this strip at the top of the screen:

Type a keyword here

When you press Return, you're teleported directly to that service.

A few of your favorite things

Here are a few typical AOL services, along with their keywords. Arm yourself with this list so that you make the most of your free ten-hour trial.

Keyword	Where It Takes You
Access	A list of local phone numbers for America Online. Use this before a trip to another city.
Banking	Check your accounts, pay bills, and so on (certain banks only).
Beginners	A collection of help topics for Mac newcomers.
Billing	Current billing info, disputes, and so on.
Classifieds	Classified ads. Read 'em for free; place 'em for a fee.

Keyword	Where It Takes You
Encyclopedia	Your choice of several different published encyclopedias. You just saved $900!
Help	Assistance about America Online itself.
Homework	A place for students to get live, interactive help with homework and research.
Macgame	Files, messages, and discussions of Mac games.
Mall	A whole mess of mail-order catalogs, from which you can order online.
News	Double-click the headline you want to read.
PCFN	Financial advice, news, and online discount brokers.
Sports	Latest sports scores in every pro sport.
Star Trek	*Star Trek*
Stocks	Check the current price of any stock. You can even see your current portfolio value.
Tech Live	"Chat" (by typing) with an actual live human being (well, live online) who'll try to help you with AOL problems.
Travel	Advice and info about traveling: passport info, travel guides, horror stories.

And how, you may well ask, do you find out what the keyword *is* for something you're looking for? Easy — just type in keyword: "keyword"! You'll get a screen that offers a complete list of keywords.

How to get back to the good stuff

With several hundred places worth visiting on AOL — and several *million* places worth visiting on the Internet — it'd be nice if there were a way to mark your place. Suppose you stumble onto this *great* English Cocker Spaniel Owners' area, for example, but you've already forgotten which buttons you clicked to get there.

Simple solution: On every America Online screen or *Web page* (described later in the chapter), there's a tiny red heart in the upper-right corner. When you're looking at a screen you might someday like to return to, click that heart:

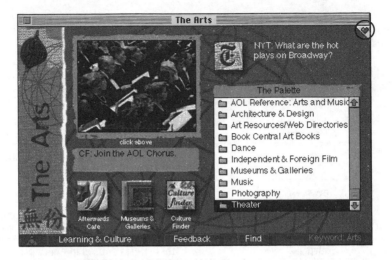

You'll be asked if you want to add this screen to your Favorite Places; click OK.

Well, great: Now you've added it to the list of places you may want to visit again. But how do you *see* your list?

  ✔ **America Online 3 or earlier:** From the Go To menu, choose Favorite Places. Or click the heart icon on the toolbar at the top of your screen.

  ✔ **America Online 4:** Use the Favorite Places icon/menu, like this:

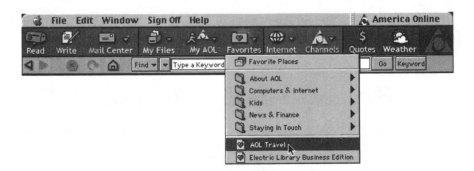

From here, just choose something's name to go there.

To delete something from this list, open the Favorite Places window like this:

  ✔ **America Online 3 or earlier:** From the Go To menu, choose Favorite Places.

  ✔ **America Online 4:** From the Favorite Places icon/menu, choose the very first command (Favorite Places).

Now, just click a place's name once and then choose Clear from the Edit menu.

The e-mail connection

Naturally, one of the best things about America Online is the e-mail — mainly the sheer, ego-boosting joy of *getting* some.

If, in fact, anybody has bothered to write to you (which you'll hear announced by Mr. "You've got mail!"), click the You've Got Mail button on the welcome screen to see your messages. After you've read the message, you can (a) reply to it (by clicking the Reply button); (b) save it on your hard disk (by choosing Save from the File menu); or (c) close its window without saving it. If you do that, the message hangs around in your Old Mail folder for about one more week, then disappears forever.

To *send* a message to somebody, choose Compose Mail from the Mail menu (before AOL version 4), or click Write on the toolbar (version 4), or press ⌘-M (any version). Type your lucky recipient's e-mail address, a subject, and your message in the appropriate blanks. (Don't forget to press the Tab key to move from blank to blank.) When you're done typing, just press Enter (or click the Send Now button). This picture is from AOL version 4, but the elements (although moved around) are the same in previous versions:

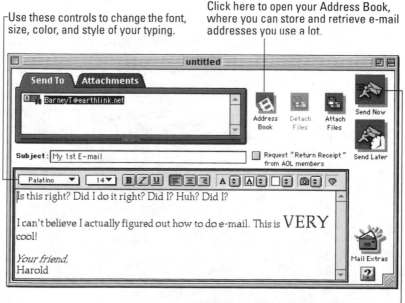

Use these controls to change the font, size, color, and style of your typing.

Click here to open your Address Book, where you can store and retrieve e-mail addresses you use a lot.

Click here to send your mail (or press the Enter key).

If you need to look up somebody's screen name, use keyword: *members*.

The party line

By far the most mind-blowing aspect of AOL is, of course, the *chat rooms*. In a chat room, you'll find up to 23 people chatting away (by typing). The nutty thing is that everybody's talking at once, so the conversation threads overlap, and hilarious results sometimes ensue:

```
Kiwi:       Since we're discussing computer terms, maybe
            someone can tell me what's this Scuzzy thing in
            my Mac? My friend Pauline told me it's a type of
            screen saver.
The King:   I totally disagree, Uhuru. Spock never said he
            had a sister.
Weinstein:  Actually, it's SCSI, Kiwi. And no, it's not a
            screen saver.
Uhura:      How about the one where Bones falls in love with
            that woman, but it turns out, in fact, that
            she's really a salt creature...?
The King:   Was it salt? I thought it had something to do
            with antimatter pods.
```

Nonetheless, the chat rooms are an unusual social opportunity: For the first time, you can be the total belle of the ball (or stud of the studio) — the wittiest, charmingest, best-liked person — without so much as combing your hair.

To get to the chat rooms, use keyword: *lobby* (or click the appropriate toolbar icon). If you click the button called "find a chat," "List Chats," or "Rooms," you'll discover that dozens of parties are transpiring simultaneously, each founded on a different topic. Double-click a room's name to go there.

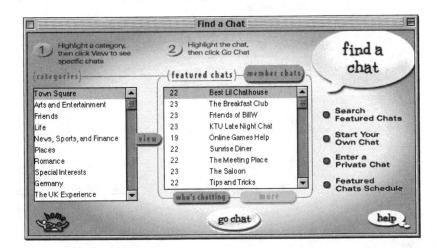

Things to know before entering the Party Zone

If it's your first time in a chat room, you may be nonplused by the gross excesses of punctuation that seem to go on there. Every five minutes, it seems that somebody types {{{{{{{{ Jennifer!!!}}}}}}}} or ****BabyBones!****

Actually, there's nothing wrong with these peoples' keyboards. The braces are the cyberspace equivalent of hugging the enclosed person; the asterisks are kisses. That's how you greet friends who enter the room — online, anyway.

You may also see a colon festival now and then. Somebody might say ":::::quaking in fear:::::." Don't ask where that designation came from, but it indicates some kind of action — the writer claims to be *doing* whatever is written there.

Finally, you sometimes see a crude typed *arrow* pointing to the left, like this:

FrogMan: < —— has no life

This, naturally, indicates that this person is pointing to himself.

Talking behind their backs

What makes the live chats even more fun is that you can whisper directly into the ear of anybody there — and nobody else can hear you.

This kind of behind-the-scenes direct communication is called an Instant Message. To send one, choose Send Instant Message from the Members menu (or press ⌘-I). You get a box like this:

As soon as you type your whispered message and click Send (or press Enter), the window disappears from your screen — and reappears on the recipient's screen! That person can then whisper back to you.

Meanwhile, somebody *else* in the room may have been Instant-Messaging *you:*

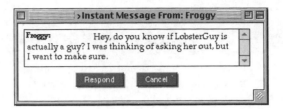

If you try to maintain your presence in the main window *and* keep your end of all these whispered conversations in *their* little windows, the hilarity builds. *Nothing* makes a better typist out of you than the AOL chat rooms.

How to find — and get — free software

Of course, for many people, the best part of AOL is the free software. Heck, for many people, that's the *only* part of AOL.

Here's how it works:

1. **Click the Disk icon on the toolbar (version 3) or use keyword:** *filesearch* **(any version).**

   A window appears. If it offers you a choice of Commercial or Shareware, click the Shareware button.

2. **Type the name of the file (or kind of file) you're looking for.**

3. **Press Return (or click Search).**

In a moment, you're shown a complete listing of all files in the AOL data banks that match your search criteria. Keep in mind that roughly 300,000 files hang out on those computers in Virginia, so choose your search words with care.

You can restrict your search by using the little checkboxes. For example, if you wanted to find a picture of Santa to use as clip art in a Christmas card you're designing, you could click the Graphics checkbox and search for the word *Santa.* After clicking Search, you'd get a list of 200 Santa Claus pictures.

If you think a file sounds good, double-click its name to read a description. If it *still* sounds good, click Download Now. Your modem will begin the task of *downloading* (transferring) the picture file to your hard drive.

Be sure to read "When You Can't Open Your Downloaded Goodies," later in this chapter, for a follow-up discussion on downloading stuff.

Signing up for an Internet Account (ISP)

If you've decided to sign up for a direct Internet connection (instead of going the America Online route), send a thank-you note to Apple; in Mac OS 8 and later, signing up for such an account is as easy as signing up for AOL. (If you have something *before* Mac OS 8, getting started with a direct Internet account is somewhat harder. You have no choice but to contact the ISP company you hope to sign up with — EarthLink, MindSpring, Concentric, or whatever — and follow the instructions they give you.)

Here's how to get started. Locate (in Mac OS 8 or later) the icon called Internet Setup Assistant. (It's probably right there on your desktop or in the Internet Access command of your menu. If not, use your Find command to locate it, as described in Chapter 4.)

The Internet Setup Assistant walks you through a series of screens, asking for your name, address, credit-card number, and so on. Your modem dials an 800 number. After a moment, you're shown either the EarthLink ISP's sign-up screen (if you have Mac OS 8.5 or an iMac) — or the logos of several Internet-access companies, like this:

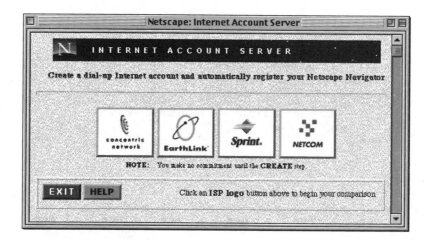

Click a logo to read about the terms of that company's offerings. (The main criterion: Do they offer a modem phone number that's local for you?)

After you've read all about your options, you'll be asked to click onto additional screens and complete the application process. Along the way, you'll be asked to make up a cyber-name for yourself (such as *CashewNut83*) and a password that protects your account.

When it's all over, you'll be an official, card-carrying member of the Internet. Now you, too, can have an e-mail address with an @ sign on your business card. Now you, too, can banter at cocktail parties about the ghastly new color scheme on the Microsoft Web site. Now you, too, can slowly drift away from family, job, and reality as you recede into cyber-hermitdom.

Now it's time to discover What's on the Internet (read on).

What's on the Internet

On the following pages, you'll read about the various things you can do on the Internet. The most useful of these features are called *e-mail, newsgroups, FTP,* and the *World Wide Web.*

As you read, keep in mind that all of these features are available to you regardless of whether you have an AOL account or a real Internet (ISP) account. The difference is that with an ISP account, you generally need a separate software program to access each Internet feature; with an AOL account, the only software you need is the AOL program you've always used.

E-mail

If you have America Online, see "The e-mail connection" earlier in this chapter. If you've signed up for an ISP instead, see Chapter 14. Either way, get psyched for a feature that'll change your life; as a technology, e-mail ranks right up there with cable TV, frequent-flyer miles, and microwave popcorn.

Newsgroups

The next important Internet feature is called *newsgroups.* Don't be fooled: They have nothing to do with news, and they're not groups. That's the Internet for ya.

Instead, newsgroups are electronic bulletin boards. I post a message; anyone else on the Internet can read it and post a response for all to see. Then somebody else responds to *that* message, and so on.

By the way: You might notice, in the following illustration, that the writer is somewhat nastier online than he might have been in your living room. That's an interesting Internet lesson — people tend to be ruder than they would in person. There are two reasons: First, you're anonymous — nobody can see you, so it doesn't seem to matter as much if you're a jerk. Second, millions of messages appear here every day; some people think they need to be extra-dramatic just to be noticed.

The little > symbols mean that this portion of the message is being quoted from a previous message, so everyone will know what this guy is responding to.

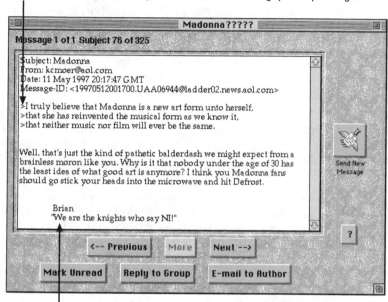

It's typical for Internet weenies to sign their names with some kind of whimsical quotation. Don't ask me why; personally, it drives me crazy.

There are about 20,000 different newsgroups, ongoing discussions on every topic — chemists who like bowling, left-handed oboists, Mickey Mouse fans who live in Bali — anything. Here's how you reach these discussion areas:

- ✔ **On America Online:** Use keyword: *newsgroups*. If you then click Read My Newsgroups, you see a starter list of topics; just keep double-clicking topics that interest you until you're reading the actual messages. (To add newsgroup topics to your starter list, use the Search All Newsgroups button.)

  Once you've read a message, you can either respond to it (click the Send New Message button) or just keep reading (click the Next→ button).

- ✔ **With an ISP:** To read newsgroups if you have a direct Internet account, use a program like Outlook Express, a free program that's included with Mac OS 8 and later — or you can get it from *www.microsoft.com*. (If that last part is gibberish to you, read the next chapter.)

Once you're online and running Outlook Express, click the Microsoft News Server icon on the screen. You'll be shown a new window containing dozens of newsgroups that all pertain to Microsoft software.

Now, I'll be the first to admit that reading about Microsoft products all day is not what you'd call, er, realizing the full potential of the Internet. Therefore, if you think you're up for the full list of 20,000 discussion topics, call up your ISP and ask: "What's your *news server address?*" They'll tell you what theirs is — a long Internet code like *news-s01.ny.us.ibm.net.*

From Outlook Express's Edit menu, choose Preferences, click the News icon, click New Server, type *Newsgroup List* (or something), click OK, tab to the Server Address blank, and type out the long Internet code your ISP gave you. Click OK.

From now on, whenever you feel like reading several million bulletin-board notes, launch Outlook Express. You'll see an icon called *Newsgroup List* (or whatever you called it) at the left side of the screen; double-click it. Finally, from the View menu, choose Get Complete Newsgroup List. Wait five minutes for the full list of thousands to arrive on your screen — and then, at last, you can begin reading the messages on the world's largest bulletin board. Just double-click a topic name; choose Refresh Message List from the View menu; and then double-click a message name to read it. (Click the Reply icon at the top of the window if you'd like to respond to something somebody has written. But be nice.)

I realize that this involves 500 steps, but as I said, nobody ever called the Internet easy.

FTP (software to download)

FTP is short for *file transfer protocol.* (Doesn't it make you feel more technically competent just *saying* that?) FTP just means software to download: games, *shareware* programs (written by amateur programmers; you pay by the honor system), and so on. It's not what you'd call user-friendly; most people ignore it altogether.

To gather some software using FTP, try this:

✔ **On America Online:** If you're accessing the Internet through AOL, using FTP may seem a little silly, since it's *way* easier to just get whatever-you're-looking-for directly from the incredibly complete software collection on AOL (see "How to find — and get — free software," earlier in this chapter).

If you want to do it the Internet way, though, here's what you do. Use keyword: *FTP.* Then click the Go To FTP button.

✔ **With an ISP account:** If you've got an Internet account, you can access FTP libraries using your ordinary Web browser, described in the next chapter; just type the address of the FTP library (which always begins with *ftp://*) into the address strip at the top of the window.

The World Wide Web

Except for e-mail, by far the most popular and useful Internet feature is the World Wide Web. In fact, it gets a chapter all to itself (the next chapter). For now, all you need to know is this:

✔ **On America Online:** A Web browser is built right into your AOL software. In many cases, you wind up on the Web just by innocently clicking some button within AOL — that's how tightly the Web is integrated with America Online these days.

✔ **With an ISP account:** You have your choice of two free Web-browsers: Netscape Navigator and Microsoft Internet Explorer, both described in the next chapter.

How to Hang Up

When you're finished with an America Online session, hanging up is no big deal; just choose Quit from the File menu. The AOL program quits, making your phone line available once again to the other members of your family — such as your spouse, child, and fax machine.

Getting off the Internet if you have a direct Internet account (ISP), however, is trickier. Allow me to propose an analogy: Imagine that you call another branch of your family tree on New Year's Day. You yourself place the call, but then you hand the phone off to various other family members. "And now here's little Timmy! Timmy, talk to Grandma. . . ."

Using the Internet works the same way. Your Mac places the call. But aside from tying up the phone line, your Mac doesn't actually *do* anything until you launch one of the programs you've read about in this chapter: an e-mail program or a Web browser, for example. Each of these Internet programs is like one of your family members, chatting with the Big Internet Grandma for a few minutes apiece.

The point here: When you quit your e-mail or Web program, *the phone line is still tied up,* just as though Timmy, when finished talking to Grandma, put the phone on the couch and wandered out to play. When you're finished Internet-ting, therefore, you should end the phone call by doing one of the following:

✔ From your ✦ menu, choose Control Panels, and open the one called PPP, Remote Access, or FreePPP (whichever you have). Click the Disconnect button.

✔ Wait. After about 15 minutes (or whatever time you've specified in the abovementioned PPP, Remote Access, or FreePPP control panel), your Mac hangs up automatically.

✔ If you have Mac OS 8.5 or later, choose Remote Access Status from your ✦ menu and click Disconnect.

✔ Or — here's another Mac OS 8.5-or-later feature — choose Disconnect from the Remote Access tile on your Control Strip (see Chapter 8), like this:

When You Can't Open Your Downloaded Goodies

It's easy to download software — either from America Online or the Internet. Maybe you find something on a Web page worth downloading (see the next chapter). Maybe somebody sends you a family picture as a file that's attached to an e-mail. Unfortunately, the first word out of the beginning downloader's mouth, upon examining the freshly downloaded loot, is generally this:

"Wha — ?"

First of all, people often can't *find* whatever-it-was that they downloaded. (***Hint:*** Downloaded stuff usually winds up in a folder called Downloads, inside the folder of the Internet program you were using — inside the America Online folder, the Claris Emailer folder, the Outlook Express folder, and so on.)

Second of all, the first thing many people read when they double-click a file they've just downloaded is this: "The application is busy or missing."

And *that's* because of *compression*. As you sit there waiting for your Santa Claus graphic to arrive on your Mac, you're tying up the phone line and drumming your fingers. Therefore, almost everything on America Online (or the Internet, or *anywhere* in cyberspace, for that matter) arrives in a compact, encoded format that takes less time to transfer.

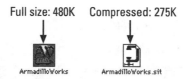

Full size: 480K   Compressed: 275K

ArmadilloWorks   ArmadilloWorks.sit

Which is terrific, except for one thing: How are *you* supposed to expand your downloaded file back into usable form?

Expand-o-matic

Any file whose format is indicated by the suffix *.sit* has been "stuffed" using a program called StuffIt. As an added convenience, the America Online software unstuffs these files *automatically* when you log off the service.

If a file's name ends in *.sea,* it's a *self-expanding archive*. You don't need *any* little program to unlock these babies — all you have to do is double-click the .sea file, and it unfolds automatically into its usable, fatter form.

Okay, this is all well and good for America Online users. But what if (a) you're getting your goodies straight from the Internet, or (b) the letters at the end of your precious loot's name *aren't* ".sit" or ".sea"? Ohhh, noooo, don't think the geniuses behind the Internet would do anything as simple as confining themselves to *one* compressed-file type. That would be *way* too logical.

The solution to all of these problems is the one-size-fits-all, does-it-automatically, set-it-and-forget-it answer to the downloader's prayers: StuffIt Expander. It comes on every new Mac (use your Find command!), or you can download it from AOL or www.aladinsys.com.

Once you install this little program (just by double-clicking), it gracefully re-expands just about any geeky Internet file you drop on it, from *.sit* to *.cpt* and *.hqx*. While you're at it, you may as well download its companion program, too, called, awkwardly enough, DropStuff with Expander Enhancer — it's a little steroid pill that lets StuffIt Expander *also* open *.gz, .z, .ARC, .ZIP,* and *.uu* files, too.

After you've got this thing safely installed on your hard drive, here's the handy two-step scheme for expanding something you downloaded from cyberspace:

1. Drag the downloaded mystery item on top of the StuffIt Expander icon.

2. Your downloaded mystery item is automatically restored to human form.

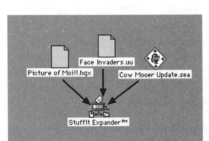

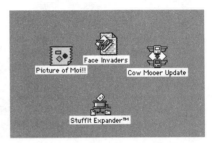

The only thing the illustration doesn't make clear is that, after the expanding process is over, the original, compressed .sit file is *still there,* along with the actual, unstuffed goodie. You should feel absolutely guilt-free about simply throwing the now-worthless .sit file into the Trash.

After it's expanded

But even *after* unstuffing your downloaded prize, you may not be immediately aware of how to open it. For example, suppose you've just downloaded what's described as a "numbingly gorgeous full-color 24-bit photo of the *Letterman* show's Paul Shaffer having soup." There it sits on your hard drive, and you've even unstuffed it from its original *.sit* condition. Yet when you double-click the icon, you get the dreaded message:

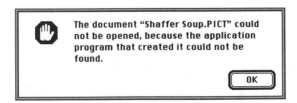

Wha — ?

In this case, you've got yourself the Classic Graphics File Dilemma: You've downloaded a graphic — whose name, even *after* being decompressed, ends with *.GIF, .JPEG, .TIFF,* or *.PICT* — but don't know how to open it. The solution is simple: You *first* have to launch a program that can open such graphics, like ClarisWorks, Photoshop, Netscape Navigator, America Online itself, or even most word processing programs. Once that program is running, *then* you can use the Open command. Navigate until you spot the file you're trying to open:

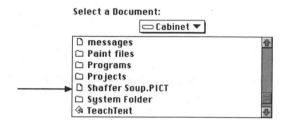

 At last, the prize is yours. If it's a graphics file that none of your current programs can seem to open, consider tracking down a super-graphics-opening shareware program, such as GraphicConverter. Like everything else worth getting in this life, you can download *it* from America Online or the Internet, too.

Top Ten Best/Worst Aspects of the Net

No question: The Internet is changing everything. If you're not on it now, you probably will be within a few years. Here's what's to look forward to:

1. Best: Everyone is anonymous, so everyone is equal. It doesn't matter what you look, sound, or smell like — you're judged purely by your words.

2. Worst: Everyone is anonymous, so everyone is equal. You can pretend to be someone you're not — or a *gender* you're not — for the purposes of misleading other Internet surfers.

3. Best: the cost. $20 a month for unlimited access.

4. Worst: the cost. $20 a month is a lot, especially when you consider the required equipment.

5. Best: The Internet connects you to everyone. You're only an e-mail or a Web-page away from anyone else on the planet.

6. Worst: The Internet *disconnects* you from everyone. You become a hermit holed up in your room, as family, friends, and relationships pack up and leave.

7. Best: The Internet is drawing people away from TV. Statistics show that as more people discover the Web, they spend less time in front of the boob tube.

8. Worst: The Internet is drawing people away from TV. The TV industry is going crazy wondering what to do.

9. Best: The Internet is complete freedom of speech for everyone. No government agency looks over your shoulder; the Net is completely unsupervised and uncontrolled.

10. Worse: The Internet is complete freedom of speech for everyone. Including pornographers, neo-Nazi groups, and others you may not want your 10-year-old getting chummy with.

Chapter 12

The Weird Wild Web

In This Chapter

- The who, where, what, and why of the World Wide Web
- A warm welcome to the wiles of World Wide Web software
- Netscape Navigator and Microsoft Internet Explorer

The most popular part of the Internet is the World Wide Web — you can't help hearing about this thing. Fourth graders run around urging schoolmates to "check out their Web pages." Web "addresses" show up everywhere — on business cards, in newspaper ads, on TV. (Have you noticed *www.sony.com* or *www.spam.com* flashing by at the end of movie ads and car commercials? Those are Web addresses.)

The Web has become incredibly popular for one simple reason: It *isn't* geeky and user-hostile, like the rest of the Internet. It looks friendly and familiar to actual humans. When you connect to the Web, you don't encounter streams of computer codes. Instead, information is displayed attractively, with nice typesetting, color pictures, and interactive buttons.

Internet Made Idiotproof: Link-Clicking

Navigating the Web requires little more than clicking buttons and those underlined blue phrases, which you can sort of see in the following figure.

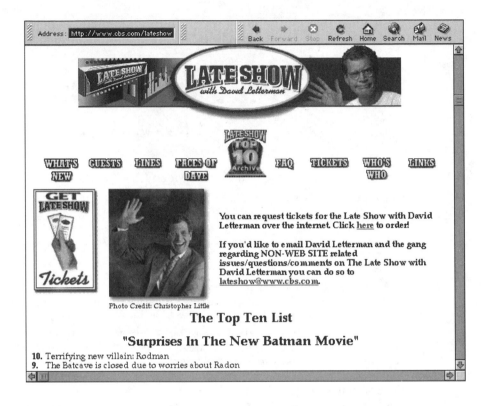

When you click an underlined phrase, called a *link,* you're automatically transported from one "page" (screen) to another, without having to type in the usual bunch of Internet codes. One page may be a glorified advertisement; another may contain critical information about a bill in Congress; another might have been created by a 9-year-old in Dallas, documenting what her dog had for lunch.

Unfortunately, all of this amazing online multimedia stuff stresses your modem nearly to the breaking point. Even with a 56 Kbps modem, the fastest standard modem there is, you still wait five or ten seconds for *each* Web page to float onto your screen. Don't even try connecting to the Web with a 14.4 Kbps (or slower) modem.

Getting to the Web via America Online

If you've got America Online version 3, you're on the Web with a single click on the toolbar globe, as shown in the following picture. (If you don't *have* a toolbar, choose Toolbar from the Windows menu.) If you have America Online 4, choose "Go to the Web" from the Internet icon, as shown here:

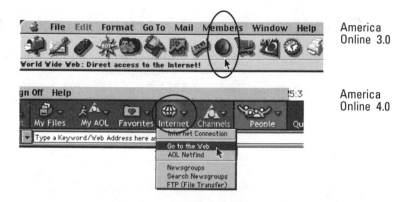

America
Online 3.0

America
Online 4.0

If you've been given a particular Web address to visit (such as *www.hamsters.com*), you can also treat it as a keyword. (See the previous chapter for instructions on using keywords.) That is, type in that Web address into the Keyword box (or the strip at the top of the AOL 4.0 screen); it'll automatically open up a Web window and take you to the appropriate page.

Getting to the Web via an ISP

If you've signed up for a direct Internet account (through an *ISP*, as described in the previous chapter) instead of America Online, you'll be using a special program for browsing the Web — called, with astounding originality, a *Web browser.*

Most people use either Netscape Navigator or Microsoft Internet Explorer browser. Both are free; both come with the Macintosh (if you have Mac OS 8 or later) or with the startup kit from your chosen ISP company.

How do you choose which browser to use? In a nutshell, Navigator is faster, but doesn't have many features. Explorer is slower, but has a lot of nice features (such as the ability to turn off blinking animations on Web pages, which otherwise drive you quietly mad).

To go a-browsing, launch your Web browser. Your Mac should dial the phone automatically, hiss and shriek, and finally show you a Web page.

Where to Go, What to Do on the Web

Once you're staring at your first Web page — whether via America Online or an Internet access company — getting around is easy. (The picture below shows Netscape Navigator, but you'll find the same basic elements in Internet Explorer, too.) Just *look* at all the fun things to see and do on the Web!

A. Click the Back button to revisit the page you were just on — or the Forward button to return to the page you were on *before* you clicked the Back button. (Does that make sense?)

B. Type a new Web page address into the thin horizontal strip at the top of the browser window and press Return to go to the site. A Web address, just so you know, is known by the geeks as a *URL* — pronounced "U. R. L."

And where do you find good Web addresses? From friends, from articles, on television, and so on. Look for *http://* or *www* at the beginning of the address — a guaranteed sign that the address points to a Web page.

C. Enjoy the little animated meteor shower in the upper-right-corner logo. It means "Wait a sec, I'm not done painting this Web page picture for you. As long as I'm animating, you'll just have to wait." (Explorer 4's indicator is a progress bar at the *lower*-right corner of your window.)

D. Clicking a picture or a button often takes you to a new Web page.

E. Clicking blue underlined phrases (called *links*) *always* takes you to a different Web page. (As a handy bonus, these links change to some other color when you see them next. That's to remind you that you've been that way before.)

F. Click in a Search blank and type what you're looking for. (Click the Search button when you're finished typing.) Similar blanks appear when, for example, you're asked to fill out a survey, type in your mailing address, and so on.

G. When you see a picture you'd like to keep, point to it, hold down the mouse button, and watch for a pop-up menu to appear at your cursor tip. From this pop-up menu, choose "Save this Image as" (in Navigator) or "Download Image to Disk" (in Explorer). After you click the Save button, the result is a new icon on your hard drive — a graphics file containing the picture you saved.

H. Use the scroll bar to move up and down the page — or to save mousing, just press the space bar each time you want to see more.

Ways to search for a particular topic

Suppose you're looking at the Kickboxing Haiku Web page. But now you want to check the weather in Detroit. Because the World Wide Web is indeed a big interconnected web, you could theoretically work your way from one Web page to another to another, clicking just the right blue underlined links, until you finally arrived at the Detroit Weather page.

Unfortunately, there are about 200 million Web pages. By the time you actually arrived at the Detroit Weather page, the weather would certainly have changed (not to mention Detroit). Clearly, you need to be able to *look something up* — to jump directly to another Web page whose address you don't currently know.

For this purpose, the denizens of the Web have seen fit to create a few very special Web pages — whose sole function is to search all the *other* Web pages. If you're on the Web, and don't know where to look for, say, information about Venezuelan Beaver Cheese, you can use the Find commands at any of the following sites:

> ✔ *www.yahoo.com*
>
> ✔ *www.altavista.com*
>
> ✔ *www.infoseek.com*
>
> ✔ *www.lycos.com*
>
> ✔ *www.hotbot.com*

All of these search pages work alike. Here, for example, is what it would look like if you used the search page called Yahoo! (the first address listed above) to find information about Venezuelan Beaver Cheese:

After clicking the Search button, you'd be shown a brand new Web page listing *hits* — that is, Web pages containing the words "Venezuelan," "Beaver," or "Cheese":

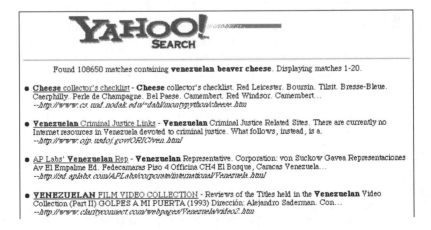

See how useful a search page is? This handy Yahoo! thing narrowed down our search to a mere *108,650 Web pages!* You're as good as home!

Not. You can see here, in a nutshell, the problem with the Web: There's so much darned stuff out there, you spend an *awful* lot of your time trying to find exactly what you want. In this case, we probably should have clicked the little Help button on the main Yahoo! screen. It would have told us that to find a page containing the three words "Venezuelan Beaver Cheese" *together,* as a phrase, we should have put quote marks around them. That would have ruled out all the "hits" containing sentences like, "The beaver population has been halved by pollution. In this photo, Venezuelan cleanup engineer José Sanchez says 'Cheese!' for the camera."

Who ever said these things were user-friendly?

Useful Web pages: The tip of the iceberg

But there's more to the Web than getting meaningful work done (as millions of American office workers can attest). Here are some good starting places for your leisure hours. Technically, each of their addresses begins with *http://,* but you can leave that off. Your Web browser will supply those letters automatically when you're finished typing.

(Disclaimer: Web pages come and go like New York City restaurants. I guarantee only that these pages existed the day I typed them up.)

- *mistral.culture.fr/louvre* — The Louvre museum home page, where you can actually view and read about hundreds of paintings hanging there.

- *amazon.com* — An enormous online bookstore, with 2.5 million books available, all at 20 percent discount (or better). Reviews, sample chapters, the works. Don't freak out about typing in your credit-card number online; you're far more likely to be ripped off by handing your Visa card to the gas-station attendant or restaurant waiter.

- *www.dilbert.com* — Today's Dilbert cartoon. And a month of past issues.

- *www.shopper.com* — Here, you can comparison shop among hundreds of computer-stuff mail-order catalogs instantaneously — with the results listed in price order.

- *pathfinder.com* — The electronic editions of popular magazines like *People, Time, Money, Fortune,* and more. Lots of graphics — nice, if you're willing to wait for the pictures to arrive.

- *www._____.com* — Fill in the blank with your favorite major company: Honda, Sony, ABC, Apple, CBS, Disney, NY Times, Macworld, McDonald's. Try it — you'll like it.

- *www.davidpogue.com* — The charming, attractive, and highly entertaining Web page of your eminently modest author.

Navigator versus Explorer: The Tip-O-Rama

Unless you're an America Online subscriber, you spend much of your Internetting time using the Netscape Navigator or Microsoft Internet Explorer browser.

Their makers, Netscape and Microsoft, are bigger rivals than Rocky Balboa and Apollo Creed (or whatever his opponent's name was). Each company has vowed to keep beating up the other until it crawls out of the ring with puffy black eyes screaming, "ADRIANNN!"

One unpleasant aspect of this rivalry is that, as they upgrade their browsers every few months by slathering on new features, these software companies tend to rush the resulting browser to market half-finished. It's a rare Mac fan who doesn't experience crashes and freezes (see Chapter 15) during ordinary Web browsing, for example, thanks to the bugginess of these programs. (Actually, Navigator 4.05 and 4.07 are pretty solid — versions before those, however, were about as stable as Seinfeld's girlfriends.)

Anyway: Unlike your America Online-subscriber comrades, you, O Internet subscriber, swallowed hard and opted for a hard-core, bona fide *ISP account,* as described in the previous chapter. One of the perks of doing so is a raft of cool features in your Web browser. Here, for example, are some time-savers and little-known features that work in both major browsers.

Type almost nothing

As you may have read earlier in this chapter, most Web addresses take the form *http://www.Spam.com,* where *Spam* is the name of the company or place. Thank goodness, you don't have to type all that! You can type (into that top strip where the address goes) *just the name of the company* — such as Apple, Microsoft, IBM, Snapple, Mentos, Pepsi, McDonalds, Spam, and so on. The browser fills in all the *http:// . . . com* junk for you automatically.

Go get the plug-in

Web browsers can show you text and pictures. But every now and then, you'll stumble onto some page where a *sound* or a *movie* is the main attraction. Unfortunately, Navigator and Explorer don't know how to play these multimedia morsels — but they know somebody who does!

What I'm driving at is *plug-ins* — small add-on programs that, once installed in the Plug-Ins *folder* on your hard drive, teach Navigator or Explorer *how* to play those extra goodies like sounds and movies. Plug-ins are free; you just have to know where to go to get them on the Web. Lucky you: I'm about to tell you.

Go to the Web address *www.plugins.com* or, if you feel like typing today, *http://home.netscape.com/plugins/index.html.* There you'll find all the little plug-ins looking for a home on your Mac. The most useful ones are:

- ✔ The *QuickTime* plug-in, which — if you're willing to wait a very long time before the movie starts — lets you watch little movies on the screen. Also available from *www.apple.com.*

- ✔ The *RealPlayer* plug-in, which lets you hear live radio broadcasts (and other recordings) over the Internet. Also available from *www.realaudio.com,* which also lists some of the broadcasts available for listening.

- ✔ The *Shockwave* plug-in, which makes a lot of splashy on-screen games and other animated snazziness possible on Web pages. Also available from *www.macromedia.com.*

I'm not saying you can't live a long, healthy, fulfilling life without any of this stuff. I'm just pointing them out in case you try to visit some Web page and get nothing but an error message saying something like, "Sorry, you can't visit this page until you spend all afternoon downloading and installing Such-N-Such™ plug-in."

Where's home for you?

Every time you sign onto the Web, your browser starts by showing you the same darned starting page — let me guess: the browser company's page. Yeah, that's *realllll* interesting. Wouldn't it be great if you could change the startup page?

You can! From the Edit menu, choose Preferences. Click the icon at the left side of the screen that says Navigator (in Navigator) or Home/Search (in Internet Explorer), as shown here:

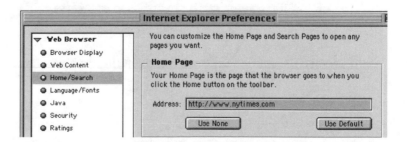

Now just change the Web address in the Home blank to a more desirable starting point. For example, you might prefer *www.apple.com,* which is all about Apple . . . or *www.macintouch.com,* which is daily news about the Mac . . . or even your own home page, if you've made one.

Faster — please, make it faster!

If the slug-like speed of the Web is making you sob quietly into your late-night coffee, despair no more. You can quadruple the speed of your Web surfing activities — by *turning off the pictures.*

Yes, I realize that graphics are what make the Web look so compelling. But all those pictures are 90 percent of what takes Web pages so darned long to arrive on the screen! You owe it to yourself to try, just for a session or two, turning graphics *off.* You still get fully laid-out Web pages; you still see all the text and headlines. But wherever a picture would normally be — wherever you would have had to wait for eight seconds — you'll see an empty rectangle containing a generic "graphic goes here" logo. Here, for example, is the Macworld magazine page (*www.Macworld.com,* of course) with all its graphics gone:

If you like the sound of this arrangement, here's how to make it so:

✔ **Netscape Navigator 3:** From the Options menu, choose Auto Load Images so that it's no longer checked.

✔ **Netscape Communicator/Navigator 4:** From the Edit menu, choose Preferences. Click the Advanced button and then turn off Automatically Load Images.

✔ **Internet Explorer:** From the Edit menu, choose Preferences. Click Web Content and then turn off Show Pictures.

The speed you gain is incredible. And if you wind up on a Web page that seems naked and shivering without its pictures, you can choose to summon them all — just on this one page — by choosing Load Images or View Images from your browser's View menu.

Bookmark it

When you find a Web page you might like to visit again, you're not con-demned to writing the address on the edges of your monitor, like some kind of geeky bathroom graffiti. Instead, just choose Add Bookmark from the Bookmarks menu (in Navigator) or Add to Favorites from the Favorites menu (in Internet Explorer).

```
┌─────────────────────────────────────────────────────┐
│ Bookmarks                                            │
├─────────────────────────────────────────────────────┤
│ Add Bookmark                                     ⌘D  │
├─────────────────────────────────────────────────────┤
│ Honda                                                │
│ Welcome to McDonald's                                │
│ AltaVista Technology, Inc.                           │
│ World Wide Web Browsers                              │
│ MacInTouch Home Page                                 │
│ Pogue's Pages (David Pogue, computer-book author)    │
│ Welcome to Pizza Hut!                                │
│ Smartcode Software                                   │
│ Welcome to the Freshest World of Mentos!             │
│ Welcome to Snapple                                   │
└─────────────────────────────────────────────────────┘
```

You're rewarded by the plain-English appearance of that page's name in the Bookmarks (or Favorites) menu! Thereafter, the *next* time you want to visit that page, you don't have to remember *http://www.madmansdream.com* or whatever; you can just choose the page's name from your menu.

To get *rid* of something in your Bookmarks menu, choose Bookmarks from the Window menu (or choose Open Favorites from your Favorites menu). Click the page's name, and then press the Delete key.

Navigator: Drag a picture off the page

Here's one that works only in Netscape Navigator: When you spot a graphic you admire enough to save for later, here's a quick way to add it to your collection of files: Just drag it out of the Navigator window and onto your desktop, like this:

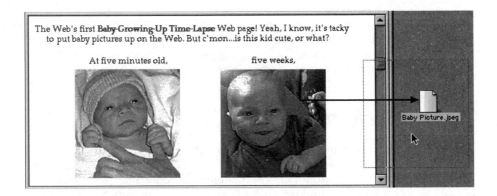

The picture turns into a Macintosh icon — a graphics file — that you and your descendants can double-click and enjoy for decades to come. (Until you trash it.)

Chapter 14

E-Mail for He-males and Females

∙ ∙

In This Chapter

▶ How to get, read, and write e-mail

▶ How to *enjoy* getting, reading, and writing e-mail

▶ The Anti-Junk-Mail Handbook

∙ ∙

*I*f you have any intention of getting the most from your expensive high-tech appliance, you *gotta* get into e-mail. E-mail has all the advantages of the telephone (instantaneous, personal) with none of the disadvantages (interrupts dinner, wakes you up). It also has all the advantages of postal mail (cheap, written, preservable) with none of *its* drawbacks (slow speed, hassle to reply, paper cuts).

Chapter 11 covers the glorious world of e-mail on America Online. If you're on the Internet courtesy of an Internet access company (an ISP), however, read on.

Getting into E-Mail

To read and write electronic mail, you need an e-mail program. The most popular are Claris Emailer and Microsoft Outlook Express; if you bought your Mac in 1997 or later, one or both probably came with it. (Emailer isn't sold any more, but several generations of Macs came with it, or its sister program, Emailer Lite. Outlook Express is free.)

If you can't find one of these programs lurking somewhere on your Mac, use the Find command, as described in Chapter 4, to look for *Emailer* or *Express*. If, on the other hand, you ordered a startup kit from your Internet access company, it probably came with one of these programs (or the very similar mail portion of Netscape Navigator), too. If you're patient, as a last resort, you can download Outlook Express for free from *www.microsoft.com* (see Chapter 12 if that's all Greek to you).

The grisliest part of joining the e-mail revolution is setting up your account for the first time. A dialog box like one of these appears when you first run the program:

Claris Emailer setup screen

Internet Account Entry

| Account Info | Options |

Account name: EarthLink acount

User name: Barney T. Dinosaur

Email account: barneyd

Email password: ••••

SMTP server: mail.earthlink.net

Email address: barneyd @earthlink.net

☐ Use Internet Config settings

[Change Password...] [Cancel] [Save]

● Proxies
▽ **Receiving Files**
● File Helpers

Outlook Express setup screen

Preferences

Mail Accounts:
EarthLink [New Account...]

Account Information

Full name: Barney T. Dinosaur

E-mail address: barneyd@earthlink.net

Organization:

Sending Mail

SMTP server: mail.earthlink.net

Receiving Mail

Account ID: barneyd

POP Server: mail.earthlink.net

☑ Save password: •••••

Account name: EarthLink

[Advanced...] [Make Default] [Remove Account]

All you have to do here is type in your SMTP address, account ID, and POP server ID.

Yeah, sure. Then after lunch, you can go out and write a thesis about molecular biophysics.

As you've probably figured out, we mere humans can't possibly figure out what to type into these boxes. To find out, you'll have to call up the Internet access company (EarthLink or whatever) and ask for help. The phone reps won't mind; they get calls for this information about 10,000 times a day.

An aside to the superstitious

No, there's no Chapter 13. There's never a 13th floor, either. It's an American tradition.

Sending E-Mail

To write an e-mail, choose New Message from the Mail menu (in Claris Emailer) or the File menu (Outlook Express). An empty e-mail message appears, filled with blanks to fill out. (The To, Subject, and message areas are the only mandatory ones.) Here's what your finished message might look like in Outlook Express:

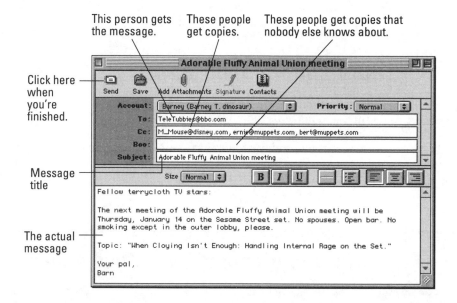

This person gets the message.

These people get copies.

These people get copies that nobody else knows about.

Click here when you're finished.

Message title

The actual message

As you'll quickly discover, e-mail addresses aren't allowed to have any spaces, always have an @ symbol in them, and must be typed *exactly* right, even if they look like *cc293fil@univ_amx.intermp.com*. Capitals don't matter.

When you're finished writing, click the Send or Send Now button at the top of the message window. If everything's set up right, your modem now dials and sends that e-message.

Sending mail in batches

If you click Send or Send Now as you write each e-mail, your Mac dials the Internet to send the single message you've just composed. In many cases, though, it's much nicer to be able to write *several* messages at a time — and send them all in a batch when you're good and ready.

If you have Outlook Express, choose Preferences from the Edit menu. Click the General icon, and turn off the checkbox called Send Message Immediately. If you have Claris Emailer, each time you finish writing a message, don't click Send Now; click Queue Message instead.

Either way, you've got a nice system now: As you write (or reply to e-mail) messages, they pile up in your Out Box. (Click the Out Box icon to see them.) When you're good and ready, choose Connect Now from the Mail menu (in Emailer) or click the Send & Receive icon (on the Outlook Express toolbar). Your modem dials and sends all of the mail at once — and *gets* all waiting mail from the Internet at the same time.

Auto-signing your mail

This *is* a computer, right? We got it under the assumption that it would save us time and make us more efficient, right?

For that reason, today's e-mail programs can stamp each outgoing message we write with our "signature" automatically — along the lines of "Love, Bob" or "Your pal, Ellen" or "Dr. Harold T. Higgenbottom, DDS, Serving the Greater Buffalo Area since 1993."

Three ways not to be loathed online

Like any foreign country, the Net has its own weird culture, including rules of etiquette that, if broken, will make nasty comments and snideness rain down upon the offender. If you want to be loved online, read up:

✔ **Don't type in ALL CAPITALS**. They'll *murder* you for that.

✔ **Don't ask what LOL means.** It stands for "laughing out loud." And while we're at it: IMHO is "in my humble opinion," ROTFL is "rolling on the floor laughing," and RTFM is "read the freakin' manual."

✔ **Quote back what you're responding to.** If someone e-mails you with a question, don't just write back, "No, I don't think so." The question-asker may have long since forgotten his/her own query!

Instead, begin your reply with the question itself. (On the Net, people generally put this quoted portion in <brackets,> like this.) *Then* follow it with your actual answer.

Oh, yeah, one more thing: You'll see these little guys all over the place:

:-)

Turn your head 90 degrees to the left, and you'll see how it makes a little smiley face. That's to indicate, of course, the writer's facial expression (which you can't otherwise see). A thousand variants of that punctuation-face are available — and an equally large number of people who absolutely can't stand those little smileys.

If this option appeals to you, here's what to do:

✔ **Outlook Express:** From the Edit menu, choose Preferences. In the list at the left side of the resulting window, click Message Composition. Turn on the "Automatically add this signature to all messages" option and type your standard signature into the box, like this:

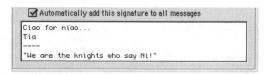

> ☑ Automatically add this signature to all messages
>
> Ciao for niao...
> Tia
> ----
> "We are the knights who say Ni!"

✔ **Claris Emailer:** From the Setup menu, choose Signatures. Click New; in the resulting window, type in what you'd like to use as your sign-off. Click Save and close the window.

Then, from the Setup menu, choose Accounts. Double-click the name of your e-mail account and, in the window that appears, use the Default Signature pop-up menu to specify the signature you just created.

Note, by the way, that *you* won't see this signature on *your* screen when you type up an e-mail message. You must trust that it'll be at the bottom of your note when your recipient gets it, however. I mention this so that you don't *manually* type "Love, Chris" at the bottom of your messages when you don't see the signature you created. The result would be "Love, Chris Love, Chris," which would make your correspondents think that either (a) you have a thing about repetition, or (b) there's an echo in your office.

Incidentally: For some unfathomable reason, it's become common on the Internet to include some cutesy little quotation as part of your signature, as shown in the previous figure. Some consider these little tag lines a form of personal expression, of quiet self-realization, of liberating freedom of speech.

Others consider them annoying.

Getting Your Mail

If the messages you send out to your friends are witty and charming enough, you may actually get a few responses.

To check your e-mail, choose Connect Now from the Mail menu (in Emailer) or click the Send & Receive icon (on the Outlook Express toolbar). In a spasm of hideous shrieking, your modem then dials cyberspace's home number and fetches any waiting mail. You'll see it in a list, as shown here in Outlook Express:

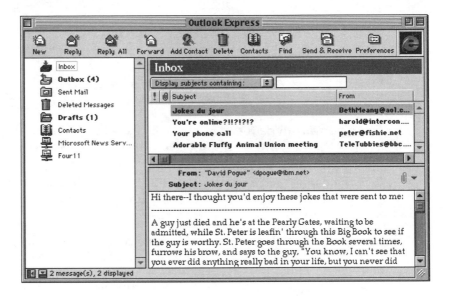

To read one of your messages, just click its name (Outlook Express) or double-click it (Emailer). A window opens, where you can read and enjoy your incoming memo.

Processing a Message You've Read

When you're finished reading an e-mail, you have four choices. You can:

✔ **Write a reply.** To do so, click the Reply button (on the Outlook Express or Emailer toolbar). Now you're back into I'm-Writing-An-E-mail-Message mode, as described in "Sending E-Mail" a couple of pages back. (Your e-mail software thoughtfully pre-types the e-mail address of the person you're answering — along with the date, time, and subject of the message. If I had a machine that did *that* for my U.S. mail, I'd be a much better paper correspondent.)

If you drag your mouse through some pertinent portion of the original message before clicking the Reply button, your e-mail program pre-pastes that passage into the reply window, like this:

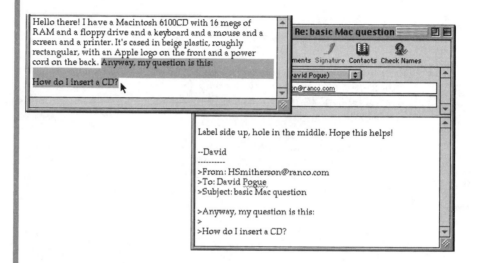

This common Internet technique helps your correspondent grasp what the heck you're talking about, especially since some time may have passed since he or she wrote the original note. As in the illustration, when the original e-mail contains a lot of irrelevant background material, this kind of bracketing helps both of you focus on the actual point (if any).

✔ **Trash it.** Click the Trash can icon on the toolbar, which sends the message to the great cyber-shredder in the sky.

✔ **Print it.** From the File menu, choose Print.

✔ **Save it for later.** To do so, close the message window. Then drag the message's name into one of the folders at the left side of the screen.

By the way: You can, and should, create your own specially named folders. Do that by choosing New Folder from the Folder menu (in Emailer) or New Folder from the File menu (in Outlook Express).

Attaching Files to E-Mail

Fortunately, there's more to e-mail than just sending typed messages back and forth. You can also send files from your hard drive — in the form of *attachments* to your e-mail messages.

Companies use this method to exchange design sketches, movie clips, and spreadsheets. Authors turn in chapters (written in Microsoft Word or ClarisWorks) to our publishers this way. And families send baby pictures this way, to the eternal boredom of most recipients.

Sending a file

To pull this off, start by writing a normal e-mail message, being sure to include a phrase like: "By the way, I've attached a ClarisWorks file. It's a drawing little Cindy did of a tobacco-company executive in a paroxysm of self-loathing and doubt."

Then locate the icon of the file you want to send. (This may involve opening some folders and rearranging some windows on your screen.) You need to adjust the windows on your screen so that you can see *both* your e-mail message *and* the icon of the file you want to send, like this:

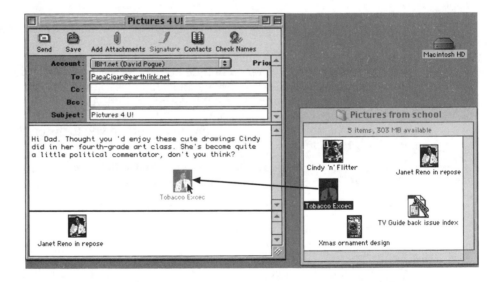

If you're using Outlook Express, drag the icons straight into the e-mail window, as shown in the preceding figure; you'll see the icons show up at the bottom of the window to indicate that your dragging was successful. If you're using Claris Emailer, drag the icons into any *gray* area of the window.

That's it! When you send the message, the attached Mac files go along for the ride.

Getting a file

You may *receive* files as part of an e-mail message, too. The telltale signs that you've received some picture or other file is (a) a special paper-clip icon and (b) a normal-looking Macintosh file icon somewhere on your message, like this:

Outlook Express

Claris Emailer

Just double-click the file icon to open it. If it doesn't open, see "When You Can't Open Your Downloaded Goodies" in the previous chapter.

The Anti-Spam Handbook

No doubt about it: Unsolicited junk e-mail, better known as *spam,* is the ugly underbelly of e-mail paradise. You'll know it if you've got it — wave after wave of daily messages like "MAKE EZ MONEY AT HOME CARVING TOOTH-PICKS!" and "SEXXXY APPLIANCE REPAIRMEN WAITING FOR YOUR CALL!"

If the names and addresses of the lowlife scum that sends out these billions of junk e-mails were ever published, the problem would take care of itself — the Internet population would drive over to the spammers' homes and rip apart each cell of their miserable little bodies.

But that's the thing — spammers hide. Their e-mail doesn't include a phone number or postal address; you're generally expected to visit a Web site or respond by e-mail. Meanwhile, our e-mail boxes fill up with useless crud that makes it harder to find the *real* messages among them.

Whatever you do, *never reply* to a piece of spam e-mail — even if the message says that you can get *off* the e-mail list by doing so! Ironically, your response to the e-mail will simply flag your e-mail address as a live, working account manned by somebody who takes the time to *read* the stuff. Your name will become much more valuable to junk e-mailers, and you'll find yourself on the receiving end of a new wave of spam.

You may have wondered: How did you wind up on these junk lists to begin with? Answer: They get your e-mail address from *you*. Every time you post a message on an online bulletin board, chat in a chat room, or even put your e-mail address up on your Web page, you've just made yourself vulnerable to the spammers' software robots. These little programs scour America Online, newsgroups, and the Web, looking for e-mail addresses to collect.

"But if I can never post messages online," I can hear you protesting, "I'm losing half the advantages of being online!"

Not necessarily. Consider setting up a second mailbox — that is, a second e-mail address for your same America Online or Internet account. (That's easy to do on AOL; go to keyword *names* to set up a new one. If you have an Internet account, call your ISP's help line to arrange an additional mailbox.)

Thereafter, the game is easy to play: Use *one* e-mail address for public postings, chats, and so on. Use your second, private one *for e-mail only*. Spam robots can't read private e-mail, so your secret e-mail address will remain virginal and spam-free.

Part V
Troubleshooting Made Tolerable

The 5th Wave   By Rich Tennant

"He must be a Macintosh user - there's a wristwatch icon etched on his retina."

In this part . . .

Now it's time to take the bull by the horns, the sword by the hilt, the fish by the gills, and really take off. I bestow unto you Chapter 15, the Mother of All Troubleshooting Guides. And then you'll find out where to go from there, with your trusty Mac ever by your side.

Chapter 15

When Bad Things Happen to Good Machines

As a new computer owner, you probably aren't cheered up very much by the fact that this troubleshooting guide is the fattest part of the book.

But let's face it: Computers are appliances. As such, they have minds of their own. And like other expensive appliances (cars, homes, pacemakers), they tend to get cranky at the worst possible times.

Fortunately, several million Mac users have been this way before, and they've already uncovered the most common glitches. You'll find those glitches and their solutions explained here. Again fortunately, most computer problems cost you nothing but time.

Some computer glitches, however, also cost you some data (that is, your work). Well, you've been told to floss if you want to keep your teeth; I'm telling you to *back up your work* if you want to keep your data, job, and sanity. Saving your work frequently and making backup copies (as described in Chapter 4) minimize the number of midnight sobbing sessions you'll have when your important projects vanish into what's left of the ozone.

Shooting Your Own Troubles

What I'd really like to teach you is how to be your *own* Mac guru — how to ferret out the solution to a problem yourself.

There are only a certain number of ways that a person can set up a Mac. The variables are what model it is; how much memory it has; what printer it's connected to; what's in its System Folder; what order you take steps in; what program you're using; and how everything's wired together. When something doesn't work, try changing *one* of those variables and repeating whatever-it-is-that-didn't-work.

A mild example

Example: Walter, a New Jersey tollbooth operator, tries to print out a picture he made of a Maserati flying off the highway at high speed — but nothing comes out of the printer. Flicking his earlobe, he wonders whether it's the *printer* that's not working or the *program*.

To find out, he goes to his word processor, types *TESTING TESTING,* and prints *that.* It works. Now he knows that the *printer* works fine; the problem is related to the graphics program. Next, he successfully prints a *different* document from the same drawing program. Therefore, he learns that the problem is with his Maserati *document,* not the drawing program in general.

See the point? He never learned *what,* technologically speaking, the problem was. But he figured out *where* the problem was, and that's the first step to working around it and getting on with your life.

The most common cause of troubles that need shooting

Get used to the computeristic-sounding word *extension.*

You know those little icons that march across your screen when you turn on the Macintosh? Those are your *extensions.* Each one is actually a little file in your Extensions folder (which is inside your System Folder). Each extension adds a specific new feature to the Macintosh: a screen saver, fax capability, and so on.

An extension runs *all the time;* it's like a program that you can't quit. It gets launched when the Mac turns on, and it's running in the background during your entire work day.

But the people who wrote the After Dark screen-saver program, for example, never met the programmers who wrote the FaxPlus faxing extension, let alone figured out how to make their two little programs coexist. Suppose you have both After Dark and FaxPlus in your Extensions folder. Also suppose that each little extension program, in the background, simultaneously reaches for the same morsel of electronic memory. You almost always get the infamous "Sorry, a system error occurred" message.

In other words, *extension conflicts* (the technical term) are among the most common causes of problems on the Mac. You'll find the solution in the following chapter.

Here, then, is a chapter full of typical snafus that typical Mac users encounter. If you never need to refer to this section, the gods smile on you — but read it anyway, to find out how lucky you really are.

About the cookbook

It turns out that about 90 percent of the things that go wrong with your Mac can be solved using the same handful of troubleshooting steps. To save you reading and me writing, I've consolidated all the fixes into Chapter 16. As you read through this chapter's symptom-by-symptom listings, I'll refer you to one or another of those steps.

The Mac Freezes or Crashes

Two scary conditions are enough to make even pro Mac jockeys swallow hard. The first of these conditions, a system *crash*, occurs when the following message appears on the screen:

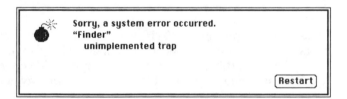

Your current work session is over, amigo; you have to restart the computer. (The safest way to restart is to press The Restart Switch, as described in "The Restart Switch" in the next chapter.) Anything that you've typed or drawn since the last time you saved your work is gone.

A System *freeze* is different — and, as horrific computer nightmares go, it's preferable. You get no message on the screen; instead, the mouse cursor freezes in place. You can't move the cursor, and nothing that you type changes anything. The Mac, as far as you can tell, has silicon lockjaw.

Escaping a System freeze right now

First resort: Try the amazing "Force Quit" keystroke (see "The Amazing 'Force Quit' Keystroke" in the next chapter). That should get you out of the locked program, at least.

Last resort: If the Magical Force-Quit Keystroke doesn't work — and sometimes it doesn't — you have to restart the Mac. This time, see "The Restart Switch" in the next chapter.

Escaping repeated System freezes

Ninety percent of the time, freezes and crashes are related either to memory or to *extension conflicts*.

First resort: Increase the amount of memory allotted to the program that you were using, as described in "Giving More Memory to a Program" in the next chapter. Give the program 10 percent more, for example.

Second resort: Something, or *several* somethings, are clashing in your System Folder. See "Solving an Extension Conflict" in the next chapter. If you're in a hurry to get your work done and can't take the time, just restart your Mac while pressing the Shift key. That turns *all* extensions off. For this work session, of course, you won't be able to use your CD-ROM drive, send faxes, use America Online or the Internet, or use Microsoft programs, but at least you can get into your Mac and do basic stuff without the hassle of system crashes.

Third resort: Maybe one of your programs is either (a) buggy or (b) out-of-date. The first problem is likely if you're using Microsoft programs or Netscape Navigator; the second problem is likely if you have recently upgraded something — your Mac or your Mac OS version, for example. You can't do anything but contact the software company and hope for the best.

Fourth resort: You may have a SCSI conflict on your hands, especially if more than one external gizmo is plugged into your Mac. See "Solving SCSI Nightmares" in the next chapter.

Fifth resort: Do you have a Power Macintosh or Performa 5200, 5300, 6200, 6300, 5215, 6205, 6214, 6216, 6218, 6220, 6230, or 6290? Then you may have one of the few Mac models that were genuinely malfunctioning right out of the box. If you can get online, go to *www.info.apple.com/swupdates* (on the World Wide Web) or keyword: *applecomputer* (on America Online) to download the program called "5xxx/6xxx Tester." This little program will confirm that your Mac has the glitch, and is therefore eligible for the free repair from Apple.

Last resort: If the crashes still haven't stopped, something in your System Folder may be gummed up. You're in for a 20-minute, but *very* effective, ritual known as a *clean reinstall* of your System Folder. For instructions, see "Performing a 'Clean System Reinstall'" in the next chapter.

Mac OS 8.5 and the Amazing Self-Repairing Mac

A system crash on a Mac running Mac OS 8.5 or later (see Chapter 1) is just as emotionally wounding as it is on any computer. Yet the feeling doesn't last — as soon as your computer starts up again after the crash, it gets to work *repairing itself.*

You'll see a big dialog box on the screen, and a progress bar showing how long the self-surgery will take. In brief, your Mac is checking out its own hard drive to make sure nothing was damaged during the system crash. If it finds anything wrong, the Mac fixes it automatically. Because this all takes place immediately following the crash, newborn problems get nipped in the bud, before they can grow up to be big, strong, meat-eating problems.

You *can* turn off this feature, if you like; open your General Controls control panel and turn off the option called "Warn me if computer was shut down improperly."

But why would you want to do that?

Problems in One Program

Suppose your Mac crashes — only when you use America Online. Or maybe it locks up — exclusively when you're in Netscape Navigator. If your troubles seem to be confined to just one application, your troubleshooting task is much easier.

First resort: Give the program more memory, as described in the next chapter under "Giving More Memory to a Program."

Second resort: First, some technical background: Whenever you launch a modern software program, it generally consults the *preferences file* in your Preferences folder. This preference file is where the program stores its little notes to itself about the way you like things set up: where you keep your toolbars on the screen (if it's Microsoft Word), what your favorite Web sites are (if it's Netscape Navigator), whether your prefer list views or icon views (if it's the Finder), and so on. If that file is damaged, so is your work session.

Now, what do we do when our government's not working? We throw out the components that aren't working and elect new ones. That's exactly the idea here: Open your System Folder, open your Preferences folder, and trash the program's preferences file. The very next time you launch that program, it automatically creates a *new* preferences file. Best of all — and here's where my political analogy breaks down — your new preference file is guaranteed to be uncorrupted.

This trick is especially useful in that most frequently used program of all, the Finder. The Finder Prefs file stores all kinds of settings important to your Mac work environment: the font and icon-layout settings used for Finder windows; window settings; whether or not the "Are you sure?" message appears when you empty the Trash; and so on.

Therefore, if you start noticing weird goings-on with your icons, windows, or Trash, try discarding the Finder Preferences file. Restart the Mac to generate a fresh, clean copy.

Last resort: If all else fails, try reinstalling the program in question — an updated version, if possible.

It's also conceivable that one of your extensions or control panels is causing trouble for this program. See "Solving an Extension Conflict" in the next chapter.

Error Messages

Let's start the troubleshooting session in earnest with a few good old American error messages. Yes, kids, these are the '90s equivalent of "DOES NOT COMPUTE." These are messages, appearing in an *alert box* like the fictional one shown here, that indicate that something's wrong.

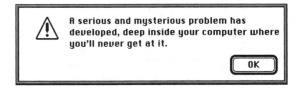

"Application not found"

First resort: Not everything in the Mac world is meant to be a plaything for you; the Mac reserves a few files for its own use. Certain items, especially in your System Folder, give you the "Application not found" message when double-clicked because they're there for your Mac's use, not for yours — such as icons in the Preferences folder, for example, or various other support-file icons for non-Apple stuff.

Second resort: In Chapter 3, you can read about programs and the documents that they produce (like parents and children). Sometimes, the "Application not found" message means that you're trying to open a document (child), but the Mac can't find its parent (the program used to create it).

So if you double-click a ClarisWorks document, but the ClarisWorks (or AppleWorks) program itself isn't on your hard disk, the Mac shrugs and asks, in effect, "Yo — how am I s'posed to open this?" To remedy the situation, reinstall the missing program on the hard disk.

More often, though, you're double-clicking something you downloaded from the Internet or America Online — something created by *someone else,* using a program you don't have. For example, let's say I send you a word processor file, but you don't have the same word processor program I do.

To read such files, launch *your* word processor *first* and then choose the Open command from the File menu (below, left).

 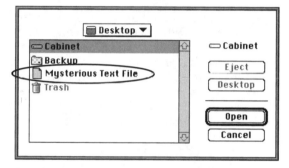

The usual list box appears, and you'll see the text file listed there (above, right). Double-click to open it.

The same applies to generic *graphics* documents. These files, in technical-sounding formats like PICT, JPEG, and GIF, can be opened by almost any program (America Online or Netscape Navigator, for example, can open all three). Yet if you try to *double-click* a generic graphics file, you may be told, "Application not found." Once again, the solution is to launch your graphics program *first* (America Online or Netscape Navigator or ClarisWorks or Photoshop, for example), and then open the file via the Open command.

(Depending on how your Mac is configured, you may instead be offered a list of programs that *can* open the orphaned file; in that case, simply double-click the name of the program you want to use.)

Last resort: Sometimes, you get the "Application not found" message even if you're sure that the document's parent program *is* on your Mac. (You double-click a ClarisWorks document, for example, and you're told that the application — ClarisWorks — can't be found, even though it's *sitting right there* on the disk in plain sight!)

In a situation like this, the Mac's genealogical gnomes have become confused: The computer has lost track of which program is associated with which kinds of documents. Don't ask me how such confusions happen; just rejoice that the problem is easy to fix. In the words of Mac gurus everywhere, "You gotta rebuild the desktop."

For instructions, see the "Rebuilding the Desktop File" in the next chapter.

"A Type 1 error has occurred"

These messages convey nothing. They simply mean that something has gone wrong inside and that you have to start over.

Turn the Mac off and then on again, or use The Restart Switch (see "The Restart Switch" in the next chapter).

As you've probably guessed, this message means that anything you typed — *and did not save* — is gone forever. Reality bites.

If you get a *lot* of these messages, however, it's time to wonder why. The Mac is not supposed to crash a lot!

Almost always, the problem is your extensions. As you read earlier, having the wrong mix of extension files inside your System Folder is an invitation to conflicts and problems. In the next chapter, you'll find a section called "Solving an Extension Conflict," which shows you how to determine which ones are responsible for ruining your life. And if you're getting a *lot* of these error messages, you may need to perform a clean install of your System Folder; see "Performing a 'Clean System Reinstall'" in the next chapter.

"Sorry, a System error has occurred"

See "The Mac Freezes or Crashes" at the beginning of this chapter.

"Not enough memory to open AppleWorks"

This message is a biggie, so it gets a section all by itself; see "Out of Memory," later in this chapter.

"You are running low on memory"

Believe it or not, this message appears even on Macs with *boatloads* of memory. It doesn't mean your *Mac* is running low on memory; it means your *program* is gasping for air, even though the computer itself has gallons and gallons of memory just sitting around.

If a program you use often is acting flaky, crashing, or giving "running low on memory" messages, you should raise the program's memory limit, allowing it to enjoy more of your machine's copious RAM. (Another good time to raise the memory amount: when America Online isn't able to open some picture file you downloaded.) Complete instructions are under "Giving More Memory to a Program," in the next chapter.

"QuickTime installation has failed because QuickTime was already installed"

You've got two copies of the QuickTime extension (as described in Chapter 8). Open your System Folder; if you see something inside called QuickTime or QuickTime 2.0, throw it away. If not, open your Extensions folder; you probably have two copies of the file called QuickTime. Throw away the older copy. (The various QuickTime support files — QuickTime VR, QuickTime Musical Instruments, and so on — don't matter.)

"Application has unexpectedly quit"

Your program has probably run out of memory. Again, even if your Mac *has* plenty of memory, the individual *program* that just "unexpectedly quit" may not have enough memory allotted to it. To find out how to give your program a more generous helping of memory, see the section in the next chapter called "Giving More Memory to a Program."

"The disk is full"

This message means that the disk is full.

It happens to the best of us: Over time, your hard disk gets fuller and fuller. Then, with only a megabyte of storage space to go, you try to do something (like saving an important file), and you're told that there's no more elbow room.

You'll have to make some more room; it's time to do some spring cleaning. From the Application menu (at the top-right corner of your screen), choose Finder. Root through your files, find some things to throw away (by dragging to the Trash can — and then choosing Empty Trash from the Special menu) or move to a different disk (such as a floppy, a Zip disk, or a SuperDisk, as described in Chapter 18). See Chapter 8 for some good ideas for stuff to throw away.

"Can't empty trash" or "Can't be deleted"

First resort: A locked file or folder is probably in the Trash can. Press Option while choosing Empty Trash from the Special menu to override its stubbornness and delete the locked item.

Second resort: Maybe the Mac has become confused about the trashability of some file or folder in the Trash. Restart the Mac and try again.

Last resort: About once in every Mac user's life, the Mac gets *so* confused that it simply will not delete a folder in the Trash, even if you've tried all the logical things. Your System Folder is simply having a psychotic break.

Here's a sneaky trick to get around its obstinacy:

1. **Drag the un-deletable folder (let's say it's called Rescued Items) to the desktop.**

2. **Change the Rescued Items folder's name to the name of another folder on your disk.**

   For example, if you have a Downloads folder, change the name of Rescued Items to Downloads.

3. **Open the original Downloads folder. Drag everything inside it into the newly named Downloads folder on your desktop.**

4. **Trash the *original* Downloads folder. Move the new Downloads folder from your desktop to the location of the *former* Downloads folder.**

You should now be able to empty the Trash, having successfully outfoxed the Mac at its own game. After all, you're now trashing a perfectly ordinary folder.

"DNS Entry not found"

You get this message when using your Web browser (see Chapter 12). It means that the Web site you're trying to visit doesn't exist. Usually this means you've made a typo as you typed the Web address, or the page's address has changed and you don't know it, or the computer the Web site is on has been taken off the Internet (for maintenance, for example).

Rescued Items? Rescued from what?

Ever wonder about the strange Rescued Items folder that periodically appears in the Trash? Usually this folder shows up when you restart your Mac after a crash or freeze.

To understand Rescued Items, you must first understand the legendary *Temporary Items* folder.

The Temporary Items folder is a locked, *invisible* folder on your hard drive. Your programs are allowed to use this hidden folder to store temporary files (such as the last version of whatever you're working on, so that the program will be able to comply if you use the Undo command). Microsoft Word, in particular, uses this folder as a temporary dumping ground.

Usually, when you finish using a program and use the Quit command, the program neatly erases everything it's put into the Temporary Items folder. But if your system crashes, the program never gets a chance to empty the Temporary Items folder!

Therefore, when you restart the Mac, and it notices that you still have files left over in the Temporary Items folder, the System automatically creates a new Rescued Items folder in the Trash and moves the files there; it's the Mac's last-ditch effort to salvage your unsaved work.

According to ancient legend, once in a blue moon, you can actually recover some of your work by poking into the rescued temp files in the Rescued Items folder. However, I've never yet found anything valuable in there; I just delete the Rescued Items without another thought.

"Launcher cannot be opened, error –39"

If you get this message when you try to use your Launcher (see Chapter 8), you've fallen victim to the dreaded Corrupted Launcher Syndrome (CLS). It means that your Launcher program, like so many great publications and government programs, has spontaneously turned to garbage.

Open your System Folder, open your Control Panels folder, and throw away the Launcher. Reinstall it using your original system-software CD (which came with your Mac). See "Performing a 'Clean System Reinstall'" in the next chapter.

Numbered error messages

This may strike you as hard to believe, but the numbers in some error messages (Type 11, Type 3, Error 49, and so on) are *no help at all*. They're valuable only to programmers, and even then not very. For example, a Type 1 error means "bus error," a Type 3 is "illegal instruction," and Type 20 is "stack ran into heap." Realllllllly helpful.

Of the 200 Mac error messages, only one lets you remedy the situation: –39, which means that the file you're trying to work with is corrupted somehow (as described in "Launcher cannot be opened, error –39," two paragraphs ago). All the others are caused by the usual problems: Some program didn't have enough memory, or you had an extension conflict, or your System Folder needs reinstalling.

Out of Memory

As a service to you, the Tremulous Novice, I've gone this entire book without even a word about memory management, which is a whole new ball of wax. I hoped that you'd never need to think about it. Memory becomes an issue only when you get the message "There is not enough memory to open Word" (or whatever program you're trying to open), and that's why you're reading about memory in a troubleshooting chapter.

Your Mac has a fixed amount of memory. Think of the Mac as a station wagon. You can pack it with camping gear, or you can pack it with your kid's birthday-party friends, but probably not with both. Even if you manage to cram in the kids and the gear, if you *then* try to cram in the dog, somebody in the family is going to say, "There is not enough room to take Bowser."

That's what the "not enough memory" message is trying to tell you.

Each program that you open consumes a chunk of the Mac's limited memory. You're entitled to run as many programs as you want simultaneously — the Note Pad, the Calculator, your word processor, and so on — *provided* that they all fit into the amount of memory your Mac has. If you try to open one too many programs, you'll get that message about the dog. (*You know what I mean.*)

Before we begin, remember that there are two different kinds of memory shortages. First, there's the "You are running low on memory" type, which indicates that a *program* doesn't have enough memory; see "Giving More Memory to a Program" in the next chapter.

Second, there's the "Not enough memory to *open* this program" problem, which means that your *Mac's* memory is all used up. The following discussion applies to this second scenario.

First resort: Quit programs

If you're told that you're out of memory, the easiest way out of the situation is to *quit* one of the programs you're already running. (You quit a program by choosing Quit from the File menu.) So if you're running Word and you try to open America Online, and you're told that there's not enough unused (free) memory, you'll just have to quit Word first.

Often, you may have programs running and not even know it. Remember that just because a program has no *windows* open doesn't mean it isn't *running.* When you're done working on something, did you just *close the window,* or did you actually *choose Quit* from the File menu? If you didn't actually Quit, then the program is still running and still using up memory.

To get rid of that program, choose its name from the Application menu (in the very upper-right corner of the screen, as described in Chapter 3). Then choose Quit from the File menu:

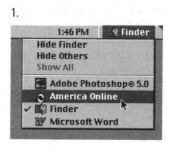

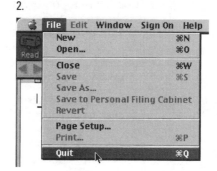

Second resort: Make the Mac give back

Quitting programs, of course, isn't a very convenient solution — especially if having multiple programs open is part of what you're *trying* to do, such as copying stuff *from* America Online *to* Word. Therefore, your next attempt to solve the problem should be to make the Mac itself use less memory.

Yes, indeed, the Mac's own behind-the-scenes operations use memory like a silicon hog — Mac OS 8 grabs at least 8MB of your memory. If your Mac has only 16MB to begin with, you can see why running out of memory is easy.

Here are some tricks to make the Mac use less memory:

> ✔ **Use fewer extensions.** Extensions, as you may recall, are the little auto-loading programs whose icons appear across the bottom of the screen when you start the Mac. Each extension (screen saver, menu clock, virus checker, and so on) eats up another nibble of your memory.
>
> A few particularly memory-hungry extensions: QuickTime (200K); After Dark (300K); Adobe Type Manager/ATM (500K or more).

And how do you turn off extensions? See "Solving an Extension Conflict" in the next chapter. And review Chapter 8 for a list of extensions you can turn off or throw away, thus saving the memory they would have eaten up.

✔ **Turn off File Sharing.** Those of you who are advanced enough to be using this complicated feature know who you are. March right up to that Control Panels command in the menu, young man/woman, choose File Sharing (or Sharing Setup), and click the Stop button. You'll immediately get back 300K of memory.

✔ **Check your Disk Cache.** This little gimmick is something that you can blissfully ignore for most of your computing days . . . until you start running out of memory.

Suppose that you're innocently word processing, and you make some text boldface. Because the word-processing program resides on your hard disk, the Mac consults the disk to find out how it's supposed to create bold type. This disk-reading business takes, say, one second. If you use boldface a lot, those one-second disk searches are going to cumulatively slow both you and your Mac.

Therefore, the Mac reserves a piece of memory, called the Disk Cache (pronounced "disk cash"), just for such frequent pieces of information. *Now* when you make text boldface, the Mac consults the disk (taking one second), but it stores the "how-to-make-bold" information in the Disk Cache. The *second* time that you need to create bold text, the Mac already knows how to do it; your text becomes bold in $1/100$ of a second (because memory delivers information to the Mac's brain 100 times faster than the disk does). Cumulatively, all the little tidbits of information that the Mac stores in the Disk Cache give you quite a speed boost.

The larger this piece of memory is, the faster your Mac will go. But there's the rub: if you make this Disk Cache memory *too* big, you'll use memory that you could be using to run programs.

Even if I've totally lost you, here's what to do when you're strapped for memory. From the menu, choose Control Panels, and double-click Memory. If you see a button called Custom Setting, click it (and click Custom in the warning box that appears). Then click the down arrow, shown here, to make the Disk Cache smaller.

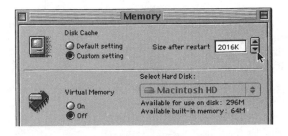

Setting your Disk Cache lower than the recommended level (which is 32K per meg of memory your Mac has, if you must know) does give usable memory back to your programs. Unfortunately, it also slows down the Mac a tiny bit; if the slowdown is noticeable, consider one of the memory tricks described in the next sections.

This has been a long explanation for a small reclamation of memory, I know, but it feels good to know what's going on behind the scenes, doesn't it?

Third resort: Defragment your RAM

Sometimes, the Mac will appall you. Here it is, the equivalent of a whole *roomful* of 1950s-style computers, yet it can't even add.

Here's the scenario. Your Mac has 32 megs of memory, let's say. You know your System uses 8MB. And let's suppose you're running two programs right now: Netscape Navigator (which wants 8), and Microsoft Word (which takes up another 8). In other words, you're using up 24 out of your Mac's 32 megs. You have 8 megs of memory not being used.

With me so far? Okay. Now suppose you try to launch America Online, which we'll suppose needs 8MB of memory — and you get the out-of-memory message! How can this be? After all, there ought to be 8MB free, right?

Memory fragmentation is going on, if you must know. It works like this. At noon, you start the Mac. You launch your favorite programs: ClarisWorks (which we'll say uses 4 megs), Navigator, and Word. At this moment, a graph of your Mac's memory usage looks like this:

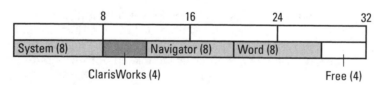

Total Memory: 32 Megs

Then, at 12:05, you *quit* ClarisWorks. Now your memory graph looks like this:

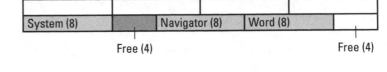

Total Memory: 32 Megs

If you look at this last drawing, you'll see that you do have a total of 8 megs free. But you don't have 8 megs of solid, *contiguous* memory left! You've inadvertently chopped your remaining memory into two smaller chunks, neither of which alone can accommodate the 8-meg America Online program.

The solution to the I-*know*-I-have-enough-memory-to-launch-this problem is to *quit* all your programs, so that only the Finder is running, and *then* launch all the programs that are supposed to fit in your Mac's memory. This time, you won't leave holes in your memory setup, and you'll be able to use all the memory you deserve.

Fourth resort: Get RAM Doubler

Here's a fascinating possibility for the RAM-shy Mac fan: Buy a $60 program called RAM Doubler.

RAM Doubler uses several potent, deeply technical tricks to make your Mac *behave* as though it has twice or three times as much memory as it really does. Most people who try it love it. The rest get their money back.

The only fundamental understanding of RAM Doubler that you need is this: It lets you run *more small programs at the same time*. It doesn't let you run one *big* program that requires more real memory than you have.

So Billy Bob, who has an 8-meg PowerBook and who wants to run ClarisWorks and America Online at the same time, is made in the shade. He no longer has to quit America Online just to free enough memory to launch ClarisWorks. RAM Doubler lets him keep both programs going.

Jenny Sue, however, wants very much to run Photoshop or Myst on her old 8-meg Power Mac. She's out of luck. Those programs require about 8 megs of memory apiece. RAM Doubler's double-memory tactics don't let you run any *big* programs that you couldn't run before.

Fifth resort: Use virtual memory

Here's another rather technical but interesting possibility for avoiding out-of-memory problems. Fortunately, this solution lets you run programs whose combined memory requirements add up to much more than your Mac should be able to handle. Unfortunately, it requires you to learn a new term. Ponder this trade-off for a moment; then read on, if you dare.

The new term is *virtual memory*. (*Virtual* means *fake*, as in "virtual reality.") Under this scheme, the Mac attempts to use the hard disk as emergency memory.

Suppose your Mac has 16MB of memory, but you want to run both LimerickWriter (which requires 5MB) and BrailleMeister (which also requires 5MB). Because your System requires 8MB by itself, you can see that 5 + 5 + 8 is going to equal more than your 16MB.

If you were using virtual memory, though, the Mac would allow you to run both programs simultaneously. Where would it get the extra 2MB of memory that it needs to fit everything in? It would use an empty hunk of *hard-disk space*.

Read this slowly: When you're in LimerickWriter, the Mac stashes the excess 2MB worth of BrailleMeister information on the hard disk. Then, when you bring the BrailleMeister window to the front, the Mac quickly feeds that 2MB worth of information back into actual memory, displacing the same amount of LimerickWriter instructions (which, needless to say, it writes back onto the hard disk). Each time you switch programs, the Mac juggles the overflow.

This switch doesn't take place instantaneously; that's a lot of information for the Mac to shuttle back and forth between memory and the hard disk. (Maybe it's time to reread Chapter 1½, which describes memory and hard disks in pulse-quickening detail.) In fact, you may have quite a lag when you switch from one program to another. But a little waiting sure beats not being *able* to run those two important programs at the same time.

For some mysterious technical reason, the amount of hard-disk space that the Mac needs to perform this stunt isn't *just* the amount of pretend memory you want to *add* to your real memory. That is, if your Mac has 16MB of memory, and you'd like your Mac to think that it has 20MB, you can't just set aside the difference (4MB) in hard-disk space. Golly, no. You have to allow a chunk of disk space that's the size of *all* the memory, real and imagined — in this case, 20MB.

Okay. All that having been said (and read), let's get to the actual process of using virtual memory. Follow these steps:

1. **From the menu, choose Control Panels; then double-click Memory.**

   The control panel appears, like this:

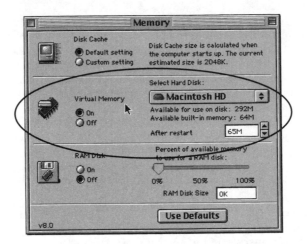

See the Virtual Memory area? (Some older Macs don't offer this feature. And don't panic because your Memory control panel doesn't look exactly like the picture — its look changes depending on your Mac model and your system-software version.)

2. **Make sure the Virtual Memory switch is On.**

   If your Mac is relatively recent (a Power Mac, iMac, or anything with "G3" in its name, for example), you'll probably notice that virtual memory is already On. And that's good: On these models, virtual memory should *always* be on, at least a little bit (see Step 4). The technical details would curl your nose hairs, but let's just say that having virtual memory turned on makes these models run faster and use memory more efficiently.

   (Geek disclaimer: The only time virtual memory should be off is if you've bought RAM Doubler, described earlier in this chapter. It replaces virtual memory.)

3. **Using the little up-and-down arrows, specify how big you want that virtual-memory file (on your hard disk) to be.**

   Remember: There has to be a chunk of empty hard-disk space that's big enough to hold the *total* of your real memory and the extra, phony memory that you'd like to have.

   As noted in Step 2, Power Macs (and other recent models) should, at the very least, have virtual memory set *1MB* higher than your actual installed RAM. If your Mac has 32 megs of RAM (consult this book's cheat sheet), set virtual memory to 33MB. Trust me.

   On the other hand, don't make this setting more than *double* your real memory. If you have 32MB of RAM, your total memory (including virtual) shouldn't exceed 64MB; things will get so slow as to be unworkable.

The Mac may tell you, by the way, that your disk does not have enough room. Maybe it's time to go on a cleaning binge.

4. **When you're done with your virtual-memory setup, restart the Mac.**

Last resort: Buy more

After a certain point, knocking yourself out to solve out-of-memory problems reaches a point of diminishing returns. You get so worn out from workarounds that they're not worth doing.

At that point (or much sooner), just spring for the $50 or $75 and *buy more memory.* You can get it from any mail-order company (such as Mac Connection). When you call, tell them what Mac you have; they'll tell you what kind of memory chips you need, and in what quantities they're available. Sometimes, the company will send you a how-to video, which is very handy — and when you're done with it, you can use it to record *Frasier.*

You can install the new memory chips yourself, fairly easily, in some models. But installing memory in other models — like PowerBooks — is trickier and requires some funky tools (or a funky repair shop). If the whole thing makes you nervous, ask a local geek from the Mac user group — or someone from your computer store — to do it for you.

Having lots of memory to kick around in is a joy. Your Mac runs faster, has fewer crashes and glitches, and acts like a new machine. It's a situation that I heartily recommend.

Startup Problems

Problems that you encounter when you turn on the Mac are especially disheartening when you're a new Mac user. It does wonders for your self-esteem to think that you can't even turn the thing *on* without problems.

No ding, no picture

First resort: Chances are very, very, very good that your Mac simply isn't getting electricity. It's probably not plugged in. Or it's plugged into a power strip whose On/Off switch is currently set to Off. Or (if it's a PowerBook) the battery is dead; plug in the adapter for ten minutes before trying again.

Second resort: On most models, you turn the machine on by pressing the triangle key on the keyboard. Maybe the keyboard isn't plugged in. Check that.

Third resort: Here's another PowerBook possibility. It may be that the internal circuitry known as the *power manager* has gotten drunk again. Unplug the PowerBook *and* take its battery out. Let it sit like that for ten minutes. Then put it together and try again.

If you're still having no luck, try slapping some sense into the power manager like this (the method depends on the model):

- **PowerBook 190, 1400, 2400, 3400, 5300, and pre-1998 G3** — Press and hold the *reset button,* which looks like a plastic hyphen on the back panel of the laptop. (It's under the monitor jack, if you have one, or near the modem and printer jacks.)

  If that restarting process doesn't work, try it again a few more times.

- **PowerBook 500 series** — After unplugging and de-batterying your laptop as described above, press ⌘-Option-Control-power key for ten seconds. Reinsert the battery and power cord.

- **1998 PowerBook G3 Series** — Press Shift-Function-Control-power button. ("Function" is the *Fn* key at the lower-left corner of the keyboard.)

Last resort: If none of those steps solved the problem, your Mac is as dead as Elvis. Get it in for repair. But that's virtually never the actual problem.

Ding, no picture

If you hear the startup chime (or ding) but the monitor doesn't light up, something's wrong with the monitor.

First resort: Is the screen brightness turned up? On most Macs, a brightness dial is on the edge of the monitor.

Second resort: Is the Mac asleep? Most recent Macs make the monitor go black after a few minutes of inactivity on your part (to save energy). Press a keyboard key and click the mouse to wake it up.

Last resort: If you have a two-piece Mac, the monitor has to be (1) plugged into the Mac, (2) plugged into a power source, *and* (3) turned on. (Not everybody realizes that the monitor has an On/Off switch.) Often, the monitor is plugged into an AC outlet on the Mac itself; that's okay.

Picture, no ding

Every Mac makes a sound when it's turned on. One some Macs (notably PowerBooks), however, the speaker-volume slider (in the Monitors & Sound control panel) actually controls the sound of the startup chime, too.

Therefore:

First resort: Open the Monitors & Sound control panel and make sure the volume slider isn't all the way down. Make sure the Mute checkbox isn't turned on.

Last resort: Look at the little speaker jack in the back of the Mac. If some kind of plug is in it — some kid's Walkman headphones, a cord connected to a stereo, or a pretzel stick — no sound can come out of the Mac speaker.

Four musical notes (or crash sound)

If you hear an arpeggio, a lick of the *Twilight Zone* theme, a drum or flute solo, or a car-crash sound, something's seriously wrong inside the Mac (Apple's sense of humor at work).

Fortunately, 50 percent of the time, you hear this sound just after installing new memory or a new expansion board (you know who you are). It means that a board, or the new memory, is loose or defective — something that you (or whoever did the installation for you) can fix relatively easily. And 40 percent of the time, it's a SCSI problem. Read on.

First resort: If you've just installed something into your computer, that's certainly the problem. Reopen the Mac. Carefully remove each memory board (or the board you installed) and reseat it. (Come to think of it, get someone who knows what he or she is doing to do this.)

Second resort: The other common source of funny startup notes is a SCSI problem of some kind. (Yes, I know that we haven't defined this in a while; for instructions, see "Solving SCSI Nightmares" in the next chapter.) For a quick fix, just unplug any external hard drive or scanner from the SCSI jack (the very wide one) in the back of the Mac, and try starting up again.

Last resort: If it's truly not a board-installation or SCSI problem, call your Apple dealer. This baby's sick.

A question mark blinks on the screen

The blinking question mark is the Mac's international symbol for "I've looked everywhere, and I can't find a System Folder."

The blinking question mark means that your hard drive's not working right — or that it's working fine, but your System Folder got screwed up somehow. In either case, here's what to do.

First resort: After ten seconds of panic, turn the Mac off and try starting again, or just press the Restart Switch (see "The Restart Switch" in the next chapter).

Second resort: Find a disk with a System Folder on it. The best bet is the startup CD that came with your Mac. The floppy called Disk Tools (which comes with every Mac ever made) will also do the trick. Put it into the drive, and turn the Mac on.

Once you're running, find the program called Disk First Aid. Run it and use the Repair button. About 40 percent of the time, Disk First Aid can repair your hard drive.

Third resort: If the hard-drive icon still doesn't appear, perhaps the System Folder is calling in sick. Reinstall from your startup CD (or your system backup floppy disks, on older Macs), as described in "Performing a 'Clean System Reinstall'" in the next chapter.

Fourth resort: Read "Solving SCSI Nightmares" in the next chapter.

Fifth resort: Try *zapping the PRAM* (pronounced PEA-ram). See "Zapping the PRAM" in the next chapter.

Last resort: If nothing has worked, and you still can't make your hard-drive icon appear on the screen, your hard drive is sick. Call your local dealer or Mac guru, and do *not* freak out — chances are very good that all of your files are still intact. (Just because the platters aren't spinning doesn't mean that they've been wiped out, just as your Walkman tapes don't get erased when the Walkman runs out of batteries.)

In fact, you can probably rescue the data from your disk yourself. Buy a disk-recovery program, such as Norton Utilities or TechTool Pro. That'll let you grab anything useful off the disk and may even help heal what's wrong with it.

Some crazy program launches itself every time you start up

In the words of Mac programmers everywhere, "It's a feature, not a bug."

Inside the System Folder, there's a folder called Startup Items. Look inside it. Somebody put a program or document in there.

Anything in the Startup Items folder automatically opens when you turn on the Mac. This feature is supposed to be a time-saver for people who work on the same documents every day.

Especially long startup times

A two-second pause between the monitor's lighting up and the appearance of the "happy Mac" icon is normal. But if the standstill is abnormally long (longer than about eight seconds), or if the disk/question mark icon briefly appears on your screen before the startup process begins, you have a problem.

First resort: If this problem is what I think it is, it's an especially easy one to fix. In the Startup Disk control panel, you may have recently selected a different disk to start up from — a disk that's no longer available, such as a Zip disk, SuperDisk, or CD-ROM. From your menu, choose Control Panels, and open the one called Startup Disk. Click the name of your hard drive, close the control panel, and restart the Mac.

Last resort: If my Startup-Disk theory isn't right, the only other tidbit I have to offer is that *memory* makes a Mac take longer to start up. The more memory you have, the longer the startup process takes (because the Mac takes a moment to test all of its memory before proceeding).

If you just can't stand sitting watching your Mac start up, consider using its Energy Saver control panel (see Chapter 8) to turn the thing on *automatically* at five minutes to nine (or whenever you haul yourself in to work). That way, no waiting: The Mac will be waiting for you, smiling, bushy-tailed, and ready.

Printing Problems

If you're like most people, you own a second computer without even knowing it: your printer. Yes, like a computer, today's printers have their own memory, microchips — and problems.

"Printer could not be opened" or "Printer could not be found"

First resort: These messages appear when you try to print something without turning on the printer first (or letting it warm up fully). Turn it on, wait a whole minute, and then try again.

Second resort: Of course, it may be that you haven't performed the critical step of selecting the printer's icon in the Chooser desk accessory. (Even if you did, the Mac sometimes gets a little feebleminded and forgets what you selected in the Chooser. Just repeat the procedure.) See Chapter 5 for step-by-step instructions.

Third resort: Maybe a cable came loose. Track the cable from your Mac's printer port all the way to the printer. (Important: make sure that it's really the printer port, because the modem port looks exactly like it.) If it all seems to be firmly connected, try replacing (1) the cable or (2) the little connectors.

Fourth resort: On some Power Mac G3 models, a weird little extension called *LocalTalk PCI* prevents your Mac from seeing its laser printer. Try turning that extension off (as described in the next chapter) and restarting the Mac.

Last resort: If you're using a laser printer, you are, believe it or not, on a network, no matter how small. A network works only if AppleTalk is *active* (check the Chooser, in your menu), and if the correct *kind* of network (such as LocalTalk or Ethernet) is selected; visit the control panel called Network or AppleTalk and confirm the setting.

StyleWriter (or other inkjet): Blank pages

It's your cartridge.

First resort: Choose Print from the File menu. Click the Options button. See where it says "Clean ink cartridge before printing?" Click that.

Now try to print something normally. The StyleWriter will, in effect, blow its nose before trying to print, just in case your cartridge nozzle has dried up and clogged. (If you have a non-Apple inkjet printer, you, too, have a "clean nozzle" command — but you'll have to consult the manual to find out exactly how you invoke it.)

Last resort: If that didn't work, your cartridge is probably empty. Buy a new one.

A million copies keep pouring out

This big-time hazard for novices has to do with background printing (see Chapter 5). When you print something, *nothing happens* for a minute or two. (The Mac is storing the printout behind the scenes so that it can return control of the Mac to you.)

Trouble is, your first time at bat, you probably don't *know* what the delay is; all you know is that the printer isn't printing. So you figure that you'll just try again. You choose Print from the File menu again. Still, nothing happens. So you print *again.*

The thing is, the Mac is duly storing all your printing requests; at some moment, when you least expect it, all those copies start to print! To stop them, choose Print Monitor from the Application menu (the tiny icon at the far right end of your menu bar); select each document; and click Cancel Printing.

Nothing comes out of the printer

Sometimes, the Mac fakes you out: It goes through the motions of printing, but nothing ever comes out of the printer.

First resort: Go to the menu. Select Chooser. Click the icon for the printer that you're using, and make sure that your actual printer's name shows up in the list on the right side of the Chooser window. (This process is explained more patiently in Chapter 5.)

Second resort: Is there paper in the paper tray, and is the tray pushed all the way in?

Third resort: If you're using a laser printer: Alas, your document is probably overwhelming the printer's feeble memory, and the printer is giving up. You can try using fewer different fonts in the document. Try printing only a page at a time. Or try using fewer *downloadable* fonts — that is, fonts that aren't built into the printer (see #3 in "Top Ten Free Fun Font Factoids" in Chapter 5).

Fourth resort: If you're printing something complicated on your laser printer, there may be a messed-up graphic. Programs such as FreeHand and Illustrator are known for generating very complex, sometimes unprintable graphics. For example, here's a graphic from FreeHand that won't print out:

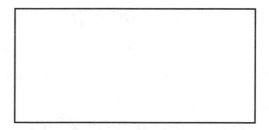

If you're printing a document that includes both text and graphics, try removing your graphics and printing the same document. If it prints without the graphics, you know where the problem is. Call the graphics-program company and complain abrasively.

Last resort: If your laser printer truly has run out of memory, you can usually pay to have it upgraded with more memory. In the computer world, as always, a little cash can surmount almost any problem.

That stupid startup page

Every time you turn on your laser printer, it prints a dumb startup page with its own logo. This is an annoying problem, but easily fixed. See #8 in "Top Ten Free Fun Font Factoids" in Chapter 5.

Finder Foul-Ups

The Finder, you'll recall, is your home base. It's the desktop. It's the Trash can and icons and all that stuff. It's where you manage your files, rename them, copy them — and sometimes have problems with them.

The Find command doesn't find a file

The Find command is pretty literal. Suppose you're looking for a letter called Mr. Ted Smith. You use the Find command, and where it says "Find what," you type *Mr. Smith, Mr.Ted Smith* (see the missing space?), *Mr Ted Smith* (no period), or *Mr. William Smith*. In any of these circumstances, the Find command will draw a blank. Try searching for *smi, Mr,* or any portion of the letters that you're certain of. (Capitalization *doesn't* matter.)

Of course, the problem may not be what you type in the "Find what" box. You may have misspelled the name of the file itself — say, **1997 Salries** — and no matter how many times you search for the word *salaries,* the Finder will always come up empty-handed.

You can't rename a file

The file is probably locked. Click it, choose Get Info from the File menu, and deselect the Locked checkbox. Or maybe the file is on a locked *disk,* such as a CD-ROM disc. You *can't* rename anything on a locked disk.

You can't rename or eject a disk

First resort: I'm gonna take a wild shot at this one. Despite your supposedly novice status, I'll bet you're using the Mac's networking feature. I'll bet you're plugged into another Mac. Right?

It's true: If you're using this feature (known as *file sharing*), you're not allowed to change your hard drive's name. You'd wreak havoc with the other people on the network, who are trying to keep straight who you are.

If you really want to bother, open your File Sharing (or Sharing Setup) control panel and turn *off* file sharing. Now you can rename your disk. (You're often not allowed to eject CDs or Zip disks when file sharing is on, either.)

Last resort: In System 7 and later, you can't rename those really old, single-sided, 400K disks. Period.

You drag a file into a window, and the file disappears

You have to watch your tip, if you'll pardon my saying so. When you drag an icon, the cursor arrow's *tip* actually marks where the icon is going, not the icon itself. What probably happened is that you accidentally released the icon when the arrow tip was on top of a *folder* within the window, as shown here:

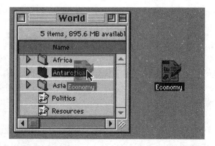

If this happens to you, and you can't even figure out *which* folder you dropped it into, use the Find command in the File menu.

All your icons show up blank

If you get zapped by the "generic icons" problem, where every document looks like a boring blank sheet of paper, your invisible Desktop file has become corrupted. See "Rebuilding the Desktop File" in the next chapter.

It's January 1, 1904

Ever wonder how your Mac always manages to know what time it is — even when it's been *unplugged?*

Turns out the Mac has a battery — a built-in, five- to seven-year battery that maintains the clock even when the computer is off.

In the olden days, nobody thought much about that battery. Lately, however, all those Macs from the late '80s and early '90s are reaching their fifth and seventh birthdays. People's lithium batteries are dying, causing a peculiar and startling problem: Suddenly, your Mac's clock resets itself to January 1, 1904 (or a date in 1957)! All your new or modified files get stamped with that date, too. And no matter how many times you reset your clock, it stubbornly jumps back to that date in antiquity.

I'd love to tell you which Eveready battery to pick up at your local drug store, but the battery's different on every model. An Apple technician will be happy to install a fresh battery of the correct type, usually at a cost of about $25.

The only virus worth worrying about

There are plenty of reasons to be glad you use a Macintosh. Consider computer viruses (computer programs written by some socio-path to gum up the works of any computer it encounters): While 10,000 different computer viruses attack Windows-compatible comput-ers, until 1998, there was not a *single virus* that could destroy Macintosh files.

Nowadays, there is one Mac virus — called AutoStart. If your Mac "catches" this virus, you'll notice three odd symptoms: First, the Mac restarts itself just after you insert a disk of some kind. (That's your Mac coming down with the virus.) Second, your hard drive starts thrashing and making noise about every half hour. Third, some of the files on your hard drive may become corrupted and un-openable.

Fortunately, it's easy to protect your Mac against this virus: From the menu, choose Control Panels, and open the control panel called QuickTime Settings. (If you don't *have* the QuickTime Settings control panel, you're all set; you can't get the AutoStart virus.) Turn off the CD-ROM Auto-Play option. That's it — you're protected. (It's perfectly OK to leave "Enable *Audio CD* AutoPlay" turned on. That option makes music CDs start playing when you insert them into your Mac, and it's com-pletely safe.)

The AutoStart virus is also very easy to eliminate once you've caught it. Visit *www. macvirus.com* on the Web (see Chapter 12). There you'll find free programs like WormScanner, which wipe out the virus instantly.

Floppy-Disk Flukes

Floppy disks are cheap and handy and make excellent coasters. But when they start giving you attitude, read on.

"File could not be copied"

This one's a pain, isn't it?

First resort: If you were copying a whole group of files, try dragging the troublesome file by itself.

Second resort: Make a duplicate of the file (click it and then choose Duplicate from the File menu). Now try copying the duplicate.

Third resort: If the unruly file is a document, launch the program that created it. (If it's a Word file, for example, launch Word.) Now choose the Open command from the File menu, and try to open the file. If it opens, use the Save As command to save it to a different disk.

Fourth resort: Eject the disk. Open and close the sliding shutter a couple times. Manually rotate the round hub. Try again.

Last resort: Try inserting the obnoxious floppy into somebody else's Mac.

The Mac keeps asking for a disk you've ejected

First resort: You probably ejected the disk by using the Eject Disk command in the Special menu. In systems before Mac OS 8, that's a no-no, precisely because the Mac will continually ask for it.

You can get out of this scrape by pressing ⌘-period several times. Next time, eject a disk by choosing the Put Away command from the File menu (or by dragging the disk icon to the Trash can).

Last resort: Sometimes, even if you use Put Away, a ghost of the disk's icon remains on the screen; the Mac keeps asking for it, and pressing ⌘-period doesn't solve anything. In this case, you probably opened a file on that disk, and it's still open. As long as something on that disk is open, the Mac won't forget about the disk; it would be like canceling the space program while some astronauts were in the middle of a mission.

Choose the program in question from the Application menu, and make sure that you close all documents. Now you should be able to drag the disk icon to the Trash can.

You can't get a floppy disk out

First resort: Press ⌘-Shift-1. That should pop out the disk, even if you can't see its icon.

Last resort: Use the paper-clip trick described in the sidebar "When the disk is too shy to come out" in Chapter 2.

"This disk is unreadable. Do you want to initialize it?"

If it's a brand-new disk fresh out of the box, there is *no* problem. *All* brand-new disks are initially unreadable (unless the box says that they come pre-formatted). Go ahead and click Erase, and follow the disk-naming process that the Mac takes you through. But if it's a disk that you've used before, you certainly don't want to destroy it.

First resort: Click Eject. *No,* you do not want to initialize (erase) the disk.

Second resort: Did this floppy come from somebody who uses a Windows computer? If so, you can still use the disk and see what's on it — but only if you have the control panel called File Exchange or PC Exchange. Turn it on by using your Extensions Manager control panel (see "Solving an Extension Conflict" in the next chapter).

Third resort: If it's a disk that you know contains data, something may be actually wrong with the disk. Eject it, shake it around a little, and try it a couple more times.

Fourth resort: Something may be wrong with your disk *drive* — not the disk itself. To find out, insert the disk into another Mac's drive.

If there turns out to be a problem with your drive, the culprit is often dust and crud. Some of my technoid friends say that it's dangerous (staticwise) to use a vacuum or blower in the disk-drive slot, but I've actually rescued a disk drive or two this way (and have never damaged one).

Last resort: If the problem is not your disk drive, the disk is really broken. Don't even erase it and reuse it: Throw it away!

One occasional source of zapped floppies, by the way, is magnetic damage. Just like an audio tape, a disk stores information by magnetizing tiny particles of metal stuff. If the disk gets magnetized by accident, the metal particles get rearranged in some random pattern that the Mac correctly deems to be unreadable.

I know that this sounds crazy, but *somebody* has to put it into print: Don't put refrigerator magnets on your Mac. That hard disk inside the machine is, after all, a disk, and magnets do to disks what gravity does to a watermelon dropped at 39,000 feet.

Your floppy disks don't hold the amount that they're supposed to

It's true — you can't fit 800K of information on an 800K disk or 1.4MB on a 1.4MB disk.

The missing storage capacity is filled by an invisible file, present on every disk, called the *Desktop file*. This file, which is the Mac's accounting department, is described in more detail in "Error Messages," earlier in this chapter.

The point is that the Desktop file takes up 7K or more on every disk. If it's taking up a lot more than that, you may have a *bloated* Desktop file; see "Rebuilding the Desktop File" in the next chapter for instructions on slimming it down.

Everything's Slow

Of course, if your Mac has seemed too slow since the day it arrived, maybe you just bought a model that's too slow for your demanding tastes. There's nothing for it except to upgrade to a faster model.

But if the Mac has begun acting slower since you've owned it, something may indeed be wrong.

First resort: After several months of using a Mac, it actually *does* slow down. The problem is a bloated Desktop file; the solution is described in "Rebuilding the Desktop File" in the next chapter.

Second resort: Choose Control Panels from your menu. Open the one called Memory. Is *virtual memory* turned on? If so, and if it's set higher than twice your Mac's *actual* RAM level, you've accounted for at least some of the sluggishness.

Third resort: While still in your Control Panels window, open the one called Views (systems before Mac OS 8 only). Is "Calculate folder sizes" turned on? If so, turn it off; it's slowing down the works.

Fourth resort: Just to be secure, read "Solving SCSI Nightmares" in the next chapter. A SCSI problem can also make your Mac act like it's on Sominex.

Last resort: If your hard drive is rather full, perhaps it needs to be *defragmented.* See "Defragmenting Your Hard Drive" in the next chapter.

Hardware Headaches

These glitches aren't as common as software problems, but they're just as frustrating.

The mouse is jerky or sticky

Like children, mops, and mimes, a mouse does its work by rolling around on the ground. It's bound to get dirty.

To clean it, turn it upside down in your hand. Very firmly rotate the round collar counterclockwise so that you can remove the little ball. (The idea is the same if you have a *trackball* instead of a mouse.) Dump the rubber or plastic ball into your hand, wash it off under the faucet, and let it air-dry completely.

In the meantime, go to work inside the socket where the ball usually is. With tweezers or something, pull out any obvious dust bunnies and hairballs. The main thing, though, is those three little rollers inside the cavity: You'll probably see stripes of accumulated gunk around them. With patience, a scissors blade (or a wad of sticky-side-out Scotch tape), and a good light, lift off that stuff, preferably making an effort not to let it fall inside the cavity. Keep turning the mouse right side up and tapping it on the table to dislodge stuff.

When you put everything back together, both you and your mouse will be much happier.

Double-clicking doesn't work

You're probably double-clicking too slowly, or you're moving the mouse a little bit during the double-click process.

Nothing appears when you type

First resort: Well, obviously, you can't just type at any time and expect to see text appear. You have to be either in a word processing program or in a text-editing area (for example, in a dialog box or in the little text-editing rectangle that appears when you're renaming an icon).

Second resort: Check the cable between the keyboard and the Mac. Make sure that it's *very* firmly plugged in at both ends.

Incidentally, the keyboard and mouse cables are especially sensitive to being plugged and unplugged while the computer is on. Be religious about shutting off the Mac before plugging and unplugging the cables. (That's especially true of SCSI cables. The same is *not* true of modem, printer, speaker, and microphone cables, though — you can plug and unplug them whenever you want. It's also not true on the iMac and other USB-jack Macs, where you can plug and unplug the keyboard and mouse to your heart's content.)

Your monitor shimmers

Of course, I don't mean that your monitor *itself* jiggles; I mean the picture.

First resort: Your screen's being subjected to some kind of electrical interference, such as a lamp, a fan, or an air conditioner running on the same circuit. Try a different plug, a different monitor location, or a different career.

Last resort: You live in an earthquake zone. Move to the Midwest.

There's a thin horizontal line all the way across your monitor

Believe it or not, many Apple monitors are *supposed* to show this faint line (it's about a third of the way up the screen); the 16-inch-and-larger models, in fact, have two such lines. They're shadows cast by a wire inside. Just grit your teeth and remind yourself, "It's a Sony." (Sony makes these monitors.)

Your monitor has a color tint

If your monitor looks like you're viewing it through rose-colored glasses (or green, or red, or any other color), you'll have a hard time retouching those scanned photos.

First resort: Check the cable to make sure it's firmly connected at each end.

Second resort: Try to isolate the problem. If you have other Macs available, test your monitor on a different Mac; substitute a different cable; substitute a different monitor.

Last resort: Your Mac's lithium battery may be dead. See "It's January 1, 1904" earlier in this chapter.

There's a wristwatch on the screen

When your cursor turns into a tiny wristwatch instead of an arrow, your Mac is thinking. It's saying, "Now computing, please wait." After a moment, the familiar arrow cursor should return. (If it doesn't, your Mac may be frozen, as described earlier in this chapter.)

And if your arrow cursor turns into an hourglass, you've got much bigger problems. You're not using a Mac at all!

Chapter 16
The Problem-Solving Cookbook

*I*f you've read the previous chapter, you've now heard about everything that can possibly go wrong and you're thoroughly depressed.

Here, then, is the literary equivalent of therapy: a chapter containing everything you can possibly do to *fix* the problem. Remember, you'll almost never find out what caused the problem to begin with; just be happy that the following techniques are almost magical in their ability to *cure* things.

Rebuilding the Desktop File

The desktop is a very important file on your disk. How come you've never seen it? Because the Desktop file is *invisible.* (Yes, Mac icons can be invisible. Remember that fact if you ever get involved in antiterrorist espionage activity.) The file is something that the Mac maintains for its own use.

The Mac stores two kinds of information in the Desktop file: the actual *pictures* used as icons for all your files; and information about the parent-child (program-document) *relationships* that you're having trouble with.

If the Desktop file becomes confused, two symptoms will let you know: the "generic icon" problem, where all your icons show up blank white, and the "Application not found" message that appears when you try to double-click something.

Another desktop-related problem: Over time, this invisible file gets bigger and bigger. Remember, it's having to store the pictures of every little icon that crosses your Mac's path. And just because you throw some icon away after using it doesn't mean that its image gets cleared from the Desktop file — it doesn't. And the bigger your Desktop file gets, the slower your Mac becomes in its efforts to open windows, display icons, and start up in the morning.

Resetting your Desktop file, therefore, has two delightful benefits. First, it cures the generic-icon syndrome and the "application not found" problem (because it re-learns the relationships between files and their pictures). Second, it makes your Mac faster (because it purges all the unnecessary leftover icon images from its invisible database).

Here's how you do it:

1. **Turn the computer on.**

2. **As it starts gearing up, press and *hold* the Option and ⌘ keys.**

   Don't let go. Keep them down until the Mac explicitly asks you whether you want to "rebuild the desktop." (Obviously, you should click OK.)

After that's done, your document double-clicking will work, your icons will return, and your Mac, having been cleansed of all obsolete icons, will run faster and more smoothly.

(P.S. If you use the child-protection program called At Ease — you'd know it if you do — turn it off before rebuilding the desktop.)

Zapping the PRAM

The PRAM ("PEA-ram") is a tiny piece of special memory that's kept alive by your Mac's built-in battery. The PRAM stores the settings you make in your control panels, such as the sound volume, mouse speed, memory, network, SCSI, and screen settings.

Rarely, rarely (but still sometimes), this tiny bit of memory gets corrupted somehow. Typical symptoms: Your control panels won't retain their settings; you can't print; you have strange networking problems.

To reset the PRAM, turn off the Mac. When you turn it on again, hold down the ⌘, Option, letter P, and letter R keys until you hear the second or third startup chord. Release the keys.

Afterward, you may have to reset your Mac's mouse-tracking speed, desktop pattern, speaker volume level, clock, and so on. Still, it's but the work of a moment to reset them using your control panels.

(PowerBook 500 or 5000 owners' note: Don't press the PRAM keys beyond the second chime. If you do, the PowerBook will shut down and can't be restarted until you press the back-panel power switch for 30 seconds.)

The Amazing "Force Quit" Keystroke

Here's the amazing keystroke for escaping a frozen program: ⌘-Option-Esc. (This is about the only time that you'll ever use the Esc key.)

You get a dialog box that says, "Force [this program] to quit?" Click Force Quit, and when it works, you exit the program that you were working in.

So what's the big whoop? Well, if you had several programs running, this technique dumps only the *one* that you were working in — the one that crashed. You now have a chance to enter each of the *other* programs that are still running and save your work (if you haven't done so). Then, to be on the safe side, restart the Mac.

The Restart Switch

Every Mac has a restart switch. Sometimes, two buttons are side by side somewhere on the Mac's casing — and the one with a left-pointing triangle is the Restart switch. Sometimes, as on older PowerBooks, there are two little back-panel *holes* that you're supposed to stick a pin into.

On most recent models, however, you have a *secret* Restart switch: Press Control, the ⌘ key, and the On button (or key) at the same time. On PowerBook laptops with a big white Apple logo, press the Fn, Ctrl, Shift, and On buttons instead. And on iMacs, press the power button for six seconds; if that doesn't work, poke an unfolded paper clip into the tiny hole on the side panel.

In every case, pressing Restart is the same as turning your Mac off and then on again, except that it's slightly gentler to your circuitry. Keep the Restart switch in mind when you have a System freeze or crash.

Solving an Extension Conflict

Okay, here it is — the long-awaited extension-conflict discussion.

See, each *extension* (a self-loading background program, such as a screen saver, that you install in your System Folder) was written by a programmer who had no clue what *other* extensions you'd be using. As a result, two extensions may fight, resulting in that polite disclaimer "Sorry, a System error has occurred."

These things are easy to fix, once you know the secret. Shut off your Mac, and then turn it on again. But as the Mac is starting up, *hold down the Shift key,* and keep it down until (1) you see the message "Extensions off" or (2) you arrive at the desktop, whichever you notice first.

Your Mac probably won't give you trouble anymore — but now, of course, you're running without *any* of your cute little extension programs. No CD-ROMs, no fax software, no Internet access, and so on.

If the point of this exercise is to pinpoint *which* extensions aren't getting along, you have two choices. One is free but takes a lot of time. The other way costs $60 but works automatically.

✔ **The hard way:** Turn off the Mac, and then turn it on again. While the Mac is starting up, press and hold the space bar down. Eventually, you'll be shown a complete list of your extensions, like this:

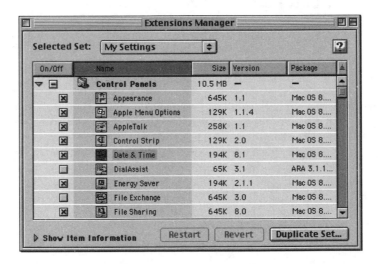

The point here is that you can *turn off* selected extensions and control panels just by clicking their names. (The little X means *on.* Or, in older versions, *black* — highlighted — means on.)

Special bonus feature! If you have System 7.6 or later, your Extensions Manager has an *extreeeemely* useful feature. In the previous picture, see the tiny triangle where it says Show Item Information? Click that to see a top-secret panel that tells you *exactly* what each extension is for. Click an extension's name in the list, and you'll be shown a little caption for it, such as "Warranty Minder Pro: This extension keeps track of how long it's been since you bought your Mac, and makes sure nothing goes wrong until after the warranty period is over."

But I digress. Using your Extensions Manager list, turn off a few of your extensions and control panels. Then restart the computer (click the Restart button at the bottom of the window).

If the Mac doesn't exhibit whatever unpleasant behavior you've been having, you can pretty much bet that one of the extensions you turned off was the guilty party. If the Mac *does* crash or act balky again, repeat the whole process, but this time turn some more extensions off.

Through trial and error, you eventually should be able to figure out which pair of extensions doesn't get along. Sometimes, just renaming one so that it alphabetically precedes its enemy is enough to solve the problem.

✔ **The easy way:** Buy a program called Conflict Catcher. This program does many useful things for managing your extensions, but its main virtue is catching conflicts. It can figure out, all by itself, which extension (or extensions) caused your Mac's problems. All you have to do is sit there, restarting the Mac over and over, each time telling Conflict Catcher whether or not the problem has been solved yet. By the time the process is over, the program will emblazon the name of the errant extensions on your screen; you then can dismember, disembowel, or trash them as you see fit.

(Yes, yes, okay, I wrote the manual for Conflict Catcher, but that's not why I'm mentioning it. Here's how I can prove my objectivity: I'll leak to you the fact that you can get a *free,* seven-day demo version from America Online or on the Internet at *www.casadyg.com*. It lasts just long enough for you to figure out which extensions were driving you crazy.)

Solving SCSI Nightmares

I've tried to shield you as much as possible from the term *SCSI* and all that it entails. But it's a common source of trouble — which may be why current Mac models (including iMacs) don't even *have* a SCSI jack — so it's time to put on the overalls and get dirty.

If there's nothing attached to your SCSI jack in the back of the Mac (for example, a scanner or a Zip drive), you *have* no SCSI problems, and you should skip this entire section. You don't know how lucky you are.

What's SCSI?

They pronounce it "scuzzy," for some reason. Here on the East Coast, we used to pronounce it "sexy," which I prefer, but the Valley girls and boys held sway.

Anyway, SCSI stands for Small Computer System Interface (or *Serial* Interface, or *Standard* Interface, depending on where you look it up; it's such a messed-up technology that nobody can even get the *name* right). SCSI describes the widest connector on the back of your Mac: the *SCSI port*. It also describes the fattest cable of any Mac appliance: the *SCSI cable*. It describes the kind of hard drives, scanners, SyQuest drives, computer CD players, and other gadgets that you attach to this jack: *SCSI devices*. It also describes the type of information that flows from those devices through those cables to that jack along the SCSI chain.

But frankly, the term that you hear most often is *SCSI problems*.

Examples: Some SCSI appliance (a scanner, a CD-ROM, a Zip drive, whatever) doesn't work right. Or your whole Mac is acting slow and weird. Or your Mac won't start up at all.

What's especially frustrating to people who write computer books is that you can't pin SCSI down. Even if you obey the "rules" (which I'll give you), things still go wrong.

The only good thing to say about SCSI problems is that once you figure out the problem with your setup, that problem is gone for good.

The rules of SCSI

Rule #1: You can string multiple SCSI devices together — or *daisy-chain* them, which is how you can use both an external drive and a scanner (for example), even though the Mac only has one SCSI jack. When the Mac attempts to talk to various devices along this SCSI train, it must be careful not to say "Start scanning!" to the hard drive or "Start spinning!" to the scanner. In other words, it has to address its messages carefully.

For that reason, every SCSI device in the world has a *SCSI address* between 0 and 7. Usually, a little number wheel that looks like a one-digit odometer is on the back or the bottom of your SCSI device. Each SCSI device connected to your Mac must have a *different* SCSI number (address) so that the Mac can speak to each appliance individually.

The Mac, which is part of the chain, has a SCSI number, which is always 7. Your internal hard drive has a SCSI number, too — it's always 0. If your Mac has a built-in CD-ROM player, its address is 3. So for your external drives, scanners, and so on, you can choose numbers 1, 2, 4, 5, or 6; just make sure that no two devices have the *same* number, or you're cruisin' for a bruisin'.

Rule #2: I wish I didn't have to mention SCSI Rule #2: The last device on the chain has to be terminated.

When I say *terminated,* I mean taken out and shot.

The second meaning for *terminated* is a little bit more complicated.

As the Mac sends its little instructions to the various SCSI devices attached to it, it shoves those instructions out the door with such force that they sometimes go all the way to the end of the cable and *bounce back* toward the Mac. Sometimes, the instructions make it all the way back, in which case you get nutty problems like a hard-drive icon showing up *twice* on the screen.

To soak up any messages that were pushed with too much oomph, you're supposed to put an electronic shock absorber at the beginning and the end of the line of devices. This absorber is called a *terminator,* Arnold Schwarzenegger notwithstanding.

Fortunately, you don't have to worry about the beginning terminator: Your SCSI chain is already terminated inside. And if you also have only *one* SCSI device outside your Mac, you don't need a terminator on the outside end. (I'm perfectly aware that this contradicts Rule #2, but it doesn't contradict **Rule #3,** which is that these rules don't always apply. Including Rule #3.)

After you have two or more SCSI things attached to the back of your Mac, though, it's time to start thinking about termination. You add termination by attaching a three-inch stopper plug (called, obviously, a terminator) to the empty SCSI jack of the last device on the chain. Some devices (such as the Zip drive), however, have a terminator *switch* on the back or bottom. You can just flip this switch between the terminated and unterminated positions.

There's hope for us all, by the way; progress, marching on the way it tends to do, has brought us *automatic* termination on a few sweet devices (such as the Jaz drive). On these SCSI gizmos, you don't have to buy a terminator plug at all; these gadgets self-terminate automatically when necessary.

Rule #4: Your SCSI *cables* can make or break the entire operation. Use thick, expensive ones. And if everything else seems hunky-dory, it's conceivable that the trouble is their *combined lengths*. They're not supposed to add up to more than 18 feet or so, and, as with speeches and Willie Nelson songs, the shorter the better.

Oh, and while we're talking about SCSI cables, you should know this: They go bad. It's true. One rich guy I know threw out an 800MB hard drive because he thought that it had died permanently. Upon rescuing it from the dumpster, an enterprising Mac buddy discovered that the drive was fine; the *cable* had been crimped by a piece of furniture. After he spent $30 on a new SCSI cable, the drive was as good as new. It's probably worth replacing, or at least switching, the cables if you're still having SCSI problems.

Rule #5: If your SCSI setup isn't working, try rearranging the physical order of the devices in your SCSI chain. It makes no sense, but sometimes rearranging makes things work when nothing else does. Anyway, at this point, you're entitled to be a little irrational.

Rule #6: Okay, you've made sure that every device has its own address. If you have more than one external SCSI device, you've terminated the last one. But things *still* aren't working right.

In this case, try taking *off* the terminator. I'm perfectly serious. SCSI **Rule #7** is: If a rule isn't working, try breaking it. Here at home, for example, I have both a scanner and a Zip drive plugged into the back of my Mac — and *no* external terminators. What sense does that make? I don't know — but I do know that if I follow Rule #2 and add a terminator, nothing works, and my hard-drive icon doesn't appear on the screen.

Someday, we'll laugh and tell our grandchildren, "Why, when I was your age, we used to have to *add terminator plugs to our external devices!*" Until that golden day, though, we have to put up with this cranky and unpredictable technology. Good luck to you.

Giving More Memory to a Program

When you turn on your Mac, several megabytes of its available RAM (memory) get used up by your System Folder's contents — your operating system. Then, every time you launch a program, a little bit of the leftover free RAM gets used up.

Here's how to find out where your memory is going at any particular moment:

Go to the Finder. From the menu, choose About This Computer. This helpful dialog box appears, showing several important numbers about your use of memory:

This is how much real memory your Mac has, not counting "fake" memory contributed by RAM Doubler or virtual memory.

About This Computer
Mac OS computer	Mac OS	Mac OS 8.5
Built-in Memory: 64 MB
Virtual Memory: 65 MB used on Macintosh HD
Largest Unused Block: 38.6 MB	™ & © Apple Computer, Inc. 1983-1998
America Online	10.2 MB
ClarisWorks	2.5 MB
Mac OS	14.2 MB

This is the largest chunk of memory you have left, into which you can open more programs. (There may be smaller chunks available, too.)

In the bottom part of the box, you can see what's already taking up memory and how *much* memory each program is taking up (see those bars?).

You may find it useful, however, to *change* the amount of memory that each of your programs uses. If you're experiencing a lot of system crashes, for example, the program may need a bigger memory allotment. If memory is at a premium, you may occasionally be able to give a program *less* memory, freeing some for other purposes.

Here's how:

1. *Quit* **the program whose memory appetite you want to change and then click its icon.**

   This step frequently confuses beginners; for help in quitting a program, see "First resort: Quit programs" in Chapter 15. And don't be fooled into clicking the *folder* a program's in, either — open the folder and click the *program icon itself.*

2. **From the File menu, choose Get Info.**

   A dialog box appears; if you're using Mac OS 8.5, choose Memory from the Show: pop-up menu.

   In any case, you should now see a window like this:

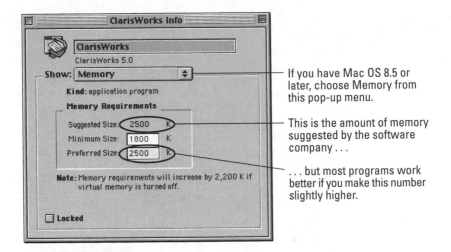

3. Change the number in the Preferred size box.

This number is the amount of memory that the program will actually consume when you run it. If your aim is to make this program stabler or faster, try increasing this number by, for example, 10 percent.

Unless System crashes make your life more interesting, don't set the Preferred size much *below* the Suggested size, though.

Performing a "Clean System Reinstall"

This procedure is just a wee bit technical. But it's *amazing* how many problems it solves. Font problems, crash problems, freeze problems, glitch problems, weird things you can't even describe very well — all of them go away when you do a *clean install.*

As the gears of your System Folder grind away day after day, little corruptions and rough edges can develop. The following procedure replaces your old, possibly corroded System Folder with a brand-spanking-new one. It's nearly *guaranteed* to wipe out any erratic, bizarre crashes or freezes that you've been having; after all, it restores the Mac to the exact condition it was in the day it left the factory.

This process requires the System Software Installer that came on a CD with your Mac.

Step one: Install the fresh software

This first step depends on which system version you have.

If you have System 7.6-point-something or **Mac OS 8.5:** Insert the System CD. Double-click the Installer icon. After you've clicked the Start button on the Software Installations screen, click the Options button on the regular Installer screen. You'll be offered a "Create additional System Folder (clean install)" option — that's the one you want.

If you have Mac OS 8 or **8.1:** Insert System CD. Double-click the Installer icon. Click Continue. On the Select Destination Screen, click the Perform Clean Installation checkbox.

If you have System 7.5-point-something: Insert System CD (or the first Installer floppy disk). Double-click the Installer icon. Click Continue. At the main installation screen — where you'd normally click the Install button — press ⌘-Shift-K, of all things. You'll be asked which you want: a *brand-new System Folder,* or just an updated *existing* System Folder. You want the whole new one. Click your choice, click OK, click Install, and then follow the directions.

Regardless of which option you used, click whatever OK, Continue, or Install buttons you're offered until the installation process is complete.

Step two: Restore your personal belongings

The result of all these shenanigans is a virgin, clean System Folder, free of any corruptions. Your Mac will run smooth, fast, and trouble-free — I guarantee it.

Unfortunately, all your customized fonts, control panels, preferences, and menu items are stranded back in your *old* System Folder!

Ideally, you should install each of these items from their original, store-bought disks. If that's too much hassle, set up your old System Folder and your new System Folder side-by-side in tall, skinny, list-view windows. Now copy anything that's not in your *new* System Folder, item by item, from your old System Folder to your new System Folder. (Key folders to compare with their newer counterparts: Preferences; Extensions; Control Panels; Apple Menu Items; and Fonts.) Do so with care, however, so that you don't simply reinstate whatever problems you were having.

Defragmenting Your Hard Drive

Over time, you create and throw away a lot of files.

Your hard drive, if you'll indulge me, is like a closet maintained by a guy who's always in a hurry. When guests are coming over, he cleans up the living room by throwing everything into the closet, not particularly neatly. Every now and then, when he gets time, he unpacks the closet and repacks it neatly, putting everything in a tidy, organized place.

The hard drive, too, is in a hurry. When you ask it to save a file, it doesn't wait around: It shoves that file wherever it can find space. Sometimes, that even means sticking the file in *two* places, splitting it as necessary. Over time, more and more files are stored on your hard disk in pieces. It's no big deal: When you need that file again, the hard drive remembers where all the pieces are and is perfectly able to bring the file back to the screen.

But all this hunting for pieces slows the drive down, especially when your drive gets 80 percent full and stays that way for awhile. And like our busy closet keeper, you'll find it very satisfying, every six months or so, to reorganize the files on your disk so that they're each in one piece, neatly placed end to end on the hard-drive surface.

You can *defragment* your drive (which is the term for it) in two ways. First, you can copy everything onto other disks, erase the hard drive, and copy the files back onto it. Second, you can buy a program just for defragmenting your drive. These programs are called things like Norton Utilities and DiskExpress. (Back up your work before using these programs, however; if you're into living dangerously, go skydiving.)

Chapter 17

Beyond Point-and-Click: Where to Go from Here

In This Chapter

▶ Facing the future, credit card in hand

▶ Where to turn when things go wrong

▶ Now get outside for some fresh air

You own the world's most forgiving, self-explanatory computer. But things will go wrong. And not even this astoundingly complete book can anticipate the problems you may encounter while running BeeKeeper Pro™ or No Namo™ Scanner Doodad Plus.

Where to Turn in Times of Trouble

When things go wrong, the world is crawling with help possibilities. For example, during the first three months you've owned your Mac, you can call Apple's delightful toll-free hotline at 800-500-7078 and ask your questions of the gurus there.

Beyond those 90 days, Apple charges you for your use of their experts (unless the computer actually turns out to need fixing, in which case the fee is waived). The number for this service is 888-275-8258 (toll-free again), and you can choose to have your wallet milked in any of the following quantities: One call for $35, three for $70, fifteen for $340. (They're not quite that stingy, by the way — if it takes several calls to resolve your problem, that's still considered one call.)

The bottom line: Try to have all your problems in the first 90 days.

If spending moolah isn't your way of problem solving, consider these all-expenses-paid avenues:

- **www.info.apple.com:** Part of Apple's Web site (which you can visit if you have an America Online or Internet account — see Chapter 11). You can get software updates, ask questions in electronic bulletin-board discussion areas, and access the Technical Information Library — a searchable electronic encyclopedia of all things Macintosh.

- **AppleFax:** Call 800-505-0171 by telephone, listen to the instructions, punch in your own fax number when you're asked for it, put in a fresh roll of fax paper, and stand back. You'll be sent a list of pre-typed answers to common questions.

- **800-SOS-APPL:** This phone number brings you to a voicemail labyrinth that would freak out Theseus. Dig deep enough into the maze, and you can find automated, pre-recorded tips, tricks, and troubleshooting techniques.

- **No Wonder Web page:** Visit this page for free, 24-hour, personal computer help at *www.nowonder.com.*

- **MacFixIt Web page:** You get hundreds of discussions of little tweaky specific Mac problems at *www.macfixit.pair.com.*

- **Tech Exchange bulletin boards:** Apple reps offer advice and answers. Go to this Web page: *support.info.apple.com/te/te.qry.*

Otherwise, your next resort should be a local user group, if you're lucky enough to live in a pseudo-metropolitan area. A user group, of course, doesn't exist to answer *your* personal questions; you still have to do some phoning and hobnobbing and research. But a user group *is* a source of sources. You can call up and find out who will know the answer to your question.

The other great source of help is an electronic meeting place like America Online, where you may get your question answered instantly — and if not, you can post your question on a bulletin board for somebody to answer overnight. Try keyword *MOS,* for example. (See Chapter 11 for details on keywords.) If you're Internet savvy, you can visit a *newsgroup* (see Chapter 11) called *comp.sys.mac* for similar assistance.

As for your continuing education — after you spend a month's salary on a computer, I'll bet you can afford $20 more for a subscription to *Macworld, MacAddict,* or *MacHome Journal* magazine. Agreed, huge chunks of these rags may go right over your head. But in every single issue, you'll find at least one really useful item. You can learn all kinds of things just by reading the ads. And if you're not in touch with the computer nerd world at least by that tenuous thread — via magazine — then you might miss stuff like free offers, recall notices, warnings, and other consumer-oriented jazz.

Buy a book — clothe an author

The publisher of this book has decided that, by gum, there's a market for this stuff, so he persuaded me to write two more — the David Pogue Macintosh Library. Without even thinking about it, I've wound up writing an entire course in Macintosh.

First, there's *MORE Macs For Dummies,* which:

✔ Goes into greater detail about what to do on the Internet, including making your own Web page

✔ Describes and rates the top 200 most-advertised Mac programs

✔ Reveals a bunch more of those cool hidden Option-key stunts

✔ Shows how to connect two Macs

✔ Helps you fake your way through Photoshop, Illustrator, Freehand, Quick-Time, and other programs

And then, when you *really* become an expert, you'll be ready for *Macworld Mac Secrets,* which has 1,400 pages, comes with a CD-ROM filled with cool programs, and requires a fork-lift to move.

A New Leash on Life: Upgrading

Here's the thing about upgrading your Mac: It's a psychological trap. Your *thinking* goes like this: "I've got so much invested in this thing, I'll just pay for a little bit of enhancement. That way, I retain my investment."

But the reality goes like this: While you were happily owning your Mac, *new* Macs got a lot faster and a lot less expensive. Buying an upgrade (in the sense of replacing the guts of your Mac) almost always costs more than buying a new Mac (and selling your old one)!

Now, despite the astounding genius of Pogue's New Upgrade Math, some Mac add-ons are worth adding: *memory* and *storage.*

For example, if your hard drive has become full, and you're spending ten minutes a day weeding through old stuff to throw out, it's time to get a Zip drive (see Chapter 18). And if you're getting out-of-memory messages all the time, and you've tried all the tricks in Chapter 16 for making do with what you have, consider installing more memory chips (known as *SIMMs* or *DIMMs*).

Adding memory or storage doesn't quite qualify for the term *upgrade,* really, but it does make using your Mac a happier experience for not much money.

Save Changes before Closing?

If you do decide to pursue this Macintosh thing, I've listed contact information for magazines, mail-order businesses, a user-group info line, and Web pages in Appendix B.

But wait a minute — the point of this book wasn't to convert you into a full-time Mac rabbit. It was to get you off the ground. To give you just enough background so that you'll know why the computer's beeping at you. To show you the basics and help you figure out what the beanie heads are talking about.

Don't let them intimidate you. So *what* if you don't know the lingo or have the circuitry memorized? If you can turn the thing on, get something written up and printed, and get out in time to enjoy the sunshine, you qualify as a real Mac user.

Any dummy knows that.

Top Ten Topics Not Covered in This Book

If you have any interest in any of these topics, the shelves are full of geekier books than this one.

1. Programming
2. Networking
3. Any add-on that costs over $1,000
4. Color separations
5. Multimedia
6. Hard-disk partitioning
7. Publish and Subscribe
8. Java
9. Security
10. The terms *ROM, interleave, user-centric, initiate, V.32 bis, TCP/IP, user-definable, DRAM, implement, CDEV, nanosecond, kerning, VRAM, magneto-optical, token-ring, Ethernet, directory,* or *AUTOEXEC.BAT*

Part VI
The Part of Tens

The 5th Wave   **By Rich Tennant**

THE COMMITTEE FOR THE PROLIFERATION OF MACINTOSH COMPUTERS FINALLY PAY A VISIT TO LARRY.

In this part . . .

Here's what *...For Dummies* book authors often refer to as "great stuff that didn't quite fit the outline" — a list of top 10 lists, for your infotainment pleasure.

Chapter 18

Ten More Gadgets to Buy and Plug In

● ●

*I*n this chapter, you'll find out about several impressive and high-tech gadgets you can spend money on — yes, it's Credit Card Workout #4. These devices give the Mac eyes and ears, turn it into a national network, and turn it into an orchestra. You're not obligated to purchase any of them, of course. But knowing about some of the amazing things your computer can do will help you understand why a Mac is such a big deal.

When you're all done spending money, your Mac setup may look as luxurious as this one:

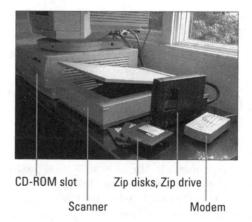

CD-ROM slot   Zip disks, Zip drive

Scanner   Modem

A Scanner

If the point of a printer is to take something on the screen and reproduce it on *paper,* then a scanner is the opposite — its function is to scan an image on paper and throw it up on the Mac *screen.* After the image has been scanned and converted into bits and bytes that the Mac understands (meaning that it's been *digitized*), you can manipulate it any way you want. Erase unwanted parts, make the background darker, give Uncle Ed a mustache, shorten your brother's neck, whatever. The more dignified use for a scanner is grabbing real-world images that you then paste into your own documents, particularly in the realm of page layout and graphic design. Got a potato-industry newsletter to crank out? Scan in a photo of some fine-lookin' spuds, and you've got yourself a graphic for page one.

Unfortunately, when you scan a page of *text,* the Mac doesn't see English words. It sees lots of itty-bitty dots in funny patterns. When the image pops up on your screen after being scanned, you can't correct a typo — because it's not really text anymore, just a picture of text. (Analogy time: If you take a Polaroid of a handwritten grocery list, you can't then erase *Charmin 8-Roll Pack* from the *photo,* because it's no longer handwriting — just a picture of some writing.)

To convert that picture of text into a true text document, you need a piece of highly brainy software designed for *optical character recognition,* which is so unhelpful a term that people abbreviate it OCR out of sheer disgust. Using OCR, you can save yourself massive amounts of retyping; you can just roll the magazine article, book page, or other text document through your scanner and wait while your OCR program examines each letter to decide its identity. The result is a text document that's about 98 percent correctly typed.

So how much is all this gonna cost you? A middle-of-the-line color scanner costs between $200 and $400. An OCR program costs between $200 and $800, depending on its sophistication.

A Digital Camera

Ordinarily, the concept of paying $500 for a camera that lacks any way to insert film would seem spectacularly brain-dead. Yet that's exactly the point of *digital cameras,* like those from Apple, Casio, Olympus, Ricoh, Sony, and others. They store between 10 and 150 photos without film — actually, in *RAM,* now that you know what that is — and when you get home, you can dump them into your Macintosh (after connecting a cable), thereby freeing your camera's RAM for another round of happy-go-lucky shooting.

For people who need instant, no-cost developing (doctors, people needing pictures for World Wide Web pages, real-estate hounds, fraternity party animals, and so on), these cameras are a godsend. As a matter of fact, just to prove the point, I took all the photos in this chapter using a little Olympus jobber. The results aren't pro quality — you'll have to pay $5,000 or more for digital cameras that take magazine-quality photos — but they're great for, say, illustrating computer books.

A Modem

A modem is a phone hookup — a box that sits between the Mac and a phone jack. Of course, if you're already using the Internet or America Online, you've already encountered the wonderful world of modems.

Some Macs, such as the iMac and the more expensive PowerBooks, come with a built-in modem. Just use a piece of normal telephone wire to connect this jack to the phone jack in the wall, and you're ready for cyberspace. If your Mac didn't come with one, you can buy one for about $100. For more scoop on modems, and what they're good for (such as America Online and the Internet), see Chapters 11 and 12.

Actually, it's hard to find a plain old modem these days. Today, almost every modem is a *fax modem,* meaning that instead of just being a modem, it can also turn your Mac into a big gray fax machine. A fax modem can receive any kind of fax; the incoming document appears on your Mac screen, where you can read it, print it on your printer, or throw it away.

To *send* a fax, you prepare the document (that you want to send) on your Mac. For most people, that means typing it up in a word processor. This, of course, is the one disadvantage to owning a fax modem instead of a real fax machine: You can only send documents that are on the Mac. You can't fax someone, for example, an article from *MAD* magazine, because it doesn't exist on your Mac screen. (Unless you go to the trouble of buying a scanner and scanning it in.)

A CD-ROM Drive

Nothing spices up a good discussion like a baffling computer equipment acronym, y'know?

Fortunately, you already know half of this one: CD stands for Compact Disc, just like the ones that you play on your stereo. Instead of holding music, though, a CD-ROM holds computer information — *tons* of it. And the hot new CD-ROM sibling that's slowly becoming available on new Mac models, DVD-ROM, is exactly the same — but a DVD disc holds *seven times* as many tons of data. (Don't even worry about what ROM stands for. It'd leave you even more confused.)

Every Mac made today, even a laptop, comes equipped with a CD-ROM player built right in; it spits out a sliding CD tray when you press a button on the front panel. (If you have an older model, you can buy a CD-ROM player as a separate gadget that plugs into the back of your Mac.)

Into this tray, you can insert a CD-ROM. CD-ROMs contain pictures, sound, movies, graphics, and text . . . enough to keep you busy for days. One CD-ROM contains an encyclopedia, complete with color pictures, some of which are movies that show the motion of, say, the Venezuelan Sun Gekko. Another is a dictionary where you actually hear a guy read the pronunciation of each word. Another CD-ROM is a video game — an *interactive* one, like a TV show where *you* control where the main character goes next.

CD-ROMs worth taking for a spin

So you got the Mac with the built-in CD-ROM. Now what do you feed it?

Aside from the sampler discs that came with the drive, here are some ideas. Get Myst, a gorgeous, multiple award-winning, mysterious game/story set on an abandoned misty island, and/or its even more impressive sequel, Riven. Get the Living Books discs (Just Grandma and Me, Arthur's Teacher Trouble, The Tortoise and the Hare, and so on) if you have kids of any variety. The encyclopedias are generally a dis-

appointment, but Encarta is pretty good. You might consider Street Atlas USA, which is a U.S. map you can zoom in on, right down to the individual side streets — you can look up an individual street address and be shown where in the country it is. Similarly, the Electronic Arts 3-D Atlas is really a killer — it lets you fly over the whole world, zooming down in on spots you want to visit.

Those suggestions ought to tide you over until Christmas, anyway.

Most software programs these days come on one CD-ROM disc instead of 45 floppies, so a CD-ROM player is a worthy asset. But here's a tip: Don't get stressed about the speed rating of these things. In reading ads and browsing computer stores, you'll hear all about "8X" drives, 12X, 24X, and so on. Don't make the mistake of attributing some logic behind this naming scheme! Each is only *slightly* faster than the model with the next lower "X" rating — nowhere near double the speed — and you should save your money accordingly.

Speakers

Oh, yes indeedy: The Mac is more than hi-tech — it's hi-*fi,* capable of churning out gorgeous stereo signals from its back-panel speaker jacks. When you listen to the Mac's tinny two-inch built-in speaker, though, you don't hear it.

If you get a pair of miniature speakers designed for the purpose, you're in for a tintinnabulating treat. If you play Mac games, particularly CD-ROM discs, you won't believe what you've been missing; the sounds are suddenly much richer and deeper. And, of course, in stereo.

If you don't do much more with sound than listen to your Mac's startup chord, don't bother buying speakers. But if you *do* want speakers, not just any old speakers will work. They must be *self-powered,* and they must be *shielded;* the magnets inside normal stereo speakers are enough to distort the image on your monitor like the Sunday comics on Silly Putty. In other words, buy speakers designed for the purpose; Apple, Yamaha, Sony, and many other companies make lines of Mac-ready speakers.

Of course, you can also plug your Mac into your existing stereo system. You just have to (a) get the right cables, and (b) learn to live with the cord trailing across the floor and into the back of your amplifier.

Music and MIDI

Oh, groan . . . another abbreviated computer term! All right, let's get it over with.

MIDI, pronounced like the short skirt, stands for Musical Instrument Digital Interface. What it *means* is "hookup to a synthesizer." What it *does* is let your Mac record and play back your musical performances using a synthesizer attached to it. When you record, the Mac makes a metronome sound — a steady click track — and you play to the beat. Then, when you play back the music, your keyboard plays *exactly* what you recorded, complete with feeling, expression, and fudged notes; you'd think that Elvis's ghost was playing the instrument, except that the keys don't move up and down. Then you can edit your fudged mistakes and wind up sounding like [insert your favorite musician here].

All you need is a little box that connects your Mac to the synthesizer. It's called a *MIDI interface,* and it shouldn't cost more than about $50. You also need a program that can record and play back the music, called a *sequencing program.* Some easy-to-use and inexpensive ones are MusicShop and Freestyle. And, of course, you need to get your hands on a synthesizer. Or, for making sheet music, investigate Encore, Overture, or Finale (in increasing degrees of completeness and complexity). Check out a music store and get jammin'.

A Trackball

People who don't like computer mice often take great delight in replacing their Mac mouse with a trackball. A trackball looks like an eight ball set into a six-inch square base; you move the pointer on the screen by rolling the ball in place with your fingers.

SuperDisks, Zip Disks, and Jaz, Oh My!

There's only one thing wrong with hard disks: Like closets, garages, and land-fills, they fill up. No matter how much of a neatness nerd you are, even if you promptly throw away anything you're finished working on, you'll gradually watch your "MB available" count go down, down, down over the months, until your hard disk is completely full. (Thousands of experienced Mac users all over the world are sagely nodding their heads in sorrowful acknowledgment.)

So what are you supposed to do? Go back to writing on Post-it™ notes? Well, you could buy another hard disk. The one *inside* your computer is called an *internal* hard drive. If you buy another, you could plug it into the back of your Mac and have access to its contents as well. (This, as you may have guessed, would be called an *external* hard drive.) But that's an expensive proposition, and the darnedest thing of all is that *that* hard drive will fill up, too.

For thousands of storage-starved people, the solution is to get a *removable-cartridge* system. This device looks just like an external hard drive, except when the spinning platters get full, you can just pull them out of the machine (they're sealed into a plastic cartridge) and put in a new, blank, virgin cartridge. Since a 100-megabyte Zip disk, for example, only costs about $15, you can see why a removable cartridge is an attractive idea.

A removable-cartridge system solves another chronic problem, too: how to *back up* your data. To back up is to make a spare copy of your important files, so if something should happen to your main hard disk (or *you* do something to it) and all your files get erased, you haven't lost your life's work.

But placing a second copy of everything on the *same* hard disk doesn't make much sense; if the hard disk croaks, then you lose both copies. Many people copy their data onto floppy disks, as discussed in Chapter 3. That's certainly cheap, but it's inconvenient, especially if you work with large files like graphics. With a removable-cartridge system, you can back up your entire hard drive in five minutes.

Iomega is the primary maker of removable-cartridge systems; especially popular are its amazing Zip disks. These things look like floppy disks that have been hitting the Ben & Jerry's a bit too often. As mentioned earlier, each holds 100MB or 250MB and costs about $15; the Zip drive, the player, costs $150. These Zip disks are fantastically convenient, sturdy, and easy to work with. (The same company makes an even fatter and faster version called the Jaz drive; each $50 disk holds 1,000MB or 2,000MB, and the drive costs $400.)

Another popular option, especially with iMac and blue Power Mac owners, is the SuperDisk drive (from Imation). It acts just like a Zip drive, accepting its own special kind of fattened-up floppies (which hold 120MB each) — but it *also* accepts ordinary floppy disks, a handy bonus for otherwise floppyless Macs.

A Digitizing Tablet

So you say you're an artist. Why, of *course* you are, dear — you bought a Macintosh!

So you say you're finding it a tad difficult to draw with a mouse that's about as precisely shaped as a chalkboard eraser? Then a digitizing tablet is just the ticket for you. As you can see in the photo, it's simply a pad that connects to your Mac; it comes with a *pen* (usually cordless) that lets you manipulate your on-screen cursor just by *drawing* (dragging your pen around on the pad).

Especially when used with programs that respond to the pressure of the pen by drawing fatter lines, like Photoshop and Painter, a tablet is the closest you can come to making your Mac act like natural painting tools.

A Network

You already know what a *network* is. It's the television company that broadcasts stuff like *Baywatch* so you'll have something to watch when you're burned out from computer work.

In the computer world, though, a network is defined as *more than one Mac hooked together*. In some offices, hundreds of Macs are all interconnected. Some advantages of being networked: You can send e-mail to other people, which pops up on their screens; you can have access to each others' files and programs; and you can save money by buying just one printer (or scanner or modem) for use with a whole bunch of Macs.

The goal of this book is to get you going with your *own* Mac. If you really, truly, honestly want to read about connecting Macs together (normally the domain of gurus, computer whizzes, and paid consultants), read *MORE Macs For Dummies.*

A Surge Suppressor

This thing looks like an ordinary multiple-outlet extension cord from the hardware store, but it's supposed to have an additional benefit — circuitry that can absorb an electrical voltage surge, and thus protect your Mac from such electrical anomalies. Not many people realize that the Mac already has a *built-in* surge suppressor, however. Furthermore, a surge suppressor's value has long been debated. (They're not designed to protect you from acts of God, though. I've known people with surge suppressors whose Macs got fried by lightning, as well as people *without* surge suppressors whose houses were struck by lightning without affecting the Mac.) Let your paranoia be your guide.

Plugging the stuff in

Suppose you win the lottery. You buy every Mac add-on there is. Only two things left to do: (a) give half your winnings to the IRS and (b) figure out where to plug the stuff in.

The answer is clear: It depends. Today's iMacs, blue Power Macs, and other recent models offer a totally different assortment of jacks than previous Mac models. Therefore, where you plug things in depends on which model you own. Let's take the two generations of Macs separately:

iMacs, blue Power Macs, and other models with USB jacks: Whatever add-on doodad you've bought, it probably plugs into one of the two skinny horizontal *USB jacks* on the side or back of your machine. That goes for *scanners, Zip drives, SuperDisk drives, digital cameras, MIDI adapters, inkjet printers, PalmPilot cradles, keyboards,* and *mice.* (If you have older versions of these gizmos that don't have

USB connectors, a wealth of adapters awaits. Visit *www.imacintouch.com* for exhaustive lists of these products.)

"Great," you're saying, "but I can't plug all that jazz into my Mac, which has only two USB jacks!" Ah, but that's the beauty of *USB hubs,* inexpensive boxes that offer four, eight, or more *additional* USB jacks. You can have everything plugged in at once, all working at once, and you can plug and unplug them without turning off the Mac. (Don't try *that* on older Macs!)

If you've got a *laser printer* or *network,* you plug that into the Ethernet jack instead (looks like a telephone wall jack that's been enlarged in a radioactive accident).

Older Mac models: Plug *scanners, external CD-ROM players, external hard drives, Zip drives, Jaz drives,* and *SuperDisk drives* into

(continued)

(continued)

the SCSI port. It's the wide one with screws on each side. So how are you supposed to plug in so many different things if there's only one port? Simple — by *daisy-chaining* them, one to another. Daisy-chaining is an act of utter bravery, however, and should not be undertaken until after you've read the "Scuzzy SCSI" section in Chapter 16 and had a nice cool drink. Until then, plug *one* machine only into the SCSI jack of your Mac.

Meanwhile, you plug *modems, MIDI interfaces (music), label printers, digital camera, digitizing tablets,* and *PalmPilot cradles* into the modem port. It's the little round jobber marked by a telephone icon. So how are you supposed to plug more than one of these into your Mac?

You have two choices, both of which involve using only one device at a time. First, you can just unplug one device before using the next. Second, you can get an A/B switch box that acts like a Y-splitter; you plug both modem port pluggables into this box and then turn a knob to select which one you want the Mac to pay attention to. (You can even buy an A/B/C/D box that accommodates *four* devices if you've really gone crazy with this kind of peripheral.)

If you have a *camcorder* or *VCR,* you'll find a built-in jack for this on certain models (see Chapter 20), marked by a little movie-camera icon.

You've probably figured out, all by yourself, that the *printer* gets connected to the printer port (another small, round jack, next to the modem port, and marked by a printer icon). But it's good to know that this is where you plug in the cabling for a *network,* too, if you have one, and if it's the *LocalTalk* variety. (See *MORE Macs For Dummies* if you want to set up a network or if you haven't the vaguest notion of what I'm talking about.)

So where does the printer go if your printer port is used up by a network connection? Easy — it gets hooked into the network so that anyone can use it. (See your resident guru for details.)

Finally, if you're on an *Ethernet* network, your guru can help you. (The cable goes into the Ethernet jack, which, as noted above, looks like a fattened telephone wall jack.) *MORE Macs For Dummies* lurks, too, with Ethernet-setting-up instructions.

Chapter 19

Ten Screamingly Important Things Nobody Tells You

• •

*1*t's amazing anybody can use computers at all, really. You're sold a computer, you're handed a manual written by people who read *Popular Semiconductor,* and you're kicked out of the nest.

Think about every important lesson you've learned in life. You learned about con artists only after being swindled. You learned to drive more carefully only after your first accident. You learned how to be careful in relationships only after having your heart broken.

It's the same way with computers. Sure, you'll learn sooner or later; but most people have to learn everything the hard way. *You* get to sit back in your La-Z-Boy and *read* about it.

It Doesn't Need to Be Repaired.

Even if something funny's going on with your Mac, the machine itself is probably fine.

Most beginners, though, immediately suspect the circuitry. I understand the instinct. I mean, when VCRs, lawn mowers, or electric razors go on the fritz, you're right — you need a repair shop. But a computer's different; it has *software.* When your Mac starts behaving oddly, it's probably a software problem, not a mechanical one. That means you can fix it yourself, for free. Almost always.

Chapter 16 shows the steps you can take to restore your Mac's software to health. Until then, just remember: These machines are built like rocks and almost never "break."

(PowerBooks are another story. You would be, too, if you were hauled around in a briefcase.)

Don't Buy Version 1.0 of Anything.

This principle isn't just true of software or Macs; it's true of cars and houses and medicines, too. The rationale is simple: If it's brand new, there's no way all the bugs and kinks have been ironed out.

Even if the software company's 20 paid testers can't find any problems, it's amazing what happens when 100,000 ordinary mortals start banging away on it. Problems crop up from nowhere, hidden bugs emerge, and the "early adopters" (people who bought the 1.0 version) pay the price.

The software company rushes to correct the problems, and it releases a new version called something like 1.01. *That's* the version you should buy.

Any New Program Must Be Installed.

You buy a new program. Let's say it's After Dark: The Oprah Winfrey Collection. You admire the handsome disks, turning the cool plastic squares over and over in your hand until you get really bored.

At last you decide you want to install the software and start seeing talk-show characters parading across your screen. You manage to insert the disk correctly (metal side first, label side up). And then you stare dumbly at the screen, not knowing what to do next, and definitely not seeing any signs of Oprah.

Today's store-bought programs are much too complicated for the typical college-educated American to install correctly, having a multitude of files that must all be carefully deposited in specific places on your hard drive to work. Therefore, the vast majority of them come equipped with some kind of automatic *Installer*. In other words, when you shove the disk or the CD-ROM disc into your Mac, you'll usually see something like one of those on the next page.

I'm sure you get the point: You're looking for the word *Installer* somewhere on your screen. Double-click whatever says Installer. From here on, you're on autopilot. The program shows you a few welcoming messages, explains what's about to happen, and maybe lists what's about to be dumped onto your hard drive. Just keep smiling and clicking OK buttons until it's over.

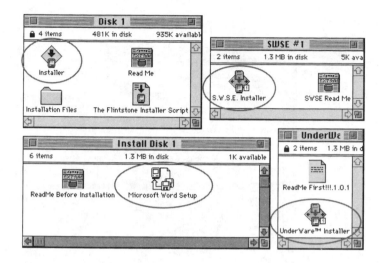

Do the Shift-Key Trick before Installing.

One more thing about installing. Unless you find that computer headaches make life more interesting, do this. Before you install any new program, restart your Mac. As it's starting up again, hold down the Shift key until you read "Extensions off" or "Extensions disabled" on your screen.

You've just disabled any antivirus programs or other startup programs that give most software Installers fits.

Of course, if the software you're installing arrived at your place aboard a CD-ROM disc, you're probably sneering in disgust at this advice. "I happen to know," you're probably muttering, causing funny looks from the passersby, "that if I turn all my extensions off with the Shift key, *I can't use my CD-ROM drive!* So how am I supposed to install my new software?"

This is, of course, true: If you start up the Mac with the Shift key down, you can insert CDs into the disc tray from now till Doomsday, and the Mac will completely ignore you; no CD icon will show up on the screen.

Therefore, the safest way to install new software from a CD is to turn off all your extensions *except* those needed for your CD-ROM! To do so, restart the Mac; as it's starting up, press the space bar; you'll be shown a nice neat list of all your extensions, like this:

Step 4

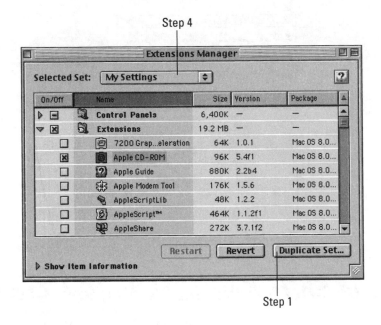

Step 1

Now try this:

1. **Click the Duplicate Set button. Type** *CD-ROM Only* **and press Return.**

2. **Turn all of your extensions off, clicking the little boxes so that the X's disappear,** *except* **for the ones with the words** *CD* **or** *Access* **in their names. Click Continue.**

   Now your CD-ROM will work fine.

3. **Install your new software.**

4. **After you're finished installing the new program, restart the Mac** *again.* **Hold down the space bar** *again.* **View your list of extensions** *again.* **This time, however, choose My Settings from the pop-up menu at the top of the window; the extensions you normally use will turn themselves back on.**

   (And *next* time you want to start up with only your CD-ROM extensions, you can skip Step 2 — just choose CD-ROM Only from this same pop-up menu.)

I realize this is about 1,402 steps more than you anticipated when you bought the new program in the first place, but the result will be a Mac that runs much more smoothly and quickly in the long run.

"Read Me First" = "Ignore Me First."

In the picture of Installers you saw a page or so ago, you may have noted that, along with an Installer, almost every program comes with a little icon that says Read Me First, ReadMe, *Lisez s'il vous plaît,* or something.

Most of the time, if you double-click this item, you'll be shown a screenful of fine print pertaining to the program you're about to install. Example: "Part 45. If you have a Performa 3100/23 with 45 MHz acceleration and no Shift key, and you've previously installed a 32-bit Addressing software, note that your screen saver may take two seconds longer to appear."

The point is that it's usually pretty trivial stuff. And it's usually pretty technical stuff. The software company is basically warning you about bugs you may be about to encounter. So skim the material, but don't sweat it if you have no clue what they're talking about. Nobody else can understand programmers, either.

Most Stuff You Buy You'll Never Use Again.

This happens to be a fact. The vast majority of programs bought by computer fans wind up on the shelf, unused. I guess that's perfectly understandable; after all, we retire old sweaters, appliances, and unlabeled jars in the refrigerator. Why not software?

Because it's darned expensive, that's why. Therefore, read the magazine reviews before you buy something; at $300 a pop, programs aren't sweaters. Also, consider downloading (getting from America Online or the Internet) the trial version of the software before buying it; almost every software company offers such demo versions, almost always from Web pages named after the company itself (such as *www.adobe.com, www.microsoft.com,* and so on). Also, buy software from places (such as a mail-order joints) that will let you return it. They're insane to give you that opportunity. You may as well take advantage of it.

Every Piece of Equipment Needs Software in Your System Folder.

Your Mac is a regular little Ellis Island. It greets every piece of incoming add-on equipment with open little silicon arms. You can attach all kinds of things to it: printers, CD-ROM players, scanners, modems, musical instruments, or anything else described in Chapter 18.

When it comes to understanding and troubleshooting your Mac, though, here's a key piece of news: Every single *hardware* item you add requires a corresponding *software* program. Think of it as the paperwork for newcomers.

These little programs, called *drivers,* translate between the Mac and whatever equipment you're attaching. They usually hang out in the folder called Extensions (inside your System Folder). If you look right now, you'll see one for your printer and probably a bunch for other printers. If you have a CD-ROM, scanner, modem, Zip drive, SuperDisk, or whatever, you'll find corresponding files somewhere on your Mac for them, too.

Now you know the technical reason you can't just unhook your printer, attach it to *my* Mac, and expect it to work, without copying over that little driver file. (Another technical reason: I live in Connecticut. Your cables won't reach.)

Error Messages Are Useless.

I've recently been notified by the Guinness Book of World Records that my e-mail box has been nominated in the category of Most Overflowing. The funny thing is, about half the mail I get poses the same kind of question:

"What does 'Bad F-Line Instruction (Error Type –93)' mean?"

It means: "Does not compute."

Of *course* you know that. After all, you only *got* that message when something terribly wrong went down, and your cursor froze on the screen, and a loud electrostatic buzzing filled the room. What you *really* want to know is whether that "Bad F-Line, Error of Type –93" can help you figure out what happened.

And the answer is no. Oh, sure, they publish lists of these codes. But no kidding: They are *totally* unhelpful. Chapter 15 offers a few examples; here are some more:

Error code	Message	Meaning
−1	qErr	queue element not found during deletion
−2	vTypErr	invalid queue element
−3	corErr	core routine number out of range
−4	unimpErr	unimplemented core routine

Okay? Now do you believe me?

As an Apple programmer once explained it, it's like finding a car smashed into a tree with its tires still spinning. All you can say for sure is that something went wrong. But you have no idea what *led up* to the crash. Maybe the guy was drunk, or distracted, or asleep. You'll never know.

Same thing with your Mac. The machine knows that *something* happened, but it's way too late to tell you what. Restart it and get back to business. If the problem recurs, read Chapter 16.

Click the Label instead of the Button.

Here's a wonderful shortcut. Whenever you're presented with a set of options, they usually look something like this:

Checkboxes   Radio buttons

☐ **Rhinoplasty**   ┌**Anesthetic**─┐
☐ **Liposuction**   │ ○ **Local**   │
☐ **Augmentation**   │ ◉ **General** │
                          │ ○ **None**   │
                          └───────────────┘

You're allowed to choose as many *checkboxes* as you want; a little X appears in each one when you click it. Like the pop-out buttons on a car radio, however, only *one* of the round ones — called *radio buttons* — can be selected at a time.

Anyway, your instinct is probably to click the little square or the little circle button to make your selection. But it's far quicker to sloppily slash away with your mouse at the *label* of a button instead of the tiny square or circle itself. Click the *words,* and the button gets clicked.

Click anywhere on the words

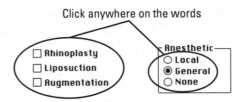

The Control Strip Is Faster.

What's so great about the Mac is all the different ways you can tailor it to fit your own personal eccentricities. You can make it burp instead of beep, or plaster your desktop background with dancing pandas, or view everything in shades of gray — all thanks to the amazing Control Panels. (See Chapter 8 for a blow-by-blow description of your control panels.)

On Macs equipped with System 7.5.3 and later, though, you can make many of these settings changes directly on the *Control Strip* instead of trudging the 14 miles to your Control Panels folder. By the Control Strip, of course, I refer to this little item —

— that's probably hugging the edge of your screen.

For complete instructions, see the Chapter 8 entry called "Control Strip." No need to thank me.

Chapter 20

Ten Cool Things You Didn't Know Your Mac Could Do

● ●

Play Music CDs

Yup, it's true. Pop your favorite music CD — Carly Simon, 10,000 Maniacs Smashing Pumpkins, the soundtrack to *Lethal Weapon XIV* — into the Mac's CD-ROM drive. Some Macs are set up to begin playing such music CDs automatically; others you have to command to begin playing.

Either way, if you'd like to control your music CDs the way you would on a $300 CD player, use the "front panel" in your ⌘ menu called AppleCD Audio Player. It should look familiar:

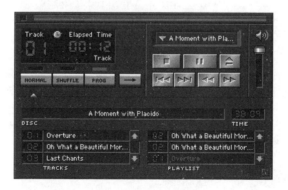

Hunt around long enough, and you'll figure out how to make your CD play, stop, skip randomly among the songs, play louder or softer, and so on.

In fact, if you click the tiny down-pointing triangle (below the NORMAL button), you'll expand the panel so that you can view the names of the individual songs on the CD. Unfortunately, they start out being called "Track 1," "Track 2," and so on — it's up to you to click on such names and type the correct song titles. (Press Return after each title to move down to the next blank, or Shift-Return to move upward. While you're at it, click the words *Audio CD,* just above the track list, and type the name of the disc, too.) After you do all this, the Player will automatically remember the album and song titles the next time you insert the disc.

But here's the best part: Click the PROG button. Now you can drag any title on the left side to any slot on the right side, as shown in the illustration. (Drag it back to the left if you change your mind.) You also can drag titles up or down on the right side. What's great about this feature is that you can drag your favorite songs into the "playlist" on the right side *more than once* — and leave the annoying songs out of the playlist completely.

Talk

It's been said that we spend the first year of a child's life trying to get it to talk, and the next 18 years trying to get it to shut up. Well, with the Mac, getting it to talk is fantastically easy.

Lots of Mac programs are capable of talking. Word 98, ClarisWorks, America Online, and WordPerfect are some examples. But the program that requires by far the least manual-reading (when it comes to talking) is the delightful, bargain-basement word processor known as *SimpleText.*

SimpleText is a baby word processor. Apple installs it on every Mac it makes so that you, the purchaser, will have *some* program with which to read important text files, such as Read Me First documents, even if you haven't bought a genuine word processor program. (If you're like most people, you've probably got about *54* copies of SimpleText; according to ancient Mac lore, this little program quietly replicates itself when you're not looking.)

Find one of your copies of SimpleText (use your Find command). Launch it, then type up something you've always wanted to have said to you, such as, "You are *such* a god! Holy smokes, everything you do turns out fantastically! I'd give anything to be more like you."

Then move that mouse on up to your Sound menu, and choose Speak All. Aren't computers great?

(If your Sound menu is dimmed and unavailable, you must not have the special files in your Extensions folder — within your System Folder — called MacinTalk. Launch the Installer on the System Software CD that came with your Mac, and install the item called PlainTalk Text-to-Speech.)

Now: For added hilarity, go back to the Sound menu. There you'll find a Voices command that lists as many as 18 different voices to choose from. They're great: male, female, kids, deep voices, shaky voices, whispered voices. You'll spend hours, I predict, making up funny sentences for each character voice to say.

Of course, Apple didn't create a talking Mac just for you to fool around making up silly sentences. This technology has some actual, useful uses. For example, there's no better way to proofread something important than to listen to it being read to you.

Sing

While it may be a little humbling that your Mac may be more talented than you are, it does indeed sing. It has a somewhat limited repertoire — in fact, it only knows four songs — but it can use any lyrics you want, and it never even stops to take a breath.

To make your Mac sing, you simply need to get it talking, as described in the previous section. Then choose one of these voices from the Voices menu:

- **Pipe Organ:** Sings to the tune of the Alfred Hitchcock theme.
- **Good News:** Sings to the tune of "Pomp & Circumstance," otherwise known as the graduation march.
- **Bad News:** Sings to the tune of the funeral march.
- **Cellos:** Sings to the tune of "In the Hall of the Mountain King," from *Peer Gynt,* by Edvard Grieg. Such culture!

Hint: Punctuation marks make the Mac start over from the beginning of the melody. Sample lyrics for the Good News graduation-march melody, for example, should look like this:

You just won the jackpot good luck and God bless

Too bad you owe half to good old IRS!

Play Movies

Your Mac is quite handy with movies. It can make them, record them, and show them.

The cornerstone to all of this is a technology bundle called *QuickTime,* which takes the form of some files that are probably sitting in your System Folder at this very moment (in your Extensions folder).

Getting movies to play on your screen is simple: Just double-click a movie file's icon to open it. It'll probably launch good old SimpleText and appear as a smallish rectangle, as shown next.

Click here to start
or stop playback

Drag this doodad to
jump around in the
movie

Click to move one "frame"
of the movie forward or
backward

To play the flick, click the little "play" triangle to make it play back. You'll
quickly discover a few disappointing facts about digital movies: They often
play back kind of jerkily, they're small (playing in a small window), and
they're generally short. That's because QuickTime movie files take up
obscene amounts of hard drive space for each minute of footage.

The bigger challenge, therefore, is simply *getting* a movie you want to watch.
Several sources spring to mind: You can download movies from the Internet
or America Online (see Chapter 11), although these enormous files take
enormous amounts of time to transfer to you by modem.

You can also make your *own* movies, as long as you've equipped your Mac
with the appropriate circuitry. For the gory details, I recommend this book's
fine sequel, *MORE Macs For Dummies*.

Make Movies

"Say *what?*" you're saying. "This crazy author is suggesting I plug my
camcorder into my computer? What's next, plugging my microwave into the
vacuum?"

It's true. The hottest use of a Macintosh is as a movie-making machine. You
can actually plug your VCR or camcorder into the computer and watch in
awe as your home movies pop up on the Mac screen. After you've captured
your videos onto the Mac (or, more correctly, *digitized* them), with full color
and sound, you can edit them, play them backward, edit out the embarrass-
ing parts, or whatever. The technology and the movies are called QuickTime.

Any Mac can *play* QuickTime movies. You need special gear, though, to *make*
them. Again, *MORE Macs For Dummies* has the details.

Send Faxes

If your Mac has a fax modem, you're in for a delicious treat. Faxes sent by a Mac come out looking twice as crisp and clean when they're received by a real fax machine. And sending faxes couldn't be more convenient for you — no printout to throw away, no paper involved at all. Your Mac sends the thing directly to another fax machine's brain.

Connecting a phone line to your fax modem (or the phone jack on your PowerBook) is the easy part. Now you have to figure out how to *send* what you want to send. Sure, you could read the manual — but who's got the time?

Here's what you do. Begin by typing (or opening) whatever it is you want to fax. Usually, this means a letter you've written in your word processor. Make sure it's in front of you on the screen.

Now take a look at your File menu, and note where it says Print. Got it?

Okay, let go of the mouse now. With one hand, press and hold down the *Option key* on your keyboard. With the other, go back up to the File menu and look at the word Print. If your fax/modem is like most, that word Print has now changed to say *Fax*!

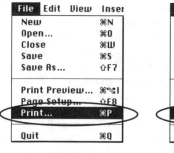

Normal   With Option key

If you choose the Fax command, you'll be shown some kind of address book, where you can type in your friend's fax number; you'll also see a button called something like Send, which will get the fax merrily transmitting away.

Now then. If your menu *doesn't* change to say Fax when you press the Option key, then maybe you don't have one of the standard modem brands (such as Global Village). You may have a different brand, as follows:

✔ **iMac:** Your computer's built-in fax modem uses the ⌘ key along with Option. You can, fortunately, change this special keystroke to anything you like. Find the program called Fax Browser, choose Settings from the Edit menu, and click Fax Menu; you'll see the controls to change the keystroke.

✔ **Apple:** Try pressing the *Shift and Control* keys together. (That's the key combo if you have an Apple modem.) Or try it again pressing the ⌘ key.

✔ **SupraFax:** This fax software puts a fax *menu* on your menu bar; you're supposed to choose the Fax command from *it*.

If *none* of those combinations works, then something else is afoot. Maybe you don't have the fax/modem software installed; rustle up the original disks and install it.

But you shouldn't have to open up the Chooser every time you want to send a fax! Many people aren't aware of the Option-key (or whatever-key) shortcut. They still open the Chooser in the ⌘ menu, switch to the Fax icon, send the fax, open the Chooser again, and switch back to their printer — a colossal waste of time and effort. Remember, the computer should *save* you time.

Transfer Files through the Air

Many of today's Macs, such as the iMac and PowerBook laptops, offer a feature that's so cool, it could freeze water: the ability to send files to other iMacs and PowerBooks *through the air,* beaming them invisibly using infrared signals. (If you inspect the front of your iMac — or the back of your PowerBook — closely enough, you'll see the dark red plastic lens that serves as the transmitter-receiver.) This is a great feature for Ye Who Travel, for example, or Ye Who Upgrade From an Older Mac to a Newer One and Wish to Transfer All Your Documents Without a Lot of Hassle. Here's how it works:

1. **Open your AppleTalk control panel. (If you don't have it, use the Network control panel instead.) Choose Infrared Port from the pop-up menu. (You've just told the Mac what connection to use for its networking.) Close and save the control panel.**

   If your Mac has the Infrared control panel, now open it, click Options, and select either IRTalk or IrDA (you and your fellow beamer should agree on one or the other — it doesn't matter). Close and save.

2. **Double-click Apple IR File Exchange.**

   Apple IR File Exchange is a program in the Apple Extras folder on every PowerBook and iMac hard drive.

3. **Position the two Macs a few inches apart so that their transmitters are facing each other.**

   The icons of any PowerBooks or iMacs in range show up as "drop-box" folder icons.

4. **The person sending the files or folders simply drags icons *from the desktop* onto the appropriate folder, as shown here:**

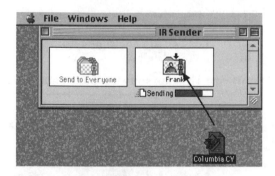

5. **Wait.**

When the progress bar indicates that the job is over, the recipient should open his own Apple IR File Exchange folder. Inside is a folder called IR Receiver — which contains the stuff that was beamed through empty space!

Fit in Your Pocket

You've truly integrated your Macintosh into your life. It's got your calendar, your phone numbers, your to-do list — everything you need. And now you need to leave the house. What's a Mac fan to do? Your options are:

- ✔ **Buy a PowerBook laptop.** Spend $3,000. Transfer everything onto it before each trip or outing — and transfer everything back to your main Mac when you return. Wait two minutes for the PowerBook to start up each time you turn it on.

- ✔ **Stuff your Macintosh into your pocket before each trip.** Shred your clothes, look like an imbecile as you walk into business meetings with unsightly bulges.

- ✔ **Get a PalmPilot.** The PalmPilot is an amazing $300 handheld computers, about the size of an audio cassette. It plugs into your Mac and sucks out a copy all your critical information: your calendar, phone book, to-do list, memos, and even e-mail.

You can't run Mac *programs* on this thing, but you *can* keep your life's critical information with you without buying a second computer or new wardrobe.

The really great part is that when you return home from your trip, you plug the PalmPilot back into your Mac — and any changes you made while on the road are automatically sent *back* to the calendar and address book on the Mac.

Run Windows Programs

It's true: Never again must you feel game-deprived. The Macintosh can run almost any Windows program alive. All you need is plenty of memory (32MB or more) and a program like SoftWindows or Virtual PC. No, your Windows programs won't run quite as fast as they would on the fastest actual Windows *computers* — but if you get one of today's Macs (an iMac or something with the letters *G3* in its name), you'll find it fast enough.

Print Photos

Armed with a digital camera (see Chapter 18) and an Epson color printer (see Chapter 5), there's no reason for you to spend money and time waiting for your photographs to get developed. Now you can spend money and time printing them from your Macintosh, instead. The bad news: The glossy photo paper costs $1 per letter-sized sheet. You can't make enlargements — if you try to enlarge your digital photos, they start to look grainy. The digital camera (but not the printer) is expensive.

The good news: The printing (which works exactly as described in Chapter 5 — but in color) is fairly fast. It looks amazing, especially on the $1-a-sheet glossy paper. And you can edit your photos before you print them, correcting the color tint, adding or removing bushes, adding or removing family members.

Part VII
Appendixes

The 5th Wave   By Rich Tennant

All right fellows - basketball today! Get changed and make sure everyone's wearing a mouse pad!

In this part . . .

Here they are: the appendixes you've been waiting for. How to shop for, and buy, a Mac; where to buy more stuff for it; and how to translate what the geeky magazines say when they talk about it.

Appendix A

How to Buy (and Set Up) a Macintosh

● ●

*G*etting started with a Mac involves three steps: deciding which model to get, figuring out where to buy it, and setting it up. This delightful appendix will guide you through all three steps with as few tension headaches as possible.

The Only Specs That Matter

You'll hear all kinds of numbers and specifications tossed around when you go Mac-shopping. But the only four that matter are (1) how big its hard drive is, (2) how much memory it has, (3) what processor chip is inside, and (4) how fast it runs.

✔ **Hard-disk space.** The first number that matters is the *size of the hard disk inside the Mac.* The size is measured in *gigabytes.* (If you're at a cocktail party, you can say *gigs* for short.)

How much do you need? Well, the stuff that you'll be creating — letters, manuscripts, whatever — is pretty small. A 500-page book might take up *one* megabyte of the 4,000 available on your hard disk. But today's software programs, such as word processing programs, are huge. Count on each program taking up several megabytes by itself. (Count on anything from Microsoft taking up *50* megs all by itself.) And if you plan to work with graphics or digital movies, your hard drive could actually fill up over time.

Otherwise, you can't *buy* a Mac with a too-small hard drive anymore; today's models usually offer four to eight *gigs* of space (4,000 or 8,000 megs), which should last you through the next couple of presidential administrations.

✔ **Memory.** When you press Play on a VCR, the machine reads the videocassette's contents and throws the video information onto the TV screen. When the TV is off, you can't watch your movie, but you sleep well knowing that it's still safely stored on the tape.

Similarly, your Macintosh reads what's on the *hard disk* and throws an electronic copy of it up on your computer screen. There, you can look at it, make changes, whatever. While it's on the screen, it's *in memory.* (Details on this stuff are in Chapter $1^{1}/_{2}$.)

But memory is much more expensive than disk space, so you get a lot less of it. Whereas hard drives typically are 4 or 8 gigs (which is 4,000 or 8,000 megs), a Mac usually comes with 32 or 64 megs of memory. The more memory you have, the more you can do with your computer simultaneously (type in one window, surf the Web in another, and so on).

Intelligent Computer Question Number Two, then, is "How much RAM do I get in this Mac? Sixteen megs? Forget it! I can't even *breathe* in sixteen megs."

Newspaper ads often give you both of these critical numbers (memory and disk space) separated by a slash. You may read, for example, "iMac **32/4G**." In your newfound savvy, you know that this model has 32 megs of memory and a four-gig hard drive for permanent storage.

✔ **Processor chip model.** The third important number is the name of the primary processor chip. (As endless *Newsweek* articles and specials on "Nova" have no doubt informed you, a *chip* is a rat's nest of tiny circuits etched into a piece of silicon the size of a postage stamp.) The heart of a Macintosh is a chip, about an inch square, that's actually manufactured in the millions by a completely different company. (It's Motorola; that's why *Apple* stock goes down when there are negative headlines about Motorola.)

Before the Power Macintosh line, several models of processor chips were used in Macs: 68000, 68020, 68030, and 68040. The higher the model number of this chip, the faster the Mac.

All of today's models, on the other hand, and all Macintosh clones, use a newer kind of Motorola "brain" chip: the famous *PowerPC* chip. These chips have all kinds of names — 601, 603, 604, G3 — but in this case, higher numbers *don't* necessarily mean faster Macs; read on to find out why.

✔ **Processor chip speed.** A chip's speed is something like blood pressure; it's how fast the data moves through the machine's circuits. The range of speeds, measured (get this) in *megahertz,* is 8 (on the original 1984 Mac) to 366 or more (the latest Power Macs).

Now, I've racked my brains trying to come up with an intelligent, logical way to explain the following mystery, but I'm stumped. I'll just lay it on you:

A higher megahertz computer isn't necessarily faster.

Isn't that odd? It's true: For example, you might think that a 300 MHz Power Mac would be just as fast as a 300 MHz IBM-compatible clone. Nope! The Power Mac would be *way* faster.

This paradox comes about because — ready for this? — you can't compare megahertz across *different chips!* In the previous example, most Power Macs use a chip called the G3; IBM-compatible computers use one called the Pentium II.

Here comes the geekiest fact you'll have to learn in this entire book, but also one of the most useful: MHz ratings are useful only for *comparisons between identical chips*. You can't compare the MHz ratings between a 604 and G3 chip. You also can't compare the MHz ratings between a Power PC and a Pentium, although I'll bet a lot of your less-informed friends try to do that all the time.

So how on earth are you supposed to buy a computer if there's *no* number that directly compares their speed? With great difficulty. In short, here are the PowerPC chip models, listed in order of decreasing speed: G3, 604e, 604, 601, 603e, 603. Of these, the G3 chip is the most desirable — if you had to choose between a G3 Mac with a *233* MHz speed and a 604 Mac with a *300* MHz speed, you'd probably want the first one.

Macintosh as a Second Language

To make newcomers feel as much like outsiders as possible, the computer stores and newspaper ads run all this information together in a cryptic little line. This is pretty important information for comparison shoppers, so I thought that a translation might be in order. Let's see how much of that tech talk you were able to absorb.

The newspaper-ad test

Stay calm. Don't let your eyes glaze over. You *do* know what this means. Take it morsel by morsel.

GREAT BLOWOUT PRICE!

Power Mac G3

32/8G/24x, 300 MHz PowerPC G3

Memory, hard drive size,
CD-ROM speed

Main processor
speed and kind

Translation: This Mac model is the **Power Mac G3**. As I write this, Apple sells only three basic models — Power Macs, PowerBook laptops, and iMacs; you don't have nearly as much name-deciphering to do as in the days when Apple sold 40 different models simultaneously.

Next, you see how much memory and hard-drive space you get in this computer (**32/8G** means 32 megs of RAM, and an 8-gigabyte [8,000-meg] hard drive). The memory comes before the slash, and the hard drive size after it. You're also told the speed of the built-in CD-ROM drive (**24x**), which isn't very meaningful; anything above 4x plays at about the same speed.

Next, you'll generally find the speed of the computer's chip, which here is **300 MHz** (*megahertz,* which you can think of as miles-per-hour). The clock speeds of older, non-Power Mac models range from 16 MHz to 40 MHz; for Power Mac models, speeds range from 66 to 366 or more, so this one, at 300, is pretty decent. (On most of today's Mac models, the speed is no longer part of the name. You have to read the fine print to see what the speed of the chip is.)

Finally, there's the chip model. As I mentioned a page or so ago, the central processing chips in Macs with four-digit model numbers (or in Mac clones) are the 601, 603, 604, G3, and so on, and there's no system to it — a higher number doesn't mean faster speed. You just have to learn that G3 is better than 604, and so on.

Cache and carry

You sometimes run across the term *Level 2 cache* ("cash"), too. This is a bonus chip, a sidecar chip that boosts a computer's speed by about 15 percent. It's a great feature to have; most modern Macs have such a chip. (I wouldn't worry much about how big yours is; just make sure you have one.)

The Product Line

Look, it's hopeless to try to keep up with Apple in a Mac book. Since the Macintosh first appeared on the scene, there have been 150 different models.

Still, I think you should have some idea of what's happening on the Mac shelf when you walk into the computer store. Here are some representative model names, past and present, along with information on what you might use them for.

Black-and-white one-piece

Macintosh Plus
Macintosh SE and SE/30
Macintosh Classic and Classic II
Performa 200

These one-piece, long-since discontinued models are about two feet tall. All you do is plug in the keyboard and the power cord, and you're off and running. The screen is built in; you can see a five-inch-tall slice of a page all the way across.

They're quite old and slow; almost none of today's software runs on them. They're still okay for word processing and old versions of Quicken.

Color one-piece

Color Classic
LC 500 series
Performa 500 series

These discontinued machines are bigger, heavier, and more expensive than the black-and-white compact Macs. On the other hand, they're easy to expand; and they have built-in color screens. The LC 500-line Macs also have built-in stereo speakers and a built-in CD-ROM player. They contain the

68030 or 68040 chip — particularly the later 500 models like the LC580. These Macs are still considered slow by today's standards — too slow for the Internet, for example — but still fine for kids' programs, basic graphics and page design, and word processing.

The LC series

Macintosh LC, LC II, and III (Performa 400 series)
Macintosh LC 500 series (Performa 500 series)
Macintosh LC 630 (Performa 630 series)

Except for the 500 line, the LC (for *low-cost color*) Macs are two-piece Macs (now discontinued). In other words, you had to buy two pieces of equipment: the computer itself and a separate screen (the *monitor*).

Two-piece Macs are easy to expand. The lid pops right off like the lid of a shoebox. Of course, the inside of the computer looks *nothing* like the inside of a shoebox — there are a lot of wires and chips and stuff, but they're very neatly arranged, and whatever you want to install (more memory, an accelerator card, whatever) slips into a very obvious place.

The LC models' speeds vary widely within the family, ranging from the dog-slow LC (with an '020 chip) to the LC 580 (with a fairly decent '040 chip); speeds run from 16 to 33 MHz.

They're good for basic page layout and graphic design (because you can attach a big screen), basic spreadsheets, and so on. (The LC 475 and higher-number models have the necessary horsepower for more challenging tasks, such as those described under "Mac II series," next.)

Mac II series

Macintosh II, IIx, IIfx, IIcx, IIsi, IIci,
IIvx (Performa 600)

These, too, are discontinued modular Macs, generally with more horsepower than the LC line. Furthermore, most of these Macs have multiple expansion slots. Techie details: All but the '020-based Mac II contain a 68030 chip running at speeds from 16 to 40 MHz. They've got enough oomph for complex spreadsheets, pro-level page layout, medium and complex databases, music notation (sheet music), and electronic mail.

The Quadra series

*Macintosh Quadra 605, 610
(Centris 610), 650 (Centris 650)
Macintosh Quadra 700, 800, 900,
950, 660AV, 840AV
Macintosh Quadra 630 (LC 630,
Performa 630-638)*

The name *Quadra* comes from the
chip on which these Macs are
based: the '040, which, when it
debuted, made everybody's hair
stand on end with its blistering speed.

Anyway, the now-discontinued Quadras introduced one other notable
feature: You could get other Mac devices, such as CD-ROM players and
removable SyQuest cartridge drives, built right in. A Quadra 610 or 650 Mac
can house one such device; Quadras 800 and higher are huge, "tower-style"
Macs, with enough room for two such built-in gadgets.

These machines were popular for color photo retouching and Photoshop (a
professional painting program) art; morphing (making QuickTime movies
that melt one image magically into another); high-level statistical analysis;
programming; and use as an office *server* (a central Mac whose files can be
accessed by every desktop Mac in the office).

PowerBooks

*PowerBook 100, 140, 170, 145,
145b,150, 160, 165, 180
PowerBook 520, 540, 165c, 180c,
520c, 540c
PowerBook Duo 210, 230, 250, 270c,
280, 280c
PowerBook 190, 5300, 1400, 3400,
2400
PowerBook G3 and PowerBook G3
Series*

PowerBooks are portable, laptop
Macs. They're dark gray, two
inches thick, weigh seven or eight
pounds, and are every bit as powerful as most of the models that you've
read about so far. A PowerBook opens like a book when you're using it; one
side has the keyboard, and the other has the screen. (See Chapter 10 for
additional PowerBook scoop.)

Typing on a PowerBook is slightly less comfortable than on a desktop Mac, and you can expand one only with considerable hassle and expense. But a PowerBook is indispensable for anyone who travels. And a PowerBook is definitely the Mac to have if you're trying to catch the eye of an attractive stranger across the airplane aisle.

The biggest differences among PowerBook models have to do with the *families* they belong to. At four pounds, the Duos (and the PowerBook 2400), for example, are much smaller and lighter than regular PowerBooks. That's because you can leave the floppy-disk drive at home on your desk and take just the computer itself on your travels.

PowerBooks with four-digit model names (5300, 1400, 3400, and 2400) are Power Mac laptops. They feature bigger, brighter screens, still faster speeds, and (in most models) a CD-ROM drive. Then there's the very fast PowerBook G3 (a 1997 model) and — don't be confused by the confusing name similarity — the completely redesigned, curvy, very large (but super-deluxe) PowerBook G3 *Series* models.

All modern PowerBooks have a special *PC card slot* — like the slot in a cash machine where you stick your card, except that into *this* slot you can insert an add-on, credit-card-sized gizmo like a PC-card modem.

Power Macintosh

Power Macintosh 6100 (and Performa 6100 series), 7100, 8100
Power Macintosh 7200, 7300, 7500, 7600, 8500, 8600, 9500, 9600
Performa and LC 6200, 6300, 6400, 6500
Power Macintosh 4400, 5200, 5300, 5400
Power Macintosh G3

These Macs, called the Power Macintosh series, look, feel, and smell like the Macs that came before them. They work fine with all existing normal Mac programs. But if you buy (or upgrade to) special PowerPC versions of your programs — the so-called "native" programs (doesn't that have a wild, jungly sound?) — these Macs really scream. Native programs run several times faster than on the fastest of yesteryear's Quadras.

In the last two years, every existing Mac model was quietly snuffed out to make room for a PowerPC-based model. Throughout the 1990s, Apple continued to crank out models built on faster and faster PowerPC chips, such as the amazingly fast G3 chip.

iMac

In Apple's entire history, few Macs generated as much excitement and anticipation as the iMac. It's a compact, two-toned, one-piece Macintosh shaped like a small, rounded pyramid (or alien egg, as some call it). It's got see-through aquamarine plastic panels that let you catch shadowy glimpses of the hardware inside the case, mouse, and even cables.

Despite its low price, the iMac offers state-of-the-art technology; it's equipped with a 233MHz G3 processor, level 2 cache, a big hard drive, a fast CD-ROM drive, a 15-inch monitor, and a 56K modem.

If you've got an iMac, of course, you know all this already. And you also know what the iMac *doesn't* have — a SCSI jack, modem or printer jacks, standard Mac keyboard or mouse jacks, or a floppy drive. Instead, the iMac has something called *USB jacks* — shiny, metal, small, rectangular connectors that accommodate, among other things, the iMac's special keyboard and mouse.

You can buy adapters that let many Mac add-ons (printers, modems, digital cameras, PalmPilots, and so on) work with these USB jacks. Some add-on gadgets (Zip drives, SuperDisk drives, some printers) are sold especially for the iMac and don't need adapters.

The missing floppy disk is a bigger problem for some people; you can transfer files from one Mac to another over the Internet, using an Ethernet network cable, or using infrared beaming (see Chapter 20). But if you really want to use floppy disks on your iMac, you have to buy a Newer Technology, USB-compatible floppy drive or Imation's SuperDisk (which can read standard floppies in addition to its own 120MB-format disks).

If you crave more details, see *The iMac For Dummies* (same author, same publisher).

Buying a Monitor

If you've decided to become the proud owner of a two-piece Mac, you have to decide what kind of screen (monitor) to get.

How big is your view?

Your biggest buying headache will be deciding what *size* monitor to get: 14, 15, 16, 17, 20, or 21 inches. (The 15- and 17-inch sizes are the most popular.)

Today's monitors — even on the iMac and the current PowerBook models — come with the fancy high-tech adjective *multisync* at no extra charge. This simply means that you can zoom in or out, magnifying or shrinking everything on the screen. Of course, when you're zoomed out, everything's smaller — but you can see a larger area. For example, you can zoom out the 17-inch screen and see two entire pages side by side. (To do so, use the Control Strip, described in Chapter 8.)

A bit about color bits

(*Note:* I'm providing the following discussion so that you'll understand the chatter in your favorite computer magazines. Unless you retouch photos for a living, there's no reason to know this stuff.)

The technobullies of the world have foisted several different *kinds* of color upon us: *8-bit, 16-bit,* and *24-bit* color.

All you need to know is that 16-bit and 24-bit color is relatively more expensive, slower to appear on the screen, and much more realistic. *Realistic* is a term that matters only if you plan to work with photos or movies on the screen. If not, 24-bit is for the pros; it's overkill for everyone else.

Which degree of colorness you have depends on your *Mac,* not the monitor. All of today's Macs provide at least 16-bit color: They can show thousands of different colors on the screen. All you have to do is plug your monitor into the built-in jack. If you one day decide that you can't live without photorealistic colors on your screen, you can buy and install more *video RAM* to get 24-bit color; you don't need a new monitor.

Where to Buy Your Mac

I'm going to assume that you're not in Donald Trump's tax bracket. I'm going to assume that you're looking for ways to get the most Mac for the least lira.

The Apple school discount

Apple grants hefty Mac discounts to students and teachers. In Apple's younger, healthier days, the discount was 40 percent; it's not nearly as much of a giveaway today, but there are still great deals to be had on Mac equipment. If you're affiliated with a college, find out whether the school's bookstore is a member of this delightful program.

Mail order

The next-least-expensive way to get a new Mac is probably through a mail-order company. These outfits take out big ads in the Macintosh magazines, such as *Macworld* and *MacAddict*. Some places even sell Macs over the World Wide Web. Of course, you can't exactly browse the merchandise, so it's assumed that you already know what you want when you call one of these places.

If everything goes smoothly, mail order can be a nifty deal: You save hundreds by avoiding sales tax, you get a pretty good price, and you don't have to haul anything home in the car. The trouble with mail order, though, is that life can get pretty ugly if things *don't* go right. What if the thing is broken when it arrives? Suddenly, you've got the burden of packing it up, shipping it back, and persuading the company to replace the equipment (if they'll even consider it).

Computer stores

A computer store is likely to have higher prices. You'll have to pay sales tax. But you also get a human being to blame when things get fouled up.

So how are you supposed to know good dealers (and their repair guys) from bad? There's only one way: Ask around. Depending on where you live, though, getting the word-of-mouth report may be easier said than done. If you're at a loss as to whom you should ask, start by finding the nearest Macintosh user group; call Apple's user-group-listing hotline at 800-538-9696.

Used Macs

Finally, you can buy a used Mac. Once again, the luck of the draw determines how satisfied you'll be. To a certain extent, you can tell how much abuse a Mac has taken by looking at it. But a visual exam won't tell you about the funny noise that the hard drive makes only after it's been on for 20 minutes, or about the monitor that's been in for repairs three times already, or about the ball of cat hair wedged inside the disk drive.

In other words, there are three rules for buying used equipment:

✔ First, determine whether you're willing to forgo the comfy Apple warranty for the sake of saving money.

✔ Second, be sure that the asking price really is low enough to make the savings meaningful, particularly on discontinued Mac models. Some naïve sellers who don't understand the Inviolable Rule of Instant Obsolescence think they can recoup the full purchase price when they sell their used Macs. Don't fall for it — be sure to compare the asking price with a computer store's new-Mac price. (If you have an Internet or America Online account, you can find out the going rate for used Macs at the Web site *www.uce.com.*)

✔ Finally, test the Mac as much as possible before you buy it. Above all, test the disk drive (by inserting a floppy disk and copying a file onto it), the printer port (by printing something), and the mouse (by rolling it around on the desk).

Credit cards

As long as you're committed to this plunge, a word of solemn advice: Put everything on a credit card, especially when you're buying by mail order. Thousands of Mac users have avoided getting ripped off by the occasional fly-by-night operation because they charged it. (As you probably know, the credit-card company doesn't pay your bill if you're disputing the charge. This is an incredible layer of protection between you and companies that send you the wrong item, a broken item, and so on.)

I Took Off the Shrink Wrap! Now What?

Setting up the Mac should take less than 20 minutes; all you have to do is plug in a few cables. (See Chapter 5 for instructions on plugging in your printer.)

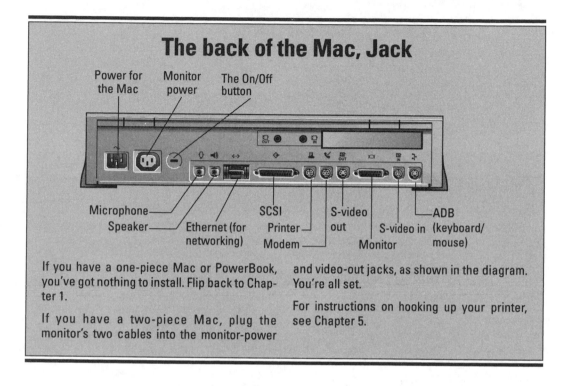

The back of the Mac, Jack

Power for the Mac · Monitor power · The On/Off button

Microphone — Speaker — Ethernet (for networking) · SCSI · Printer — Modem — · S-video out · S-video in · Monitor · ADB (keyboard/mouse)

If you have a one-piece Mac or PowerBook, you've got nothing to install. Flip back to Chapter 1.

If you have a two-piece Mac, plug the monitor's two cables into the monitor-power

and video-out jacks, as shown in the diagram. You're all set.

For instructions on hooking up your printer, see Chapter 5.

Ergo . . . ergonomics

First, figure out where you're going to put the most expensive appliance you've ever bought. In my opinion, the principal principle is this: When you're seated at your desk and you're in typing position, *your elbows can't be lower than your wrists*. Otherwise, if you plan to do a lot of work at the computer, you may wind up with nasty and painful wrist or arm ailments, which don't go away until you stop using the computer.

Finally, your Apple manual offers some good advice about your chair: If you spend a lot of time at the Mac, invest in a good one.

Getting plugged

If your new Mac is a laptop or an iMac, there's not much to set up. Plug in the power cord (and the iMac's keyboard/mouse) and flip back to Chapter 1.

If not, study the diagram in the sidebar. Using it as your guide, plug the power cord into the power jack and the keyboard into the ADB jack. Then plug the mouse into the other side of the keyboard. Do whatever feels good.

Switching the Mac on

Quick! Flip to Chapter 1!

The Resource Resource

• •

Magazines

MacHome Journal
(For beginners, students,
at-home Mac users)
(*www.machome.com/*)
415-957-1911

Macworld
(News, reviews, analysis;
more advanced)
(*www.macworld.zdnet.com/*)
800-288-6848
303-447-9330

MacAddict
(Fun, irreverent, lots of
games and gadgets; every
issue comes with a CD-ROM
filled with goodies)
(*www.macaddict.com/*)
800-666-6889
415-468-2500

User Groups

Apple User-Group Info Line
800-538-9696, ext. 500

Call to get the number of
your city's Mac club; every
major city has one, and
many towns do, too.

Deep-Discount Mail-Order Joints

Contact these outfits when
you're interested in buying
any of the programs or add-
ons described in this book.

MacConnection
(*www.macconnection.com*)
800-800-4444

MacWarehouse
800-255-6227

Mac Zone
(*www.maczone.com*)
800-248-0800

Cyberian Outpost
(*www.outpost.com*)
(800) 856-9800
(860) 927-2050

Great Mac Web Pages

MacSurfer
(*www.macsurfer.com*)

A daily roundup of articles
about the Mac from
newspapers and maga-
zines around the country.
Click a listing to read that
article.

Macintouch
(*www.macintouch.com*)

Updates, news, and bug-fix
reports. Fascinating, dry,
reliable.

EvangeList
(*www.evangelist.macaddict
.com*)

Facts, surveys, articles,
and success stories to give
you ammunition when
Windows bigots put down
the Macintosh.

SiteLink
(*www.sitelink.net*)

A Web page that's nothing more than a link to other Web pages about the Mac. You'll be on the Web until you're 90.

O'Grady's Power Page
(*ogrady.com*)

The PowerBook lover's paradise.

MacOS Rumors
(*www.macosrumors.com*)

The *National Enquirer* of the Macintosh world — wild, juicy, sometimes erroneous rumors about Apple's secret plans for the future.

Appendix C
The Techno-Babble Translation Guide

● ●

accelerator — An expensive circuit board that you can install to make your Mac faster and slightly less obsolete.

access privileges — Permission to do something on the Mac, as in: "You can't do that because you don't have access privileges." Pertains either to File Sharing (you haven't been allowed access to a certain networked folder) or System 7.5 or later (somebody turned on "System Folder protection" in your General control panel).

active window — The window in front. Usually, only one window can be *active*; you can recognize it by the stripes across the title bar, like this:

ADB — An acronym (for *Apple Desktop Bus*) that describes the cables and jacks used by the keyboard and mouse (on pre-iMac machines), as in "Can you believe that dimwit!? He plugged his printer into the ADB port!"

alert box — A message that appears on the screen; the Mac's attempt to maintain an open and communicative relationship with you. Unfortunately, as in most relationships, the Mac tends to communicate only when something is wrong. An alert box is marked either with the International Exclamation Point or a warning hand, like this:

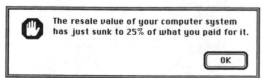

alias — A duplicate of a file's icon (not of the file itself). Serves as a double-clickable *pointer,* or reference, to the original file, folder, or disk. Indicated by an italicized icon name.

Apple Guide — The high-tech Help feature. Choose Help or Macintosh Guide from the Help menu (which, before Mac OS 8, is marked by a question mark) and choose from a list of topics, such as "How do I make a printout?" or "What should I do if I'm going crazy from frustration?" — and the Mac actually *shows* you, step by step, right on the screen.

Apple menu — The menu at the far left end of your menu bar, marked by the symbol — a piece of multicolored fruit. In the menu, you'll find a list of your desk accessories (miniprograms, such as the Calculator), as well as any files, folders, documents, control panels, and even disks (or their aliases) that you care to see there.

AppleShare — Some kind of trademarked name for the way that interconnected Macs communicate with one another. (You'll never need to know this.)

AppleTalk — Another trademarked name, also having to do with Macs talking to one another. You *may* need to know this term if you have a laser printer, because AppleTalk is the language that it speaks to your Mac.

application — Nerd word for *program.*

Application menu — The rightmost menu in the menu bar, marked by an icon. You can switch from one program to another by choosing names from the Application menu.

ASCII — The most interesting thing about this term (which means *text file*) is its weird pronunciation: ASKie. Good name for a Labrador, don't you think?

ATM — Short for *Adobe Type Manager,* a piece of software that makes certain fonts look really great on the screen (and in nonlaser printouts).

background printing — A feature that returns control of the Mac to you immediately after you use the Print command. The alternative, known as *background printing is off,* takes less time to print but takes over the Mac, preventing you from working and displaying a "now printing" message until the printing is over.

back up — To make a copy of a file for use in case some horrible freak accident befalls your original copy (such as your throwing it out).

Balloon Help — See the little question mark in the upper-right corner of your screen, or the word Help in Mac OS 8 or later? It's a menu. Choose Show Balloons from it; then point to various elements of your little Mac-screen world. Cartoon balloons pop out to identify what you're pointing at.

baud rate — The speed of a modem (see *modem*).

BBS — An electronic bulletin-board system. That's where a Mac in somebody's house is connected to a phone line or two so that you can dial in with a modem (see *modem*) and post messages for other people to see.

beta test — Means *test,* but adding a Greek word makes it sound more important. Used exclusively when applied to software: When a program is still so buggy and new that a company doesn't dare sell it, the company gives it away (to people who are called *beta testers*) in hopes of being told what the bugs are.

bit — You'd think that it's the past tense of *byte* (see that entry). Actually, it's a tiny piece of computer information that's not even big enough to bother with.

bitmap — A particular arrangement of black dots on your white screen. To your eye, a particular bitmap may look like the letter *A* (bitmapped text) or a coffee mug (a bitmapped graphic); to the computer, it's just a bunch of dots whose exact positions it has to memorize.

boot — (1) (v.) To start the computer. (2) (n.) Western footwear.

bps — Bits per second. The technically proper way to measure the speed of a *modem* (instead of *baud,* which everybody still says out of force of habit).

bug — A programming error in a piece of software, caused by a programmer too wired on Jolt and pizza, that makes the program do odd or tragic things when you're working to beat a deadline.

bus — The wiring between any two components *inside* your computer.

button — You'll have to deal with two kinds of buttons: the big square one on the mouse, and the many oval or round ones on the screen that offer you options.

byte — A piece of computer information made up of bits. Now *that* made everything clear, didn't it?

cache — A trick, involving a special piece of memory, that makes a Mac faster. You can adjust the everyday cache in the Memory control panel; some Mac models also have a cache *chip,* which uses high-speed memory to pull off the same speed enhancement.

CAD — An acronym for *computer-aided design* (for example, architectural programs).

Caps Lock — A key on your keyboard that makes every letter that you type come out as a capital; it doesn't affect numbers. Press it to get the capitals; press it again to return to normal.

CD-ROM — A computer compact disc. CD-ROMs can show pictures, play music or voices, display short animations and movies, and display reams and reams of text. (A typical CD holds 600 megs of information; compared with the 4,000- or 8,000-meg hard disks that come in typical Macs, or the 1.4 megs on a floppy.)

character — (1) A single typed letter, number, space, or symbol. (2) The scoundrel who got you into this Macintosh habit.

Chooser — A desk accessory, therefore listed in the menu, that lets you specify what kind of printer you have. Failure to use this thing when you set up your Mac is the #1 reason why beginners can't print.

click — The cornerstone of the Macintosh religion: to point the cursor at an on-screen object and then press and release the mouse button.

clip art — Instead of possessing actual artistic ability, graphic designers can buy (or otherwise acquire) collections of ready-made graphics called *clip art* — cutesy little snowmen, city skylines, Santa Clauses, whatever — that they can use to dress up their newsletters, party invitations, and threatening legal notices.

Clipboard — The invisible holding area where the Mac stashes any text or graphics that you copy by using the Copy command.

clock rate — The speed of your computer's main processor chip, measured in *megahertz.*

clone — A Mac made by a company other than Apple.

close box — The little square in the upper-left corner of a window (as opposed to the little square who sold you the Macintosh), which, when clicked, closes the window.

Close box

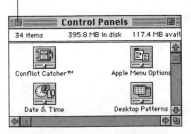

color separation — The technique used in offset printing, where four separate metal plates (each one sopped in ink of a different color) are used to print a full-color image.

command — Something that you'd like the Mac to do, such as Print or Save or Make Me Rich. See also *menu*.

Command key — The one on your keyboard, right next to the space bar, that has a ⌘ (Command) symbol on it. When you press this key, the letter keys on your keyboard perform commands instead of typing letters — for example, ⌘-P = Print, ⌘-S = Save, ⌘-Q = Quit, and ⌘-Z = Undo. (Well, they can't *all* be mnemonic.)

Control key — A keyboard key that generally does absolutely nothing — except in Mac OS 8 or later, where it makes secret menus pop out of windows and icons you click.

control panel — A window full of settings that pertain to some aspect of the Mac's operation. To view the selection of control panels, choose (what else?) Control Panels from the ⌘ menu.

CPU — What it *stands for* is *central processing unit*. What it *means* is the actual computer — the box that contains the real brains. As distinguished from things like the monitor, the printer, and the keyboard.

crash — A very ugly moment in every Mac user's life when the Mac abruptly malfunctions, usually with scary sounds and visuals. Requires restarting.

CRT — The CRT is the screen. If you must know, it stands for *cathode ray tube*.

cursor — The pointer on the screen that moves when you move the mouse across the desk.

DA — Short for *desk accessory*.

daisy chain — A string of different add-on appliances, such as a CD player, a hard disk, and a scanner, plugged one into the back of the next, very much like an elephant conga line.

data — Isn't he that white-makeup guy on *Star Trek: The Next Generation*?

database — An electronic list of information — for example, a mailing list — that can be sorted very quickly or searched for a specific name.

default — (1) The factory settings. For example, the *default* setting for your typing in a word processor is single-spaced, one-inch margins. (2) De blame for hooking you on de Mac hobby.

defragment — To restore, in one continuous chunk, something that's all broken up and scrambled. Usually refers to the information in memory or on a

hard disk, but can also be applied to hamburger meat.

Delete key — In the typewriter days, this key was named Backspace. In my opinion, it still *should* be called that.

deselect — To *un*highlight some selected text or graphic. (You usually do it by clicking someplace else.)

desktop — (1) The top of your desk, where the Mac sits, as in "I don't want a laptop; I want a desktop computer." (2) *(Capitalized)* The home-base environment, where you see the Trash can, icons, and all that stuff. Also known as the Finder. (3) The actual (color-patterned) background of that home-base view. You can drag an icon out of its window and onto this tablecloth, and announce to your coworker that you've just placed an icon on the desktop.

Desktop file — A file the Mac maintains for its own use, in which it stores information such as what your icons should look like and which kinds of documents can be opened by which programs. This file is invisible, but when it becomes damaged or bloated and starts causing problems, it's not quite invisible enough for most people.

desktop publishing — The act of cranking out nice-looking printouts from your Mac instead of paying to have the work typeset. Despite the fact that the PowerBook is equally adept at creating beautiful printouts, the term *laptop publishing* still hasn't quite caught on.

dialog box — The message box that the Mac puts on the screen when it needs more information from you (for example, the one that appears when you print, asking how many copies you want).

digitize — Computerese for *digest*. To convert sound, pictures, video, or any other kind of real-world sensory experience into the Mac's own numerical digestive tract.

digitizing board — A circuit board that converts video or TV pictures into files on your Mac.

DIMMs — The memory chips for Power Macs made in 1995 or later (see *SIMMs*).

disk — Oh, come on; you know *this*.

disk cache — A secret feature for making your Mac faster at the expense of memory. The Mac memorizes a few things that you do a lot and keeps them in a wad of memory called the *disk cache*, where they'll be immediately accessible. You set the size of the disk cache (the amount of memory reserved) in the Memory control panel.

disk drive — The machinery that actually reads what's on a disk. If we're talking hard disk, the disk and the drive are built into a single unit. If we're talking floppy, the disk drive is the slot in the face of the Mac into which you insert a floppy disk.

document — A file that you create with a *program*. Examples: a memo (using a word processing program), a logo (using a graphics program), or a spreadsheet (using a spreadsheet program).

documentation — A five-syllable way of saying *user's guide*.

DOS — Synonym for *IBM-style computers,* meaning the computers of the world that aren't lucky enough to be Macs. Stands for Disk Operating System.

dots per inch — A gauge of visual clarity, both on printouts and on the screen. A laser printer is capable of printing at 300 or 600 dpi.

double-click — Double-clicking involves placing the on-screen pointer on an icon and, without moving the mouse, pressing the mouse button twice quickly. If you double-click an icon, it always opens into a window. In word processing, you double-click a word to select it.

download — To transfer a file from one computer to another over phone lines. If you're on the receiving end, you *download* the file. If you're on the sending end, you *upload* the file. If you're the phone company, you *love* the file.

dpi — See "dots per inch."

drag — (1) To position the cursor on something, hold down the mouse button, and move the mouse while the button is still down. (2) What it is when your disk drive breaks the day after the warranty expires.

drawing program — A graphics program (such as MacDraw or ClarisDraw) that creates circles, squares, and lines. The Mac stores each object that you draw as an object unto itself, rather than storing the status of each screen dot. See also *painting program* and *bitmap.*

driver — A smallish file on your disk that tells the Mac how it's supposed to relate to a specific piece of equipment (such as a printer or a scanner) that it's never heard of before. A translator.

DVD — A new kind of CD, capable of storing an entire movie on a single disc. Some expensive Macs and PowerBooks have DVD drives instead of ordinary CD drives (although the DVD drives can *also* play the older CD discs).

e-mail — Electronic mail; messages that you read and write on the Mac screen without ever printing them.

Enter key — A key (obviously) with the word *Enter* on it. It almost always does the same thing as the Return key.

EPS file — A type of graphics file. Characterized by extremely sharp, smooth printing on a laser printer; a large file size on the disk; and, often, difficulty in printing.

Ethernet — A system (wiring, connectors, software) of connecting Macs together in an office network. Faster than the free, built-in system (LocalTalk) that comes with every Mac.

expansion slot — The connector socket for an add-on circuit board inside most Mac models. Used to add circuit boards for fancy new features like networking, pro graphics, and so on.

extension — Miniprogram that you install by dropping it in your System Folder (whereupon the Mac puts it in the Extensions folder). From that moment on, the extension will run itself when you turn on the Mac and will be on all the time. Examples: virus protectors and screen savers.

fax modem — Like a modem (see *modem*), but also lets you send or receive faxes from your Mac screen.

field — Computerese for *blank,* such as a blank in a form.

file — The generic word for one of the little icons in your Macintosh. There are two kinds of files: *programs,* which you purchase to get work done, and *documents,* which are created by programs. See also *program* and *document.*

file compression — Making a file take up less disk space by encoding it in a more compact format, using a *file-compression program* such as StuffIt or DiskDoubler. The trade-off: Stuffing something down (and expanding it when you need it again) takes a few seconds.

File Sharing — A built-in Mac feature, wherein you can make any file, folder, or disk available for other people to go rooting through (as long as they're connected to your Mac by network wiring).

Finder — The "home-base" view when you're working on your Mac. It's the environment where you see the Trash, your icons, and how little space you've got left on your disk. Also known as the desktop or "that place with all the little pictures."

Fkey — Can refer to (1) the row of keys across the top of some keyboards: the *function* keys, labeled F1, F2, and so on. Or (2) a special built-in keyboard shortcut involving the ⌘ and Shift keys plus a number. The ⌘-Shift-3 function key, for example, takes a snapshot of the screen, and ⌘-Shift-1 ejects a floppy disk.

floppy disk — The hard 3¹/₂-inch-square thing that you put into your disk-drive slot. Comes in three capacities: 400K (single-sided), 800K (double-sided), and 1,400K (quadruple-sided, or high-density). After being accidentally zapped by a refrigerator magnet, often used as a windshield scraper.

folder — In the Mac world, a little filing-folder icon into which you can drop other icons (such as your work) for organizational purposes. When you double-click a folder, it opens into a window.

font — (1) Apple's usage: a single typeface. (2) Everyone else's usage: a typeface *family* or package.

FPU — See *math coprocessor.*

fragmentation — When something gets broken up into little pieces. Usually refers to the files on your hard disk (see *defragment*).

freeze — When your cursor becomes immovable on your screen, you can't type anything, your Mac locks up, and you get furious because you lose everything you've typed in the past ten minutes.

function key — See *Fkey.*

GB — Short for *gigabyte.*

GIF — A kind of graphics file, most often used on America Online and the Internet. (Stands for *graphic interchange format.*) Nobody quite knows whether to use a hard or a soft "G."

gig — Short for *gigabyte,* which is 1,024 megabytes, or a nicely big hard drive.

grayscale — A form of color image on which all the colors are different shades of gray, like all the images in this book.

grow box — Slang for *resize box* (see that entry).

hang — (1) Freeze (see *freeze*). (2) Knack, as in "Hey, I'm actually getting the hang of this. I'm no dummy!"

hard copy — A synonym for *printout.* A term used primarily by the kind of people who have car phones and say, "Let's interface on this."

hard disk — A hard drive.

hard drive — The spinning platters, usually inside your Mac but also available in an external form, that serve as a giant floppy disk where your computer files get stored.

hardware — The parts of your computer experience that you can feel, and touch, and pay for. Contrast with *software.*

header — Something that appears at the top of every page of a document, such as "Chapter 4: The Milkman's Plight" or "Final Disconnection Notice."

highlight — To select, usually by clicking or dragging with the mouse. In the Mac world, text and icons usually indicate that they're selected, or highlighted, by turning black or colored-in.

icon — A teensy picture used as a symbol for a file, a folder, or a disk.

iMac — The one-piece, high-speed, low-cost, see-through, blue-plastic, rounded-cased, G3-based Macintosh that debuted in late 1998 and became a huge smash hit.

initialize — To prepare a new disk for use on your computer. Entails *erasing it completely.*

injket — A kind of inexpensive, high-quality printer, such as an Epson Photo or DeskWriter, that makes its images by spraying an incredibly precise plume of ink at the paper.

insertion point — In word processing, the short, blinking vertical line that's always somewhere in your text. It indicates where your next typing (or backspacing) will begin.

The insertion point is right before this|word.

Internet — The worldwide network of computers joined by phone lines. Incorporates the World Wide Web, e-mail, and other features (see Chapter 11).

jaggies — Ragged or tiny stairstepped edges on lettering or graphics, appearing either on the screen or in your printouts.

Jaz drive — A $300 gadget that accepts $100 disks, about five inches across. Each disk holds 1,000 megabytes, making these great for backups and storing stuff when your hard drive gets full.

JPEG — Another graphics-file format found most often on America Online and the Internet (see *GIF*). This one has higher quality than GIF.

K — Short for *kilobyte,* a unit of size measurement for computer information. A floppy disk usually holds 800K or 1,400K of data. All the typing in this book fills about 2,500K. A full-screen color picture is around 1,000K of information. When your hard disk gets erased accidentally, it's got 0K (that's not OK).

kerning — In type-intensive Mac work, such as creating a newspaper headline, the act of squishing two letters slightly closer together to make better use of space so that you can fit the phrase AN ALIEN FATHERED MY TWO-HEADED BABY on one line.

label — A text tag or color tag, used to identify icons by category. You apply a label to an icon using the Label menu or, in Mac OS 8.*x*, the File menu.

landscape — The sideways orientation of a piece of paper.

laser printer — An expensive printer that creates awesome-looking printouts.

launch — To open a program, as in "He just sits at that computer all day long, moving icons around, because he hasn't figured out how to launch a program yet."

Launcher — The window containing jumbo, one-click icons that launch your favorite programs and documents. You open it by choosing Launcher from the Control Panels command of the menu.

LCD — The technology that creates the flat screen on the PowerBook laptop computer, marked by the tendency for the pointer to fade out if it's moved too quickly. Stands for either *Liquid Crystal Display* or *Lost the Cursor, Dammit.*

leading — *(LEDding):* The vertical distance between lines of text in a document. Single-spaced and double-spaced are measurements of leading.

LocalTalk — The hardware portion of a Macintosh network: the connectors and cables that plug one Mac into another.

logic board — The main circuit board inside your Mac. Often at fault when your Mac refuses to turn on.

Mac OS — The System software (the behind-the-scenes operating software) that makes a computer act like a Mac. As distinguished from DOS or Windows.

Mac OS 8 — The 1997 System software that give the Mac a cool new look, secret Control-key menus, super-tuggable windows, and other goodies described in Chapter 9. The phrase "Mac OS 8.*x*" can mean Mac OS 8.0, Mac OS 8.1, or Mac OS 8.5.

Mac OS X — The late 1999 version of the Mac system software. Advertised to be faster, crash less, and do your dishes. Pronounced "Mac O. S. ten."

macro — A predefined series of actions that the Mac performs automatically when you press a single key — such as launching your word processor, typing **Help! I'm being inhabited by a Mac poltergeist!**, and printing it — all by itself. Requires a special macro program such as QuicKeys or OneClick.

mail merge — Creating personalized form letters with a word processing program. Considered to be perfectly polite unless somebody catches you.

math coprocessor — The kid whose algebra homework you used to copy. (Just kidding.) Actually, a specialized chip inside certain high-level Macs that kicks in to handle certain very intense number-crunching tasks — data analysis and stuff. Also called an *FPU* (floating-point unit).

MB — Short for *megabyte.*

megabyte — A unit of disk-storage space or memory measurement (see *K*). There are 1,024K in a megabyte.

memory — The electronic holding area that exists only when the Mac is turned on; where your document lives while you're working on it.

menu — A list of commands, neatly organized by topic, that drops down from the top of the Mac screen when you click the menu's title.

menu bar — The white strip, containing menu titles, that's always at the top of the Mac screen. Not to be confused with *bar menu,* which is a wine list.

modem — A phone attachment for your Mac that lets you send files and messages to other computer users.

modifier keys — Keys that mess up what the letter keys do. Famous example: the Shift key. Other examples: (Command), Option, Control, and Caps Lock.

monitor — The screen.

motherboard — See *logic board.*

mount — To bring a disk's icon onto the desktop so that its contents may be viewed or opened.

mouse — The rounded hand-held thing that rolls around on your desk, controls the movement of the cursor, and is such an obvious target for a rodent joke that I won't even attempt it.

mouse pad — A thin foam-rubber mat that protects the mouse and desk from each other and that gives the mouse good traction.

multimedia — Something involving more than one medium, I guess. On the Mac, anything that gives you something to look at *and* listen to, such as a CD-ROM game.

native software — Specially written programs that run nice and fast on a Power Macintosh.

network — What you create when you connect Macs to each other. A network lets you send messages or transfer files from one Mac to another without getting up and running down the hall with a floppy disk in your hand (a networking system fondly called *SneakerNet*).

NuBus — The special kind of expansion slot (see *expansion slot*) found in any Mac II-style computer and most Quadra-style computers. Contrast with *PDS,* the slot in a Macintosh LC, or *PCI,* the slot in recent Power Macs. (And no, there was never an OldBus.)

NumLock — A goofy key, named by numskulls, on the keyboard. Pretty much does nothing except in Microsoft Word, where it switches the functions of the keys in the number pad.

OCR — Short for *optical character recognition*. You run an article that you tore out of *Entertainment Weekly* through a scanner, and the Mac translates it into a word processing document on your screen, so you can edit it and remove all references to Cher.

online — Hooked up, as in "Let's get this relationship online." In Mac lore, it means hooked up to another computer, such as America Online.

painting program — A program with the word *Paint* or *Photo* in the title that creates artwork by turning individual white dots black on the screen.

PalmPilot — A tiny, hand-held computer, about the size of a deck of cards, that quickly and automatically exchanges your address book, calendar, notes, and to-do list with your Mac, so that you can keep your info with you at all times. Recent models drop the word "Pilot," as in "Palm III."

partition — To use special formatting software that tricks the Mac into thinking that your hard disk is actually *two* (or more) disks, each with its own icon on the screen. Like subdividing a movie theater into a duplex, but less expensive.

paste — To place some text or graphics (that you previously copied or cut) in a document.

PC — Stands for *personal computer,* but really means any non-Macintosh computer; an IBM clone.

PCI — A 1995-era new style of NuBus slot in certain Mac models (see *NuBus*).

PDS — Stands for *processor direct slot* and is the kind of *expansion slot* (see that entry) in a Mac LC. Incompatible with *NuBus* (see that entry, too).

peripheral — Any add-on: a printer, scanner, CD-ROM drive, dust cover, and so on.

Performa — A line of Macs sold in the early 1990s as a complete package (monitor, keyboard, software, modem, Mac) for one price in one box.

PICT — A confusing-sounding acronym for the most common kind of picture file.

pixel — One single dot out of the thousands that make up the screen image. Supposedly derived from *pi*cture *el*ement, which still doesn't explain how the *x* got there.

pop-up menu — Any menu that doesn't appear at the *top* of the screen. Doesn't actually pop *up;* usually drops down.

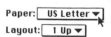

port — A jack or connection socket in the back of your Mac.

portrait — A right-side-up piece of paper; the opposite of *landscape* (see that entry). Also a right-side-up monitor that can display a full page (as in "a portrait display monitor").

PostScript — A technology, a printer, a trademark, a kind of font, a computer code language for displaying or printing text or graphics, a way of life. All of it means high-quality type and graphics, and all of it means heaping revenue for Adobe, the company that invented it.

PowerBook — A Mac laptop.

Power Macintosh — A Mac whose primary brain is the PowerPC chip.

PowerPC chip — The very fast main processor chip inside a Power Macintosh, such as the G3 chip.

PRAM — *Parameter RAM:* the little piece of memory maintained by your Mac's battery. Helps explain why the Mac always knows the date and time even when it's been turned off.

printer font — The printer half of a PostScript font (the other half is the *screen font*). Must be in your System Folder, and you must have one printer font for each style (bold, italic, and so on). An eternal nuisance.

PrintMonitor — A program that launches itself, unbidden, whenever you try to print something when background printing is turned on (see *background printing*). PrintMonitor is also the program that tries to notify you when something goes wrong with the printer, such as when a piece of paper gets horribly mangled inside.

program — A piece of software, created by a programmer, that you buy to make your Mac do something specific: graphics, music, word processing, number crunching, or whatever.

Publish and Subscribe — A fancy version of copy-and-paste. Lets you paste information (such as a graphic) from one document into another (such as a memo) in such a way that when you make a change in the original (the graphic), the copy (the memo) is changed automatically.

QuickDraw — A behind-the-scenes technology used to draw all the familiar pictures on your screen, such as lettering, windows, and icons.

QuickTime — The technology (and the little software extension) that permits you to make and view digital movies on your Mac screen. Does nothing by itself; requires QuickTime recording, playing, and editing programs.

QuickTime VR — A special kind of QuickTime movie that lets you change the camera angle by dragging your cursor around inside the picture. Increasingly common on the World Wide Web.

quit — To exit or close a program, removing it from memory. Or to exit or close your job, having gotten sick of working in front of a computer all day.

radio button — What you see in groups of two or more when the Mac is forcing you to choose among mutually exclusive options, such as these:

> A System error has occurred. What result would you like?
>
> ○ Loud, static buzzing
> ◉ Quietly blink to black
> ○ A two-minute fireworks display

RAM — Term for memory (see *memory*) designed to intimidate non-computer users.

RAM disk — A way to trick the Mac into thinking that it has an extra floppy disk inserted. The RAM disk is actually a chunk of memory set aside to *resemble* a disk (complete with an icon on the screen). Explained in *MORE Macs For Dummies.*

reboot — Restart.

rebuilding the desktop — One of several desperate methods that you can use in the event that something screwy goes wrong with the Mac. Involves holding down the ⌘ and Option keys while the Mac is starting up.

record (n.) — One "card" in a database, such as one person's address information. Contrast with *field,* which is one *blank* (such as a Zip code) within a record.

relational database — A complex information list that you hire somebody to come in and set up for you, in which each list of information (such as a mailing list) is connected to another list (such as People Who Never Pay on Time).

ResEdit — A free program that lets anybody do some hacking in any program — changing what the menus say, altering the keyboard shortcuts, or really screwing up the works.

resize box — The small square in the corner of a window that, when dragged, changes the size and shape of your window.

resolution — (1) A number, measured in dots per inch, that indicates how crisply a printer or a monitor can display an image. (2) A New Year's vow, such as "I will spend five minutes away from the computer each day for family, exercise, and social activity."

restart switch — A plastic switch or — more commonly — a keystroke (⌘-Control-power key) that, when pressed, safely turns the Mac off and on again.

RISC — Stands for *reduced instruction-set computing* and means a very fast processor chip, such as the PowerPC chip inside a Power Macintosh.

ROM — A mediation mantra that you can use when contemplating the ROM chips, where the Mac's instructions to itself are permanently etched.

sans serif — A font, such as Helvetica or Geneva, with no little "hats" and "feet" at the tip of each letter. See Chapter 5.

scanner — A machine that takes a picture of a piece of paper (like a Xerox machine) and then displays the image on your Mac screen for editing.

Scrapbook — A desk accessory, found in your menu, used for permanent storage of graphics, text, and sounds.

screen saver — A program (such as After Dark) that darkens your screen after you haven't worked for several minutes. Designed to protect an unchanging image from burning into the screen, but more often used as a status symbol.

scroll — To bring a different part of a document into view, necessitated by the fact that most computer monitors aren't large enough to display all 60 pages of your annual report at the same time.

scroll bar — The strips along the right and bottom sides of a Mac window. When a scroll bar's arrows, gray portion, or little white (or gray) square are clicked or dragged, a different part of the window's contents heaves into view (*scrolls*).

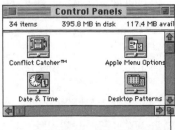

Resize box

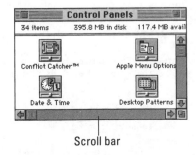

Scroll bar

SCSI — Stands for Small Computer [something] Interface. The second *S* may stand for *standard, system,* or *serial,* depending on whom you ask. Used only in the following five terms.

SCSI address — Refers to a number that you must give each SCSI device (see *SCSI device*) that's plugged into your Mac, using a little switch or thumbwheel on the back. If two SCSI devices have the same SCSI address, you're in big trouble.

SCSI cable — A fat cable with a 25- or 50-pin connector at the end, used to join SCSI devices.

SCSI device — A scanner, CD player, external hard drive, printer (sometimes), removable-cartridge drive, external floppy-disk drive (some-times), or other piece of equipment that you attach to the wide SCSI port in the back of your Mac.

SCSI port — The wide connector in the back of your Mac. See Chapter 16.

SCSI terminator — A plug that is supposed to go into the last SCSI device attached to your Mac.

serif (n., adj.) — A term used to describe a font that has little ledges, like little "hats" and "feet," at the tip of each letter, such as Times or this font.

shareware — Programs that are distributed for free, via the Internet or on a floppy disk from user groups. The programmer requests that you send $10 or $20 to him or her, but only if you really like the program.

Shut Down — The command in the Special menu that turns off your Mac.

SIMM — Stands for *Single In-line Memory Module,* which I suggest that you immediately forget. It refers to the little epoxy mini-circuit board that you install into older Macs when you decide you need more memory.

SimpleText — A basic word processor that comes free with every Mac.

sleep — Sort of like Off, except that the Mac remembers everything that you had running on the screen. When you want to use the computer again, you just touch a key; the whole computer wakes up, the screen lights up, and you're in business again. Used to conserve power.

slot — An *expansion slot* (see that entry).

software — The real reason you got a computer. Soft-ware is computer code, the stuff on disks: programs (that let you create documents) and documents themselves. Software tells the hardware what to do.

spreadsheet — A program that's like an electronic ledger book; you can type columns of numbers in a spreadsheet program and have them added automatically.

startup disk — *A* startup disk is a floppy or hard disk that contains a System Folder. *The* startup disk is the one that you've designated to be in control (in the event that you have more than one to choose among).

stationery — Click a document icon, choose Get Info from the File menu, and select Stationery Pad. Thereafter, when you double-click that icon, it won't open; instead, an exact *copy* of it opens. This saves you the hassle of pasting the same logo into every memo that you write because you can paste it into your Stationery Pad document just once.

StyleWriter — A quiet, low-cost, high-quality, slow-speed Apple inkjet printer.

submenu — In some menus, you're forced to choose among an additional set of options, which are marked in the menu by a right-pointing triangle, like this:

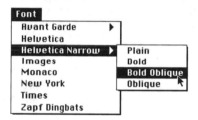

System 6 — An old version of the Mac's controlling software.

System 7 — A more recent version of the Mac's controlling software, circa 1991. More attractive, easier to use, more powerful, and slower than System 6. Generically, refers to any flavor of System 7: version 7.0, 7.1, 7.5, or whatever.

System 7.5 — Yet another version of the System Folder, which, again, you had to purchase unless your Mac came with it. Under the hood, System 7.5 is much the same as System 7.1. But it came with about 50 new control panels and extensions that perform stunts such as giving submenus to your menu to providing a floating "control strip" for your PowerBook.

System 7.6 — Pretty much the same as System 7.5, but faster and much stabler.

System 8 — There's not really a System 8. They renamed it *Mac OS 8.*

System crash — When something goes so wrong inside your Mac that a bomb appears on the screen with the message "Sorry, a System error has occurred" — or not. Sometimes, the whole screen just freaks, fills with static, and makes buzzing noises, like a TV station that's going off the air.

System disk — A *startup disk* (see that entry).

System file — Contains the Mac's instructions to itself, and stores your fonts, sounds, and other important customization information. A Mac without a System file is like a broke politician: It can't run.

System Folder — The all-important folder that the Mac requires to run. Contains all kinds of other stuff that's also defined in this glossary: the System file, the Finder, fonts, desk accessories, printer fonts, and so on. Always identified by a special folder icon:

In System 7 through System 7.6: System Folder

In Mac OS 8 and later: System Folder

telecommute — To work in T-shirt and slippers in a messy apartment, spending not one penny on transportation, and sending work to the office over the phone lines. Requires a modem and an ability to be alone for days on end without going insane.

terminator — See *SCSI terminator.* Or see an Arnold Schwarzenegger movie.

third party — (1) A company other than Apple, as in "You didn't get a mouse pad with your Mac? Well, of course not; you buy that from a third party." (You, by the way, are the second party.) (2) The New Year's Eve get-together at which you get the drunkest.

TIFF — Stands for *tagged image file format* and is the kind of graphics-file format created by a scanner.

title bar — The strip at the top of a window where the window's name appears.

toner — The powder that serves as the "ink" for a laser printer. Runs out at critical moments.

trackball — An alternative to the mouse. Looks like an 8-ball set in a pedestal; you roll it to move the pointer.

TrueType — A special font format that ensures high-quality type at any size, both on the screen and on any printer. Rival to PostScript but costs much less (nothing, in fact; it comes with the Mac).

upload — To send a file to another computer via modem. See also *download.*

USB — Describes rectangular metal jacks (USB *ports*), cables that plug into them (USB *cables*), and add-on appliances (USB *devices,* such as printers, modems, digital cameras, disk drives, and so on) that plug in there. On the iMac and some later Mac models, USB jacks, cables, and add-ons replace the keyboard, mouse, and printer ports of previous models.

user group — A local computer club. Serves as a local source of information and as a place to unload your obsolete equipment to unsuspecting newcomers.

virtual memory — A chunk of hard-disk space that the Mac sets aside, if you want, to serve as emergency memory (see Chapter 16).

virus — Irritating, self-duplicating computer program designed (by the maladjusted jerk who programmed it) to gum up the works of your Mac.

volume — A disk of any kind: floppy, hard, cartridge, or anything represented on your desktop by its own icon.

VRAM — Stands for *video RAM.* Memory chips inside your Mac that are dedicated to storing the screen picture from moment to moment. The more VRAM you have, the more colorful your picture (and the more you paid for your Mac).

window — A square view of Mac information. In the Finder, a window is a table of contents for a folder or a disk. In a program, a window displays your document.

word wrap — A word processing program's ability to place a word on the next line as soon as the current line becomes full.

WYSIWYG — Short for *what you see is what you get.* Means that your printout will precisely match what you see on the screen.

Zip disk — A slightly thickened floppy disk that holds 100MB (as much as a hard drive) and costs $15. To be used in Zip drives, sold by Iomega.

zoom box — The tiny square in the corner of a window (in the title bar) that, when clicked, makes the window jump to full size.

Zoom box

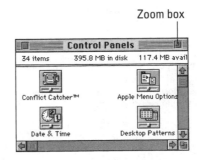

Index

Playing games is really fun...
The Dummies Way™!

Pressman®
©1998 Pressman Toy Corporation, New York, NY 10010

Crosswords For Dummies™ Game
You don't have to know how to spell to have a great time. Place a word strip on the board so that it overlaps another word or creates a new one. Special squares add to the fun. The first player to use up all their word strips wins!
For 2 to 4 players.

Trivia For Dummies™ Game
You're guaranteed to have an answer every time! Each player gets 10 cards that contain the answer to every question. Act quickly and be the first player to throw down the correct answer and move closer to the finish line!
For 3 or 4 players.

Charades For Dummies™ Game
Act out one-word charades: when other players guess them, they move ahead. The special cards keep the game full of surprises. The first player around the board wins.
For 3 or 4 players.

...For Dummies and The Dummies Way are trademarks or registered trademarks of IDG Books Worldwide, Inc.

Discover Dummies™ Online!

The *Dummies* Web Site is your fun and friendly online resource for the latest information about ...*For Dummies®* books on all your favorite topics. From cars to computers, wine to Windows, and investing to the Internet, we've got a shelf full of ...*For Dummies* books waiting for you!

Ten Fun and Useful Things You Can Do at www.dummies.com

1. Register this book and win!
2. Find and buy the ...*For Dummies* books you want online.
3. Get ten great *Dummies Tips™* every week.
4. Chat with your favorite ...*For Dummies* authors.
5. Subscribe free to *The Dummies Dispatch™* newsletter.
6. Enter our sweepstakes and win cool stuff.
7. Send a free cartoon postcard to a friend.
8. Download free software.
9. Sample a book before you buy.
10. Talk to us. Make comments, ask questions, and get answers!

Jump online to these ten fun and useful things at
http://www.dummies.com/10useful

For other technology titles from IDG Books Worldwide, go to
www.idgbooks.com

Not online yet? It's easy to get started with *The Internet For Dummies®,* 5th Edition, or *Dummies 101®: The Internet For Windows® 98,* available at local retailers everywhere.

Find other ...*For Dummies* books on these topics:

Business • Careers • Databases • Food & Beverages • Games • Gardening • Graphics • Hardware
Health & Fitness • Internet and the World Wide Web • Networking • Office Suites
Operating Systems • Personal Finance • Pets • Programming • Recreation • Sports
Spreadsheets • Teacher Resources • Test Prep • Word Processing

IDG BOOKS WORLDWIDE BOOK REGISTRATION

We want to hear from you!

Register This Book and Win!

Visit **http://my2cents.dummies.com** to register this book and tell us how you liked it!

- ✔ Get entered in our monthly prize giveaway.

- ✔ Give us feedback about this book — tell us what you like best, what you like least, or maybe what you'd like to ask the author and us to change!

- ✔ Let us know any other *...For Dummies*® topics that interest you.

Your feedback helps us determine what books to publish, tells us what coverage to add as we revise our books, and lets us know whether we're meeting your needs as a *...For Dummies* reader. You're our most valuable resource, and what you have to say is important to us!

Not on the Web yet? It's easy to get started with *Dummies 101*®*: The Internet For Windows*® *98* or *The Internet For Dummies*®, 5th Edition, at local retailers everywhere.

Or let us know what you think by sending us a letter at the following address:

...For Dummies Book Registration
Dummies Press
7260 Shadeland Station, Suite 100
Indianapolis, IN 46256-3917
Fax 317-596-5498

FOR DUMMIES™

BESTSELLING BOOK SERIES